THE REFORMS OF PETER THE GREAT

The New Russian History

Series Editor: Donald J. Raleigh,
University of North Carolina, Chapel Hill

This new series makes examples of the finest work of the most eminent historians in Russia today available to English-language readers. Each volume has been specially prepared by the author with an international audience in mind, and each will be translated and introduced by an outstanding Western scholar in the same field. The next title in the series will be a sweeping study of nineteenth-century Russia by Nikolai A. Troitskii, the great historian of Russian populism, in a translation by American historian Deborah Hardy.

THE REFORMS OF PETER THE GREAT

PROGRESS THROUGH COERCION IN RUSSIA

Evgenii V. Anisimov

Translated with an introduction by **John T. Alexander**

M.E. Sharpe

ARMONK, NEW YORK
LONDON, ENGLAND

Library of Congress Cataloging-in-Publication Data

Anisimov, E. V. (Evgenii Viktorovich)
[Vremia petrovskikh reform. English]
The reforms of Peter the Great : progress through coercion in Russia /
Evgenii Anisimov; translated by John T. Alexander.
p. cm.
"Condensed version of . . . Vremia petrovskikh reform" —
CIP galley, p. 4.
ISBN 1-56324-047-5 (cloth)
ISBN 1-56324-048-3 (paperback)
1. Russia—History—Peter I, 1689–1725.
I. Title.
DK133.A5513   1993
947'.05'092—dc20
92-22280
CIP

Printed in the United States of America

The paper used in this publication meets the minimum requirements of
American National Standard for Information Sciences—
Permanence of Paper for Printed Library Materials,
ANSI Z39.48–1984.

ED (c)   10   9   8   7   6   5   4   3   2   1
ED (p)   10   9   8   7   6   5   4   3   2

Contents

The New Russian History

It is my pleasure to invite readers to enjoy the first volume in a series of historical works in translation, *The New Russian History*, whose purpose is to make available to English readers the finest work of the most eminent historians of Russia today. Addressing a broad readership, our authors hope their works will appeal to both students and general readers as well as to those with a specialized knowledge of Russia.

It is fitting that the inaugural volume in the series presents a fresh view of that giant of Russian history, Peter the Great, whose daunting image has played a central role in the evolution of Russian historical writing and in how Russians have understood their country's place in the world. As Marc Raeff observed years ago, "the historiography of Peter the Great provides an almost perfect mirror for the Russian intelligentsia's views on the past and future of Russia, their relationship to the West, and the nature of the social and political problems confronting their country."[1] Raeff's remark remains valid nowadays, as historians search for ways to explain how Russia's political culture and historical traditions contributed to the rise of Bolshevism and shaped Marxism's peculiar development in Russia.

In fact, the shadow Peter cast over the centuries fell on a young boy growing up in Moscow province, who found in Peter his childhood hero as well as an object of his later scholarly investigations. Evgenii Viktorovich Anisimov, author of *The Reforms of Peter the Great: Progress Through Coercion in Russia*, moved to Leningrad to study with R.G. Skrynnikov, one of the Soviet Union's most prolific students of Muscovite Russia, and certainly one of its historical profession's most notable stylists. Drawn to the banks of the Neva by his childhood hero, Anisimov made Peter's city his home, where he has had a successful and productive career and enjoyed considerable international attention and acclaim.

A great historical figure with one foot in the Russian past, the other stepping brashly westward toward an abstract sense of the common good, Anisimov's Peter the Great is every bit a product of his century. Peter built more than Russia's first navy: he crafted a ship of state that loaded horrendous burdens on his subjects. Its features, Anisimov intimates with irony and insight, are all too familiar to hapless Soviet citizens, precisely because many realia of the Petrine era became fixed in the public's consciousness. Peter's reign marked the apotheosis of statism and his forcible experiment at creating a social utopia—or at least a rational state—transformed Russia into a regulated police state that extolled a cult of militarism and of military force. Moreover, Anisimov shows how Peter's "reforms" bred apathy, social dependence, and lack of freedom, arguing there was something conservative in his revolutionary program, which was aimed, after all, at making Russia a great power while preserving its traditional regime.

To be sure, any drawing of analogies and links between Soviet realities and the tsarist past risks charges of ahistoricism. Anisimov's notion of Peter as the founder of a totalitarian system in Russia, however, compels the reader to take stock of the similarities between Peter's approach to statecraft and that of his Soviet counterparts. In 1924 the poet Maximilian Voloshin branded Peter Russia's first Bolshevik. Historical objectivity, to be sure, is not the same as literary flair, but Voloshin's judgment reflected a sentiment widespread at the time. Indeed, in his magisterial biography of Stalin, Robert C. Tucker reminds us that "Peter was a cult figure in some historical literature that Stalin perused in the 1920s."[2] At the very least, reading Anisimov's reevaluation of Peter the Great, now available in John T. Alexander's lively translation, will improve our understanding not only of the birth of Imperial Russia, but also of contemporary Russian society. At the very least, we will come to appreciate Anisimov's contention that "Russia's future is more tightly bound up with its past than may appear at first glance."

Donald J. Raleigh
Series Editor

Notes

1. Marc Raeff, ed., *Peter the Great Changes Russia*, 2d ed. (Lexington, Mass.: Heath, 1972), p. 195.

2. Robert C. Tucker, *Stalin in Power: The Revolution from Above, 1928–1941* (New York: Norton, 1990), p. 61. See also pp. 62–64.

Translator's Introduction

The recent historical works of Evgenii Viktorovich Anisimov may be seen as important products and multifaceted reflections of the ferment in process in what used to be known as the USSR. Born in 1947, Anisimov received his higher education in Leningrad—now Saint Petersburg—where he is currently senior researcher at the St. Petersburg Branch of the Institute of History of the Russian Academy of Sciences. He has been strongly influenced by the examples of Ruslan Skrynnikov and Nikolai Pavlenko in writing history addressed to a broad readership. Prior to the publication in 1986 of his scholarly popular book, *Russia in the Mid-Eighteenth Century: The Struggle for the Heritage of Peter the Great*—a strikingly revisionist treatment of the reign of Empress Elizabeth (1741–61), copiously illustrated, issued in a printing of 100,000 and reissued in 1988—Anisimov was known primarily to a narrow circle of Petrine specialists. In the more relaxed era of *perestroika* and *glasnost'*, however, Anisimov, described by Donald J. Raleigh as a "rising star" of the Russian historical profession, has emerged as one of the more outspoken professional scholars and has commented frequently on academic and cultural politics. He has been critical of the rather stodgy academic journals for shying away from controversial questions such as nationality policies in the past and for ignoring the repression of the historical profession in the Stalin era, particularly the purge of Leningrad historians in 1930. At the same time Anisimov has rankled conservative nationalists by his sharp criticism of the popularized history purveyed by novelist Valentin Pikul'.

Indeed, the field of history has recently been enlivened by the spill-over of current political debates, as attested by Anisimov's own shocking application of the term "totalitarian" to Peter the Great, a figure singled out for praise by Stalin himself and glorified in the widely seen film of the late 1930s *Peter the First*. Some of the stir engendered by Anisimov's revisionist account of Peter the Great may be detected in a roundtable discussion convened at Saratov University on 16 June 1990. Sergei Alekseevich Mezin, a junior faculty member (docent), offered this appraisal:

It has become very interesting lately to teach and research Petrine history. People are introducing original points of view, and current debates sometimes turn into historical journalism. I believe that it is incorrect to compare Peter I with Ivan the Terrible and Stalin. The basic difference, as I see it, lies in the enormous constructive significance of all of Peter's activity. It is difficult to overestimate the importance of the cultural turning point that took place thanks to his reforms. To be sure, Peter's despotism is perfectly evident (although it never turned into senseless brutality), as is his growing imperial ambition in foreign policy.[1]

Equally revisionist in the contemporary Russian context is Anisimov's emphasis on the "police" dimensions of Peter's regime and its encouragement of "a culture of denunciations," a phenomenon sorely likened to Stalinist and more recent Soviet regimes. Anisimov also offers a rather revisionist account of Russo-Ukrainian relations and the supposed "treason" of Mazepa, the Ukrainian hetman—quite a contrast to the damningly negative portrayal given by Pavlenko (Ukrainian by birth) in his recent large-scale biography.[2] Similar dissent marks Anisimov's presentation of economic policies, where he denies any parallel to the New Economic Policy of the 1920s and questions whether Petrine policies did much to foster capitalism—a standard contention of previous Soviet historiography.

Beyond Anisimov's revisionism on specific topics, his work is unorthodox in terms of style. He makes abundant use of irony and sarcasm, for instance, in comparing Peter's expansionist dreams vis-à-vis Persia to Stalinist plans for the transformation of nature by diverting rivers, and in citing a Petrine decree banning defecation in nonprescribed places. Anisimov displays an expert eye for pithy expressions and striking scenes: for example, his depiction of a peculiar time-out during the Russo-Swedish combat at the fateful battle of Lesnaia in 1708 and his dramatic portrayal of the murder/execution of Tsarevich Aleksei. He also indulges in periodic direct addresses to his readers. Throughout he shows his wit and humor. He possesses a charming personality and is not afraid to reveal himself to his readers. In short, he is a modern-day historian concerned with accuracy and balance, yet also devoted to the literary and dramatic qualities that should enliven the writing of history.

It is a professional honor and a personal pleasure to assist Evgenii Anisimov in making more of his fascinating scholarship accessible to broader audiences outside Russia.[3] The text presented here is a condensed and modified version of his book *The Time of the Petrine Reforms*,[4] the condensation having been performed by the author himself. In paring the text substantially from the Russian original, the author dropped or paraphrased many lengthy quotations and generally condensed all of the chapters. He also rewrote the introduction to provide some historiographical guidance for non-Russian readers. I added the brief bibliographical note.

In translating Anisimov's stylish prose, I have attempted to convey both his meaning and his style—no simple assignment in view of his fondness for irony and sarcasm and for structural and lexical complexity. For reasons of readability I have chosen to minimize the use of untranslated technical terms and have sought to find rough English equivalents for most of such terms. Where Anisimov quotes from English-language sources I have returned to the originals, and I have used a number of existing translations of sources such as Alexander Muller's edition of the *Spiritual Regulation*, several quotations from the scholarship of James Cracraft, and the 1722–23 translation of F.C. Weber's account of Petrine Russia. All of these citations have been added to Anisimov's notes. Finally, as a translator and a historian now seeking to become better informed about the Petrine era I wish to acknowledge the guidance I have derived from the superb edition by A.P. Vlasto and I.R. Lewitter of Ivan Pososhkov's tract. My wife, Maria Kovalak Alexander, answered my pleas for assistance as I labored to understand Russian usage, and she patiently provided informed counsel on many points large and small. Maria (Manya) Carlson, my colleague in the Russian and East European Studies program at the University of Kansas, also advised me on several points of puzzlement. Pam LeRow of the Word Processing Center managed the printouts efficiently and clarified some of my confusion about word processing. Pat Kolb, Don Raleigh, and Max Okenfuss helped greatly to improve the text's readability. I thank them all for their help and absolve them of any responsibility for what I did with their advice.

John T. Alexander
Lawrence, Kansas

Notes

1. "Perestroika in the Provinces," *Soviet Studies in History*, vol. 30, no. 1 (Summer 1991): 62.

2. *Petr Velikii* (Moscow: "Mysl'," 1990).

3. Anisimov's scholarship has only recently begun to appear in English translation. The summer 1989 issue of *Soviet Studies in History* was devoted to "E.V. Anisimov on Petrine and Post-Petrine Russia," edited by Carol B. Stevens and translated by Hugh F. Graham. His article "Peter I: Birth of an Empire," appeared in the same journal of translations (vol. 30, no. 2 [Fall 1991]: 6–29), and another, "Progress through Violence: From Peter the Great to Stalin," was published by *Russian History* 17 (1990): 409–18. My own translation of his book on Elizabeth's Russia is currently in press with Academic International Press, Gulf Breeze, Florida.

4. *Vremia petrovskikh reform* (Leningrad: "Lenizdat," 1989).

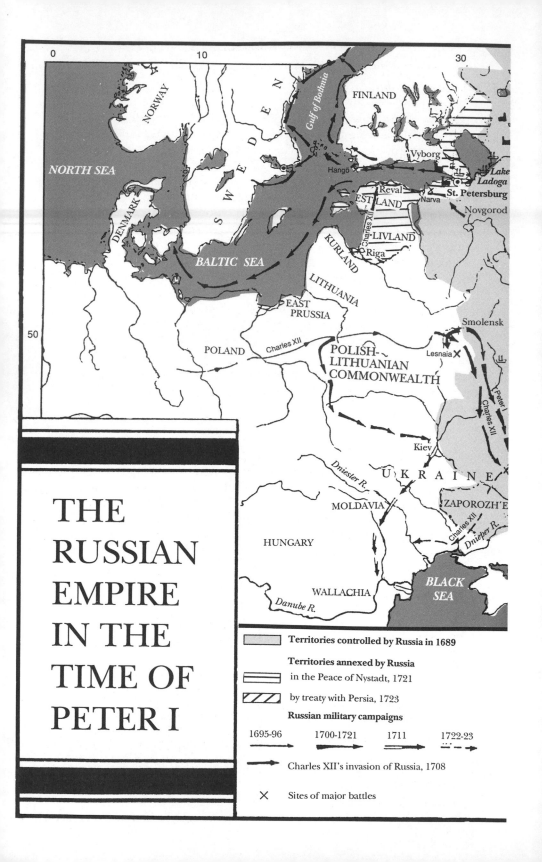

THE
RUSSIAN
EMPIRE
IN THE
TIME OF
PETER I

Territories controlled by Russia in 1689

Territories annexed by Russia

in the Peace of Nystadt, 1721

by treaty with Persia, 1723

Russian military campaigns

1695-96   1700-1721   1711   1722-23

Charles XII's invasion of Russia, 1708

×   Sites of major battles

Map labels:

NORWAY, SWEDEN, FINLAND, NORTH SEA, Gulf of Bothnia, Vyborg, Hangö, Lake Ladoga, Reval, St. Petersburg, ESTLAND, Narva, Novgorod, Charles XII, LIVLAND, BALTIC SEA, KURLAND, Riga, DENMARK, LITHUANIA, EAST PRUSSIA, Smolensk, POLAND, Charles XII, POLISH-LITHUANIAN COMMONWEALTH, Lesnaia ×, Peter I, Charles XII, Kiev, UKRAINE, Dniester R., MOLDAVIA, ZAPOROZH'E, HUNGARY, Charles XII, Dnieper R., WALLACHIA, Danube R., BLACK SEA

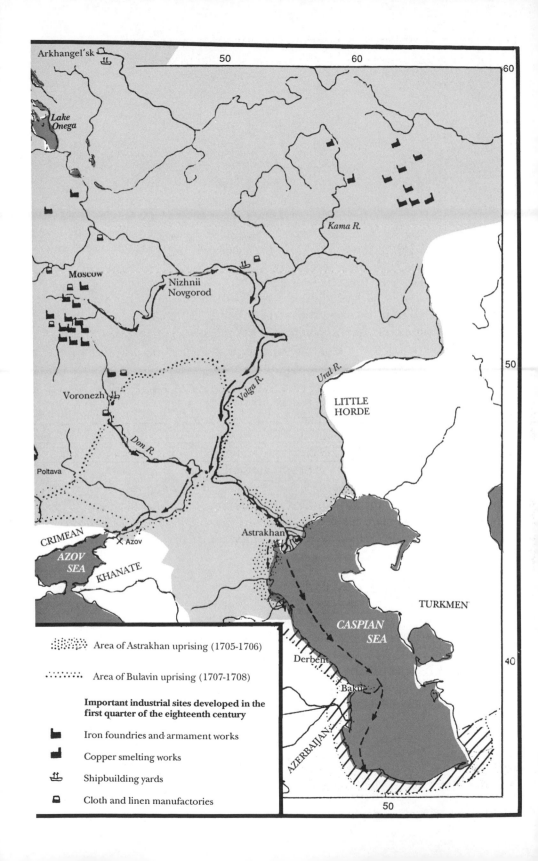

Arkhangel'sk

50   60   60

Lake
Onega

Kama R.

Moscow

Nizhnii
Novgorod

Volga R.

Ural R.

LITTLE
HORDE

Voronezh

Don R.

50

Poltava

Astrakhan

CRIMEAN

AZOV
SEA

× Azov

KHANATE

TURKMEN

CASPIAN
SEA

40

Derbent

Baku

.... Area of Astrakhan uprising (1705-1706)

.... Area of Bulavin uprising (1707-1708)

**Important industrial sites developed in the
first quarter of the eighteenth century**

Iron foundries and armament works

Copper smelting works

Shipbuilding yards

Cloth and linen manufactories

AZERBAIJAN

50

THE REFORMS OF PETER THE GREAT

Introduction

"He wrought out of Russia a real metamorphosis, a transformation."
These words of Piotr Shafirov, the vice-chancellor of Petrine times,
from his 1717 treatise *Considerations on the Causes of the Swedish War,*
suggest that Peter I's contemporaries already understood clearly the significance of the transformation of Russia going on before their eyes. The
upheaval was especially violent because underlying this "metamorphosis"
was the will of a single person, like an ancient titan lifting an overwhelming
burden. This is beyond doubt, whatever we may say about the role played
by his supporters, by "productive forces," and so forth.

The grandiose, all-encompassing nature of the Petrine transformations was such that even after a century and more they had not become
merely history but continued to be something real and vital that affected everyday life. Historian Mikhail Pogodin, a contemporary of
Pushkin, wrote in his essay "Peter the Great":

> We wake up. What day is it? 1 January 1841—Peter the Great ordered
> that years be counted from the birth of Christ and months of the year
> from January. It's time to get dressed—our clothing is sewn in the
> fashion given by Peter the First, a uniform by his pattern. The cloth is
> woven at a factory that he established, the wool is shorn from sheep
> that he introduced in Russia. A book catches your eye—Peter the
> Great put the script into use and himself cut out the letters. You start
> reading—this is the language that under Peter was made into a book-
> ish and literary one, forcing out the previous church idiom. Newspa-
> pers are delivered—Peter the Great launched them. You need to
> purchase various things—all of them, from the silk neckerchief to the
> sole of the boot, will remind you of Peter the Great. . . . At dinner,
> from the salted herring to the potatoes that he ordered sown to the
> wine that he introduced, all the dishes remind you of Peter the Great.
> After dinner you go out for a visit—this is Peter the Great's assemblies,
> public social functions. You meet ladies there who were permitted
> into men's company at the demand of Peter the Great.

3

If it were only a matter of neckerchiefs, salted herring, and assemblies! Pogodin continues:

> A place in the system of European states, the administration and its subdivisions, court procedures, the rights of the estate groups, the Table of Ranks, the army, navy, taxes, censuses, recruiting levies, manufactories, mills, ports, canals, highways, postal service, agriculture, forestry, cattle raising, mining, gardening, viticulture, domestic and foreign trade, clothing, external appearance, pharmacies, hospitals, drugs, chronology, language, the press, printing, military schools, academies—these are essentially monuments to his indefatigable activity and his genius.[1]

Time showed the astonishing viability of many of the institutions Peter created. The colleges lasted until 1802, that is, eighty years; the soul-tax system of assessment introduced in 1724 was not abolished until 163 years later, in 1887. The last recruiting levy took place in 1874—almost 170 years after the first. The synodal administration of the Russian Orthodox church remained unchanged almost 200 years, from 1721 to 1918. Finally, the Governing Senate, created by Peter in 1711, was liquidated only in December 1917, some 206 years after its formation.

It is hard to find examples in Russian history of other institutions known for their longevity and created by the conscious will of one person. One can understand the admiration that the great reformer of Russia evoked and still evokes.

Peter has always been particularly celebrated on the banks of the Neva, where he founded a great city with an amazing destiny, the city in which everything is linked to its founder's name. "It was born to become an imperial capital," and here began, flourished, and declined the "Petersburg" period of Russian history, filled with names, dates, and events without which world history is unthinkable. At the beginning of this memorable period stands the gigantic figure of Peter, whose life in history proved to be extraordinarily vivid and durable.

As Alexander the Great has remained a historical figure equally celebrated and respected in the West and the East for three millennia, so too is Peter perhaps the single figure in Russian history who almost painlessly crossed over the divide of 1917, so fatal for the old regime, to remain in public awareness as a reformer of genius who converted Russia into a great power.

Around Peter's name many legends and stereotypes have taken shape and become imprinted on public consciousness. These stereotypes are so alive that both for those who write about Peter and for those who read about him it is sometimes hard to resist the inertia of the ready-made clichés—"the tsar-carpenter, the worker on the throne," who "made a window to Europe," who was "harsh, but just and democratic, far beyond his successors," and so forth—which have persisted and long since become axioms of judgments and definitions. These positive stereotypes are usually accompanied by current ideological innovations to the effect that in instituting reforms necessary for Russia, Peter "expressed the interests of the ruling class" and skinned the laboring peasantry three times over. Further, as a rule there follows the all-reconciling notion that in history results are what is important in the final analysis, whatever the directions and the means used to attain them, whether we speak about a ruler who created an empire or one who built what he himself and his apologists called "socialism."

In our day historians and commentators are trying hard to resolve the problematic relationship between ends and means. It is no accident that the theme of Peter and the theme of Stalin have proved to be closely related, and no accident that some commentators and historians have subtly turned to Peter's epoch in search of the first causes and sources of the "Stalinshchina."

Disputes about the significance in Russian history of Peter's personality and his reforms have not subsided for three centuries, and it is doubtful that they will ever end. The historiography of the Petrine transformations is exceptionally broad and many-sided. Its sources extend back to the end of his reign when Peter started to write "The History of the Swedish War." This unfinished book was supposed to sum up his rule, to immortalize both the glorious victories of Russian arms on the battlefield and the achievements in the sphere of reforms. And although "The History" never saw the light, its purpose was attained via other means—the next generation of historians began to celebrate the significance of the reforms and the majesty of the genius-reformer. From the moment of his death Peter entered into Russian national consciousness as one of the greatest geniuses of Russian history, an outstanding personality who struck everyone by the scale and profundity of what he had accomplished. How this actually came about after his death has been well delineated by Xenia Gasiorowska and Nicholas Riasanovsky.[2]

In the historical scholarship of the eighteenth century, apologetics predominated in evaluating the tsar's personality and his aims. The works of Vasily Tatishchev, Mikhail Lomonosov, belles lettres and poetry lauded all the aims and deeds of Peter the Great. The apogee of this kind of literature was *The Feats of Peter the Great, the Wise Transformer of Russia*, issued by Ivan Golikov in twelve volumes that were later supplemented by eighteen more volumes (1788–97). The very same purpose, to celebrate the great monarch, was also served by the popular historical anecdotes that flowed from the pen of Peter's turner Andrei Nartov, academician Yakov Stählin, and Ivan Golikov. Concurrently, in the second half of the eighteenth and the beginning of the nineteenth century, the historiography of the Petrine era started to sound some critical notes. The celebrated aristocratic critic of Catherine II's reign, Prince Mikhail Shcherbatov, in his *On the Corruption of Manners in Russia*, and then also Nicholas Karamzin, in the "Memoir on Ancient and Modern Russia," saw in Peter's reign not only victories and outstanding achievements, but also "horrors of despotism" that led to the damage of the "good" patriarchal manners of old, to the destruction of the significance of the hereditary estate of the nobility, and to the dominance of luxury and corruption at court and in the higher echelons of Russian society.[3]

The great Russian poet Alexander Pushkin (1799–1837) occupies a special place in the historiography on Peter. In the last years of his life he collected material for a book on "The History of Peter the Great." In this as in Pushkin's other works there are many valuable observations and comments about the role of Peter's personality and the meaning of his reforms. Pushkin's ruminations proceed partly in the doubting vein of Shcherbatov and Karamzin, yet Pushkin does not stop there: he incisively grasped the most profound internal contradiction of the Petrine epoch and of the very personality of the tsar-reformer, the combination of rationality and irrationality in his actions, the necessary firmness in implementing the reforms, and, at the same time, the exceptional brutality in their implementation on Russian soil.

The post-Pushkin period (1830s–50s) is notable for the unfolding battle of "Westernizers" and "Slavophiles" over Russia's past and the paths of its movement forward. "Westernizers" such as Alexander Herzen, Timofei Granovsky, Konstantin Kavelin, and others, and "Slavophiles" such as Ivan Kireevsky, Aleksei Khomiakov, Yuri Samarin, and the Aksakov brothers made Peter the Great the very center of their disputes. If the "Westernizers" saw in Peter the tsar-revolutionary who with the aid of strong central authority managed to make Russia into a great power, then the "Slavophiles" vehemently denounced Peter for introducing into Russia alien Western principles of life, institutions, and mores that were harmful for the Russian individual and the society as a whole. As a consequence, in their view, the internal harmony of Russian life was destroyed, and there was a split between the authorities and the people, the state and "the land." One should note that for the most part both sides disputed without new facts in hand, but the centrality of their dispute was manifest, and it did not subside even later.

The Petrine epoch of reforms was reflected most fully in *The History of Russia from Earliest Times* by Sergei Solov'ev, who had access to previously closed state archives. Three volumes of his multivolume *History* were published in the 1860s and 1870s and were dedicated entirely to the Petrine epoch of reforms.[4] A plethora of historical facts combined in these volumes with Solov'ev's unambiguous concept of the sense and significance of the Petrine reforms. In concentrated form Solov'ev's views were reflected in his *Public Lectures about Peter the Great*, which appeared in 1872, the bicentennial of Peter's birth. Solov'ev saw in Peter not only the great reformer who accomplished the great feat of converting Russia from a backward and uncultured country into a great and enlightened power, but the personification of the spirit of the Russian people whose genius he represented.

Solov'ev's tremendous labor became the genuine fount of a historiographical river: from it flowed all of Russian historiography about Peter. Here and in Vasily Kliuchevsky's brilliant lectures, which gave much fresh evaluation of the reforms, were also specific historical works on law, the economy, social relations, and the system of authority at the center and at the local level.[5]

Paul Miliukov's book, *The State Economy of Russia in the First Quarter of the Eighteenth Century and the Reforms of Peter the Great* (second edition, St. Petersburg, 1905), occupies a special place in the historiography. The book addressed the sociofinancial aspect of Peter's reforms. This work, as well as Miliukov's later writings on the history of Russian culture, developed the notion of the accidental nature, chaos, and senselessness of many of the reforms of Peter, who in Miliukov's opinion lacked the ability to think and to act consistently and logically. Miliukov's "destructive" point of view later became the subject of a long-term scholarly debate. In the 1880s and 1890s scholarship on Peter was enriched by the first volumes of *The Letters and Papers of Peter the Great*, edited by academician A.F. Bychkov on a high scholarly level, which still constitute the documentary basis of research on the Petrine epoch.[6]

After 1917 the historiographical traditions about Peter and his reforms were broken in many respects. At first a crudely sociological view predominated in treating the reforms of the Petrine epoch: all the efforts of Mikhail Pokrovsky and his school were aimed at seeking out "class essence" and "commercial-industrial capitalism" in the Petrine epoch. The rebirth of imperial designs in the politics of the 1930s and 1940s led to the exaggeration of Peter's personality and concerns, even though he was deprived of the title "Great" and was indicted by Josef

Stalin for "skinning the peasant three times over." Nevertheless, Peter
was evaluated as a great statesman who, while surrounded by enemies,
gave the example of a decisive, brutal but necessary break with the old.
A special place in the historiography about Peter is occupied by the
talented novel of Aleksei Tolstoi, *Peter I*, which elaborates the apologetic
idea of the powerful personality, the boss, among his subjects. In Peter's
features contemporaries palpably perceived Stalin.

At the same time, the definite rehabilitation of Peter accomplished
under Stalin facilitated the reactivation of scholarly research on the
Petrine epoch. Publication of *The Letters and Papers of Peter the Great* was
resumed, a valuable collection of documents prepared in 1945 by N.A.
Voskresensky, *Legislative Documents of Peter I*, appeared, and the first five
volumes of Mikhail Bogoslovsky's biographical chronology of the
Peter's life, *Peter I: Materials for a Biography* (Moscow, 1940–48), were
released, as were other books and articles.

Among contemporary historians in the Commonwealth of Independent States Nikolai Pavlenko's writings must be singled out. His works
address the problems of the socioeconomic policies of the Petrine era
as well as the problems of Peter's domestic policies, with special attention devoted to the personality of the tsar-reformer himself and his
entourage.

Peter's vivid personality has constantly attracted the attention of historians in the West, where the number of books about Peter published
in the past twenty years manifestly exceeds the number published in the
USSR during the entire seventy years of the Soviet era. These books are
not of equal value; many of them are superficial and devoid of deep
analysis. The most valuable of these appear to be studies of a general
nature: those written by the German historian Reinhard Wittram, the
English historian M.S. Anderson, and the American Marc Raeff, the last
of whom has long studied the Petrine epoch in the context of Russian
history in general and the history of the intelligentsia in Russia in particular. Especially important is the research on specific subjects: James
Cracraft on Peter's church reforms, Claes Peterson on the administrative reforms, Robert Crummey and others cited in the bibliography of
the present book on the social structure of Petrine society.

To be sure, I have not set out to reconsider all aspects of the enormous theme of the Petrine reforms, and have striven to avoid the traditional exposition of the great reformer "from birth to death." The book
comprises four basic parts. The first is devoted to Peter's personality
and analyzing its makeup, for therein lay the essence of all that later
took place in Russia. How Peter implemented his ideals and ideas, what
goals he pursued in the different spheres of life, and what it all

amounted to make up the following parts of the book.

One should not forget that the reforms were only part of the life of society. People are born, live, work, fall ill, and die in times of acceleration and stagnation alike. In this indivisibility, the variegated mix of the exalted and the banal, the extraordinary and the traditional, are found the color and particularity of history, just as in life in general. In the book presented here many aspects of the life of the society of the Petrine epoch are reconsidered, but its main theme is the history of the Petrine reforms. Besides, as a researcher it seemed to me not so important merely to recount to readers the results of the reforms as to try to understand how, when, and why the idea developed under Peter—that social utopian and peculiar "Petersburg dreamer"—of saddling his own people with a grandiose, forcible experiment in creating a "regulated" police state where, for the sake of an abstract idea of the "common good," the private interests of the individual were sacrificed.

FATHER OF THE FATHERLAND

The Personality of the Reformer

In considering the early years of the life of this extraordinary tsar, one unwittingly seeks to find on the banks of the notorious river of time early testimony to Peter's exceptional qualities, and therefore one reviews his copybooks, first letters, and notes with special care.

But nothing alerts us to the coming genius. The boy born on the day of Saint Isaac of Dalmatia, 30 May 1672, was not distinguished from his numerous brothers and sisters by anything special. Tsar Aleksei Mikhailovich's marriage to Natalia Kirillovna Naryshkina on 22 January 1671 had been the second for the forty-year-old tsar. From the previous marriage with Maria Il'inichna Miloslavskaia had been born thirteen children, among whom were Fedor, Ivan, and Sophia. In 1676 Aleksei Mikhailovich died, leaving the throne to the oldest of his sons, Fedor Alekseevich, a sickly and feeble young man. Fedor ruled only briefly and died at the end of April 1682. A council of high-ranking dignitaries decided to offer the throne not to the next eldest son, sixteen-year-old Ivan, but to nine-year-old Peter. This unexpected decision was taken through the intrigues of the Naryshkins, relatives of Peter's mother who had followed the young tsaritsa into the palace, but there was also the circumstance that the lively, healthy young man greatly outshone his older brother Ivan, who seemed to bear signs of degeneration. Possibly awareness of this fact, and not only the political struggle, had influenced the dutiful decision of the Boyar Council, the highest governmental body, to violate the tradition of transmitting the throne via the direct male line of descent from older (Fedor) to younger (Ivan).

Yet the Naryshkin faction underestimated the foe. Headed by the imperious, ambitious Sophia, the Miloslavskys contrived to arouse the discontent of the strel'tsy (the palace guards) and with their aid to stage a bloody coup d'état on 15 May 1682. On the throne a triumvirate was instituted: Peter was joined by Ivan as co-tsars while Sophia was declared co-ruler with the rights of regent. For Peter the situation was a political dead end. The widowed tsaritsa Natalia Kirillovna left the Kremlin palace with her household retainers and settled in Preobrazhenskoe—one of the suburban residences that then ringed Moscow.

All these events, which took place independently of Peter's will and wishes, became as it were the backdrop to the beginning years of the future reformer of Russia, and they also determined many of the unusual qualities that later constituted his genius. The main thing was that he abandoned the Kremlin. The Moscow Kremlin of the seventeenth century was not just buildings and churches, it was a world of ceremonies and conditions, of stereotyped conduct shaped by the centuries, and a closed system hallowed by tradition that as a whole hardly facilitated the development of individuality. Not one public enterprise with the tsar's participation occurred without the observance of rather severe ceremonial procedures. The sovereign's progresses beyond the bounds of the Kremlin—as a rule these were pilgrimages to surrounding monasteries or churches—were treated as events of state significance. Even the tsar's coming to "the Jordan," out onto the ice of the Moscow River on 6 January for the ritual cutting of ice holes in the traditional festival of blessing the waters, was organized as an important event and called a "march," while in the Kremlin—"Above" in the terminology of the time—there remained a commission of boyars and other council ranks appointed by the tsar so that during his absence the state "would not be at loss and would not have losses."

By force of political circumstance Peter had apparently been ejected from this system. To be sure, he appeared in the Kremlin on official holidays and for audiences, but all this was alien to him and even, knowing the hostility of relatives on his father's side, threatening. Preobrazhenskoe, as the tsar's summer residence surrounded by fields and forests, gave him that which abruptly eased the development of his abilities—freedom to pass the time with a minimum of obligatory duties and a maximum of games, which, as always happens with little boys, bore a military character and with the years became complicated because their participants were not dolls but live persons. The training and developmental significance of these games was huge. The native endowments typical of Peter already appeared here: lively impressionability, turbulent and indefatigable energy, the passion and self-absorbed enthusiasm for play that imperceptibly turned into serious business. Thanks to this the "play" soldiers and the English boat found in a barn did not remain mere toys, but became the foundation of the future grandiose cause of transforming Russia.

One other circumstance is important. Near Preobrazhenskoe was the so-called Foreign Settlement—Kokui, the settlement of foreigners who had come to Russia from various European countries. By the tradition of that time this settlement of merchants, diplomats, and mercenaries was separated from the city by a barrier. Kokui was a peculiar model of Europe where side by side and just as closely as in Europe lived Catholics and Protestants, Germans and French, English and Scots. This strange world of Kokui, so different from Moscow, captured Peter's curiosity and attention, probably because it was so unlike the world of the Kremlin and Preobrazhenskoe. Acquaintance with foreigners—interesting, educated people like Franz Lefort and Patrick Gordon—unusual things, customs, multiple languages, and later also intimate impressions in the house of the wine merchant Mons where his beautiful daughter Anna lived all made it easy for Peter (whose ancestors had washed their hands from a silver bowl after the ceremony of "offering the hand to" a foreign envoy) to surmount the invisible but solid psychological barrier separating two alien worlds from one another—Orthodox Rus' and "ungodly" Europe—a barrier that even now is not so easy to surmount.

Peter's assumption of power in the summer of 1689 served to resolve the long simmering political crisis stirred by the unnatural status of a dual-power in practice. But, just as in May 1682, so in August 1689 Peter had largely been swept away by the course of events without governing them. Propitious circumstances facilitated Sophia's overthrow and the practically bloodless transfer of the sovereign's authority to him.

At the time Peter did not need this authority as a lever for reforms, because they had not yet matured in his consciousness. Thus Russia's "real" seventeenth century lasted ten more years, coinciding exactly with the calendar century. But this decade did not pass in vain for Peter; it ripened his genius so that at the end of the decade, at the turn of two centuries, a whole flood of ideas poured over the country, transforming it.

One should single out three important events of these years that influenced the formation of Peter the Reformer. First, there are the trips to Arkhangel'sk in 1693–94. An ordinary "play" journey to the town on the White Sea became, undoubtedly, a great event in the life of the young tsar. For the first time he saw a real sea and real ships and made his first voyage on the restless and dangerous element so unlike the quiet ponds of the Moscow hinterland. This gave a powerful impetus to the imagination, the dream of the sea appeared for Russia, and a genuine cult of the ship and the sea arose. From this Arkhangel'sk experience, as the Russian historian Mikhail Bogoslovsky wrote, "the roar of the waves, the sea air, the watery elements drew him in and with the years made themselves an urgent requirement for him. In him an elemental urge to the sea exploded."[1]

In actuality, how did it happen that the sea and ships filled a special place in the life of this man, all of whose forebears had died having seen with their own eyes only the hilly expanses of the Great Russian plain? Like a mother hen who had raised a duckling that floated away from her, Peter's mother, Natalia Kirillovna, worried on the shore, sending anxious letters to Arkhangel'sk one after another.

But it was already too late to change anything: ships and the sea had become Peter's destiny, appearing to him while awake and even in his dreams. Concerning dreams, notations have been preserved that the tsar made in his mature years and which reflect this all-consuming passion of Peter's: "1714, November 9 to 10: had a dream of [a ship] with green flags in Petersburg. . . . I saw this dream when we entered Pomerania: I was in a galliot, whose masts and sails were out of proportion, on which galliot we sailed off and in making it come about we capsized and swamped it with water, into which we fell and swam to the other side, and turned it toward home and then set out thither, and at home I ordered the water bailed out."[2]

The experienced eye of an old salt and shipwright could not over-look even in a dream the incorrect setting of the sails on a ship, on which he had been placed by Morpheus.

Peter's turner Andrei Nartov recounts in his memoirs the tsar's rap-ture at the sight of the maneuvers of the English fleet in 1698: "From the multitudinous ships of the fleet constituted in his presence various formations were deployed and the master was thereby brought to such delight that as if from joy he said unabashedly to the commanding admiral with the other naval officers on this occasion he would prefer the rank of an English admiral to that of the tsar of Russia. So much was Tsar Peter in love with naval service! But I know for sure inasmuch as I heard it from the monarch's lips that he said the following: 'If I were not tsar, I would wish to be an admiral of Great Britain.' "[3]

This rapturous reaction to the sea and ships he preserved till the end of his days. Not one launching of a ship or great naval engagement happened without his involvement. He pined when kept away from his beloved maritime affairs.

I think that his enthusiasm for the sea is no accident or caprice. It was a kind of elusive correspondence and concordance of Peter's inner world to an image, the idea of the ship under sail, a symbol of the rational organiza-tion of the world toward which Peter strove by all means; it also refers to the struggle with the resistant, blind, and powerful element of the waves. A little later I shall dwell on this in more detail.

The second important event of these years was the Azov campaigns of 1695–96—the war with Turkey for egress to the Sea of Azov. Here on the southern borders a dress rehearsal of those events took place that in other, more grandiose and dramatic settings unfolded at the start of the eighteenth century on the western borders. The first failures to capture Azov, the building of a fleet at Voronezh, finally the military victory over a serious opponent, and the foundation of a new town, Taganrog, different from traditional Russian towns—all this we encounter later on the banks of the Neva and the Baltic. For Peter the Azov campaigns were the first military school which, although even he appraised it skeptically later, still brought him incalculable benefit. The experience of guiding a large army, siege operations, and the storm of a powerful fortress did not pass in vain for Peter's military genius. No less important is that here too, under the walls of Azov, the concept entered Peter's consciousness of his own place, "duty," and role in the life of Russia. Precisely from the Azov campaigns and not from the moment of his accession, as historian Nikolai Pavlenko has justly remarked, Peter would later date the account of his own "service" on the throne.[4] And it was the idea of service to Russia, as he understood it, that became the chief fulcrum of his life, fulfilling for him in the highest sense all his acts and steps, even the most unseemly and dubious ones from the perspective of the morality of the day.

The third event that affected the formation of the personality of the future reformer of Russia was his extended trip abroad to Western Europe in the company of the Grand Embassy of 1697–98. Peter traveled not as a member of the diplomatic delegation but as an accompanying personage among the other nobles and servants. This gave him substantial freedom, and allowed him to acquaint himself in detail with many aspects of the life of Holland, England, and other countries. And the point was, of course, not only in studying the shipwright's skills at the Dutch and English dockyards. Peter for the first time caught sight of Western European civilization in all its military and cultural might, experiencing its spirit, sense, and strength. He brought back from Europe not only knowledge, impressions, and the calluses of a laborer, but also the idea that he formulated for himself quite simply: in order to make Russia just as strong as the great powers of Europe, it was urgent to borrow all the essentials from Europe as quickly as possible. Precisely then was Peter's orientation to the Western European model of life formulated, and this automatically signified the negation of the life of Old Russia, the consistent and at times violent enmity toward and destruction of the old and the hated things associated with enemies: Sophia, the strel'tsy, the boyars.

One curious testimony dates to the time of the Grand Embassy, a

letter of Princess Sophia of Hanover in which she candidly enumerates
her impressions of meeting the young Russian tsar on 11 August 1697
in the town of Koppenbrucke. This letter—a vivid document for its
time—is especially valuable in that its author is free of the a priori and
literary influences that contemporaries inevitably experienced when
they met Peter later, when the glory of his genius and victories had
widely spilled over Europe.

> The Tsar is very tall, his features are fine, and his figure very noble.
> He has great vivacity of mind, and a ready and just repartee. But,
> considering all the advantages with which nature has endowed him, it
> could be wished that his manners were a little less rustic. We im-
> mediately sat down to table. Herr Koppenstein, who did the duty of
> marshal, presented the napkin to His Majesty, who was greatly embar-
> rassed, for at Brandenburg, instead of a table-napkin, they had given
> him an ewer and basin after the meal. He was very merry, very talkative,
> and we established a great friendship for each other, and he ex-
> changed snuff-boxes with my daughter. We stayed, in truth, a very
> long time at table, but we would gladly have remained there longer
> still without feeling a moment of *ennui*, for the Tsar was in very good
> humor, and never ceased talking to us. My daughter had her Italians
> sing. Their song pleased him, though he confessed to us that he did
> not care much for music.
>   I asked him if he liked hunting. He replied that his father had
> been very fond of it, but that he himself, from his earliest youth, had
> had a real passion for navigation and for fireworks. He told us that he
> worked himself in building ships, showed us his hands, and made us
> touch the callous places that had been caused by work. He brought
> his musicians, and they played Russian dances, which we liked better
> than Polish ones.
>   . . . He is a very extraordinary man. It is impossible to describe him,
> or even to give an idea of him, unless you have seen him. He has a
> very good heart, and remarkably noble sentiments. I must tell you,
> also, that he did not get drunk in our presence, but we had hardly left
> when the people of his suite made ample amends.

In another letter describing a new meeting with Peter and remarking
on his "many good qualities and depth of mind," the princess intro-
duces an amusing detail: "but in dancing, they took the whalebones of
our corsets for our bones, and the Tsar showed his astonishment by
saying that the German ladies had devilish hard bones."[5]

These letters mention those features of Peter's personality to which it
would later become a peculiar collective obligation to draw attention on
the part of memoirists and later of historians as well. In wishing to give
a full picture, however, one cannot avoid in future discussions similar

remarks, characterizations, and observations, for they really reflect the extraordinary features of this autocrat "of all Rus' " that were not typical of his contemporaries, the crowned heads of the West.

First, that which struck observers most about Peter was his exceptional appearance, the simplicity of his life-style, and his egalitarianism in dealing with people from different levels of society.

He might pop up in any corner of Petersburg, drop into any house, sit down at table and not shun the simplest food. He did not remain indifferent to popular diversions and games. Here are only two excerpts from the diary of Bergholtz, chamberlain of Duke Charles Frederick of Holstein, from 10 April and 5 November 1724 that amply illustrate the aforementioned traits: "We learned that on this day after dinner the emperor with many officers played on the swings at the Krasnye Gates that had been set up there for the common folk on the occasion of the holiday, which had already happened once several days before"; "there was a wedding at the house of one German baker who lives in the neighborhood of the emperor's Winter Palace. . . . The emperor, probably driving by, heard the music and being curious to see how they celebrate weddings in that class of foreigners, completely unexpectedly went into the baker's house with several of his people, ordered two special tables set there, one for himself, the other for his suite, and watched the wedding ceremonies and dancing more than three hours. During all this time he was unusually merry."[6]

Peter consciously avoided widespread manifestations of that special semisacrosanct respect for the person of the Russian tsar with which his predecessors on the throne had surrounded themselves from time immemorial. Indeed, one gets the impression that Peter did this deliberately, demonstratively violating the accepted etiquette hallowed for centuries. At the same time it would be incorrect to think that by similar disdain for custom he strove to destroy the respect for supreme authority, to cast doubt on its omnipotence and sanctity for his subjects. In his attitude toward the majesty and significance of the autocrat's authority one observes a different approach, founded on the principles of rationalism, about which we shall speak in detail later.

Such a mode of behavior by Peter struck observers: to some it seemed capricious and eccentric, to others—especially in the folk milieu—"deceitful" and false. Be that as it may, the fidgety, active tsar chose the sole convenient, natural mode of life for himself, one that was impossible with the observance of traditional ritual forms. It is impossible to imagine Peter's dealings with his subjects on the streets of Petersburg if, according to tradition, they groveled in the mud and were afraid to raise their heads when he appeared.

A decree of 1722 has been preserved that serves, apparently, as a supplement to the *Articles of War*. Enumerating in it the modes of greeting the emperor, Peter writes that it is essential to ask him beforehand, because "marching out all the soldiers in formation with weapons is not always required, for sometimes he wishes that his passage not be much noticed, and sometimes thanks to this particular use he will be bored."[7]

In the history of Russia we know very few rulers who could ever be "bored" by the magnificent ritual of semisacrosanct reverence and submission. Of course, the tsar's unusual conduct—that of "a worker on the throne"—could only elicit great sympathy for his personality from posterity, which more often contended with quite a different manner of behavior and a different life-style from later rulers who sometimes lacked even the slightest of Peter's innate genius. But what was the essence, the sense of such behavior on his part?

For a start we will not be unduly seduced by the first emperor's "democracy," which is not so simple and uniform. In the Soviet film *Peter the First* there is one episode remarkable for its expressiveness. A foreign diplomat, who has turned up at a Petrine assembly for the first time, is astonished to catch sight of Peter at table surrounded by seamen and merchants. He inquires of Piotr Shafirov standing nearby: "They say the tsar is simple?" To which the vice-chancellor responds with a smile: "The master is simple in manner."

It is generally known that at Peter's court there reigned, to express oneself in "high style," the cult of Bacchus, or speaking more plainly, rather disgraceful drunkenness. Official state, religious, and other festivities were often accompanied by drinking bouts lasting many days in which all the greatest figures of state participated. "Service to Bacchus" was considered a peculiar kind of valor that it was acceptable to take pride in, anticipating the tsar's approval.

Peter himself much encouraged such an attitude toward disgraceful drinking bouts. Though they became typical of court life, such phenomena were quite unusual at the courts of his successors and even rarer at those of his predecessors, with the possible exception of Ivan the Terrible's Oprichnina court, where outrageous Bacchanalias sometimes took on the coloration of drunken executions.

There are many explanations for this regrettable, by contemporary standards, spectacle. There were the established traditions of carnival, holiday culture—carousing was still not an everyday phenomenon and mostly occurred in connection with holidays and masquerades—and there was the rather low level of everyday culture and notions about recreation. But in this case something else attracts our attention. Just Juel, who was often compelled to attend such gatherings and to drink against his will, wrote:

At all feasts as soon as the guests assemble, before they start to drink, the tsar has already ordered the guard doubled at the door so that nobody is let out, not excluding even those who vomit. But still the tsar himself rarely drinks more than one or, at most, two bottles of wine, so that I rarely saw him drunk as a cobbler. In the meantime he compels the remaining guests to drink until they cannot see or hear anything, and then the tsar undertakes to gossip with them, attempting to find out what each has on his mind. Disputes and curses among the drunken are also after the tsar's heart, because from their mutual recriminations their thievery, crookedness, and cunning are revealed to him.[8]

What can one say? Such a mode of conduct manifestly does not fit the image of the great tsar's conduct known to us from other sources. I think there is no contradiction here. Peter was convinced that in the name of the state's aims one might ignore many ethical norms. On this basis the institution of fiscality (fiscal surveillance) took root and, more broadly, the culture of denunciations that flourished under Peter. This happened all the more easily because, to the tsar's way of thinking, the ethics of a private "particular" person did not resemble those of a ruler who lived in the name of the state's highest aims.

But this is only one side of Petrine democracy. Much more important is another, which had far-reaching consequences. The same Juel noted down on 10 December 1709: "After noon I set off for the Admiralty wharf to be present at the raising of the stem of a 50-gun ship, but on that day was raised only the forestem because the derricks proved to be too weak to raise the stem. The tsar, as the chief shipwright (a post for which he receives a salary), supervised everything, took part in the work along with the others and, where necessary, swung an axe, which he wields more skillfully than all the other carpenters present there."[9]

It was not enough that Peter served and worked as a carpenter; he even appeared as a "subject" of the jester "prince-caesar" Fedor Romodanovsky, to whom he wrote reports and petitions, and addressed him as subject to ruler. At once we note that Romodanovsky and others treated this uniformly as a game, and Peter's letter-requests were taken as decrees that one was obliged to fulfill. Here comes to mind the memory of Simeon Bekbulatovich—the vassal khan of Kasimov to whom Ivan the Terrible "transmitted" the throne and wrote submissive petitions in the name of "Ivashka." "Giving up" the throne to a puppet, Ivan strove thereby to untie his hands for a new cycle of bloody revenge against real and imagined opponents.

Though he respected Ivan, Peter was playing other games. Their essence consisted of the fulfillment of "service." For Peter "service" was a synthetic concept that gathered together a distinct awareness of the duties of each toward the state and the sovereign, their zealous and honest fulfillment, even if that was accompanied by risk to health and life, unconditional obedience to the will of the chief commander, and the right to reward for selfless labor or feats in war (regarding this his letters have been preserved addressed to Romodanovsky in gratitude for the award of the next military rank). Several insightful contemporaries recognized this, correctly interpreting the tsar's conduct as a method of training his subjects and as propaganda of the new image of life.

In 1705 the English ambassador Charles Whitworth wrote: "When the Czar is with his army, he has not hitherto appeared as general, but only as captain of the bombardiers, and acts according to that post, and his son, the young prince, is a cadet in the Preobrazhensky guards, which they probably do with a design of obliging the first nobility to follow their example, and breed themselves up to a knowledge of military affairs, whereas formerly it seems they thought they were born generals as well as lords and princes."[10]

It is crucially important to mention that Peter understood service not simply as the conscientious fulfillment of obligations and obedience to superiors, but as service to the state. Precisely in this he saw the meaning and main aim of his life and the lives of his subjects.

This observation allows us to give an explanation of Peter's deeds and acts that sometimes, it might seem, palpably contradicted his character as an impulsive, lively, impatient person. This appeared especially clearly in diplomatic activities. Suffice it to recall the history of his relations with unfaithful allies—Frederick IV of Denmark and Augustus II, King of Poland and Elector of Saxony—a history in which Peter, an outstanding diplomat, displayed rare patience and tact, restrained his own outbursts, and managed to attain the most important aim: to restore after 1706 the Northern Alliance against Sweden.

An unusually capable and diligent man, he delighted in work, especially that which bore real results that were visible to everyone. In the most diverse spheres of activity he was notable. As John Perry, an Englishman in Russian service, wrote, "it may be said of him, that he is from the Drummer to the General, a compleat Soldier; besides his being Engineer, Cannoneer, Fire-worker, Ship-builder, Turner, Boatswain, Gun-founder, Blacksmith, etc. All of which he frequently works at with his own Hands, and will himself see that every thing be carried on and perform'd to his own Mind, as well in these minutest things, as in the greater Disposition of Affairs."[11]

No doubt the personal example of service to the state that Peter selflessly demonstrated for the eyes of thousands of people on the blocks of dockyards, in the forests of construction sites, on the bridge of ships, or on the battlefield was exceptionally effective, infectious for some and obligatory for others. Peter was sincerely convinced that reigning was his service to Russia; that in reigning he was fulfilling his duty to the state. By his own example he challenged all of his subjects to fulfill their obligations just as selflessly.

Archbishop Feofan Prokopovich, a theorist of absolutism, put forward a whole concept of the tsar's "exemplary, higher obligations" for his "service." Placed at the summit of "ranks," the autocrat represents, according to Feofan, the highest "rank" to which God Himself has assigned him, entrusting him with the difficult "service" of administering the subjects. Such a godly-bureaucratic conception wholly corresponded to the ideas of the creator of the "Table of Ranks."

The monarch's obligations were set forth in the well-known postulates of the law concerning the church, *The Justice of the Monarch's Will*: "The duty of tsars is ... to maintain their subjects in felicity and to formulate for them every kind of good instruction for piety, and also for honest living." Obviously, for the successful accomplishment of these basic obligations of the monarch he must, according to Feofan's thinking, possess absolute authority, to wit: "legislative authority that is supremely effective, bearing supreme justice ... and his own not subordinate to any law."[12]

Attempts to determine the monarch's obligations and to formulate rather precisely the bounds or, more exactly, the boundlessness of his authority were the result of new ideas that affected the political culture of Russia at the turn of the seventeenth and eighteenth centuries.

Feofan's notions about the monarch's "service" and authority were not original; they stemmed from ideas current at that time in the juridical and philosophical thought of Western Europe. These require somewhat more detailed consideration.

From the many customary symbols of the Petrine epoch one should specially single out the ship under sail with the captain on the bridge. About this Alexander Pushkin has spoken best of all in his poem "My Family Tree":

> This captain was the captain glorious
> By whom our earth was moved.
> Who imperiously imparted the strong course
> By the helm of our own ship.

Why a ship? I think that for Peter too it was not only a means of transport for freight across the water's surface. The ship—Peter's eternal love—was for him a symbol of a structure organized and calculated to the inch, the material embodiment of human thought, complex movement by the will of rational man. Furthermore, the ship for Peter was a peculiar model of the ideal society, the best form of organization relying on knowledge of the laws of nature in man's eternal struggle with the blind elements.

Behind this symbol is a whole layer of culture, the world of intellectual treasures of the epoch of rationalism of the European seventeenth century, the successor to the Renaissance of the sixteenth century and the predecessor of the Enlightenment of the eighteenth century. A pleiad of outstanding thinkers shaped the circle of ideas, creating the atmosphere in which breathed the poets, artists, scholars, and statesmen. Among the rulers of minds were Bacon, Spinoza, Locke, Gassendi, Hobbes, Leibniz. Their ideas began actively to reach Russia along with Peter's reforms, and the names of the great philosophers of the century of rationalism were not alien to Russian ears.

What were these ideas? Simplifying matters, one may single out several of the more important ones. The people of the seventeenth century, as never before, felt the force of experimental knowledge in which they discovered the means of attaining dominion over nature. In this struggle a special place was reserved for the organization of human society, more specifically for the state. It was conceived to be an institution that had arisen through the will of free people who had made, for the sake of their own security, a contract by which they ceded their rights to the state. The state thus appeared to be a purely human institution; people might perfect it depending on the common purposes that they set for themselves. The state, Hobbes contended, is constructed like a house (and like a ship, we should add, following the metaphor cited). This notion was often repeated in different variations, for it was the weapon that forced out the medieval idea of the immutability and God-given nature of state forms.

Derived from this idea was another: that the state is an ideal instrument, the universal institution of the training of people that converts them into conscious, virtuous, useful citizens of society. Laws and organization serve as the state's levers. Law, like the state itself, is the creation of man, and in perfecting laws and attaining their fulfillment with the aid of institutions, one may attain the flowering of universal happiness, of universal good—a cloudy purpose, but one which has always enticed people.

For mankind, which had emerged from the obscurantist shade of the Middle Ages, it seemed that the key to happiness had finally been found—one only need formulate laws correctly, to perfect the organization, to attain absolute, universal, and exact fulfillment of the state's initiatives. It was no accident that there was a reinforcement in society of the influence of deism—the teaching whereby God was relegated to the role of prime mover. Furthermore, the deists considered that nature and man developed according to their own, natural laws, which one needs only to discern and to record. Hence the (for us) astonishingly optimistic naive faith of people of the seventeenth and eighteenth centuries in the unlimited powers of rational man, who erects his own house, ship, city, and state according to plan on the basis of experimental knowledge. This era had its own hero too: Robinson Crusoe, who was not so much a literary image as a symbol of the century of rationalism that showed the whole world that man can surmount all adversity and misfortunes, believing in his own powers and relying on his own knowledge and experience.

It is likewise important to note that in an appraisal of social phenomena and institutions, mechanism held sway—more precisely mechanical determinism. The outstanding successes of mathematics and the natural sciences created the illusion that one might treat life in all its manifestations as a mechanical process. With equal ardor such an approach was applied to physiology, psychology, society, and the state, for according to Descartes's teaching on universal mathematics (*mathesis universalis*), all sciences were seen as another form of mathematics, which appeared to be especially important then as the only certain knowledge shorn of mysticism.

Without taking account of all these ideas one might misunderstand Peter's intentions as well as his vital concept. Of course, it would be a great exaggeration to think that Peter had mastered the entire corpus of the philosophical ideas of the epoch. He was not a philosopher and probably did not even possess a philosophical turn of mind. Nevertheless it is impossible to dismiss the wide currency (even if in popularized, simplified form) of these ideas in public consciousness and their role in shaping the intellectual atmosphere of thinking persons of those times. It is impossible to forget, too, that Peter was acquainted with Leibniz, possibly with Locke as well. Finally, one should consider the intense interest that the tsar-reformer displayed for the works of the jurists and state theorists Hugo Grotius and Samuel Pufendorf. The latter's book *On the Duties of Man and Citizen* was translated into Russian under Peter, who respected it very much. It is significant that these authoritative works refracted the philosophical ideas of the century of rationalism as applicable to the state. It is no accident that in Leibniz's correspondence with Peter the problem of state reforms is touched upon and that Leibniz presents an image of the state in the form of clockwork, all the gears of which work in ideal conjunction. There can be no doubt that this image was close to Peter's view of the world, as a true son of his century.

In his approach to life and to people we see features that predominated at that time: extreme rationalism and practicality. Peter was a typical technocrat. Displaying interest in many spheres of knowledge, he manifestly gave preference to the exact sciences and in general to knowledge that had an applied, practical significance.

Medicine—particularly surgery—enjoyed Peter's special respect. Peter had long been fascinated in observing it, and later he himself performed rather complicated operations, the risk of which could in truth be appraised only by the patients themselves. Peter's love for medicine was greater than that which he felt for sailing on the uncertain seas or for the roar of cannon; it caused anxiety to those close to him, for Peter considered himself an indisputable authority in this and, indeed, in many other spheres of knowledge. He carefully looked after the health of his own courtiers and relatives, eagerly offering his services, the more so as he always carried with him a valise of surgical instruments, while he carefully kept in a special sack the teeth he had pulled. When an operation proved to be unsuccessful, Peter dissected the corpse of his patient in the anatomy theater with no less knowledge, for he was a good pathologist-anatomist.

Peter's rationalist approach may be exemplified, of course, in his personally fashioning a new alphabet, from which he discarded everything that struck him as overloading the letter or which had become old or imperfect.

Peter also evaluated art from the position of a technocrat. Artistic works ought to serve, according to the tsar's thinking, either as decoration or as symbol, a visual training aid that gives people knowledge or instructive examples for their moral perfection. In other cases Peter displayed utter indifference toward the artistic treasures of Paris, Dresden, Vienna, and London. Maybe only fireworks and all kinds of "pyrotechnic games" were Peter's true aesthetic passion. Possibly in them he found the rare combination of the beautiful and the useful.

In the literature the question has often been posed whether Peter was religious. The majority of scholars have not come to a definite answer, so contradictory is the historical material that has come down to us. Actually, on one hand we see indubitable toleration (excluding the traditional negative attitude toward Jews professing Judaism), friendship with assorted foreigners, an interest in world religions and problems of natural science, rejection of the ritual standards of old Russian "piety" as the most important features of the autocrat, an ex-

tremely negative attitude toward superstitions, the avarice of churchmen, disdain for monasticism as a form of existence, the blasphemous
joking of the "most-all-drunken conclaves," and, last and most important, the reform of the church that brought it into final subjection to
the state's authority. All this created for Peter among the broad masses of
the people the ingrained reputation of a "tobacco-stained atheist" and
"Antichrist" whose name was cursed by many generations of Old Believers.

On the other hand, in reading thousands of Peter's letters, one sees
in them that God's name is not just a tribute to tradition or custom that
occurs even now among atheists ("Glory to God," "God willing," etc.),
but testimony of real religious feeling. To be sure, in this regard I
deliberately cast aside the words, formulas, and ritual expressions used
exclusively for propagandistic, political purposes. More important is
something else. Peter's antichurch policy never became antireligious.
In Peter's church policy there is no hint of Protestantism. It is impossible not to notice, too, Peter's complete passivity and deprecation when
Catholic militants solicited him to reactivate the old idea of the Union
of Florence of the fifteenth century, reuniting the Catholic and Orthodox churches. The same thing was proposed by Protestant bishops.
They knew what they were doing, for in principle it completely corresponded to Peter's ideas about the quickest and closest rapprochement
of Russia with the West.

Despite Peter's inclination to joke about religion, he certainly did
not neglect the obligations of an Orthodox Christian. Remarkable is a
notation on a writing pad that advances one of the arguments of a
dispute (possibly imaginary) between the tsar and atheists: "Against
atheists. If they imagine that laws are imaginary, then why does one
animal eat another, and we [eat them]? For what reason is such a
calamity done to them?"[13] The point here, apparently, concerns the
thesis regarding the reasonable beginnings of the universe. According
to this thesis, its forms arose in correspondence with internal, rational
laws innate to nature that have nothing in common with God's laws. An
argument against this widespread rationalist thesis, Peter proposed, appears to be the incompatibility of the rationality ("imaginary things" in
Peter's terminology) of nature with the prevailing bitter struggle for
existence, which in Peter's thinking destroys the extragodly harmony of
nature. This same thinking also serves Peter as weighty proof of the
error of atheists who repudiate God, the creator and ruler of the universe, who in Peter's conception comes forth as the awesome Yahweh
the despot, in whose image and likeness the tsar may possibly have
thought of himself.

On the whole I think the tsar had no problems with God. He proceeded from a series of principles that reconciled his faith with reason. He considered that there is no sense in killing soldiers on campaign and denying them meat during fasts—they needed strength for the triumph of Russia, and that meant for Orthodoxy too.

Notable too is the saga of Peter's excursion to the museum of Luther in Wittenberg. Examining the library and burial place of the great reformer, Peter with those accompanying him "were in the room where he lived and under a seal on the wall of that room they pointed to drops of ink, and said that when he, sitting in the room, had been writing the devil came to him, and then he supposedly threw the inkwell at the devil, and the ink had supposedly remained there on the wall till now, which the master himself looked at and found that the inkdrops were new and darkish; later the local clergy requested that the master sign something personally in the room in memory of his being there and on their request the master signed this in chalk: 'The ink is new and this is utter nonsense.' "[14]

But in speaking about similar, quite typical manifestations of Peter's rationalism, one should not rush to extremes and pronounce them to be testimony to his atheism. Noteworthy and not unlikely is Nartov's account of a visit to Novgorod's Saint Sophia Cathedral by Peter and Jacob Bruce, the well-known bookman, or, more precisely, magician and alchemist, about whose unbelief and contacts with the devil many contemporaries gossiped. Standing with the tsar next to the shrine of some saints, Bruce recounted to Peter the causes of the incorruptibility of the bodies lying inside. Nartov writes: "But as Bruce was attributing this to the climate, to the nature of the earth in which earlier the bodies had been buried for embalming and for preservation, and dryness and fasting, then Peter the Great, stepping up finally to the relics of Saint Nikita, archbishop of Novgorod, opened them, lifted them out of the shrine, set them down, spread the arms, folded them, put them back, and then asked: 'what do you say now, Jacob Danilovich? How does this come about that the joints of the bones move as if he were alive, and they are not decaying, and the look of the face is like that of somebody who had recently died?' Count Bruce, having seen this miracle, was extremely moved and in astonishment replied: 'I don't know this, yet I know that God is omnipotent and all wise.' "

It may be that Bruce really did lose his head somewhat and could not immediately find words to answer Peter, who, according to Nartov, remarked instructively at the time: "This I believe and I see that the secular sciences are still far behind the secret knowledge of the majesty of the Creator, to Whom I pray, may He convince me by the Spirit."[15]

Let us imagine this phantasmagorical situation where, standing at

the opened shrine of the saint with the corpse sitting there, the autocrat of all the Russias and the scholarly general-grand master of ordnance conduct a philosophical discourse about the limits of knowledge
in explaining the world. This scene astounds by its blasphemy (for one
cannot forget that it is occurring not in the Kunst Kamer [Chamber of
Curiosities] but in one of Orthodoxy's holy places with sacred remains
to whom generations of the faithful have paid reverence) and at the
same time by how it reflects Peter's faith, devoid of mysticism and
superstition, proof for which he seeks again in the impotence of science
to explain phenomena the source of which consequently may be, in
Peter's opinion, only God.

In general, the impression has been created that Peter's thinking was
far from religious: phenomena that he observed and in which he participated elicited in him (in accordance with the language of European
culture of the seventeenth century—a time of classicism) not biblical
but classical images; the imagery of comparison was not strained but
natural and precise. Thus, in one of the letters from the victorious
battlefield near Poltava he compares the fate of the Swedish army with
the fate of Helious Phaeton, the proud son of the sun-god who could
not contend with the sun's rays, and in another he compares the retreating foe with the nymph Echo fleeing from her pursuer.

Remarkable are the dreams that the tsar remembered and which he
immediately noted down or ordered his secretary to record. Reflecting
the man's unbridled consciousness, they vividly show the special symbolic mentality of his thinking. These dreams consist of blocs of allego-
ries that enjoyed wide currency in the culture of that time, and it may
be possible to use them as a description of some festive firework, an
allegorical group sculpture designated for the next calendar festival.

> His Majesty on the 26th day of April 1715 had a dream: It was as
> though an eagle were sitting in a tree, and beneath it had crept or
> crawled some sort of large wild beast, like a crocodile or a dragon,
> onto which this eagle immediately leapt, and gnawed its head from its
> neck—that is, chewed away half the neck and killed it. And then,
> while many people gathered to watch, another such beast crept up,
> whose head this eagle also gnawed off, it seemed in plain view of
> everybody.[16]

Can any contemporary reader recall such a vivid allegorical dream? The
cat's wish for the mice will not figure.

The idea of rationalism was distributed in full measure over the state,
which ought to have been subjected in the first instance to the action of

the principles of reason, logic, and order. Proceeding from these principles, Peter lived, showing an example of serving and service, and in accordance with the spirit of the time he formulated the idea of the monarch's obligations to his subjects.

But, carried away by such rare simplicity for a ruler, Peter's capacity for work, purposefulness, and selflessness, one cannot forget two crucial nuances: first, the monarch himself defined his circle of obligations in "serving" the people that varied with his discretion and was not recorded anywhere in legislation; second, the tsar's "service" and the service of his subjects were essentially distinguished from one another. Indeed, for the latters' service to the state, regardless of their wishes, merged with service to the tsar, more broadly to the autocracy. In other words, by his daily toil Peter showed his subjects the example of how they should serve him, the Russian autocrat. The memoirist Perry underscored this point: "As the Czar has taken particular Regard to have his own Subjects qualify'd to serve him on all these Occasions, and has spared no Pains for it, but continually busies himself amongst these Men. . . ."[17]

Of course, here one should not simplify things. To be sure, serving the Fatherland, Russia, was the most important element of the political culture of the Petrine era. It fed upon well-known traditions of the struggle for independence, for survival, which was unthinkable without national statehood. One may find many examples of such a struggle in pre-Petrine history. Suffice it to recall the civic feat of Minin and Pozharsky, who at the start of the seventeenth century defended "the land," a concept for the inhabitant of medieval Rus' that was capacious and multilayered and included the community, the town, and the state. They took action against the Poles not only in the name of the ruler— the Orthodox tsar, whom they were still to select, but thanks to "the cause of all the land." The tradition of "the Land" was one of the most important in the history of old Rus'. But in post-Petrine and especially in Petrine times another tradition also dating from ancient times remained fundamental, defining—the identification of supreme authority and the tsar's personality with the state. The development of this tendency had led to a merger of notions about statehood and Fatherland—concepts hallowed for each citizen and which symbolized independent national existence—with a notion concerning the bearer of nationhood, a fully real, alive, and, as a rule, far from faultless person to whom (by force of the position occupied) were imputed the standards of nationhood. In recent history the identification of the ruler's personality with the state, the Motherland, and even the people has been exhibited in the cult of Stalin.

For Russia's political life this entailed, as we know, the most sorrow-ful consequences, for any move against the bearer of supreme author-ity, whether he be the supreme ruler or a petty official, could be treated as a move against him who exemplified in his person nationhood, Rus-sia, and the people, and that means it could lead to accusations of treason, crimes against the state, and recognition by the foe. The idea of identifying culpability for insulting the monarch's person with insult-ing the state had been set forth with particular clarity in the Law Code of 1649—the most important legal document of Russian history in the seventeenth century that consolidated the system of autocracy and serf-dom. The apotheosis of these ideas emerged under Peter and was re-flected in full measure in legal standards.

In the military's oath of fidelity confirmed under Peter there is no concept of Russia, Fatherland, or land. There is only the concept of the "tsar-master," while the state itself is referred to as "his tsarist majesty's — state and lands." But even these words are not in the oath of servitors included in the General Regulation that regulated the life of the state. The oath was given "to his own native and true tsar and master, the most serene and most mighty Peter the First, tsar and all-Russian auto-crat, et cetera, et cetera, et cetera." Then came the oath of fidelity

> to the august lawful heirs who have been designated and are to be desig-nated henceforth by H. Ts. M.'s wish and autocratic authority as worthy of accepting the throne, and to H. M. mistress and tsaritsa Ekaterina Alekseevna [Catherine I], to be a loyal, good, and obedient servant and subject, and all the rights and prerogatives (or privileges) appertaining to H. Ts. M.'s august autocracy, power, and authority that have been legis-lated and will be legislated by the utmost reason, to protect and defend as far as possible without sparing his own life if need be.[18]

Concerning any duty to the Fatherland or to Russia there is not, as we see, a word.

Under Peter the traditional idea of autocracy received new impetus, when an attempt was undertaken to substantiate rationalistically the absolute authority of one man over millions. The urgency of this was caused by the fact that for Petrine society acknowledgment of the divine origin of the tsar's authority as the single argument for its reverence was already insufficient. Its foundations needed different, new, rationalistic principles. Therefore, Feofan Prokopovich introduced into Russian po-litical culture concepts taken from the contract theory of law, according to which people, in order to guard against self-destruction, ought to give themselves to a ruler who is obligated to defend them but in exchange receives full supreme authority over them. In the conditions of Russia, which was undergoing fundamental transformations, the paternalistic idea was set forth as a derivative of these conceptions; there was formulated the image of a rational monarch who saw far beyond the horizon—a father of the Fatherland and of the people. In *The Justice of the Monarch's Will* Feofan reaches the at first glance paradoxical yet logical deduction that if the master "by his supreme authority" is "father" to all his subjects, then by the same token he is "father" to his own father.[19]

Peter's turner Andrei Nartov explains in peculiar terms the tsar's frequent reprisals against his own errant dignitaries: "I often saw how the master applied the club here (i.e., in the turner's shop) to persons of eminent rank for abuses, and how afterward they went out into other rooms with a merry face and the master, so that outsiders would not notice, that same day invited them to dinner." And further the main point: "But all such correction was done not as from emperor to subject, but as from father to son: one was punished and honored on the same day." Close to this is Stählin's account about how on a broken bridge the tsar beat with a club the senior policemaster of Petersburg, Andrei Devier, who was driving with him in a single-seated carriage, resolving: "Henceforth you will try harder to see that the streets and bridges are in proper repair, and yourself will look after them." "Meanwhile," continues Stählin, "the bridge was repaired, and the master's wrath passed. He climbed into the one-seater and talked to the senior-policemaster quite kindly, as if nothing had happened between them: 'Sit down, brother!' "[20]

Here it is essential to make a brief digression. The notion about a monarch or a president or some other ruler being "father" to his subjects and fellow citizens is a phenomenon widely spread among different peoples at different times. Max Weber in his studies of authority introduced the concept of "the charismatic leader" as a transition between the traditional and the democratic. The term "charisma," which was borrowed from early Christian literature and applied to the Christian-godly elect, allows us to single out a series of elements and peculiarities of such a figure's authority. The charismatic leader is a state figure who possesses a number of qualities thanks to which he or she is singled out of the milieu of ordinary people and "is considered to be endowed with supernatural, superhuman or, at least, exceptional skills and qualities. These are not accessible to the ordinary person, and they are seen as stemming from God or are exemplary, and on their basis the given individual is considered a leader." Also important are other peculiarities of the charismatic leader. As a rule, he scorns material interests (at least in the beginning); he is surrounded by associates who bolster the leader's charisma and who, as a rule, derive from it real material advantage, authority, and riches. "In the sphere of his own pretensions the charismatic leader rejects the past and in this sense he represents a specific revolutionary force." Finally, the title "Father of the Fatherland" and "Father of the nation" is strongly individualized. Leadership of the charismatic type is not transmitted by heredity, like a throne.[21]

For Peter there are, no doubt, many features typical of the charismatic leader. His authority was based not so much on divine sanction, but mainly on recognition of his distinctive traits, their demonstrative-pedagogical "exemplarity" in the fulfillment of "duty."

All the same, Peter was not capricious. Simple in his mode of life, he lived in a modest little house, and later in the quite unpretentious—for the time—Summer and Winter palaces. Receiving the salary of a general and ship-captain, he did not dine at home on goldplate or even silverplate, and his crowned spouse diligently darned stockings for him.

Concerning his negative attitude toward many traditional forms of reverence for the autocrat, as well as his constant orientation toward reforms, I shall discuss these matters further later on. He was truly revolutionary. We know that revolutions are diverse; the main thing is that they entail a consistent and deep urge to transform, to make a fundamental break in society. To be sure, the question of the aim of the revolutionary break remains open (we recall the recent victory of Islamic revolutionary fundamentalism in Iran). In Petrine Russia such a break led, in the final reckoning, to the consolidation and solidification of structures of bondage.

Celebrating the tsar-reformer's personality, stressing his special personal distinctions, was a most typical feature of the publicity of the Petrine era. It inevitably brought in its wake the creation of an actual cult of personality of the transformer of Russia, which was allegedly obligated only to him for all that had been attained and which had been raised only through his efforts to heights unattainable earlier. As Ivan Nepliuev, a contemporary of Peter, wrote, "whatever you look at in Russia, we have everything through his initiative, and whatever is done henceforth, we shall mine it from this source."[22] Such a cult of the monarch's person is a phenomenon not unknown in earlier Russian political culture.

The Petrine publicists (Feofan, Shafirov) floridly lauded Peter's personal merits. During Peter's lifetime they already compared him with outstanding figures of Russian and world history: Alexander Nevsky, Alexander the Great, Julius Caesar, and so forth.

It is difficult to exalt a personality that has already been elevated to such heights through coronation. Thus, the thinking of the ideologues turned to the experience of the Roman Empire. On the day of the

celebration of the Peace of Nystadt with Sweden, 30 October 1721, the
Senate submitted a request in which it underlined the tsar's special role
in "producing" Russia and asked him to accept a new title never seen in
Russia before: "Father of the Fatherland, All-Russian Emperor, Peter
the Great, as customarily such titles were publicly awarded by the
Roman Senate to the emperors for eminent deeds and were written on
statues for the memory of eternal ages."[23]

Resorting to Rome's experience was no accident. The orientation to
Imperial Rome, and to the city of Rome as the capital of the world in
general, may be traced back in the symbolism of Imperial Russia, in fact
to its earliest stages. This appears, as Georgii Villinbakhov has remarked
in his studies, both in naming the new capital and the patron cathedral
in honor of Saint Peter—Saint-Petersburg—and in the city's crest,
which repeats the crossed keys from the state flag of the Vatican.

It is important to note, however, that in accordance with the principles of charisma the title "Father of the Fatherland" was Peter's privilege alone and did not represent an obligatory attribute of all Russian
emperors. Although the successors of the first emperor were praised for
insignificant personal merits and for "generosity" to the Russian people,
officially they did not have the title. To be sure, in likening herself to
her great father, Elizabeth I (reigned 1741–61) was named "Mother of
the Fatherland," but this did not elicit any images to inspire the soul or
comparisons from her contemporaries.

Peter perceived the reforms and the onerous toil in peacetime and
wartime as constant training, a school in which the Russian people
attained knowledge unknown earlier. A manifesto of 16 April 1702 inviting foreign specialists to Russia mentioned that one of the autocracy's
most important tasks is "to institute changes for the greater training of
the people, so that our subjects may be conveniently made into trained
people in manners the longer and more thoroughly they are exposed
to every kind of society and intercourse with all other Christians."[24]

The Northern War was likewise persistently linked to the concept of
study. Upon receiving word of the conclusion of the Peace of Nystadt,
Peter interpreted the event as certification of graduation (somewhat
late, to be sure) from a peculiar school. In a letter to Vasily Dolgoruky
on the occasion of the peace he wrote: "All students usually finish their
studies in seven years, but our school has been thrice as long [21 years],
yet, God be praised, it has ended so well that it could not be better."[25]
Well known too is his expression "Just as I have been in the ranks of
students so am I demanding of my students."

In reality, the conception of life as study and training is typical of a
rationalist perception of the world. It is also typical of Peter, a person

exceptionally inquisitive, active, and capable. But in the school into which he had converted the country, he reserved for himself the post of the Teacher who knows what the students need. In a setting of stormy transformations whose aims—except in the most general sense—were not clearly visible and comprehensible to everyone and were met by open and more often by concealed resistance, the idea of the wise Teacher with which Peter identified himself was reinforced in his consciousness in contrast to the unreasonable children-subjects. Stubborn in their stagnation and laziness, they could be trained for study and good work only with the help of coercion, by the stick, for they understood nothing else.

Peter spoke of it often. In a decree of 5 November 1723 to the College of Manufactures concerning the difficulty of fostering manufacturing industry in the country, he wrote: "It is true that few are eager, inasmuch as our folk are like unschooled children who will never take up the alphabet if not compelled by the master and who find it vexing at first, but once they learn it, are grateful; and this is clearly true of all the current undertakings carried out under compulsion, for already gratitude is heard for much that has borne fruit."[26]

The notion of coercion, of compulsion as the universal means of resolving internal problems, was not new in the history of Russia, as we know. But Peter was perhaps the first who so consistently and so systematically employed coercion for the attainment of the state's highest aims, as he understood them.

Among the stories that compose the memoirs of Andrei Nartov there is one that attracts special attention. Nartov recounts an integrated concept of the autocrat's authority, as the tsar understood it: "Peter the Great, conversing in the turner's shop with Bruce and Osterman, told them vehemently: 'The foreigners say that I order servitors around like slaves. I order them like subjects who obey my decrees. These decrees contain good and not harm for the state. *English freedom is not relevant here, like a blank wall. One must know the people to rule them.* He who sees the bad and thinks up the good can speak to me directly without fear. You are witnesses to that. I am glad to hear something useful from the least subject; hands, feet, and tongues are not bridled. Access to me is open—if only they do not burden me merely with trifles and do not vainly take up my time each hour of which is dear to me. Ill-wishers and miscreants to me and to the fatherland cannot be content: their bridle is the law. He is free who does not do evil and obeys the good.' "[27]

Although Nartov's *Anecdotes* contain much that it is unreliable, this deserves belief, for it is confirmed by other documents and reflects Peter's cast of mind.

The idea of paternalism defines everything: Peter is the only one who knows what the people need, and his decrees, because they contain only unconditional good, all subjects are obliged to fulfill. Those dissatisfied with the laws issued by the tsar are "miscreants to me and to the fatherland." Notable also is the tsar's conviction that in Russia, as distinct from England, such is the single path of leading the country toward the good. Besides, this hymn to the regime of single authority (in essence, veiled tyranny under which the ruler's will is the only source of law) is based on all those above-enumerated duties of the monarch whom God has called to power, and this means he has the right to command and knows what is best by the power of God's will.

Count Brümmer, a courtier of the Duke of Holstein (and the future supervisor of Peter III), recounted to Stählin Peter I's quite positive reaction to the analogy between his reign and the rule of Ivan the Terrible. Peter supposedly said: "This master (indicating tsar Ivan Vasil'evich) is my predecessor and example. I have always taken him as an example in wisdom and courage, but I cannot yet compare to him. Only blockheads who do not know the circumstances of his time, the traits of his people, and his great merits call him a tyrant."[28]

I think that the memoirists scarcely grasped the tsar's political sympathies. These are self-evident and stem from his philosophy of supreme power. The contention that Peter knew little about his predecessor Ivan the Terrible and was therefore fascinated by him can have no bearing here. Indeed, it is well known that the profound knowledge of Ivan's bloody tyranny assembled by generations of historians could still not undermine a stubborn political sympathy for Stalin's medieval tyranny and for that "murderer and muzhik-slayer" of recent times (Osip Mandelstam).

The concept of compulsion was based not only on the completely traditional idea of paternalism, but, quite likely, on the peculiarities of Peter's personality as well. In his attitude toward people there was much that one may call brutality, intolerance, and hardness of heart. It was as if man with his weaknesses, problems, personality, and individuality did not exist for him. One gets the impression that he often looked on people as tools and raw materials for the creation of that which he had conceived for the good of the state, for the empire. I think that the notions of Ivan the Terrible in punishing Kurbsky and the like for disobedience on the basis that "God delegated them [subjects] to work" for him, the autocrat, would have been close to Peter's heart. Of course, one should note that for Ivan the concept of "work" is identical to "slavery," and "workers" are all without exception subjects committed to slavery. All the same, the attitudes of Peter and Ivan toward their subjects had much in common.

Quite expressive is a letter to Petrozavodsk on the occasion of the illness of Peter's personal physician Dr. Robert Erskine, who for many years had belonged to the tsar's inner circle. On 2 December 1718 Peter wrote Wilhelm Henin, the local chief official: "Sir colonel. Your letter of 25 November has reached us in which you write that doctor Erskine is already dying, about which we are very sorry, and if (God preserve us) his life has already ended, then inform doctor Policala that he should cut him open and examine the internal organs, [to see] what illness he suffered from and whether some poison had been given him. And having inspected him, write to us. And then send his body here, to Sankt-Piterburkh. *Peter.*"[29]

The tsar's astonishing anticipation stemmed from suspicions of poisoning in the death of Erskine, who had persuaded Peter to support the "Jacobites," the supporters of James Stuart, pretender to the English throne. It is quite possible that Peter apprehended a conspiracy somehow threatening him. But in this instance our attention is directed to the cold pragmatism, the slightly sinister businesslike tone in relation to a person quite close to him. With the same businesslike tone in 1709 he directed Apraksin how to interrogate an ailing state criminal: "As concerns the archpriest of the Trinity Monastery, you may proceed at your own discretion. If there will be time for you, then proceed to take him to Moscow and, although it is impossible to torture him because of illness, nonetheless it is possible to squeeze it out without hanging him up, namely to beat him, applying whips or sticks, and ask him in the meantime."[30]

It would be untrue to presume some kind of pathology for the tsar—Peter did not exhibit pathological tendencies. He lived in a cruel century, whose children rushed to the scaffold as if to a festival, and troops with difficulty restrained crowds surging closer to enjoy the spectacle of the next criminal's agonizing execution. True, the century was harsh, but as the poet A. Kushner has rightly said: "every century is an iron century and one cannot overlook that in Peter's attitude toward people much stemmed from his own personality, from the traits of soul of this harsh, brutal, and high-handed person toward his associates."

No doubt Peter was a person of strong and harsh feelings, impetuous in their manifestation. These feelings occasionally possessed him entirely. Even everyday letters sometimes transmit this passion. Here is only one example. On 6 February 1710 Peter received the long expected confirmation from Istanbul that the Turks had halted military preparations against Russia and thereby untied his hands for operations in the Baltic region. On 7 February Peter wrote Alexander Kikin: "Yesterday we received the long and ardently awaited courier from Constantinople . . . and now we have eyes and thoughts already in only one direction."[31] In Peter's epistolary legacy there are many such expressive, eloquent letters.

After what has been said it is not difficult to understand how terrifying and boundless Peter's wrath could be. It is noteworthy that in a state of strong irritation he would suddenly suffer an attack that horrified his associates.

Here is how Just Juel describes such an incident when in January 1710 with chancellor Golovkin he took part in the solemn ceremony of the Russian army's entry into Moscow as the victor at Poltava:

> We had driven along in this fashion for a good distance, when suddenly the tsar galloped past at full speed. His face was exceptionally pale, contorted, and distorted. He was making various terrible grimaces and movements of the head, mouth, arms, shoulders, hands, and feet.
>
> There we both got out of the carriage and caught sight of the tsar, who had driven up to one common soldier carrying a Swedish flag and started mercilessly beating him with a bared sword and raining blows on him, perhaps because the latter had not marched as the tsar wished. Then the tsar halted his horse, but he still continued to make the aforementioned terrible grimaces and jerked his legs back and forth. All the most important officials surrounding him at that minute were frightened by this, and nobody dared to approach him because everybody saw that the tsar was angry and infuriated by something. . . . The tsar's terrible movements and gestures described above are called convulsions by doctors. They happen to him often, primarily when he is angry, has received bad news, in general when he is dissatisfied with anything or is sunk in deep thought. Not infrequently similar spasms in the muscles of the arms find him at table while eating, and if he is holding a fork and knife, then it draws them in the direction of his face. They say that the spasms come from poison that he swallowed sometime, yet it is more likely and more plausible to suppose that their cause is a sickness and acid of the blood and that these movements which are terrible to see—stamping, jerking, and nodding— are elicited by a well-known attack similar to an apoplectic fit.

The incident of punishing the soldier in 1710 is quite typical. Ten years later, in 1720, at a different parade another contemporary, V.A. Nashchokin, observed almost the same thing: "When the prisoners were led in . . . the master himself, dressed in the uniform of the Guards, organized a convoy and started to go into the fortress with the prisoners, whereas the senior captain of the Life Guards Semenovsky

Regiment, Peter, the son of Ivan Vel'iaminov, interfered with the convoy by his presentation, whom the master on this occasion beat with his cane."[32]

It would hardly be necessary to focus the reader's attention on these unpleasant scenes of reprisals against people who could not respond, if the stick were not a peculiar symbol of the system of brutality cultivated by Peter.

Probably there is no point in talking about the successes of "cudgel" pedagogy. Nartov recalled the tsar's ruminations on that count: "The master, trimming a human figure at the lathe and happy that the work was going well, asked of the mechanic Nartov: 'How am I trimming?' And when Nartov answered: 'Good,' then his majesty said [with a sigh, we might add in Nartov's place]: 'Just so, Andrei, do I trim bones very well with a chisel, but I cannot shape up the stubborn with a cudgel.' " On another occasion "the master," writes Nartov, "returning from the Senate and seeing his small dog greeting him and jumping around, sat down and petted him and then said: 'If the stubborn would mind me as well as Lizeta [his favorite dog] minds me, then I would not pet them with a cudgel. My dog minds me without beating, he knows what to do instinctively, whereas those others are sunk in obstinacy.' "[33]

Peter's letters to officials and commanders are full of demands to show discipline, initiative, and dispatch—whatever was required at the moment for the business at hand. Almost every such demand was accompanied by threats of force and reprisal.

Numerous summons and threats could not compel people to do as the tsar demanded: precisely, rapidly, with initiative. Few of his associates felt confident when it came to acting independently at their own terror and risk without the tsar's petty decrees. This was inevitable, for Peter, according to Vasily Kliuchevsky, who put it so well, "hoped by the threat of supreme authority to stimulate spontaneous activity in an enslaved society and through the slave-owning nobility to establish in Russia European science, public enlightenment as an essential condition of public spontaneous activity; he wanted the slave, while remaining a slave, to act spontaneously and freely. The simultaneous operation of despotism and freedom, enlightenment and slavery—this is the political squaring of the circle, the dilemma that we have been trying to resolve for two centuries since Peter's time and which has not yet been resolved."[34]

Typical of many Petrine associates was a sense of helplessness, of desperation, when they did not have the tsar's exact directives, or, bending under the terrible weight of responsibility, they did not win his approval. Our attention is drawn to a letter of 31 December 1716 from the president of the Admiralty College, Fedor Matveevich Apraksin, to a secretary: "In relying on you I beg you for God's sake not to leave us without word, would you be so good as to come to us, truly in all matters we wander like blind men and we know not what to do, there is great disarray everywhere, but whither to run and what to do in the future we know not, there is no money from anywhere, all affairs are stopping."[35] And writing this is one of the most influential persons of the time, a man invested with the trust of the awesome tsar!

Reading such letters, Peter had every reason to suppose that without him all matters would come to a halt and that he was the single one who knew what needed doing and how. Together with this feeling of Peter's uniqueness, far from self-love and empty vainglory, there must have prevailed another feeling—a feeling of loneliness, an awareness that people feared him but did not understand him, that they acted as if they were working hard, but they were waiting for the time when he would turn away, when he would die at last. This was the inevitable and tragic consequence of every kind of authoritarianism and coercion, which naturally gave birth to the apathy of the slave, the thievery of the official, the social dependence, and the indifference that became a sorry tradition of Russian history:

> State monies are not prized
> a word of honor does not resound for you
> till such time when with a thick stick
> the state beats you.
>   —B. Slutsky

Toward the end of Peter's life, having lost his son—his heir and hope—the tsar might have exclaimed as once he did in a letter to the slain tsarevich Aleksei: ". . . for I am a man and consequently I must die, then to whom shall I leave the seedling I have planted and that, with God's help, is already growing?"[36]

Yes, he was mortal, and it pleased fate to condemn him to a painful death. In it there was much that was symbolic and unclear, just as there was in the fate of Russia, which faced living without Peter. . . .

First we shall turn to the events of the Northern War, to the start of that cruel school of life, in passing through which the young Russian tsar became Emperor Peter the Great.

VICTORY AT ANY COST

The Narva Confusion

On 9 September 1700 one could have observed from the bastions of the fortress of Narva a mass of troops and strings of supply carts—Peter's army of almost 40,000 was approaching the Swedish fortress on the river Narva that bordered on Russia. So began for Russia the Great Northern War, and nobody then could have surmised that it would last more than two decades (until 1721) and that it would end only when a new generation had been born, grown up, and even settled in on both sides of the Baltic—a generation for whom the memory of "ill-fated" Narva would be a legacy.

Nor could Peter have surmised in those autumn days that Narva in 1700 would be a divide in his life and in the life of the huge country of which he had become the ruler. Along with his commanders he was reconnoitering the locality, considering where to build palisades (stockades), where to erect walls that would keep even a mouse out. The men worked confidently and calmly: a protracted siege was being prepared of this powerful fortress—the keystone of the defense of the junction of the kingdom of Sweden's two overseas provinces, Ingria and Estland. The young tsar who supervised the works was not a novice in the matter, and after Azov the siege of Narva very likely struck him as an ordinary affair the success of which was obvious. There was every reason for such assurance: Peter had already passed with honors the school of combat on the southern frontiers far from Narva where fate had assigned him to launch his amazing "career."

To be sure, he knew nothing about the military genius of the young king of Sweden, Charles XII; he patently underestimated the might of the kingdom of Sweden with which he faced such a long war. Indeed, a state of war would become routine for Peter: of the fifty-two years of his life Russia was at war for thirty-seven years!

In 1700 the war against Ottoman Turkey and its Crimean vassal that had dragged on for fourteen years had just ended. Of course, the Russo-Turkish War of 1686–1700 was not as grandiose as the Northern ——

War, but it also had shed blood, and thousands of people had perished. In one sense war with Turkey and the Crimea was inescapable, incited not so much by severe internal problems as by the general international situation, by that system of international relations which included Russia.

In the 1670s and 1680s the pressure of Ottoman Turkey on the lands of the Austrian Empire, the Polish-Lithuanian Commonwealth, and Russia had been substantially increased. The battles of Russian and Ukrainian troops against the Turks near Chigirin in 1677–79 had not yielded a decisive advantage to either side, but all the same they had contained Turkish expansion northward. Austria and Poland found themselves in a more dangerous position: the Turks stood on the Polish-Lithuanian Commonwealth's southern frontier at Kamenets-Podol'skii; the capital of the Austrian Empire, Vienna, had been saved from the Ottomans only by the feat of Jan Sobieski's Austro-Polish army.

Interested in activating anti-Turkish forces, Austria had achieved a truce between the Polish-Lithuanian Commonwealth and Russia—sworn foes who, after finishing a most acute conflict in 1617, had renewed it twice more in 1632–34 and 1654–66. These wars had brought little success to Russia, and the territorial losses of the Time of Troubles (1598–1618) had not been recovered. Therefore, in agreeing to peace with the commonwealth, Russian diplomacy had demanded the return of the Smolensk lands and recognition of the annexation to Russia of Left-Bank Ukraine including Kiev, for which the Russian side promised to pay 146,000 rubles and to declare war on Turkey. On 6 March 1686 "eternal" peace with Poland was signed on these conditions. It culminated a long period of bitter conflict between Poles and Russians and signified a brief moment of a balance of forces in Russo-Polish relations, after which Russia's side of the scales began to prevail more and more manifestly. But at that time nobody sensed the turn dictated by fate, and a natural consequence of the peace with Poland became war with Turkey and the Crimea, which Russia could not avoid any longer.

Russian forces under the command of Vasily Golitsyn twice—in 1687 and 1689—mounted campaigns against the Crimean Khanate, but both proved to be fiascoes and brought Russian arms no glory. Steppes set ablaze, inept leadership, skillful operations by the nomads—and many other circumstances made the withdrawal from under the unbreached walls of Perekop, the fort at the narrowest place on the isthmus, into a real rout accompanied by tremendous losses.

The young tsar's new government had inherited old foreign policy problems. One must admit, it did not hasten to resolve them: the situation in Europe remained confused, Turkey and the Crimea ceased their military operations for a time, and a mass of domestic affairs that were more important for the young tsar preoccupied his mind for a long time until finally in 1695, yielding to his allies' demands, it was decided to renew the war. And although the campaign's Crimean direction officially remained foremost, the basic blow was aimed directly at Turkey's possessions on the northern littoral of the Black Sea, the mouth of the Dnieper and the mouth of the Don.

Peter adopted such a decision, of course, primarily because he did not wish to repeat the fate of his unlucky predecessor, Vasily Golitsyn. All the same, the main intention of the new campaign was to establish control over the mouths of the Dnieper and the Don, which would allow him to gain a hold on the shores of the Black and Azov seas that represented Turkish lakes, and at the same time to control the entire course of both rivers. This direction of strategic blows became fundamental in the prolonged Russo-Turkish wars for the northern Black Sea littoral in post-Petrine times. A raid on the Crimea could yield only temporary advantage.

Therefore, the main aim of the first Azov campaign of 1695 became the Turkish fortresses of Kazi-Kerman and Arslan-Ordek at the mouth of the Dnieper and the fortress of Azov at the mouth of the Don. Peter resolved to deliver the basic blow at Azov inasmuch as it would be easier to convey troops and supplies there from the Russian-controlled upper Don and Voronezh.

The siege of Azov began in July 1695 and continued almost four months, but without success. There were many causes for this: the poor preparation of the troops, the absence of unified command, the shortage of good engineers capable of correctly conducting the siege and pre-assault works, and a good deal of muddle, fuss, and unjustified sacrifices. This cost the explosion of mines that caused loss not only to Azov's fortifications but also to the besiegers themselves, and two unsuccessful assaults wherein the activity of some detachments combined with the irresolution and passivity of others led to huge losses. Neither could Russian forces interdict the free delivery of supplies and reinforcements to the fortress from the sea.

In sum, the order had to be given to withdraw. It began in the late autumn when Russian forces traversed the naked steppe. Frosts and hunger decimated people and animals such that Peter's soldiery returning to Russia scarcely differed from that of Vasily Golitsyn several years before.

The period between Peter's first and second campaigns against Azov was extremely important for the future. It showed that the young tsar, who in the first campaign had only observed the generals' inept operations, possessed a statesman's will, mind, talent, and the desire to alter an unfavorable situation and to that end to force thousands and thousands of people to work intensely.

In a short time thousands of peasants were driven into the sleepy Voronezh woods and set to work felling timber for building, then to haul and to float it to Voronezh, where at the dockyard founded by Peter under the supervision of English and Dutch masters work was in full swing. There are two more astounding dates separated by only two months: 2 April 1696, when the first galley left the yards for the waters of Voronezh, and 27 May of the same year, when the Sea of Azov first caught sight of the Russian naval flag—a fleet of twenty-two galleys accompanied by a mass of smaller vessels emerged on the open sea. All this resembled a fairy tale, particularly if one recalls the time when this occurred. Peter's dream of the sea suddenly started to come true.

But then humdrum days followed, filled with harsh trials. The young Russian fleet, poorly manned and immobile, obviously avoided engaging the Turks, whose attempts to deliver supplies and men to Azov were decisively blocked not by the galleys but mainly by cossacks, light craft which captured several transports and drove the larger Turkish ships into the open sea. As a whole the siege, thanks to the presence of naval forces, went more smoothly than the year before. Peter successfully blockaded the mouth of the Don: on both banks forts armed with cannon were built—a peculiar "padlock" on the mouth that thwarted the unhindered entry of enemy vessels into the Don to besieged Azov.

The army under the command of "generalissimo" Aleksei Shein had in the meantime disembarked from the ships and occupied anew, as in the past year, the trenches and approaches (ditches and tunnels) that had not been destroyed by the Turks, who foolishly supposed that the Russian tsar would long recall "impregnable Azov" and forget the way to its walls.

The siege of the fortress proceeded according to the old pattern, the more so as they were afraid to dig tunnels for mines and to tempt fate with storming ladders. A gigantic work was begun that was senseless from a military point of view—the erection around the fortress of a wall higher than the wall of the Turkish fortress that would have filled in its moat. This extremely archaic form of siege for the seventeenth century recalled, as historian Nikolai Ustrialov wrote, the chronicle's account of the siege of Cheronesus in the tenth century by Prince Vladimir.[1] It is not known how long the siege might have dragged on if not for a new, more adept arrangement of cannon the accurate fire of which destroyed the Turkish fortifications, a "providential" raid of Zaporozhian and Don cossacks that captured the wall of the fortress, and finally the blockade from the sea. Seeing all this, the Turks began parleys about capitulation, and in mid-June 1696 the Russian forces entered Azov.

This event brought in its wake two consequences: one diplomatic, the other strategic. The Azov success gave Russia the right to demand loudly from her own allies help in the war against Turkey.

In this regard it is scarcely likely that Peter's summons to his currently inactive allies were sheer rhetoric, a desire to raise Russia's low international prestige. The seizure of Azov was not simply a "raid"—a march there and back, like the Crimean campaigns. Peter ended one of his first letters to Moscow after the capture of Azov with the words: "Written in our conquered town of Azov,"[2] underscoring then and there that he intended to consolidate his hold on the sea forever. Furthermore, Peter viewed the capture of Azov and the consolidation there as only the first step of long-term strategic plans involving profound political and military prospects. One must admit that for many people both in Russia and abroad this, apparently, proved to be utterly unanticipated.

Immediately after the Russian flag had been raised over the bastions of the fortress, Peter began reconnoitering it according to the most recent achievements of fortification art. Specially hired foreign military engineers executed his directions. Day and night the victorious army reconstructed and expanded the Azov fortifications. Noteworthy also was the consecration of the town and two Orthodox churches, remodeled from mosques. This was supposed to symbolize Russia's intention to remain on the Sea of Azov for the long term. Peter himself set off with the galley fleet along the seacoast in search of a convenient harbor. The vicinity of the cape Tagan-Rog struck the tsar and his suite as the most suitable. Here it was decided to found a fortress, a town, and the harbor of Taganrog—a decision of extraordinary importance, for it signified that the ships built at Voronezh would be needed by Peter not only for transporting troops to Azov, but as a whole for the defense of the Azov region, in pursuit of which Peter also began to create a base for naval forces on the Sea of Azov.

Peter confirmed the seriousness of these unseen and grandiose plans for Russia at that time right after celebrating the Azov victory in Moscow. On 20 October 1696 he sent an inquiry to the Boyar Council: "Suitable articles, which are related to the fortress (or *fartetsyi*) of Azov captured from the Turks." Considering it essential promptly to renovate and to settle Azov, Peter writes that ". . . a fleet or sea caravan is required, comprising forty or more vessels, concerning which one must begin without losing time: how many of which vessels, and from how many households and trades, and where to build it?" In an autocratic state such an "inquiry" automatically entailed a corresponding decree, which appeared on 4 November 1696. This decree signaled the organization of "kumpanstva"—companies in which landowners, clergy, and townsmen were summarily enrolled. By the spring of 1698 these "kumpanstva," having hired contractors and masters beforehand and having prepared timber, were supposed to launch fifty-six ships at Voronezh, not counting the dozens that Peter had undertaken to build at the tsar's expense.[3]

Peter's plans did not look utopian, for the experience of constructing the galleys in 1695–96 had been completely successful; the human and the material resources of the country seemed inexhaustible. True, there had been a shortage of shipwrights, hence young nobles in large numbers were sent abroad for training, and from abroad experienced shipwrights and seamen were recruited.

The matter quickly assumed serious scope. Besides Venetians working at the Voronezh dockyards there were Dutch, Swedes, English, and Danes. Ships, galleys, and various seacraft started to come down the ways one after another. By the efforts of a force of 20,000 soldiers at Taganrog a fortress and town started to arise. Thirty-five thousand peasants from south Russia were thrown into another grandiose construction project—digging the Volga-Don canal, the significance of which (in case it had really been built then) would be difficult to overestimate in strengthening Russia's military and economic position in the south.

All these measures combined attest indubitably to Peter's serious intention to consolidate a hold on the Sea of Azov. In essence, Peter assigned to Azov and Taganrog in the south the same role that still stood to be won in the north for Petersburg and Kronstadt. As diplomatic insurance the guarantee of the Azov bridgehead became the treaty of alliance Russia, Austria, and Venice concluded on 29 January 1697, which bore a clearly expressed anti-Turkish offensive character.

In line with such actions by the Russian government it would seem logical to place the Grand Embassy, which, judging by the charters sent off beforehand, was intended to visit Austria, Brandenburg (Prussia), the Vatican, Venice, Holland, and England. The embassy, which was headed by Franz Lefort, Fedor Golovin, and Peter Voznitsyn, departed Moscow in March 1697. In the scholarly literature there is no unanimous opinion about the true causes that impelled Peter to organize this grandiose diplomatic action. Most scholars consider that the embassy, sent to Western Europe ostensibly to form a broad anti-Turkish alliance, was in fact a cover for a training orientation trip to the West by the Russian tsar, who concealed himself among those accompanying the embassy under the name of Sergeant Peter Mikhailov.

I think that in the literature Vozgrin has greatly exaggerated the initial anti-Swedish tendency of the Grand Embassy.[4] One thing is beyond doubt: the Grand Embassy was not simply a cover for the tsar's curiosity as a tourist. It was undertaken for the purpose of deep diplomatic reconnaissance, which was then beyond the power of Russia's puny and inert diplomacy. The Grand Embassy was supposed to ferret out the real balance of forces in Europe, to study it in the making of Russia's future policy.

The necessity of such a diplomatic search was acutely felt in Russia. Peter, as subsequent events showed, was an advocate of an active policy of imperial scope. He had just begun his career, having made a decisive step into the Azov region; he "had squeezed out" of a situation created by his predecessors the maximum that one could have imagined at the time. Now, after the Azov triumph he could not help thinking of the future, of the next step.

As we know, three main directions dominated Russian foreign policy in the seventeenth and the eighteenth centuries—Polish, Swedish, and Turkish. The following step in the southern (Turkish) direction meant nothing less than full-scale war with all the land and sea forces of the then mighty Ottoman Empire on the shores of the Azov and Black seas. In that case Peter knew where he would move his ships and regiments. In 1698, discussing peace terms with the Ottomans, he wrote the Austrian emperor Leopold: ". . . in all ways it is necessary that the conquered fortress called Kerch be ceded to the possession of his tsarist majesty."[5]

Suffice it to glance at the map in order to understand why Kerch was Peter's next aim: it is the "key-town" of the Black Sea. Yet to wage full-scale war with the Ottomans was possible only in alliance with Austria, Venice, and Poland, for the fate of the northern Black Sea could be decided only in confrontation with great armies. The sounding of Austrian intentions carried out by the Grand Embassy in Europe showed that after the deterioration of the situation concerning the Spanish Succession the treaty of 29 January 1697 was simply a scrap of paper, for the Austrians at the time (in 1698–99) were thinking only of a separate peace with Turkey. Nor could there be any thought of Poland as an ally: a difficult "interregnum" had become the country's lot since 17 June 1696, when King Jan III Sobieski had died.

Here it is important to stress that the "Polish" direction of policy had never been taken off the government's agenda and with the onset of the "interregnum" Poland transfixed Peter's attention. Russia did not intend to remain an outside observer of Polish internal affairs and launched an active struggle against the candidacy of the Prince de Condé, a protégé of Versailles, for the kingship that was put forward by part of the nobility. Peter's charter of 31 May 1697 to Cardinal-Primate Radziwill, who was temporarily acting supreme ruler of Poland, contained an undisguised threat "to break the eternal peace" in case a representative of France allied with Turkey should come to power. Further there followed a rather tough recommendation about whom the Poles should elect or not elect as king: "Therefore, we, the great master, our tsarist majesty, having constant friendship toward your master, the king of Poland, and also to you, gentleman of the council, such a king from the French and the Turkish side do not desire, whereas we desire for you to have on the throne of the kingdom of Poland and the grand duchy of Lithuania a king . . . from whatever people, only not from the opposing side."[6]

Thus was the fragile balance of "eternal peace" first broken, and subsequently the language of ultimatums became quite widespread in Russia's relations with its nearest neighbor.

Then, too, actions were undertaken in support of words that subsequently became traditional: in the autumn of 1697 by Peter's decree the 60,000-man corps of Mikhail Romodanovsky crossed the Polish border and played a decisive role in the election to the Polish throne of a candidate preferred by Russia—the elector of Saxony, Frederick August I—who became Augustus II the Strong, king of Poland. Subsequently, Peter in a dispatch to Queen Anne of England wrote of this episode: "This army was given into his [Augustus] command as soon as he arrived there, in order to put him in a position to chastise his enemies; besides, the side opposed to him we threatened with fire and sword, which frightened many of them, compelled them to recognize him as their master and thus by our aid he was firmly established on the throne."[7] It is believed that Peter's wager on the Saxon candidacy was a consequence not of some special sympathy toward Saxony, but merely a determination not to see a protégé of France on the throne of Poland, which would have led to strengthening the influence of Louis XIV, a dangerous and powerful opponent, in the lands bordering Russia.

One should not forget that Peter's directives about concentrating troops on the border with Poland and interfering in Polish affairs were issued when, after changing the plan of the embassy's itinerary, he had gone to Prussia for negotiations with Elector Frederick III. Between these facts—interference in Polish affairs and the trip to Prussia—a connection definitely existed, for Prussia, avid to strengthen itself at the expense of its own neighbors (Poland and Sweden), saw in Russia a potential ally. One should recall the whole history of Russo-Prussian relations in the seventeenth and eighteenth centuries. In the second half of the seventeenth century Prussia was still trying to nudge Russia into action against Poland, whereas it also proposed more than once to attack Sweden's Baltic provinces as a means of recovering Ingria and Karelia. The situation had not changed by the moment of "kingless-ness" in Poland, either. It is known that a point about joint operations against some third party had figured in Frederick's discussion of a Prusso-Russian treaty with Peter, by which Poland was obviously meant (in case of the triumph there of the supporters of Condé).

The results of the elections in Poland in the autumn of 1697 were quite favorable for Russia, however, and after the victory of the Saxon "party" there could no longer be any talk about an anti-Polish variant of Russia's foreign policy. It is possible that right after the victory of Augustus, Russia's protégé, the last alternative variant of Russia's foreign policy—the anti-Swedish—rose to the surface as the most promising for the country's interests at that moment, and the most favorable for realization.

The point is that by the end of the seventeenth century the international setting in Europe was becoming ever more strained. In London, Paris, Vienna, and other capitals statesmen were waiting for news from Madrid about the health of the king of Spain, Charles II, who had no heirs. The specter of war "for the Spanish Succession" hovered over Europe.

Peter, who had just returned from abroad, deftly evaluated the significance of the impending conflict in connection with the Spanish Succession and hence began to follow the development of the situation carefully.

Given these conditions, one can understand why Peter harbored real hopes that the hastily arming opponents—England and France with their allies—would not be able to interfere in a conflict for the Baltic or, more bluntly speaking, help Sweden, on which the great powers had long since looked as their northern ally.

Possibly, just these propitious circumstances for action against Sweden were discussed during the tsar's meeting with Augustus II at Rawa when Peter, returning from Vienna in the summer of 1698, stopped in Poland. He immediately found a common language with Augustus, who was obligated to him for his throne. The latter, sensing the fragility of his position in Poland, sought to strengthen it through a victorious war against Sweden in alliance with the Russian tsar and Sweden's other opponents. And there were plenty of those.

In order to understand why, we need to make a short excursus into the history of the sixteenth and seventeenth centuries. The foe against whom Peter and Augustus intended to unsheathe their swords was the true ruler of the North at that time. For almost a century, starting from the mid-1500s, Sweden had conducted prolonged wars with all of its neighbors: Russia, the Polish-Lithuanian Commonwealth, Denmark, and Brandenburg (Prussia). These wars had ended with almost unbroken success for the Swedes and had led to the gradual extension of Swedish possessions along the shores of the Baltic Sea, making it, in essence, a Swedish lake. Later, substantial stretches of the littoral of the North Sea had also fallen under the authority of the Swedes. The formation of the Swedish Empire had begun in the time of Eric XIV, who had seized Revel in 1561 and northern Estland. The peace treaty of Tiavzin with Russia in 1595 had consolidated Livonia for the Swedes and reinforced the unhindered Swedish colonization of Finland.

Taking advantage of the prolonged Russo-Polish conflict at the start of the seventeenth century, Sweden under the remarkable command of King Gustavus II Adolphus managed from 1610 to the 1620s to take Russia's Baltic territories (the Karelia district, Ingria, the Izhora, and Novgorod lands) and then Riga and Livland from the Polish-Lithuanian Commonwealth. These gains were secured by the Peace of Stolbovo with Russia in 1617 and the Altmark truce with the Polish-Lithuanian Commonwealth in 1629.

The Peace of Westphalia of 1648—the result of the Thirty Years' War—was a real triumph for Sweden: it annexed the north German territories of West and East Pomerania. The last wave of Swedish expansion during the wars with Denmark (1640–50) and the Northern War of 1655–60 with Poland and Russia had brought Stockholm equally rich spoils: the southern part of the Scandinavian peninsula (Scania), eastern Norway, and the general consolidation of Swedish power on the southern littoral of the Baltic.

A series of peace treaties in 1658–61 had recognized Sweden's undisputed primacy in the Baltic and in Northern Europe in general. By the second half of the seventeenth century the empire of the Swedes had been finally formed and had attained the zenith of its might. Therefore it is not surprising that on the eve of the Northern War of 1700–21 in Europe there was not a more peace-loving state than Sweden, which constantly fought for the preservation of the peace that guaranteed its dispersed possessions extending from the North Sea almost to the Barents Sea. Its neighbors held a different opinion.

One of these neighbors, Denmark, eagerly embarked from the spring of 1697 on a rapprochement with Russia, for it had serious pretensions toward Sweden, a rivalry that had not subsided for a century and a half. The rivalry manifested itself most distinctly in the Holstein question. Bordering on Denmark, the north German duchy of Holstein-Gottorp had by the end of the seventeenth century fallen completely under the sway of the Swedes, who felt quite at home on its territory and thereby threatened the southern frontiers of Denmark. This threat had become stronger by the end of the 1690s, when Sweden sent troops into the duchy.

Russia's aims in the negotiations that had begun with Saxony and Denmark were formulated quite definitely: to recover the Izhora and Karelian lands taken by the Swedes through the Peace of Stolbovo of 1617 and to obtain, as it was written then, "firm footing on the Baltic Sea."

During the negotiations of 1698–1700 it did not prove possible to create a solid front among Sweden's opponents. Prussia, dependent on the general European situation, did not feel strong enough to enter the alliance and awaited the development of events as an observer on the sidelines. The Polish-Lithuanian Commonwealth, however, true to its political principles, did not support its king. Nor did it achieve the internal unity necessary for war, which had been destroyed by the painful "kinglessness."

The negotiations of the various sides were pursued with a further aim—partition of the Swedish Empire. Long before the Swedish lion had been trapped, his skin had been divided.

The initiator of these proposals was Johann Reihold von Patkul—an influential Livland nobleman and staunch opponent of Swedish hegemony in the eastern Baltic, which threatened the noble landholding of Livland with a reduction (confiscation) of lands that had already been carried out in Sweden itself. Condemned to be executed by the Swedes, Patkul had fled and, becoming an unofficial counselor of Augustus II, had given the king at the end of 1698 several projects that considered possible military action against Sweden and terms of partitioning its possessions. It is impossible to overlook in these projects the cynicism so typical of Patkul's calculations or his intrigues with anti-Russian implications.[8]

In the forthcoming war Russia was assigned the unappealing role of providing cannon fodder, while Peter was to be a kind of mighty bear with a ring through its nose dancing to his trainer's tune. As life later showed, Patkul and many others did see very clearly with whom they were dealing. Jumping ahead, it should be noted that Patkul's worst fears were completely realized—Russia occupied both Estland and Livland.

The treaty Russia and Saxony signed at Preobrazhenskoe on 11 November 1699 was the second agreement laying the basis of the Northern Alliance; the first was the Dresden agreement between Saxony and Denmark on 14 September the same year. The road to war had been opened. It is symbolic that many years later, celebrating in Moscow the conclusion of the Peace of Nystadt of 1721, Peter personally torched the Preobrazhenskoe palace in which his childhood had been passed but from which in 1699 the invisible flames of war had burst forth.

The treaty specifically envisaged that Russia would enter the war immediately upon the conclusion of peace with the Ottoman Empire— Peter did not wish to risk waging warfare on two fronts. From his side, Augustus promised to occupy Livland and Estland solely to aid Peter. In fact Augustus nursed far-reaching (and secret from Russia) plans in regard to Livland. Formally, Livland was supposed to go to the Polish-Lithuanian Commonwealth as a fief that would preserve its own aristocratic administration with the right of possessing armed forces, about which an agreement had been concluded between Augustus and Patkul as the representative of the German knights of Livland.

It should be mentioned that at this time the Swedish government and fifteen-year-old Charles XII, who had just come to the throne in 1697, were disturbed by rumors about the formation of an anti-Swedish coalition and were making every effort to head off war with Russia. With regard to Russia in general, Sweden in the second half of the seventeenth century had been following a policy that combined uncompromising firmness in the question of altering borders and unusual flexibility and tolerance in everything else. It is known that after the Peace of Stolbovo of 1617 the Russian side had raised more than once the question of changing borders, but each time the Swedish response had been negative.

In fact, however, the Swedes, confronting numerous foreign policy problems in Germany and on the borders with Denmark, were seeking to avoid war with Russia. Therefore, when the Russian government at the beginning of 1697 approached the Swedes with a request to buy six hundred cannon for the Azov fleet, the king of Sweden, concerned that Russia's conflict with Turkey not die down anytime soon, made a gift to Peter of three hundred iron cannon "out of his own neighborly friendship to Russia." On coming to the throne, Charles XII had immediately dispatched an embassy to Moscow with a pledge "to preserve as sacred all treaties with Russia." For his part, Peter, especially after the meeting at Rawa, likewise sought to display his own love of peace—falsely in this instance. In conducting negotiations with the Swedes, Petrine diplomats applied maximum effort to liberate their master from the oath of fidelity to previous treaties with Sweden.[9] This was done so that with the outbreak of war there would be no grounds to accuse Peter of violating his oath. This was the more urgent because at the moment of the Russo-Swedish negotiations Peter had already concluded with Augustus's representative at Preobrazhenskoe an agreement about war against Sweden.

But the Swedes were still anxious. In order to pacify and to divert them, Peter dispatched to Stockholm the embassy of Prince Yakov

Khilkov, who was received on 19 August 1700 by the king in camp near Landskrona and who handed over Peter's dispatch to Charles with the usual assurances of friendship. It was a matter of fate that on that very day, 19 August, and possibly at that very hour in Moscow the rupture with Sweden and the start of war had been announced.

Actually, the war of the Northern Alliance against Sweden had already begun: on 2 February 1700, without a declaration of war, Augustus II's Saxon troops had invaded Livland and had attempted at once to seize Riga. A month later King Frederick IV of Denmark invaded the duchy of Holstein-Gottorp, exploiting the fact that in defiance of treaties the Swedes had sent troops there.

In both instances the allies' military operations had proved unsuccessful. Augustus did not manage to grab Riga, and he had to undertake a regular siege of its formidable fortifications. The Danes also settled down for a long time under the walls of the Holstein fortress of Reneburg. And at that moment the lion under three crowns [the Swedish royal crest] awakened: a Swedish squadron bombarded Copenhagen in the summer of 1700 while Charles XII on 14 July landed on the Danish coast and surrounded the capital.

Caught in a situation without escape, the Danes sued for peace. Not far from Lübeck at the castle of Travendal the peace negotiations began and quickly ended: Denmark left the war, having escaped with only a slight scare and not even losing the foundation of its might—its navy. For such mild peace terms with an opponent who earlier had shown no mercy to the Danes, Frederick was obligated to the maritime powers interested in peace in the north, England and Holland, which quickly hired a Danish army of 18,000 men for four million talers and dispatched it to the battlefields of the recently begun War of the Spanish Succession.

Having taken Denmark out of the war, Charles XII decided to deal just as quickly with the other members of the Northern Alliance.

The events of late autumn 1700 unfolded precipitously for those times. Augustus, learning of Travendal, apprehended that the Swedish king would move directly against Dresden, the capital of Saxony, and treat him much worse than Frederick. Therefore, on the eve of the Swedes' descent on Livland the Saxons lifted the siege of Riga, which had gone quite badly till then, for they had failed to surprise the fortress, and Augustus's army had proved to be unprepared for a prolonged siege and assaults. In sum, upon the appearance of the Swedes, the Saxons withdrew.

Charles disembarked at the Estland port of Pernou (Piarnu) in November and force-marched toward Narva; on 18 November he was already at the approaches to the camp of the Russian besiegers. On 19 November, taking advantage of the bad weather and the passivity of the Russian troops inside the palisade, he successfully attacked an army that outnumbered him four to one. The next day the Russian army capitulated and, laying down its banners and weapons, withdrew to the right bank of the Narva. All the artillery was left to the foe; almost all the Russian generals were taken prisoner.

There was a certain predictability in this defeat suffered by the allies. From the very start they had taken a passive, waiting stance in the war they had unleashed, sitting under the walls of the fortresses they had besieged. The initiative proved to be in the hands of Charles XII, whose military-strategic abilities had obviously been underestimated by his opponents. Besides, the allies had no plans of joint operations in case of attempts by the Swedes to relieve the besieged fortresses. Finally, the passivity so untypical of Peter is explained by the subordinate role that had been allotted him in the alliance with Augustus at an awkward time for him as he set off not into Ingria, which was directly contiguous with Russian possessions, but toward Narva to carry out the secondary task of diverting the Swedish forces from Riga. This did not permit him to operate independently and actively in his own interests.

Indeed, the Russian army near Narva had not been ready for the operations that were expected of it. This became obvious the night of 19 November 1700 and was the consequence not only of mistaken strategy and tactics, but also of the vices of the whole state system, a part of which was the army.

"Seek to overthrow the foe"

Peter did not see his army's defeat—he was no longer in camp under Narva's walls: literally on the eve of the engagement he left for Novgorod, taking along his favorite, Alexander Menshikov, and Field Marshal Fedor Golovin.

Of course, the fact that the tsar abandoned the army on the eve of a decisive engagement does not decorate a great commander. But this deed was not a sign of cowardice or faintheartedness. It manifested the harsh rationalism typical of Peter, a sober recognition of the imminent, inevitable defeat, a desire to survive so as to continue the struggle with redoubled energy.

Subsequently, many years later after the Narva engagement, Peter in fleshing out his celebrated *Journal, or Daily Notations* came to think not only about the inevitability of defeat back then in 1700—the predictability of this disgrace—but also about the undoubted benefit that "ill-starred" Narva had contributed to the entire cause just begun.[1]

To be sure, thoughts came later about the benefit of defeat at the beginning stage of a war far distant from the country's crucially important centers, whereas in the first days after "the Narva confusion" he thought about something else: how to save what remained and not succumb to panic and desperation, for truly the victory of the Swedes was for Peter at the time "sadly painful."

To utilize the surviving units of the gentry cavalry that Sheremetev commanded for raids on the Swedish possessions in the Baltic was only part of Peter's plans for immediate military operations. More worrisome were domestic affairs: after Narva, Peter distinctly recognized that the Russian army had proved to be unprepared for battle with its opponent, the Swedish army of Charles XII.

For many readers the pre-Petrine army is associated above all with an untrained mass of gentry cavalry and the regiments of refractory strel'tsy. Such a notion is mistaken. The records of the Appointments

Bureau, which in the seventeenth century oversaw the majority of the armed forces, indicate that by the mid-seventeenth century there were sixteen regiments of strel'tsy (16,900 men), whereas the gentry cavalry comprised 9,700 men. At the same time there were fifty-eight infantry regiments with 59,200 men and twenty-five regular cavalry regiments with 29,800. To put it differently, by the mid-seventeenth century, out of 115,000 men (not counting the irregular units of cossacks, Tatars, Kalmyks, and others) more than three-quarters, or 76 percent, comprised regiments of infantry and cavalry of the "new formation."

In 1680 the proportion of "new formation" regiments as compared with the gentry cavalry and strel'tsy was as follows: 61,300 infantry and 30,500 cavalry for a total of 91,800 men; 15,800 gentry cavalry and 20,000 strel'tsy for a total of 35,800 men; that is, the previous proportion had been maintained.[2]

The "new formation" regiments date to 1630, when analysis of previous experience had revealed the necessity of forming fighting units trained for European modes of warfare. The first regiments "of the new formation" (i.e., trained according to new patterns, in a new style) were the regiments of Alexander Leslie and Franz Pentzner. Three more regiments were soon formed and trained with the assistance of instructors recruited from abroad. They immediately underwent baptism under fire in the so-called Smolensk War with Poland in 1632–34. The "new formation" regiments also played an important role later.

The question naturally arises: why was reform of the army an urgent matter after Narva? The point is that the defeat at Narva ranked on par with the defeats that had dogged the Russian army in the second half of the seventeenth century. Peter clearly understood that. He subsequently commented in the preface to the Articles of War of 1716, in reviewing military history since the start of mustering "new formation" regiments and creation of *The Study of the Skill of Military Formations*—the first war code of Aleksei Mikhailovich's time—that success in the wars of the first half of the seventeenth century with Poland and Sweden had yielded to setbacks in the Russo-Turkish war (the so-called Chigirin campaigns of 1677) and in the Crimean campaigns of 1687 and 1689, setbacks culminating in the first campaign against the Turkish fortress of Azov in 1695.

Peter understood the cause of the chronic defeats of the army; he recognized that it was essential to change the very basis on which the military organization had been founded.

At bottom the "new formation" regiments had been another form of gentry militia, a new graft on an old tree. As we know, the gentry militia had undergone special development in the sixteenth century, serving as it was said then "from the land," that is from those landed estates (*pomestiia,* singular *pomestie*) that had been allotted to servitors in conditional tenure (for the term of service). At the ruler's first summons the servitor, "the pomeshchik," was obligated to appear for inspection or action completely armed and equipped—on pain of confiscation of his estate. The pomeshchiks, who held estates with serfs, were supposed to bring with them a unit of auxiliary forces from their slaves, that is, to appear as they wrote then "with horse, people, and arms." Thus, the pomestie system of maintaining military contingents was also extended to the soldiers of the "new formation" regiments, who were recruited from servitors of various categories including gentry. The officers and soldiers of the "new formation" regiments served "from the land" and enjoyed pomestie rights; that is, they were pomeshchiks.

In the second half of the seventeenth century the pomestie form of landholding was evolving under the influence of many factors, above all the development of serfdom, toward a merger of the pomestie—a temporary possession—with the patrimony—permanent, hereditary property. The growth of this trend culminated in the economic and legal fusion of the patrimony and the pomestie into inalienable pomestie property—the basis of the pomeshchik's land tenure. In a military sense this evolution signified the loss by the pomestie system, the basic means of providing military labor, of flexibility and effectiveness. Service from "the land," in view of the binding of the pomestie to its owner, turned into a fiction. All this led to a corresponding decline of the armed forces, which was becoming apparent to many.

Peter had no doubt what course to adopt. In the aforementioned preface to the Articles of War of 1716 after describing the chronic setbacks in the wars of the second half of the seventeenth century he comments:

> But later, when the troops were reorganized, what great progress was made with the aid of the Almighty, over a glorious and regulated people. And hence each may reconsider that this followed from nothing else than good order alone, for the barbarous custom of utter disorder is worthy of laughter and one cannot expect any good from it. Therefore, having been a witness of both in this matter, we deemed it best to institute this book of the Articles of War so that each rank would know its duty and be obligated by its calling, and would not excuse itself through ignorance, so that through our own toil everything would be assembled and multiplied.[3]

Peter saw the cause of the Russian army's failures in the seventeenth century and also at Narva notably in the absence of "disposition"—of clear-cut organization and of "regularity" (a concept encompassing and articulating the sense and aim of the reform of the army).

It should be mentioned that he had embarked on the route of "regularity" long before the war with the Swedes. As we know, in 1687 fifteen-year-old Peter had created two "play" regiments—the Preobrazhensky and the Semenovsky (from the names of the palace villages where they were quartered)—in which noble boys and the tsar's servants served. No doubt, serving in the "play" regiments became for Peter and his associates an invaluable school that gave the young tsar his initial military education and developed those native endowments that made him an outstanding commander and reformer of military affairs.

According to the methods and devices of preparing the "play" regiments, which were founded on "regularity," that is, not on the pomestie basis, they became the prototype of the army that Peter began to create on the eve of and particularly during the initial period of the war with Sweden.

The dismissal in 1699 of the strel'tsy regiments after the suppression of their rebellion of 1698 served as the signal for the creation of regular regiments as the basic units.

In Peter's decrees and the government's other ordinances during 1699 an entire program is clearly outlined of creating a new army on principles quite different from those on which the seventeenth-century army had been constructed.

In raising the new regiments, two means were selected: the acceptance of volunteers—free men as they said then—and the levy of "recruits." Among the free men were accepted all those who wished to serve, except peasants obligated by state dues, that is, those paying state impositions. The "recruits" were basically those armed slaves who previously had turned out with their master-pomeshchiks for inspection or war in accordance with the prescribed proportions; for instance, one pomeshchik was supposed to provide no less than one warrior with arms for every twenty households of his pomestie. Now the levy of free and "recruits" (in general this was the usual practice of the seventeenth century) took on a different character, being altered at the source. The volunteers were not assigned to regiments of soldiers of the old pomestie type, whereas the "recruits" no longer served as auxiliary troops as previously; all of them became "rightful" soldiers of the regular regiments. They were trained according to the new codes and were maintained by the state while becoming lifelong military servitors who were not released home after a war.

In 1705 the government took the next step: ending acceptance of "free men" and switching to a levy of so-called "recruits" directly from the peasant population, which had not been done earlier. This was motivated by an acute shortage of men in the army, the requirements of which could no longer be met by volunteers and old-style "recruits."

The source of providing the army with men became truly inexhaustible. As was confirmed subsequently, in 1705 an exceptionally durable system of providing the armed forces with men was created, a system that endured practically without changes until 1874, that is, almost 170 years! The cause of such durability stemmed from the fact that the recruiting system was completely in accord with the peculiarities of the country's social and economic structure. The obligation to provide recruits and serf relationships constituted two sides of the same coin. In the army where the nobleman was an officer and yesterday's peasant was a soldier, the serf system impressed its indelible stamp, notwithstanding the distinction in principle between the pomestie and the regiment. It is important to note that the recruiting obligation was not an individual matter, similar to universal military service, but preserved an archaic communal character including group responsibility, a regular sequence, and so forth. It is natural that recruitment—as the people termed it—lasted until the other institutions of serfdom started to decay, for it reflected the serf relationships in the country.

Like serfdom, recruitment spurred constant resistance among the people. In becoming recruits, peasants parted with their relatives forever, and they were mourned as if they had died. Documents testify that there were grounds for this. The most burdensome trials began with a recruit's first steps. In order to hinder flight, recruits were put in fetters like criminals. "Stations"—the places for assembling recruits before dispatch to the army and where they were held for months—scarcely differed from jails.

In order to forestall flight, the authorities resorted to various contrivances. One of these was traditional group responsibility. But even this seemed to Peter too little to halt flight. In 1712 he hit upon a measure that aroused universal antagonism and symbolized to many the onset of worse times.

In a letter to Senator Yakov Dolgoruky, Peter stipulated that recruits receive special brands, which among the people received the name of "the stamp of Anti-Christ": "And as a sign for recruits this means to scratch crosses on the left arm with a needle and wipe it with gunpowder. And announce publicly in the districts of all guberniias, and in the towns in church, and at the marketplaces, that whoever sees a person that has on the left arm a designated cross, these should be caught and brought to town."[4]

If the system of recruitment took shape over five years, the reorganization of the entire army was worked out in some ten years, right up to the battle of Poltava, when Peter finally became convinced of the correctness of the decisions taken.

The infantry comprised the foundation of the army. Along with the infantry regiments were created grenadier regiments, the soldiers of which, besides the usual arms, carried grenades. The cavalry underwent equally significant changes. It was made up of dragoon regiments comprising cavalrymen who had been trained to fight on foot. In 1720 Russia could field 79,000 infantry bayonets and 42,000 cavalry sabers.

The pride of the Russian army became the artillery, which was rapidly reconstituted after the Narva defeat and divided into regiment, field (108 pieces), and siege (360 heavy pieces). To the artillery were assigned the engineer units created by Peter. Furthermore, garrison troops appeared in Russia that were stationed in the numerous fortresses. In 1720 they amounted to no less than 68,000 men. In conjunction with the use of the irregular (i.e., noncombatant) forces of cossacks, Tatars, Bashkirs, and other native peoples traditional for the pre-Petrine army, the numbers of which amounted to between 40,000 and 70,000 sabers, in the 1720s the so-called land militia was created (territorial troops recruited for a term) from the single homesteaders living in the south. They guarded the dangerous southern frontiers.[5]

The system of organization and administration of the army was worked out in detail and in depth. During the first quarter of the eighteenth century the central administrations were created that oversaw the army's needs: the War, Admiralty, and Provisions bureaus that were replaced in 1718–19 by the War and Admiralty colleges.

The highest tactical unit remained, as before, the regiment. Regiments were combined into brigades, and brigades into divisions.

The army's operations were directed by the field (or general) staff headed by a general–field marshal. According to European practice, commanders were introduced for the different kinds of troops: a general-from-the-infantry commanded the infantry, a general-from-the-cavalry commanded the cavalry, a grand master of ordnance commanded the artillery. A permanent attribute of army administration was the functioning of a war council—consultations of all the highest generals on the most important questions of the conduct of war operations.

Analyzing the causes of the Narva defeat, Peter commented in his *Journal*: "the art is out of sight," that is, the state of the troops' preparedness for battle and the art of conducting warfare were most unsatisfactory. In reality, knowing of the Swedes' approach, why had the Russian army not come out of the palisades constructed around besieged Narva and met the opponent in a field engagement, where numerical superiority would have been on the side of the Russian troops? The fault was not in the high command's indecisiveness, but in the fact that the Russian troops of the seventeenth century were not used to fighting in the field and strove to fasten upon some height by fortifying it, or to conduct an engagement behind the mobile wall of a "wander-burg" or, simply, of a fortified supply train. In this way the initiative fell into the opponent's hands. The Russian commanders had operated at Narva exactly in this obsolete manner.

Peter quickly understood the fallaciousness and wrongheadedness of such a military concept. Under him a headlong restructuring of the strategic and tactical bases of Russian military art took place. For Peter the main aim of military operations was not to capture the opponent's fortresses (as it had been earlier), but to defeat him in direct, fast-moving contact—battle engagement. In this, Peter, by weighing all strengths and weaknesses of the opponent and his own forces, knew how to proceed cautiously, with certainty, with a huge reserve in readiness, as happened at Poltava, for example. The movement of a mass of infantry was coordinated with the operations of the artillery and the cavalry; at the same time the cavalry of the dragoon type (i.e., trained for maneuver on foot) exercised broad possibilities to operate independently, to pursue operations of strategic scope.

Peter clung to the principle: "It is necessary to conduct your own army, depending on the foe's forces or his intentions, so as to forestall him in all matters and seek in all ways to overthrow the foe."[6]

The preparation of the troops for battle operations was changed in accordance with the new strategic and tactical principles. In place of the earlier yearly reviews, and infrequent training in shooting, constant preparation became the norm, which did not end with the conversion of the recruit into a "regular" soldier. This preparation focused on active military operations. In it we see a combination of individual and group training that led to the necessary different kinds of automatic movement by the reorganized company, battalion, and regiment, which ensured mobility and effective maneuvering on the battlefield. Here too training was for the coordinated and accurate direction of fire skillfully combined with bayonet thrusts. Here too was the clear direction of battle on the part of the officers, which was founded on the combination of unquestioning obedience and necessary independence.

At the basis of Peter's tactical troop training lay not only some purely technical devices, but also the cultivation of responsibility, initiative, and conscious discipline, that is, everything without which an army cannot exist.

Special significance was thus assumed by military codes and regulations—in a word, the codex of military law. Peter devoted much attention to their composition, seeing in them the basis of the life of the army, and indeed of all of society. In place of Aleksei Mikhailovich's *The Study of the Skill of Military Formations*, the start of the eighteenth century saw new codes: "Drill Regulations," "Ordinance for Battle," and others.

Published in 1716, the celebrated Articles of War specified not only the organization and formation of the army, the duties of the military, and the bases of training and field service, but also laws on military crimes and administration. One may speak about the powerful influence on the Articles of War of the military legislation of Sweden, France, Austria, and Denmark that was reworked and supplemented in accordance with Russian conditions and relying on Peter's experience as a commander and organizer of military affairs. The life of the Articles of War proved to be extraordinarily long—150 years. During all these years several generations of Russian soldiers and officers took the military oath according to the text of the Articles of War, more precisely in its section "Articles of War with a Brief Interpretation." Among them for certain were the commanders Rumiantsev and Suvorov, Barclay de Tolly and Kutuzov, the Decembrists Pestel and Bestuzhev-Riumin, the writers Shevchenko and Leo Tolstoy, and hundreds of thousands, even millions of the Russian army's new inductees.

Here is the text of this "Oath or Pledge of Every Military Rank to the People":

> I (name) pledge to Almighty God to serve Our Most Serene Tsar and Master loyally and obediently, that in these stipulated articles of war and also in those to be stipulated henceforth all shall be upheld and everything executed dutifully. I shall exert myself to concert strong and brave resistance to and to harm in all ways the enemies of His Tsarist Majesty's state and lands, whatever their calling, by body and blood, in the field and in fortresses, on water and land, in battles, sallies, sieges and storms and other military occasions. And if I hear or see something opposed to or blameworthy against the person of His Majesty or his troops and also against his people or the state's interests, then I promise to inform about it without hiding anything and according to my best conscience and as much as will be known to me, but all the more to uphold and better fulfill his benefit in everything. And to my commanders set over me in everything, as regards the prosperity and increase of His Tsarist Majesty's troops, state, and people, to render dutiful obedience in guard duty, in works and other occasions, and not to oppose their orders at all. And never to separate myself from unit and banner to which I belong, be it in the field, the supply train or the garrison, but to follow after them while I am alive, directly, willfully and faithfully just as is worthy of my honor and my life. And in everything to act as behooves an honorable, loyal, obedient, brave and deliberate soldier. In which may the Lord God Almighty help me.[7]

The oath, like Peter's other military laws, clearly defined the principles of service, more broadly the service of the Petrine soldier. This involved a consistently followed hierarchy, strict subordination to military discipline and to the orders of superiors, fear of God, and obedience to the law. These principles had never before been formulated in Russia and implemented with such fullness, consistency, and purposefulness.

The military legislation would not have attracted so much attention if it had been a reflection of Peter's views only on the structure and relationships within the army. Peter's general ideas on the state found clear expression in the military legislation of Petrine times, which reflected his ideological concept. In this sense Peter followed a tradition known to have existed in Europe. P.O. Bobrovsky's remarks seem just, as concerns the coincidence of Peter's ideas with those of the Swedish king Gustavus Adolphus (1594–1632), an outstanding commander and reformer. The matter involves the urge of both to depart from primitive brutality as the sole form of treating soldiers and their desire not to convert the soldier into a walking machine but to cultivate good morals with the aid of the army, to enlighten, and to counter absurd superstitions. In full measure the influence of these advanced ideas undoubtedly found expression in the Petrine Articles of War, which had been composed under the strong influence of Gustavus Adolphus's military laws. It is no accident that the oath cited earlier literally repeats (with some additions) the 110 articles of Gustavus Adolphus's Military Codex.[8]

Hierarchy and subordination are the backbone of relationships in the army. But that is not all. The commander is not merely somebody senior in rank to whom it behooves one to be subordinate. He is the personification of something larger than military command. He is himself obligated to meet quite lofty requirements, professional as well as those common for everyone. Chapter 10 of the Articles of War, which is entitled "On the general–field marshal and on every chief," propounds the following as law: "His virtue and justice attract to him the hearts of all the army, both officers and rank and file. It behooves him to hear their complaints and denunciations willingly, to praise and reward their good deeds and for the bad to punish them strictly and zealously, so that for both he be liked and feared."[9]

Not just the last phrase but the entire text is expressive and symbolic. Although the text addresses the army, it leads us far away from the parade ground and the barracks. In the army's core, the army's structure, and the army's relationships, Peter saw the pattern for all of society. Peter felt a sincere desire "to correct" society by extending to it the norms of army life so easily formulated in the form of articles and so easily implemented on the army's parade ground. The concise organization of the army, the clearly outlined circle of the obligations of commanders and subordinates, the relationships of respect for rank on the basis of strict discipline and unanimity—all this, it seemed, would be so easily transferred to the whole society.

That is why the document cited earlier should be viewed not as a purely military one. In essence, it contains requirements obligatory and applicable to any leader. And what about deficiencies and vices? Of course, there were some. Peter singles out two of the chief ones.

The first involves banal "cupidity," by which was understood bribery, extortion, and other illegal forms of enrichment by officials. The second vice involves "flattery," that is, indulgence and connivance, the condemnation applying not so much to connivance from selfish or other undesirable purposes as to every connivance in general, for "nothing so leads people to evil as weak command."[10]

In such norms of the military codex the general principles of Peter's approach to the fulfillment by each man in service of his own duty are distinctly seen. The heart of these principles is unquestioning subordination to the leader and strict observance of orders prescribed from above.

Creation of the regular army was part of the task that Peter had set for himself after receiving the Narva lesson. In occupying Ingria in the first years of the war, he immediately evaluated the significance of its bodies of water and waterways in view of the leading role that a naval force might play here. It is also important that Peter did not think of his state's might without a navy, did not imagine his own life without ships. The creation of the navy was for him the first duty after creating the army, the natural continuation of the cause begun by his father, Tsar Aleksei Mikhailovich, under whom the first Russian ship, *Orel*, had been launched into the water at Dedinov on the Oka.

The construction, maintenance, and deployment of naval forces were always exceptionally complicated and costly matters of general state policy, which as regards the Russia of the turn of the seventeenth and eighteenth centuries may be compared, by no special stretch of the imagination, with contemporary space programs. It was not enough to build or to purchase a ship that cost a small fortune. One had to have an elaborate infrastructure that provided the fleet with everything essential, starting with nails and ending with naval commanders. An endless string of works—sawmills, sailcloth weaving, ropewalks, and others—labored for the navy's needs. Harbors and port facilities, training institutions, arsenals, and finally a full-scale shipbuilding industry—

these alone could actually breathe life into the notion of a "naval fleet."

It is essential to do Peter justice in that he recognized this and displayed rare organizational talent and energy. One may confidently assert that maritime affairs, beginning with the ship's design and ending with the lofty art of navigation and sea battle, represented his favorite preoccupation. Carrying a carpenter's axe or a sextant, Peter evidently found inspiration for the soul; he experienced the reliable clarity and simplicity of shipbuilding, the obedient submission to his will of a huge thing bearing hundreds of people and scores of cannon that was so like the country at whose helm he had been fated to stand.

Construction of the Petrine navy had begun, as we know, at Voronezh in 1695–96. Here after the setback of the first Azov campaign had been assembled substantial forces of shipwrights hired in Holland, England, and Venice, who together with Russian carpenters and laborers built a large number of galleys and other vessels in a very short time. In all there had been built twenty-eight ships, twenty-three galleys, and many smaller craft at the Voronezh shipyards before 1702. The building of ships continued later, too, right up to the time that Azov and Taganrog were surrendered to the Turks in 1712, when part of the ships of the Azov fleet were destroyed and part sold to the Turks. But by that time the Azov fleet was not Russia's only fleet. Ships had been busily built on the banks of the rivers of the Baltic basin already for ten years.

Just as at Voronezh, the experience of which had been taken into account, construction of the navy on the Baltic was pursued at breakneck speed. Its beginning had been laid in 1702 with the foundation of shipyards on the river Sias'. In 1703 on the Svir' sprang up the celebrated Olonets shipyard, one of the very largest that was rivaled only by the Petersburg shipyard founded just a bit later. In all during the Petrine period no fewer than 1,104 ships and other vessels were built, the lion's share of them coming from the Petersburg and Olonets yards—386 vessels, among which were 45 ships of the line. These figures reflect the colossal successes of shipbuilding over a little more than twenty years.

In the opinion of historians of Russian shipbuilding, Peter was himself an extraordinary shipwright who proposed many new technical solutions beginning with the design and ending with the deployment of seagoing vessels. It is odd that, in striving to achieve the nonstop work of shipyards throughout the year, Peter proposed to launch ships even in the winter—in a specially prepared hole in the ice. Over the years, the experience of the tsar-shipwright grew. Having started with the design and construction of light sailing vessels and snows, Peter finished by designing and laying the keel of a 100-gun ship. The 64-gun ship *Ingermanland*, designed by him and built by Richard Cozens in 1715 was exemplary.

At the same time that ships were being built at Petersburg and Kronstadt, powerful naval bases were created there, supplemented by a base in Estland (Rogervik, now Paltiiski). In Kronstadt a unique system of canals and sluices was built that permitted the repair, outfitting, and even storage of huge ships on shore between seasons.

Peter did not restrict himself to shipbuilding. He also purchased them from abroad; in the years 1711–14 sixteen ships of the line were thus brought to Russia. The Petrine era witnessed a blossoming of the galley fleet known from ancient times. Peter appreciated its significance for battling the enemy in the shallow skerries of the Gulf of Finland and the Gulf of Bothnia. The experience of Venetian shipwrights, which had been acquired in the course of centuries of naval wars on the Adriatic and the Aegean seas, was especially applicable here.

By the time of the Hangö battle of 1714 Peter had created a maritime shield for Petersburg—the fleet numbered twenty-two ships, five frigates, and a multitude of small vessels. Of course, one cannot call this fleet perfected: the ships were of various types, they had been built of green wood (and therefore proved short-lived), they maneuvered badly, and the crews were poorly trained. It was no accident that during the Hangö operation all the burden of military action at sea fell to the galley fleet, which thanks to its maneuverability and shallow draft could avoid engagement with large aggregations of the Swedish fleet of the line.

The experience of shipbuilding and the prospects of military operations on the expanses of the Baltic directly along the shores of Sweden—a consequence of the expulsion of the Swedes from the Gulf of Finland and of Peter's naval ambitions in general—led to the adoption around 1714–15 of an entire program of expanding and qualitatively renovating the fleet. This program was not just carried out, but even overdone by the end of Peter's reign: from 1715 to 1724 the number of ships increased from twenty-seven to thirty-four and of frigates from seven to fifteen. At the same time the fleet's firepower grew almost twofold: the total number of cannon on board rose from 1,250 to 2,226. The reinforcement of firepower was connected with the appearance of a new generation of large ships, among which were singled out the ninety-six-gun *Fridrikhshtadt*, the ninety-gun *Lesnoe* and *Gangut*, and three ships with eighty-eight guns. By comparison I should note that the average number of guns on the ships of the Russian fleet in 1715 did not exceed fifty-four.[12]

The fact that the Russian navy surpassed the Swedish had already become apparent by the second half of the Northern War. But, glancing ahead, it should be noted that after the breakthrough in Russia's favor Peter did not start cutting back on naval construction. It was clear to him as an experienced naval commander that the Russian fleet was far behind the fleet of the "queen of the seas," Great Britain: three times in the years 1719–21 the squadron of Admiral Norris had shut the Russian fleet in port. It is not out of the question that Peter's response was to lay down in 1723 the 100-gun ship that later received the name *Peter I and II.* Apparently this ship, gigantic for those times (historians of shipbuilding refer to it as the first of that type in the world), was supposed to launch a new generation of ships for which the Baltic would have been manifestly cramped.

Industrialization Petrine-Style

The successes of Peter's army on the battlefield would have been impossible without fundamental reforms in the economy of Russia: the victorious arms at Noteburg, Poltava, and Hangö had been forged in the foundries of the Petrine works of the Urals and Tula. It is beyond doubt that during Peter's reign a fundamental reform was instituted in the economy that had far-reaching consequences. It may be confidently asserted that in the first quarter of the eighteenth century an abrupt economic leap took place in Russia equal in significance and consequences to the industrialization of the Soviet period. The industrial buildup of the Petrine epoch proceeded at a tempo never seen before that time: over the years 1695–1725 no fewer than two hundred enterprises of different sorts arose—that is, ten times more than there had been at the end of the seventeenth century—and this was accompanied by an even more impressive growth in the scope of production.

The most typical peculiarity of the economic boom in Russia at the start of the eighteenth century consisted of the autocratic state's defining role in the economy, its active and profound intervention in all spheres of economic life. Many factors governed this role.

The economic concept of mercantilism then prevailing in Europe proceeded from the assumption that the accumulation of money via an active balance of trade, the export of goods to foreign markets and the obstruction of the import of goods to one's own markets, represented the basis of the state's wealth and the crucial condition for its existence. This presupposed the state's intervention in the economic sphere. Encouraging some "useful" and "necessary" forms of production, crafts, and goods inevitably entailed curtailing, restricting, or even prohibiting others that were considered "not useful" and "unneeded" from the state's perspective.

The concept of mercantilism presupposed administration of the economy in accordance with those notions about the country's wealth and the subjects' prosperity that were held by statesmen inspired by economists who promised prosperity for society. Such an approach implied a rather precise definition by the authorities of the ways and means of attaining the "common good." Among these means were encouragement and compulsion and regulation of the subjects' economic life.

Dreaming about his state's might, Peter was not indifferent to the ideas of mercantilism and its integral part, protectionism, the encouragement of industry that produces goods in the first instance for the export market. The ideas of compulsion in economic policy coincided with the general ideas of "progress through coercion" that Peter practiced throughout his reforms.

But something else is more important—in Russian conditions it was not only and not mainly the concept of mercantilism that governed the choice of direction of economic policy typical of the beginning of the eighteenth century. The strongest stimulator of the state's active, previously unseen intervention in the economic sphere was the disastrous start of the Northern War, which had brought neither trophies nor new, rich, economically developed territories. With the loss of all the artillery at Narva it had become clear that it would be necessary to re-create virtually from scratch a battleworthy army. Numerous manufactories, primarily significant for defense, started to be built not from abstract notions of encouraging industry or from calculations of revenue, but from the brutal necessities to provide the army and the navy with arms, munitions, and uniforms. A thin stream of deliveries via the port of Arkhangel'sk could not satisfy the country's growing demand for diverse goods. Furthermore, having launched the war with Sweden, Russia had been deprived of a basic source of supply of high-quality Scandinavian iron, which went for the forging of weapons, and in general it turned out to be economically isolated in practice.

It was the extreme situation that arose after the "Narva confusion" of 1700 that predetermined the character, tempo, and specifics of the industrial boom unleashed by the crash construction. Proceeding from clearly acknowledged defense interests, Peter's state emerged as the initiator of the industrialization necessitated by conditions. Possessing huge financial and material resources and the right of unlimited use of the land, its minerals, and its waters, the state took upon itself the regulation of everything linked to production, beginning with the location of enterprises and ending with the specification of essential output. The same thing happened with trade. In the system of state industry and trade created under Peter the principles and devices of the administrative management of the economy were laid down and consistently elaborated on a grandiose scale unknown previously in Russian history.

Of course, in the seventeenth century, state monopolies had already existed, and the central bureaus had occupied the most important place in the development of crafts, trade, and industry, but for pre-Petrine Russia such all-encompassing scope and depth of the state's penetration into the economy had hardly been typical.

In the years of the Northern War state enterprise developed in two directions: first, production was activated in the old industrial regions through expanding existing enterprises and constructing new ones, and second, new regions of industrial production were created. It is important to note that the newly constructed enterprises were of the manufacturing type, the most advanced for the time. The application of diverse instruments and tools, division of labor, and specialization of professions ensured adequate productivity of labor at the manufactories in comparison with craft workshops. To be sure, manufactory production had appeared long before Petrine industrialization and in the seventeenth century had already produced diverse goods for the domestic market. A genuine breakthrough in the country's industry arrived, however, only with the start of the Petrine transformations.

Both paths of developing state enterprises—the activization of old industrial regions and the creation of new ones—are clearly observed in the example of metallurgy, the basis of military might. The treasury invested huge sums in expanding the output of iron, cannon, and arms in the regions of traditional production—Karelia, the Voronezh-Tambov lands, and the Muscovite center. Here in a short time new works were built, old ones were expanded, and quite often they were taken away from entrepreneurs who could not deal expeditiously with the state's huge orders. It is quite evident that if the Lipetsk mills were "attached" to the construction of the fleet at Voronezh, then the demands of naval construction at Petersburg and around Lake Ladoga were satisfied by the Olonets mills, which, although they used poor-quality ore, were located near the theater of military operations.

A special role was played by the Urals, where in very short order a whole metallurgical complex was built. We should not picture the pre-Petrine Urals as a wild country, unpopulated and untamed. By the end of the seventeenth century there were quite a few petty trades and forges, many of the greatest orefields were known, and attempts had been made, unsuccessfully it is true, to build manufactories. But things changed when the state, subjugated to Peter's will, assumed responsibility for the industrial development of the Urals. By the summer of 1696 the Siberian Bureau had already directed the provincial governor of Verkhotur'e to prospect for iron ore. The enterprising executor of Peter's wishes, Andreas Vinius, became the chief administrator of the Siberian Bureau; he himself took part in investigating the riches of the

Urals. The most suitable was acknowledged to be the very rich iron orefields along the bank of the Tagil—the so-called Magnetic Mountain, and "amid the mountain an umbilical cord of pure magnetite." Upon returning from abroad in August 1698, Peter almost immediately arranged for the construction of a metalworks there.[1]

In Peter's decrees about founding the works one distinctly observes the methods of creating new manufactories, by which the experience of operating enterprises elsewhere was actively utilized, and the best masters were resettled to a new place under the jurisdiction of the local administration. Moreover, Peter's agents in Western Europe actively recruited foreign mining specialists and metallurgists who willingly journeyed to Russia from Germany, England, and other countries.

The foundation of works in the Urals was a difficult matter, and the first pig iron flowed out of the first furnace of the Nev'ianskii plant only on 15 December 1701. This was an outstanding event: the birth of the renowned Urals industry without which it is hard to imagine the economy of Russia. On 8 January 1702 the first forged iron that had no equal either in Russia or abroad was prepared from this pig iron.[2]

A bit earlier the Kamenskii works was founded, then the Uktusskii in 1702, and the Alpat'evskii works in 1704. In addition to these, from 1702 through 1707 metalworks were built in the Olonets region, in Ustiuzhna, on Beloozero, and also in the Voronezh lands (the Lipetskii works). No fewer than eleven works founded by the state had abruptly altered, literally in the space of five years, the situation in heavy industry, supplying the country with iron. The mighty metallurgical base allowed the expansion of metalworking production, more specifically the arms industry. In Tula, which had been famed for its armorers, an arms plant was founded in 1712, and in 1721 another appeared near Petersburg at Sestroretsk.

Peter actively promoted the creation of manufactories in light industry. In 1696–97 a translator of the Ambassadorial Bureau, Andrei Krevet, founded in Preobrazhenskoe, on the bank of the river Yauza (and using its water power), the state Weaving Court—a manufactory for the production of sailcloth, the demand for which had become great with the start of fleet construction. Krevet was commissioned to build a sawmill and to hire weavers from abroad for the Weaving Court. Also hired were Russian weavers from Moscow's Kadashevskaia settlement, where the weaving trade had a long tradition. By the start of the eighteenth century the Weaving Court was already working at full power supplying the Admiralty with sailcloth. By 1719 this was a huge enterprise with more than 1,200 specialists and workers.[3]

At the beginning of the eighteenth century in Moscow the Rope

Court was built—a manufactory for preparing ship rigging, and also the Leather Court and the Sword-knot Court, which supplied the army with accoutrements and saddles. At the same time the state took over the production of hats for the army. For this the Hat Court was built in Moscow, which operated until 1710, when hats were dropped from the uniform of the Russian army and replaced by tricornes. At the beginning of the century other state manufactories—paper, button, stocking, woolen, linen—were also feverishly established, primarily in Moscow and Petersburg. A special place among them was occupied by the Woolen Court in Moscow—the first large-scale textile production "of German woolens for the cause," the overwhelming majority of which went to the needs of the army, which required tens of thousands of tunics, coats, and cloaks. The textile manufactories in Moscow, Kazan, and Lipetsk worked on both imported as well as native wool, for which from 1710 sheep herds were established in the southern districts. The most important linen manufactory, the Ekateringof, operated in Petersburg. The treasury was the initiator of other production—glass, mirrors, flints, leather, tapestries, and so forth.

In the organization of industry, especially in the first years of the eighteenth century, the state exploited all its advantages to the maximum. The centralized administration allowed it to allocate expeditiously and rationally the regional sites, scope of production, and essential means of supply. Local authorities were directed to cooperate fully in the construction of enterprises in the shortest time possible. The construction of works (especially metallurgical) required huge means, which no single private entrepreneur or lender could muster. These means were easily found in the treasury, which had not yet been exhausted by the war and which managed gradually to increase the pressure of the tax bite on the taxable population.

In the formation and operation of the first large-scale government manufactories, whatever their designation, one observes certain common features. The enterprises were founded with optimal proximity to sources of raw materials; their construction used the cheap labor of the local population from which they recruited poorly paid and unskilled workers. For the organization of production they attracted experienced specialists both Russian and foreign. Common as well were the supply of the manufactories with technology and raw materials, part of which were purchased abroad, and the delivery of finished products, which for the most part went to the needs of the state, for which, indeed, the manufacturing industry had been created preparatory to the outbreak of the Northern War.

In setting up its own industry the state included the organization of its own commerce—primarily to obtain profit from goods inside the country and from the export abroad of such goods as would provide the state with money for the purchase of ships, arms, and raw materials for industry. The state seized control of commerce by a most primitive but quite effective method—the introduction of a monopoly on the preparation and supply of specified goods both within the country and without.

One of the first monopolies was introduced for salt. For consumers this signified a twofold price increase; that is, the state wished not merely to take into its hands a profitable branch, but even to obtain a surplus profit of 100 percent. The introduction of a state monopoly on tobacco in the same year of 1705 led to an 800 percent growth of profit to the state.[4]

Special significance arose from the monopoly on the sale of goods abroad. The introduction of "forbidden" goods had been practiced in the seventeenth century too, but under Peter it assumed huge proportions and encompassed practically all forms of goods that Russian merchants sold to foreigners at Arkhangel'sk or themselves conveyed abroad through other ports and border towns. Among the goods taken into state commerce were raw leather, hemp, flax, linseed, grain, bristles, pitch, potash, tar, caviar and isinglass, mast wood, skins, rhubarb, brimstone, tallow, wax, sailcloth, and iron.

The Petrine government's monopoly policy should not be oversimplified. Along with goods that had long since been under the state's monopoly and those that fell into the "forbidden" category for a long time under Peter, there were many that were declared under state monopoly for only a short time and were then exempted. The treasury sold a series of goods without forbidding merchants to do the same, but it remained at the same time a specially privileged "merchant" with the right of first purchase for raw materials and sale of goods on the market. Raw materials often came in the form of taxes in kind on the peasants (hemp, flax, etc.), and finished products were supplied to the treasury by private entrepreneurs at prices set by the state (nowadays these would be called state orders). Sometimes merchants were prohibited from making purchases until the treasury's orders had been completely filled; sometimes certain regions producing raw materials were declared "forbidden," that is, closed to merchants.

The participation of the treasury in commerce, which under Peter assumed gigantic scope, led inevitably to the restriction and regimentation of commercial activity by Russian merchants, and it resulted in disruption, disorganization of trade turnover, and suffocation of free enterprise based on market competition. It should be obvious that state officials themselves did not engage in trade—trade was granted as a concession to a single merchant or to several; thus the sale of goods was monopolized by a specific concessionaire who paid the treasury (all at once or in parts) a sum of money that he, of course, strove hard to recover at the expense of the consumer or the supplier of raw materials, thereby throttling his own potential competitors on the free market.

The basic goods that went for export fell into the hands of foreigners who had extensive business contacts with the West. In the correspondence of Peter and the Senate we often encounter the names of Henry Stiles, Jan Lups, Charles Goodfellow, Rodion Meyer, Christopher Brant, and other monopolists for the sale of Russian goods on European markets and for the purchase of goods that Russia needed. For all of his patriotism Peter was forced to resort to this. The absence of Russian commercial shipping, the lack of established contacts on the European market, inexperience in trade, and an acute need for money compelled him to turn to Western intermediaries, who of course did not suffer as a result.

In general the Petrine era was a most difficult time for the Russian merchantry, not only owing to the negative consequences of the monopolies on a series of goods, trade of which for centuries had made it possible for many trading houses and merchant families to enrich themselves. In the years of the Northern War the demand for different services from the merchantry increased, which diverted it from trade and compelled it to fulfill (at its own expense) duties in urban administration—"for the receipt of state monies" and "for the sale of spirits and salt"—and in the custom houses. The introduction of new taxes automatically meant that the merchantry had a new duty—"to attend the collection" of the tax. Besides, one should add that the taxes—direct and indirect—increased in the course of the Northern War not only in the village but also in the town. The townsmen—merchants and artisans—provided transport, horses, and provisions while soldiers and officers were quartered in their houses for years. Furthermore, all the payments and duties were apportioned in the urban communes "by substance," that is, in proportion to the prosperity of each inhabitant. This meant that the brunt of the burden of payments fell on the shoulders of the more substantial merchants, which, of course, scarcely facilitated the growth of merchant capital.

State monopolies, taxes, and duties—these were the powerful means the Petrine state applied to obtain the huge sums of money for the resolution of its tasks. Peter pursued the same purpose by other actions in the sphere of commercial enterprise that should be seen as devastating for trade and the merchantry. Of what value were the compulsory knocking together of companies or the establishment of firm purchase prices (depressed as a rule) for goods supplied to the treasury by merchants and entrepreneurs? These goods could then be sold by the state on the domestic or export market at the most arbitrarily elevated prices.

In 1713 a decree was issued that riled Russian entrepreneurs for years. It prohibited shipping from the interior regions to Arkhangel'sk the main goods of Russian export—hemp, raw leather, bristles, potash, and so forth. These goods were supposed to be sent to Petersburg—the new port on the Baltic.[5] The calculations and desires of the initiator of this decree—Peter—are understandable. He proceeded from notions that seemed obvious to him: Petersburg is geographically and climatically better suited for trade with Europe; it is closer for Western European merchants, too, than remote Arkhangel'sk across three seas. Yet Peter's willful decision, which was based on logic and a sincere desire to transform Petersburg quickly into a "second Amsterdam," met no support among either the Russian merchants or the foreign merchants who traded with Russia, for this decision broke the traditional trade patterns. Enterprise in Arkhangel'sk was linked with definite advantages and traditions the destruction of which would be dangerous, if a loss of revenue were to be avoided.

Indeed, the route from Moscow to Arkhangel'sk was longer than that to Petersburg, but it passed along a known, established road and along full-flowing rivers on the banks of which lived people who worked in the northern trade. Indeed, Petersburg was twice as close to Europe as Arkhangel'sk, but what awaited the merchant who traversed the difficult, poorly built route to the new capital that stood amid swamps? A lack of living quarters and trade facilitites, a high cost of living, shortages of work hands, intermediaries, storage and transshipment—the entire commercial infrastructure was missing. That is what awaited merchant's in the tsar's "paradise."

Later on, when 1713 arrived, the Swedes still controlled the Baltic. The Russian fleet was afraid not only to accompany or to convoy ships, but even to venture out of Kronstadt to the open sea. Even Western skippers preferred the risk of meeting ice on the White Sea en route to Arkhangel'sk to the risk of an undesirable encounter with a Swedish privateer. And the Swedes, to be sure, had no intention of providing the foe with the possibility of free navigation on the Baltic Sea.

But Peter was implacable. Although he subsequently somewhat softened the restrictions imposed on commerce to Arkhangel'sk, still the privileged, "hothouse" conditions for Petersburg were preserved for a protracted time and were reinforced by a 1721 decree, according to which customs duties on goods sold in Arkhangel'sk were set one-third higher than the duties on the same goods when sold at Petersburg.

It is true that Petersburg in time actually became Russia's major port. But that came about much later than the Nystadt peace of 1721, after many events that converted the country into the mighty Russian Empire. In the specific context of 1713 Peter's decree was a serious blow to commerce and to the prosperity of the Russian merchantry as well as to the population of the Russian north.

Peter, however, did not limit himself to these measures of encouraging Petersburg's commerce. He resolved to create a Petersburg merchantry by the same means that he had employed quite often before, that is, by compulsion or coercion. After 1711 several decrees were issued regarding the compulsory resettlement to Petersburg of several thousand merchants and artisans from the large and small towns of Russia.

Peter practiced compulsory resettlement in regard to other strata of the population too. Is it necessary to dwell in detail on the fact that no less than forty thousand peasants from the whole country drove pilings every year and built the houses and fortifications of the new capital, dying in their earthen quarters from the exhausting toil, malnutrition, and disease? Also resettled were noblemen who were obligated to build houses in Petersburg. But for the merchantry resettlement was an especially painful, ruinous matter: commerce relied on contacts and business relationships, and each trading house had its own assortment of goods and region of commerce. Resettlement broke these contacts; the competition in commercial activity in the new locale changed for the worse.

Everything that has been recounted here is merely part of the policy of merciless exploitation of merchant capital by the autocratic state, which aspired to obtain money and goods quickly for the resolution of its own grandiose plans at the expense of the merchantry and its professional occupation with trade. Monopolies, compulsory service, duties, resettlement, artificial restrictions on commercial activity of various kinds—all these afflicted Russian merchants: historical sources testify to the utter ruination of the more substantial group of the merchantry— the so-called "gostinaia sotnia" and "gosti."

A.I. Aksenov's research into the genealogy of the Moscow merchantry demonstrates that "right up to the end of the seventeenth century some increase in the number of gosti was under way, whereas in the first decade and a half of the eighteenth century there was a sharp decline." If in 1705 "among the gosti there were numbered twenty-seven family names (actually there were, naturally, more gosti inasmuch as in several clans there were several representatives so designated), then in 1713 in the capacity of Moscow gosti 'present' only ten were counted."

The causes of the "impoverishment" of the most substantial stratum of the Russian merchantry were the liquidation of traditional forms of trade and crafts after the introduction of numerous state monopolies and the rapid growth of taxes. As Aksenov asserts, with rare exceptions it was just in the Petrine era that the richest Moscow family firms were ruined; the gosti in this period "suffered a shattering blow. Even the few whose descendants seemingly occupied a firm position experienced this. Therefore, despite external prosperity, the clans of the Filat'evs, Chir'evs and others slowly but surely declined in the mid-eighteenth century."[6]

This conclusion repeats the observations made earlier by N.I. Pavlenko for the whole of the "gostinaia sotnia": in 1715, of 226 men, only 104 preserved their trade and crafts, and 17 representatives of the trading community's elite "changed their estate membership, having ceased occupations with trade and crafts: some turned up as orderlies, others as petty clerks, a fifth had become soldiers, whereas 6 men had taken refuge in monastery cells." It is also important that Pavlenko had indicated the deep roots of what had occurred: the basic wealth of the merchants had been borrowed and loaned capital in constant circulation. With a substantial merchant the money was in ceaseless movement, so that "behind the façade of the flowering of trade firms was concealed their unstable position, governed by the huge proportional weight of borrowed and loaned capital in their transactions."[7] To put it differently, such capital was uncustomarily "fragile," dependent on changes of situation and commercial competition. The crude interference of the Petrine state in the sphere of trade had largely destroyed the already unstable balance of the financial fulcrum of private commerce, which led to the decline of the flower of Russia's merchantry.

Hence there was no exaggeration in the assertion of the authors of the Charter of the Main Municipal Administration of 1721, who wrote that Russian "merchant and taxed crafts people in all towns abide not only scorn, but even all kinds of insult, attacks, and unbearable burdens, from which they have greatly diminished and almost all have been ruined causing significant harm to the state."[8]

Indeed, the impoverishment and decline of the once richest merchant firms, the ruin of towns, the flight of their inhabitants—this was the steep price that the Russian merchants and townspeople paid for success in the Northern War, for financing it, and for being deprived of their profits as a result of the harsh monopoly policy and various restrictions implemented by Peter's economic policy from the start of the eighteenth century.

For the sake of justice it should be noted that the townspeople shared the cost of victory in the Northern War with the country's rural population. All the burden of the war weighed on the shoulders of the Russian peasantry. And victory, as often happens in history, became possible only through overburdening the people.

A mere enumeration of the different obligations of the peasant-tax-payers during the Northern War will produce an impression on us who have been long accustomed to the imperceptible growth of taxes via the price system. The obligations took several forms: (1) people (recruits); (2) labor; (3) cartage; (4) horses; (5) quartering; (6) in kind (provisions, forage, and so forth); (7) money.

Money taxes were divided into ordinary and extraordinary. The proportions (amounts) of routine taxes remained stable for years. They were composed of several groups of taxes. "Bureau" taxes went for the needs of the central offices. The very old "drovers' and hostage monies of the Drovers' Bureau" were supplemented by "the monies of the Military Bureau for the salary of the dragoons," "the ship monies of the Admiralty Bureau," and "the recruit monies of the Urban Bureau." At the beginning of the 1710s ordinary taxes appeared for the construction of the new capital: "monies for the Saint Petersburg city affairs for bricks," "for the burning of lime," and "monies for supplies and for vessels." A sizable group of money taxes consisted of estate taxes, that is, those that the separate estate groups paid. Thus, the monastery peasants from 1707 were assessed "monies of the Monastery Bureau for the salaries of dragoons" and "monies for hiring stonemasons and bricklayers." The palace and the state peasants paid their own taxes.

The ordinary "bureau," Petersburg, and estate taxes were supplemented by local levies peculiar to each guberniia, province, and even district. If you lump them together by destination, then these were collections for the local administration, garrisons, maintenance of the postal service, roads, bridges, and so on.[9]

Notwithstanding the fearsome variety of regular money payments, one may confidently assert that if these had been the only taxes, the peasants of Petrine times might have lived quite decently. But the crux of the problem was that the regular and even the extraordinary money taxes constituted merely an insignificant part of the general burden of state imposts. Most burdensome were the extraordinary imposts, which as a rule were mixed: money and kind; money dues and labor dues; cartage dues, money dues, and labor dues; and so forth. A typical feature of such imposts was prepayment, without which the dispatch of provisions, recruits, workers, and horses could not be managed.

The collection and dispatch of provisions represented one of the most burdensome extraordinary imposts that did not cease for a single year. There were several forms of provisions that were named for their destination: "Petersburg," "Riga," "Pomerania," "Briansk," "Azov," "Voronezh," "Admiralty," and so forth. The provisions impost in each region of the country was defined differently. In some localities (primarily grain producing) the provisions were exacted in kind, in others "provisions monies" were collected, and in still others the impost was of a mixed money and in-kind type.

Besides deliveries of provisions or payment of "provisions monies," the peasants might receive a decree to pay "monies in addition to the usual." An especially heavy burden of the provisions impost was assessed on those peasants whose villages housed the army, which in essence they fed and sheltered in their households. Thus, in 1713 for the population of Kiev guberniia, where Boris Petrovich Sheremetev's army was stationed, deliveries of provisions cost three times more than in those guberniias where the army did not winter.[10]

Sizable money prepayments accompanied the levies of recruits and horses for the army. Annual recruiting levies began in 1705. The first decree about a levy of recruits from 20 February 1705 had specified taking one recruit from every twenty households, and only "the unmarried from fifteen to twenty years old, and under fifteen or over twenty not to take anyone." These same twenty households were supposed to provide money for "food, and clothing, and footwear, gray overcoats, and fur coats, and hats, and sashes, and stockings, and boots." At the same time the peasants providing a recruit bore collective responsibility for him, and in case of his death or flight they were supposed to provide a new one instead.[11]

Heavy fines were imposed for not delivering a recruit on time or for violating the rules of delivery. The recruiting levies begun in 1705 followed one after another not only annually, but more than once per year. In all, from 1705 through 1725 not less than 400,000 men were taken. Considering that the country at this time had about five or six million male souls, this meant (even figuring an annual increase not exceeding 1 percent) that under Peter every tenth or twelfth peasant was compelled to don a soldier's uniform. Besides, they naturally took as recruits those who were healthier and, consequently, able bodied.[12]

The labor impost was equally burdensome for the peasantry. Large and small construction sites cropped up all over the country: roads, canals, bridges, fortresses, buildings, redoubts, and many other objectives were provided with labor forces almost exclusively via the labor impost. Only toward the end of Peter's reign did his supporters, convinced of the ineffectiveness of compulsory labor, switch to a contract system when for the monies collected from the peasants "for working people" they started hiring furloughed peasants. Prior to that for months tens of thousands of peasants had been torn away from their homes and fields.

The flight of peasants and townsmen on a massive scale became a typical feature of Petrine times. There is no necessity to prove that only extreme, inconsolable desperation could induce the peasantry, which was attached by mode of life, customs, and traditions to the land that fed it, to take flight in whole families and villages. In the Petrine era flight became ubiquitous. In some cases peasants temporarily went off to the woods until the tax collectors or soldiers left the villages; in other cases flight was linked with a search for work or for a haven where it would be possible to hide from the recruiters and the imposts.

Many documents attest without question that the tax burden, in conjunction with harvest failures and other calamities, drove whole peasant families away in search of salvation from their pomeshchik or the tax collector on palace, state, and other lands, primarily in scantily populated outlying districts.

The intensification of the tax burden led inexorably not just to the growth of peasant flight, but also to the intensification of social stresses that took the form of insubordination to authority and not infrequently to armed resistance. A typical feature of provincial life in Petrine times were armed robberies, executed often and by large detachments headed by atamans. "In the past year of 1710, sire," reported the peasant selectmen of the Samerovskie hamlets of Petersburg guberniia, "in the Samerovskii locality and in other districts miscreants and brigands have been going around in great bands of one hundred or one hundred and fifty and more men. They have burned down many villages and hamlets and have shot and burned many people of different ranks. The miscreant ataman Savvatii Vakhrushenok, having assembled with many accomplices, came to the patrimonial village of Romanovskoe three versts away from Samerovo and torched some fifty and more households, and from that village they came along the river toward Samerovo to the hamlet of Khakhileva and destroyed and pillaged the goods of all the Karelians, and they approached Samerovo and fought with the Samerovo inhabitants some five hours and the miscreants were driven off by force. . . ."

Among those who attacked villages and hamlets were quite a few declassed elements, murderers and sadists who tortured women and children. Yet they were not the majority. The multitude of "bandit bands" was a direct consequence of the worsening position of the peasants who sought salvation from imposts, recruiting levies, and the numerous punitive detachments that the authorities sent around the country.

Noteworthy and typical is a report of an incident in the Staritskii district of Moscow guberniia. Arriving at the small village of Obuvkovo in the summer of 1710, brigands "took captive four peasants working in the fields and, putting them on blocks, broke their arms and legs in two, and then after tying three of them to a tree, they shot them to death with muskets, and released the fourth alive, saying, we have beaten you to death because, said they, your pomeshchik begged for investigators and rode with them himself, but no matter how much he rides, said they, he will be in our hands; we will chop up his body, and scatter it over the fields for the dogs."[13]

The pillaging and burning of pomeshchik estates, as well as the murder and torture of their residents, were certainly a manifestation not only of vengeance, but also of more serious social stresses. These came to the fore with special force in the Bulavin rebellion, which — erupted amid the most difficult period of the Russian army's retreat in Belorussia and in the Ukraine.

The rebellion that the Don cossack ataman Kondraty Bulavin launched in October 1707 in itself reflected all the bitterness of the social situation that had arisen in the country by the end of the first, most difficult period of the Northern War. The upper reaches of the Don and its tributaries had long since been a place of settlement for fugitive peasants from the central regions of Russia. Just as the upper reaches fed the "quiet Don" with water, so too did these fugitive muzhiks provide an inexhaustible source of cossacks on the Don. Cossackdom, no matter how well it lived, possessed a well-developed corporate consciousness, the basic element of which was a notion of the right of any man to find refuge on the lands of the free Don, to become a cossack. Every violation of this ancient right by Moscow encountered embittered resistance from the cossack democratic republic.

By 1707 the flow of fugitives from the center had intensified so much that the government, having received numerous complaints by landowners about fugitives and reports from outlying towns about the intensification of brigandage and the migration of masses of fugitives, adopted a police action common for such times. It dispatched in the summer of 1707 detachments of the "investigator" Prince Yuri Vladimirovich Dolgoruky, who had been ordered to seek out and to return fugitive peasants from the Don to Russia under guard. Dolgoruky operated according to orders, but with particular brutality. His detachments, as Bulavin wrote to the Kuban cossacks, "set fire to many cossack villages and knouted many long settled cossacks, cut off lips and noses and hanged babies from trees, and also took maidens of the female sex to themselves for carnal acts in bed."[14] Apparently,

Dolgoruky's actions received wide social resonance and became the spark in the powder magazine that set off the explosion—on the night of 9 October Bulavin with two hundred men surrounded Dolgoruky's encampment and massacred his whole detachment. Soon other detachments of investigators were destroyed too, and the officers leading them were executed.

After a brief lull, in February 1708 the rebellion erupted with new force. This force came from the link that had been established between the Bulavinites and the Zaporozhian Sech, and also from extremely effective propaganda among the peasants of Tambov, Voronezh, Borisoglebsk, and other districts of southern Russia. Bulavin sent around to nearby and distant localities "enticing" letters with summons to the peasants and all who had been suffering from the authorities and the official church to join the rebels: "Come from all towns on horse and on foot, naked and barefoot, come and fear not, you shall have horses and arms, clothing and money salary; and we have stood up for the old belief and for the house of the most holy Mother of God and for you, for all the rabble." The exhortations called for them not to obey the authorities, "to transport" the boyars, provincial governors, officials, and pomeshchiks.

Peter found himself in a very difficult position, for his army had retreated through Belorussia and the Ukraine under the constant pressure of the Swedes and was in real danger of being caught between two fires. Therefore, from the start of April, Peter undertook the most vigorous measures to localize and to suppress the rebellion. Vasily Vladimirovich Dolgoruky, brother of the "investigator" killed by Bulavin, was appointed commander of the punitive detachment.

To put down the rebellion not only the units at the disposition of the governors of Kiev and Azov were rushed in, but even dragoons from the front, and it was also decided to mobilize the gentry militia at Moscow.

By this moment the rebellion had reached its height: Bulavin entered Cherkassk, the capital of the Don region, and was chosen war ataman by the cossack circle. Judging by the dispatches he sent out, he reckoned on the Zaporozhian and Kuban cossacks joining the rebellion. After heated debates the Zaporozhians sent a large detachment to Bulavin that took part in the military operations.

After Bulavin's successes at Cherkassk the threat hanging over Azov and Taganrog had become obvious. That summer the Volga had been cut off, in essence, by the rebels.

A final circumstance, the unreliability of the local garrisons that sympathized with the rebels, worried Peter particularly. He anxiously inquired of Ivan Alekseevich Tolstoi, the governor of Azov guberniia: ". . .

are the soldiers there with you being subverted, and also (God forbid), if Cherkassk does not hold out, do you have confidence in your own soldiers?"[15]

The possible fall of Azov and Taganrog would have been a catastrophe for Peter that might have changed the whole situation in the southern theater of military operations of the Northern War. On 6 July 1708 the Bulavinites advanced on Azov, whereas on 8 July Charles XII, having triumphed over the Russian army near Holowszyń, entered Mogilev intending to cross the Dnieper and move into the Ukraine. It was impossible to foresee how the Crimean Tatars and the Ottoman Empire would react to the Swedish advance and the capture of Azov by the Bulavinites. Peter had every reason to fear the establishment of contacts among all his opponents.

In the engagement near Azov the cossacks suffered defeat, a decisive role therein being played by the ship artillery that inflicted great losses on the rebels. They withdrew and, capitalizing on the defeat, the cossack elite, dissatisfied with Bulavin, staged a mutiny in Cherkassk. During the battle that flared up around Bulavin's house the ataman perished under vague circumstances (either by the foe's hand or by his own after finding himself in a hopeless position).

At the very same time, the government decided to announce to the people, among whom persistent rumors had circulated about the rebellion, what had happened on the Don as if it were an event that had already ended in victory. In this, one cannot overlook a well-known tradition of political culture in Russia when the authorities, not wishing "to sow panic," "to distress," or "to confuse" the people, kept silent about current dramatic events right up to their favorable resolution, in order subsequently to disperse doubts and temptations by the thunder of victorious salutes. Thus, having received the report of Bulavin's demise, Matvei Gagarin noted in a protocol of a session of the boyar commission that administered affairs in Moscow: "Thanks ought to be given to God and cannon ought to be fired so that many be informed about it for the present occasion, inasmuch as this evil caused rumors heard by many people."[16]

But in two days the boyars changed their minds about staging fireworks without Peter's decree and resolved to limit themselves to publishing in *Vedomosti* (the only gazette) an extract in the same soothing spirit. Readers learned from it the whole months-long saga from beginning to fortunate end.

As often happens, the authorities in their triumphant dispatches outran the events, presenting what they desired as what actually occurred. Although the direct threat to Azov had disappeared, the rebellion did

not subside. It was headed by Bulavin's atamans—Nikita Goly, Sergei
Bespalyi, Ivan Pavlov, and Ignaty Nekrasov—who carried operations to
the Volga, capturing Tsaritsyn and besieging Saratov. All the same, by
the fall of 1708 the repressive units had achieved superiority in forces in
all directions, the rebellion had been drowned in blood, and along the
Don floated rafts with those hanged—the brutal tradition of intimida-
tion that had been preserved from the time of Stenka Razin.

Bulavin's rebellion reflected the palpable trouble in social relations
as a consequence of the intensification of the tax burden and was the
greatest link in a chain of similar outbreaks. As some novelist might
have written, the Russia of Petrine times was illuminated not only by the
victorious cannon fire of Poltava and Hangö, but also by the fires of
burning pomeshchik estates and offices of provincial governors.

"It's difficult for a man to know and direct everything sight unseen"

Preparing for the outbreak of the Northern War, creating a new army, and building the navy—all this led to a sharp upswing in the activity of government offices and to an expansion of the scope of their work. The bureaus—the central institutions of administration that Peter had inherited from the sixteenth and seventeenth centuries—could not cope with the increasingly complicated administrative tasks. Construction of the navy had been initially supervised by the Moscow Court Bureau, which had no connection to naval affairs. Hence, with the expansion of the scope of naval construction new institutions arose: the Admiralty and War bureaus. For the more rational management of the army the Cavalry and Foreigner bureaus were fused into a single War Bureau. The Strel'tsy Bureau was liquidated, whereas two new ones were founded—the Preobrazhensky and the Semenovsky bureaus.

The war required money. To obtain it, the government strove to centralize the collection of taxes and their disbursement, to introduce new indirect taxes, and to institute supervision over the riches of the church. For this, new, primarily financial institutions were created: the Municipal Administration, Izhora chanceries, and the Monastery Bureau headed by a layman, the boyar Musin-Pushkin. The necessity of activating the search for ore for industry led to the formation of the Mining Bureau.

At the same time one cannot overlook essential changes in the principles of the formation and the activities of the bureaus created on the eve and at the start of the Northern War, in comparison with the bureau system of the previous era. The centralization and specialization of administration in this period still did not bear a systematic and comprehensive character. Notwithstanding the fact that a main war office might seem to have been created in the War Bureau, there still existed no less than a dozen institutions that exercised functions of military administration. Similar situations took shape in other branches of administration.

The basic idea of all the reforms of that time did not consist of creating something new in principle and fundamentally different from the old state apparatus, but with the aid of the old institutions and their recombination to ensure at all costs the resolution of the most important task—victory in the Northern War. To attain victory it was utterly unimportant to Peter how the jurisdiction of the different offices was delineated and how they were named.

But even so the new, so typical of Peter's reforms, penetrated into the sphere of administration, sometimes weirdly intermixing with the old. Unusual in particular was the appearance of "chanceries," as the new institutions of the bureau type were named. The first and most important of them was the Inner Chancery (1701), the chief purpose of whose work was to oversee and to audit the documents of the bureaus' financial activities.

The term "chancery" started to be applied to the departments of the Moscow bureaus that were located in the new capital of Petersburg and which resolved urgent administrative matters. It is important to note that over the years the significance of the chancery departments increased and the center of gravity of the administration was gradually transferred from the bureaus left in Moscow to the Petersburg branches. This occurred above all because the directors of the bureaus were in Petersburg alongside the tsar: Fedor Apraksin in the Admiralty, Jacob Bruce in the Artillery, Gavriil Golovkin in Ambassadorial, and so forth. Noteworthy in this regard is a letter of Chancellor Golovkin to servitors of the Ambassadorial Bureau in which he expresses in exhaustive detail the notion of the irrevocability of the change that had taken place in the old institutions' status: "You have been left in Moscow solely for receiving the stipulated monies from the guberniias and for managing affairs according to the letters we sent to you, whereas the chief direction of affairs is received in the State Ambassadorial Chancery here in Saint-Petersburg, and you are not to initiate any new matters or to accept any reports from other chanceries or make responses that have not been ordered."[1] Thus the once mighty office of the seventeenth century had lost all its authority. In similar fashion the sphere of activity of the War, Admiralty, Naval, and other bureaus left in Moscow had been curtailed.

In the first years of the Northern War it had already become evident that the working mechanism of the state administration, particularly on the local level, was not keeping up with the increasing speed of autocratic initiative. The deficiencies of administration were reflected in the supply of the central offices with money and the army with recruits, provisions, horses, and so forth. Under the conditions of wartime difficulties it was apparent that the old simple system of administration— the bureaus (central institutions) and the districts (territorial institutions)—could not bear the load on account of their own archaic ways. Hence in the first years of the war there had already emerged the problem of bringing the upper and lower links of administration into conformity.

On 17 December 1707 a decree was issued on the formation of new large-scale administrative territorial units—guberniias: "Assign the towns in parts (except for those 100 versts from Moscow) to the Kiev, Smolensk, Azov, Kazan and Arkhangel'sk guberniias."[2] Later the list of guberniias was refined: two more guberniias were added to those cited in the decree—Ingermanland (Petersburg) and Siberia, and Nizhegorod and Astrakhan were detached from Kazan.

The clearly delineated financial, judicial, and administrative extraterritorial scope even became the basic status of the new administrative organization of the guberniias that arose through the regional reform of 1707–10. The crux of the new guberniia system consisted in transferring many of the functions of the central bureaus to the governors and concentrating in them information about population, finances, and so forth. An important result of the reform was to liquidate part of the bureaus, mainly the territorial ones (that supervised the outlying regions), and also some of their branches. A series of bureaus (Municipal, Estates, Urban, and others) were converted into departments of the Moscow guberniia chancery, for the extension of their authority was restricted basically to the more densely inhabited districts of the center of Russia that were now taken into Moscow guberniia. In those instances where the authority of the bureaus extended over a large territory, their functions were transferred to the guberniia chanceries.

At the same time it is important to note that the basic bureaus supervising defense (War, Admiralty, and Ambassadorial) preserved their authority. The jurisdiction of an all-Russian bureau such as the Estates Bureau was reinstituted.

In planning the regional reform, Peter was convinced that it would not weaken central authority. On the contrary, a certain decentralization should have strengthened and focused administrative, judicial, and predominantly financial authority in the hands of the tsar's representative—an official of high rank as the governor would be. He was invested with incomparably greater authority than the former provincial governor. In sum, the guberniia reform became as it were the raw material for erecting the next stage of the bureaucratic edifice of autocratic administration.

"Principals" were placed at the head of the guberniias—close supporters and persons trusted by Peter who possessed tremendous despotic authority and worked on resolving the tasks that Peter had personally placed before them. Alexander Menshikov presided in Petersburg, Tikhon Streshnev in Moscow, Fedor Apraksin in Azov guberniia, his brother Peter in Kazan, and Matvei Gagarin in Siberia guberniia.

Appointing trusted persons as governors did not mean, however, that the reform was merely a variant of the practice of commissioning high-ranking emissaries for the "correction" of local affairs. The reform led to an abrupt strengthening of the administrative apparatus and to the creation on the local level of a ramified network of bureaucratic institutions with a large staff of officials—a new infrastructure.

Under the governor, whose authority encompassed at once several of the old districts—a huge territory—were assistants who supervised military affairs (*ober-komendant*), levies from the populace (*ober-komissar*), and justice (*landrikht*). The district was headed not by the former voevoda (military governor) but by a "new-model" commandant, who likewise exercised substantial military-administrative and judicial authority.

The cumbersome size of the guberniias led to the creation of an intermediary territorial unit: in 1712–15 provinces appeared in the guberniias that were supervised by senior commandants. So, the former binary "bureau-district" linkage was converted into a quadruple one: "bureau (chancery)-guberniia-province-district." Along with the senior commandant came new staffs of officials that were headed by commissars who supervised the collection of taxes and who administered the population. A peculiarity of the new structure of local administration was not only its previously unheard of complexity, but its uniformity and strict hierarchy. In the course of the reform was finally ended the practice of appointing local officials to office as a "feeding," which had provided them with the opportunity of quickly enriching themselves, and then along with their relatives and dependents that had been appointed in the same district, of leaving for the capital in expectation of a new "cozier" place.

It would be silly to suppose that making the administration more complex appeared to Peter as an end in itself. Above all, the reformed system of local administration was supposed to provide for the needs of the armed forces. The main purpose of the guberniia reform was the wish to bring order to finances. In creating the guberniias, the budgets of the new administrative regions were defined on the basis of the old financial accounts, and the priority categories of expenses that the guberniias were supposed to finance from their own budgets were projected. These were the expenses of the four main bureaus that supervised military and diplomatic affairs and which were preserved after the reform of local administration: War, Admiralty, Artillery, and Ambassadorial. Their needs were to be given special attention.

The allotment of expenses for the war among the guberniias was important, but not the sole task of the reform of local administration. Peter strove to specify in as much detail as he could the role of administration in supplying the war, "to insert" the military principle into the administrative system. A direct linkage was established between the different army regiments and the guberniias. For this the regiments changed their names, which had been taken from the names of commanders, into geographical ones. Thus, the Chernyshov regiment became the Moscow regiment, the Bolobanov the Yaroslavl, the Nostitsev the Nizhegorod, the Golovin the Narva, and so forth.

With each regiment, no matter where it was located, there was supposed to be a commissar from "its" guberniia who was charged to take care of the supply and maintenance of uniforms and provisions, to provide people and horses, and to pay the soldiers and officers. The guberniia commissars were the lowest link of the war commissariat created then, at the head of which, with the field army, was placed the *ober-shtern-krigs-komissar*—the head of the war commissariat's office under the Senate, which was formed in the spring of 1711.

There definitely existed a connection between these two events, completion of the regional reform and creation of the Senate as the highest government organ, for the Senate from the very start of its activity had become the highest overseer of the guberniias. They were closely bound to it primarily in questions of supplying the army and the navy with all necessities. Of course, the creation of the Senate is a remarkable fact in the history of state building in the time of the Northern War, when all efforts (including organizational ones) were directed toward achieving victory, and the reorganization of local and central administration was supposed to guarantee the prerequisites for that victory.

The experience of the first years showed that with all the positive factors of the guberniia system it still retained quite a few serious defects. The old afflictions—red tape and sluggishness—proved to be typical of the new system as well. Confronting numerous instances of governors' laggardliness, Peter issued threatening decrees.

Their harshness was, of course, a powerful stimulus for the governors' zeal, but the essence of the administration's ineffectiveness lay in its structural shortcomings, notably the lack of coordination by a single center to which all information might come concerning the work of the guberniia system and from which the governors might have received directives without waiting for orders from the often absent tsar. This also became the direct cause for the creation of the Senate, the highest governmental body.

In the formation of the Senate (as in the ramified guberniia administration) we may also discern the general trend of bureaucratization without which Peter could not conceive of administration or even of the political regime of absolutism as a whole.

The creation of the Senate as a purely bureaucratic higher governmental institution had been foreshadowed by important events. In coming to power in 1689, Peter had inherited the traditional system of administration of the sixteenth century with the Boyar Council and the bureaus as central institutions. These were constituent parts of the system of administration of the estate-representative monarchy that had emerged in the sixteenth and the start of the seventeenth centuries. The main links of this system were local elective bodies that sent representatives to Assemblies of the Land. Their sessions were attended by men chosen from the peasants, nobility, and clergy—from all "the land" excluding enserfed peasants and slaves. From the mid-seventeenth century the institution of the Assemblies of the Land had fallen into decline for reasons not yet clarified. Possibly this had been facilitated by the intensification of serfdom from the middle of the seventeenth century and by the country's emergence from the crisis during which the central authorities could not manage without the aid and support of "the land," whose representatives came to Moscow for the Assemblies of the Land and approved the autocracy's actions. In the second half of the seventeenth century the strengthened autocracy no longer needed approval and could implement its decrees in practice, relying primarily on the force of its own subordinates and not on public bodies.

By the time Peter came to power the Assemblies of the Land had already been blissfully forgotten. Yet several institutions of the previous system were still in operation. This pertains first of all to the Boyar Council, the highest consultative institution, composed primarily of the hereditary elite and the tsar's relatives. With the consolidation of autocracy the Boyar Council, as a narrow estate council, was losing its significance so much that at the start of the eighteenth century it disappeared in the flood of change. This is no exaggeration—no decree has survived concerning the abolition of the Boyar Council—and most probably there was none at all. Peter had placed the council in a hopeless position by ending appointments to council rank. This meant that the

Boyar Council, the council of elders, in the absence of new blood simply started to die out: if in 1698–99 there had been 112 elders, by 1712 only 49 remained. Information about the council's sessions breaks off somewhere around 1704, although from 1701 its functions as the highest governmental body had already begun to be carried out by the so-called "Consilia of Ministers"—a council of the heads of the most important government offices among whom were quite a few non-boyars. The "Consilia" assembled in the quarters of the aforementioned Inner Chancery. Having become a standing governmental body, the "Consilia of Ministers" concentrated in its hands all authority while the tsar was away from Moscow, primarily at the theater of military operations. Specifically, it administered the bureaus and chanceries, organized the supply of the army with all necessities, and oversaw financial matters and construction.

It is curious that in the activities of the "Consilia" we distinctly detect features of the ever-increasing bureaucratization of administration—a tendency that was palpably manifest even in the seventeenth century. It showed up in the stabilization of the membership of the "Consilia," the establishment of a work routine, and the strict delineation of duties and responsibilities among its members. This trend showed up also in the introduction of different forms of clerical work—journals, protocols, and accounts that the Boyar Council had never known. The very urge to gain effectiveness and accountability for the "Consilia" by bureaucratic means explains Peter's celebrated decree of 7 October 1707 addressed to Romodanovsky: "Be so good as to announce at the meeting in the Palace to all the ministers who assemble for the Consilia that they write down all matters about which they are consulting and each minister should sign with his own hand, which is very much needed. It is also required that they not deal with any matter without doing that, for thereby every kind of foolishness will be manifest."[3]

The formation of the Senate in 1711 was the next step in organizing the bureaucratic apparatus of administration. The new institution was being created as the highest organ of administration to which all the chanceries and bureaus as well as the guberniias and the governors were subordinated.

The formal cause for creating the Senate was the tsar's forthcoming departure for the war with Turkey in the spring of 1711. Yet from the Petrine decrees it is evident that the Senate had not been created as a temporary commission similar to the "Consilia," but as a standing higher governmental institution. A decree of 2 March 1711 defined the direction of the Senate's work in broad perspective: "A decree to follow after our departure: 1. Hold a trustworthy court and punish dishonest judges by depriving them of honor and of all property; pursue the same with slanderers; 2. Oversee expenditures throughout the state and halt those that are unnecessary, and particularly those that are useless; 3. Collect as much money as possible inasmuch as money is the artery of war." Special attention was devoted to the service of the nobility, to trade, and to commercial concessions.[4] This was the whole program of measures that was entrusted to the new institution. Among them were the conduct of commerce, commercial concessions, justice, and inspections of nobles and other servitors. Peter devoted special attention to finances. This same decree contains his widely known aphorism about money as the artery of war.

Peter's decrees oriented the senators to different principles and forms of work from previously. Thus, the decree of 5 March 1711 introduced, in essence, the principle of collegiality under which equality was maintained in the resolution of affairs and a decree did not come into force without general agreement. For the first time a personal oath of loyalty, as in the army, was introduced in a state institution.[5]

Right after the formation of the Senate, it received, in contrast to the Boyar Council and the "Consilia of Ministers," a chancery consisting of numerous sections or "desks" staffed by clerks. Furthermore, over the years the Senate, which had been converted into a huge institution for those times, "sprouted" diverse auxiliary offices and chanceries.

Although a similar higher governmental institution was being created for the first time, distinct from the Boyar Council and the "Consilia" in its bureaucratic nature, it still bore many of the features of the old, archaic organization of administration typical of the system of central institution, the bureaus. To erase archaic traces, to build a new bureaucratic structure corresponding to the regime created by the autocrat's unlimited personal authority—these became the logical next tasks of Peter's government in the sphere of domestic policy toward the end of the Northern War.

On the Roads of War:
From Narva to Poltava

The economic, military, administrative, and other reforms so hastily, even feverishly, introduced by Peter right after the Narva defeat were supposed to bear fruit on the battlefield. Otherwise their sense would be lost. But the outcome of war is decided not only by the quantity of cannon and cannonballs, provisions, and recruits. War depends on both the success of long marches and the invaluable experience of fast-moving cavalry skirmishes and prolonged sieges. War is a multiyear duel of the talents of commanders and the ingenuity of diplomats; it is a test of the determination of soldiers and the loyalty of allies. War is also a moment rushing past fortune that must be seized.

All of this Peter had occasion to experience over the nine years separating the "Narva confusion" and the "Poltava victory."

Right after Narva the most acute difficulty concerned relations with the sole remaining ally. Peter strove to maintain the alliance with Augustus no matter what and not to allow Saxony to leave the war, for to battle Charles XII alone would be extremely dangerous. Moreover, departing in February 1704 for Birzhi (Birzhai) to meet with Augustus, Peter counted on dragging into the war the Polish-Lithuanian Commonwealth, which had been mistrustfully observing the foreign policy adventures of its newly elected king and which looked askance at Peter as his ill-starred ally. Peter succeeded in attaining his main aim; on 26 February 1701 Augustus signed a treaty that envisaged substantial sacrifices by Russia in the name of preserving the alliance. Peter pledged to place 15,000 to 20,000 troops and 100,000 rubles at the complete disposal of Augustus, and he also guaranteed the transfer of Estland and Livland to Poland.

So the allies resolved to continue the military operations that had been broken off in specified regions: Russia in Ingria and Karelia, the

Saxons in Livland and Estland. Yet Augustus did not succeed in implementing his plan. After wintering in Dorpat and receiving reinforcements from Sweden, Charles XII advanced on Riga and on 27 June 1701 defeated the Saxon forces of Field Marshal Steinau, who had to abandon Livland. Anikita Repnin's Russian auxiliary force afforded no aid to the ally and also withdrew toward Pskov, the main quarters of the Russian army.

Right here in the onrush of events that have departed forever into the past we may overlook a turning point that the notorious locomotive of history has thundered past. By gaining brilliant victories at Narva and Riga, Charles XII had completely fulfilled his task and had driven his opponent out of the Swedish crown's Baltic possessions. Then a dilemma confronted him: either to move toward Pskov or to pursue Augustus. If Charles had chosen the first variant, Peter would have faced a very complex, not to say dramatic, confrontation with an army of 25,000 battle-tested Swedes. But Charles moved into Poland.

I think that Charles in his choice of direction proceeded from the simple logic of a warrior fighting on two fronts who decides first to defeat the stronger and therefore more dangerous opponent, and then to deal with the weaker one. One cannot disregard two other factors: first, Charles's strong personal animosity toward the luxury-loving, cunning, and unprincipled Augustus and, second, the necessity of further expanding and consolidating the Swedish empire. For success in the war on Polish territory it was necessary to depose Augustus, according to Charles, yet first he had to be defeated. With these aims Charles crossed his Rubicon in the summer of 1701 and moved his regiments not toward Pskov, but on the road to Vilna. This step was not accidental: in the Grand Duchy of Lithuania—part of the Polish-Lithuanian Commonwealth—there were many open and hidden opponents of Augustus II who accepted neither him as the Polish king nor his policy of alliance with Russia.

Charles's decisiveness alarmed both the Saxons and the Poles. They tried to enter into negotiations with Charles, but in vain. Augustus resorted to the strongest means that he could think of to attain an agreement (of course, at that moment he hardly thought of honoring the Birzhi agreement)—he dispatched to Charles's camp his own mistress, Countess Maria Aurora von Königsmarck, an exceptional beauty who possessed such wit that the skeptical Voltaire considered her the most remarkable woman of the seventeenth and eighteenth centuries. By charming the descendant of the Vikings, Maria Aurora was supposed to incline him to peace. The king could not evaluate her virtues, however, for he simply did not wish to be seen with the countess. He received a delegation from the Polish Diet and openly announced that he did not wish to talk about peace so long as Augustus was Poland's king.

Poland confronted a choice: either accept the Swedish conditions or defend its own independence and join Augustus's side. And again, as has often happened in Polish history, in its hour of trial the country was not united. As a novelist of the past century might have written, Poland "was plunged anew into the abyss of civil strife."

Augustus started looking all the more frequently to the north where cannon thundered without a break—this was Peter learning the first lessons of the school from which he would "graduate" only twenty-one years later. It should be noted that at the start of the Northern War, Peter strongly depended on his ally Augustus in politics and military operations alike and did not undertake any kind of serious operations without his agreement. We recall that the "Narva" fiasco at the start of the war had been an obvious tribute to the allies, for according to the initial treaty with Saxony, the region of Russia's operations should have been Ingria and Karelia, not Narva, which was an Estland fortress.

The operations in 1701–2 assumed the same character of a diversion. The Russian forces based at Pskov carried out "ventures"—raids against the units of General Anton Wolmar von Schlippenbach stationed in southern Estland. Their aim was to ravage Estland and Livland, the bases of the Swedish army, by destroying homes and farms, driving off livestock and people, and also defeating the opponent's forces in the engagements unleashed upon him.

At the same time, Peter Apraksin delivered some painful setbacks to General Krongiort's group that had been left in charge of Ingria and Karelia.

In August 1702 Sheremetev took "by accord" the fortress of Marienburg (Aluksne), in southern Livland. During the surrender of the fortress, according to a notation of the *Journal of Peter the Great*, this incident took place: "The commandant Major Til and two captains came out to our supply train for the surrender of the town by accord, whereby our troops went into the town, and the townspeople started to leave; at that moment captain of the artillery Wolf and a lance-cadet entered the powder magazine (whither the lance-cadet had taken his own wife by force), and set off the powder whereby they were themselves blown up and many of them and ours were killed, for which both the garrison and the townspeople were not released according to the agreement but were taken prisoner."[1]

We should add that among the civilian townspeople that were made slaves en masse that ill-fated day was Marta Skavronskaia, the future

Empress Catherine I. Once again a historical crossroads has flashed by us—what if the citation from the *Journal* had begun this way instead: "The commandant Major Til and *three* captains came out to our supply train for the surrender of the town by the accord . . ." That is, what if Captain Wolf had not carried out his insane venture, but had come out to the Russian supply train along with the commandant, the fortress had remained undamaged, and the civilian townspeople had not become hostages of the soldiery but had gone off to Riga and, possibly, further to Sweden? Marta's fate would have been different, of course. But would the fate of post-Petrine Russia have been different too?

The "venturesome" character of the war in 1701–2 had great significance for Peter's army. The first victories, albeit quite modest ones, had been gained. They were important for the morale of the troops who remembered Narva. Furthermore, Livland, the richest granary of Sweden, had been devastated.

No doubt the civilian population of Livland and Estland had experienced all the horrors of a military invasion.

In letters to Augustus, Peter reported that he would continue the earlier "ventures" in Livland and, moreover, he planned "now to advance to the other Lithuanian frontiers and had ordered ventures made against the foe."[2]

In fact, in secret from the Swedes and even from his own ally, Peter was preparing an operation north of Livland, namely in Ingria.

Having carried out a careful reconnaissance, Peter had in mind to seize in the wintertime Noteborg (Oreshek) and Nienschanz (Nien or Kantsy) with a force of four regiments. The rest of the army was supposed to observe the Swedes and not allow them to relieve the Neva fortresses. Furthermore, Peter tried to mislead the Swedes, to give them the impression that all his attention was focused on the "ventures" in Livland.

What Peter had in mind was not an everyday "venture," but a plan for conquering Swedish Ingria. By implementing it he would be able to interdict communications between the Swedish units in Livland and Krongiort's units that controlled Ingria, Karelia, and Finland, whereas the occupation of Nienschanz and Noteborg would allow him to take control of the main water artery, the Neva, over its entire extent from source to mouth. The operation that had been planned in 1701–2 was the start of the more grandiose plan of consolidating control of the mouth of the Neva, similar to what had been done on the Sea of Azov.

For some reason, however, the idea of suddenly seizing the fortresses at the start of 1702 did not succeed: possibly the Swedes found out about the Russians' preparations, possibly the Neva opened earlier in the season. Be that as it may, Peter did not give up his intentions. In the summer of 1702 on Lake Ladoga began to be concentrated huge quantities of supplies of things that were suited only for the storm of fortresses—ladders, spades, mattocks, and bags stuffed with wool to block bullets.

It should be noted that the plan of attack on Ingria was original and unanticipated by Krongiort, who focused all his attention on defending the left bank of the Neva against the forces of Peter Apraksin. Peter I, who had set off for Arkhangel′sk under the guise of preparing the town for defense against a Swedish diversion by sea, pursued something different. On 19 August 1702 he wrote Augustus "from a pier on the sea called Niukhchi" that "we are passing time near the enemy's frontier and are intending, of course, with God's aid, to launch some undertaking."[3] Niukhcha-Niukhotskaia pier on the White Sea was located 170 versts from Povenets, which stood on the northern edge of Lake Onega. Using the tradition of Russian portages, thirteen seagoing vessels including light sailing craft were borne on the shoulders of peasants and soldiers along a road that had been cleared overland in a month, and had already been launched on Lake Onega on 26 August.

Peter sent Sheremetev on the Svir′ River a decree to leave Livland and Pskov forthwith. The same decree was also received by Anikita Repnin, whose regiments had been quartered in Novgorod. On 26 September the main Russian forces had arrived at Noteborg.

No repetition of Narva was possible; Charles XII was thousands of versts away from Noteborg, and the besiegers had long since mastered the necessary lessons. The siege lasted two weeks in all, and after a prolonged artillery bombardment the storm was launched.

Peter appraised the true worth of the resistance put up by the garrison that numbered no more than 500 men to the army of 35,000, and as the *Journal* says "on the 14th day the garrison by treaty marched out through the breach with lowered banners, beating of drums and holding musket balls in the mouth [as was standard for a garrison that had capitulated] and with four iron cannon was released to Shantsy with all its things on the vessels provided."[4]

Peter met the victory with rapture. In one letter he called it a miracle.

The capture of the most powerful fortress in Ingria and Karelia is, indeed, hard to overestimate, as is its key position in the northwest defense system. Consequently (as noted in *The Journal of Peter the Great*), right "then and there had this fortress been renamed Sliusenburg, that this name later became real with God's aid, for by this key the gates were opened into the enemy's land."[5]

In the spring of the next year, 1703, came the turn of Nien

(Nienschanz)—the rather weak fortress at the mouth of the river Okhta, and on 7 May a small but memorable victory in the history of the Northern War was accomplished by capturing two Swedish vessels at the mouth of the Neva.

The capture of Nienschanz was only the beginning of Russia's consolidation at the mouth of the Neva. At a council of war after the capture of Nienschanz the fortress was acknowledged to be unsuitable—too small, poorly defensible, and located far from the sea. Therefore it was decided not to reinforce it but to build a new one. On 16 May 1703 such a fortress was founded on the island Lust-Eland and named Sankt-Peterburg. Part of the army headed by Sheremetev advanced toward Kopor'e. Toward Yam (present-day Kingisepp), another Ingrian fortress, advanced the detachment of General von Werden.

Having occupied Yam, Peter undertook several other operations to consolidate his position in Ingria. First, after an engagement on the river Sestra the Swedish detachment of Krongiort, who had tried to seize the initiative in Ingria, was driven back toward Keksholm. Second, at Lodeinoe Pole the first ships of the future Baltic fleet were launched one after another from the yards founded in 1702. Finally, at the beginning of October 1703 when the Swedish squadron under the command of Admiral Gustav Nummers left the mouth of the Neva for winter quarters at Vyborg, Peter on a yacht reconnoitered the island of Kotlin and ordered that "a fortress be made in the sea"—Kronslot.

Thus, Ingria, or as it started to be called, Ingermanland, had been occupied in one year. Peter had firmly taken the Neva, its main communication route, from source to mouth. The victories in Ingria certainly affirmed the growing military mastery of the Russian army, buttressed by the strategic talent of its real commander—Peter. Even so we should not exaggerate these victories, for they confirmed the very worst apprehensions of the Swedish military engineer Erik Dahlberg, who had inspected the fortresses of Ingria in 1681 and had concluded that they were almost indefensible. Over the whole twenty years the Swedes in fact had done nothing to reinforce the fortifications in Ingria, indeed throughout the eastern Baltic, and Erik Dahlberg proved to be a Cassandra whose prophecies were not heeded.

In mid-May 1704 from the bastions of Narva the Swedes once more caught sight of troops advancing from the northeast—it was the Russian army, as if it had completed a huge circle in time and space, advancing again on Narva and Ivangorod three and a half years later. But it was already a different army about which one might say, recalling the Narva catastrophe, that for each man defeated there were two undefeated. At the end of May the town was blockaded, and on 8 June the Swedes fell for a military ruse. Having learned that General Schlippenbach's detachment from Revel was moving to relieve Narva, Peter clandestinely dispatched on the Revel road several regiments of infantry specially dressed in blue (the predominant color of the Swedish army's uniforms). Showing themselves in sight of the fortress, they lured part of the Narva garrison into a sally and with the besiegers surrounded the detachment that had come out to aid the phony Swedes.

I don't know whether such a masquerade with military uniforms and banners corresponded to the ethics of warfare then, but for Baron Horn, the commandant of Narva, it was a bad omen. On 17 July the Swedes could observe from the walls of the fortress a new burst of excitement in the besiegers' camp. Light vessels had come across Lake Chud and up the Narva to deliver a whole collection of captured standards from Dorpat, which had been taken by Sheremetev.

Then, too, the siege artillery was finally brought up and the ceaseless shelling of Narva began—ten days in a row.

On 6 August the captured commandant of Dorpat, Colonel Skitte, was released to Narva with a request to persuade Horn to surrender the fortress, but Horn heeded neither his advice nor the ultimatum of the commander of the Russian army, Field Marshal Ogilvy.

On the night of 8–9 August, with the dispatch into the moat of court-martialed soldiers with scaling ladders and the conventional salvo of mortars, the storm of Narva was launched very swiftly, very successfully, and with great bloodshed, for it was difficult to halt the terrible butchery of the civilian townsfolk by the soldiers that breached the fortress.

After taking Narva and Dorpat, Peter entered Estland, which along with Livland was supposed to go to Poland according to the current agreements. Peter confirmed Poland's unconditional right to these lands via a special manifesto, explaining his own conquests by the necessity of overthrowing Swedish hegemony in the eastern Baltic. In confirmation of these intentions on the eve of the siege of Narva, Sheremetev carried out a deep "search" into Estland. Regular units captured and burned Wesenberg (Rakvare), Weisenstein (Paide), Fallin (Viliandi), Ober-Pahlen, and Ruin (Ruiena) while the cossacks, Tatars, Kalmyks, and Bashkirs turned the rural regions of central and southern Estonia into a desert, destroying hamlets and fields, and herding people as well as livestock into slavery.

Being a sober statesman, Peter clearly understood that his army's successes in 1701–4 counted for little so long as the army of Charles XII remained victorious in Poland. The fate of Ingria and Karelia, Shlüsselburg, Petersburg, the navy, and egress to the sea were all being decided at that time in Poland.

So that Charles would be all the more deeply "tied down" in Poland and Peter would thereby win more time to prepare to do battle with him, the tsar exerted every effort to strengthen the Russo-Polish alliance against the Swedes, providing constant aid to Augustus and his supporters in arms, money, and troops.

At this moment, when the first stage of the war (1700–1704) was ending successfully for Russia, Peter demonstrated the qualities of an extraordinary diplomat and of a patient, tenacious statesman who deftly exploited his own initial military successes and the foe's manifest lapses. And there were many of the latter: Charles conducted himself in Poland as a conqueror, dictating his will to the Polish-Lithuanian Commonwealth. Here and in other circumstances Charles XII showed himself to be a peculiar kind of antidiplomat who frankly scorned every kind of foreign policy triumph attained through negotiation and not by arms. He was utterly indifferent as well to such a significant aspect in prolonged conflicts as the economic side of affairs. He assumed that with an opponent there could be only one discourse concerning the conditions on which the latter would yield to the victor. Throughout his reign he did everything, it would seem, to isolate Sweden and to break her international contacts. He did not understand that diplomacy is a matter no less complex and effective than victory on the battlefield.

In their approach to diplomacy—that "craft of kings"—there was a difference in principle between Charles and Peter. The Russian tsar very early understood that in the sphere of international relations Russia needed reform. The matter concerned changing the traditional forms of Russian diplomacy, rejecting embassies as peculiar kinds of diplomatic caravans in favor of standing representation made up of diplomats who know the country to which they are accredited and the international context. Peter understood that it was necessary to reject the age-old forms of protocol thanks to which Russian ambassadors might undermine negotiations critically important to the country.

One is reminded of the many anecdotal instances that had made Russian representatives ridiculous at European courts. Thus, the courier Simanovsky in 1682 brought to Berlin a message from the tsar and, according to the complaint of the Brandenburg diplomatic office, conducted himself most obnoxiously at a reception of the elector Frederick-William, "detaining the elector more than an hour and a half by his stubbornness and his importunities about where the elector should stand, where he should take off his hat, what questions he should pose himself and which his intimates should pose, declined to kiss the elector's hand and to drink to his health as an uncrowned head and so forth."[7]

Reforming the diplomatic service proved to be comparatively easy. It was more difficult to reform the principles of external policy-making. Peter distinctly grasped the direction in which they should be reoriented. "Fully aware of Russia's isolated position, he tried to fight for a place in the sun, keeping in view as opponents not the different countries or the simple sum thereof, as pre-Petrine statesmen had assumed, but the ever more complex system of states. He was the first who grasped, who acknowledged with all candor, that as long as Russia did not enter into the 'concert' of European countries and did not establish ties of alliance and otherwise with them, there would be no equal rights."[8] One should add that Peter frankly acknowledged, too, that to enter into the European "concert" and to establish oneself under the sun could be done only by force. Only military might would make an equal out of the newcomer who attempted to displace the old-timers of world politics; only military victories would make treaties and agreements real.

After the "Narva victory" the situation had changed, but to talk about equality of forces in 1704 would have been premature. Both then and later Peter did not conceal his reluctance to confront Charles on the battlefield, although he well knew the significance of a victorious general engagement.

Charles, however, exploiting his military superiority, followed his own political policy imperiously and without compromise. Astonishing the Poles by his straightforwardness, arrogance, and relentlessness, he devastated the country with burdensome indemnities and humbled the national pride of the Poles with mass executions. "This king is purely a soldier," Constantine de Turville, a participant in Charles XII's Russian campaign, writes in his memoirs. "His qualities, no doubt, are great and brilliant, but that inflexibility that has defined his character, appearing in particular in his inner being and manner of conduct, manifested itself in utter crudity and abruptness, which it was hard to tolerate."[9] After this it is hardly surprising that Charles stopped at nothing, ignoring the traditions of the Polish-Lithuanian Commonwealth and decisively demanding the deposition of Augustus and the proclamation of a new king. Unable to exploit the powerful anti-Russian and anti-Saxon attitudes of the petty nobility that had existed since the election of Augustus as king in 1697, Charles XII compelled a minority of the senators and nobles by force of arms "to elect" as king the Poznan voevoda Stanislaus Leszcyński on 12 July 1704.

The election of Leszcyński, which had been pushed through in violation of the customs characteristic of the Polish-Lithuanian Commonwealth, led to reinforcement of the confederation of Sandomir, an all-Polish militia of Augustus's supporters. They declared war on Sweden and proclaimed Stanislaus's confederation of Warsaw illegal [rokoshem], that is, an assemblage of people who had placed themselves, their families, and their estates outside the law. The conclusion on 19 August 1704 at Narva of a Russo-Polish alliance against Sweden represented a triumph for Peter. Thus, by his actions Charles XII achieved what Peter had long failed to do—ally Poland with Russia. From his side Peter dispatched to Poland at Augustus's disposal 12,000 soldiers and paid a subsidy of 200,000 rubles, for which all the Russian peasantry was assessed in 1705 a heavy supplemental money tax.

The logic of battle inevitably also drew Peter himself to the plains of Poland, where Charles pursued a fruitless "hunt" for Augustus, who deftly evaded a general engagement. Peter could not fail to understand that sooner or later he must confront Charles and that their confrontation would decide the fate of the eastern Baltic, and indeed possibly everything that was dear to them both. Therefore, from the autumn of 1704 Russian troops started to assemble in Polotsk, a point strategically suited for operations both toward the Baltic and toward Warsaw.

On 12 June 1705 Peter joined the army. Thus, in the summer of 1705 all the main actors of the drama of the Northern War—Peter, Charles, Augustus, and Stanislaus—turned up within reach of each other. Who could have thought that only a year and a half later three members of this quartet—Charles, Augustus, and Stanislaus—would sit at a common table peacefully conversing? True, of the three kings one would already be an ex-king. . . . Yet this will be discussed in greater detail later, whereas Peter in the meantime assembled forces in Polotsk and then shifted them to Grodno. Charles observed these maneuvers of the tsar attentively from Warsaw and did nothing.

Winter set in, Peter left for Russia, and then the Swedes unexpectedly took the offensive. Menshikov, who had stayed with the army, had received word of the start of the Swedish advance on Grodno long before the campaign. In a letter to Peter he calmed the tsar: "Yet Your Worship should not doubt, inasmuch as we here are in all readiness and our regiments are assembling hither and soon we shall straighten everything out."[10]

But soon Menshikov and Ogilvy "were straightened out" by Charles, who contrived in two weeks to cover 360 versts amid fierce frosts and suddenly appear before Grodno. By deft maneuver he interdicted the Russian army's communications with Russia such that Peter could not even reach Grodno, and the couriers with his orders, in order to get to Grodno, had to be dressed in peasant clothing. The Russian command had so little anticipated Charles's thrust that General of the Cavalry

Rönn found himself cut off from the main group of forces commanded by Ogilvy. Finding himself in Grodno, Augustus broke out of the trap into which the whole Russian army had fallen and in which it also lacked adequate provisions. Peter requested aid from Augustus, who dispatched to Grodno General Schulenburg's Saxon corps of 20,000, but at the beginning of February 1706 terrible news reached Grodno: the Swedish General Rehnskiöld, the strength of whose corps was barely half as great as his opponent's, had met Schulenburg head-on near Fraustadt and practically destroyed the Russian regiments among the Saxon corps.

The situation in Grodno became dramatic. Only on 24 March, by taking advantage of the ice floes on the Nieman (which prevented the Swedes from fording the river at the town), were Ogilvy and Menshikov able to lead the army out of the trap. They started to withdraw to Kiev. In this segment of the war it is quite evident that Peter still did not feel the confidence that a commander requires and still did not desire a personal meeting with Charles on the battlefield.

Turning his back on the hastily retreating Russian forces, Charles immediately set off quickly to Dresden, the capital of Augustus's Saxony. Hereby he placed the Polish king in a hopeless position: the Saxon army, in contrast to the Russian, had no strategic room for withdrawal. On 13 October 1706 at the castle of Altranstädt, which is not far from Leipzig, Saxon representatives concluded peace with the Swedes on very harsh and humiliating terms for Augustus: he renounced the Polish crown in favor of Stanislaus Leszcyński and was compelled by Charles's demand even to congratulate his sworn foe with the victory; he likewise broke the alliance with Russia, giving the Swedes as prisoners all the Russian soldiers at his disposal, and turned over to them, as a criminal, the Russian emissary to his court, Patkul, whom the Swedes subsequently executed.

A direct result of the defeat at Fraustadt, the treaty fundamentally changed Poland's position and was kept in strict secrecy. Five days after its signing, the Russo-Saxon-Polish forces under the command of Augustus himself and Menshikov gained a victory over the Swedish general Mardefelt near Kalisz, the general himself being taken prisoner with more than 2,500 of his soldiers and officers. Menshikov, meeting Augustus's request halfway, turned the captured Swedes over to the Saxons, and the latter released them to the Swedes under terms of the treaty already signed.

There is a curious subtext in the Altranstädt treaty. That such a treaty had become possible and had been made should not surprise us. Charles XII represented a huge force, frightening in Vienna, in Berlin, and even in the capitals of the maritime powers, England and Holland, which were always standing in the wings of the political theater in the north. Saxony, which had suffered defeat at Fraustadt and had proved to be without the support of Russia and the Polish-Lithuanian Commonwealth, could not resist Charles XII for long. One should note that Peter, too, had not rejected the possibility of concluding a separate peace with the Swedes: from 1703 to 1709 he constantly tested the soil for reaching such an agreement, and in case of success he would hardly have shown much concern for Augustus's interests. Altranstädt was taken by the tsar as the amoral deed of an ally mainly because, having concluded peace with the Swedes, Augustus played a double game, hiding from Peter the turnabout that had taken place and not giving Russia the possibility of recasting its policy.

It is important to underline here the personal aspect of the relations of the Russian tsar and the Polish king. For Peter, Augustus had been not merely an ally but a crowned friend with whom he was united by something larger than just the struggle against the Swedes. Not to a single one of his crowned "colleagues" did Peter write such heartfelt letters as to Augustus. In one of the missives, understanding the conditionality of the diplomatic lexicon and the strictness of the official formulas, he underscored in parentheses: "To my lord and most beloved brother (and to my friend in truth and not by politics)."[11]

These amicable relations ("special brotherly love," as Peter wrote) had apparently arisen during their meeting in the summer of 1698 at Rawa, when Peter, who was just starting out in politics and who had been inspired by his journey in Europe, first met Augustus. He was almost the same age, European educated, handsome, and gallant; had just become king of Poland; and also dreamed of glory for his fatherland. Evidently Augustus, in contrast to Charles XII, was an exceptionally charming person, as he is likewise depicted in the memoirs of Constantine de Turville: ". . . a calm and pleasant exterior, an ingratiating and gentle look, pleasant tone of voice, which by its softness enchanted the hearts of those attending him—in a word, everything that together comprises the image of a bewitching lord, which was utterly lacking in Charles."[12] It is no accident that many historians consider the Rawa meeting decisive in the reorientation of Russia's policy from the south to the north. And who knows what such a meeting of the Russian tsar and the Polish king might have led to if instead of Augustus it had been his predecessor Jan Sobieski—an old man wrapped in the laurels of victories over the Turks, possessed by the idea of crusades against the Muslims, a man of another era, other notions, and other traditions?

Many years later, while compiling his *Journal*, Peter included in it an excerpt in which resounds the already long since cooled feeling of bitterness and resentment: ". . . And he arrived in Dresden in the month of December, and on 16 December King Augustus was with the Swedish king in Leipzig and they dined openly at one table, the Swedish king, King Augustus, and Stanislaus and, sitting at table, they gave outward satisfaction among themselves and King Augustus engaged in secret conversation with the Swedish king for quite some time. And then the Swedish king was with King Augustus in Dresden as well, and they were already meeting together."[13]

Peter received the stunning news en route to Moscow and immediately hastened back to Poland, where he was a man of business and not emotions. It was necessary to start everything afresh and primarily not to permit the collapse of the single alliance left to him, that with the Polish-Lithuanian Commonwealth.

Concurrently Peter strove to soften by diplomatic means the force of the blow dealt to the Northern Alliance. In a dispatch to Queen Anne of England he summoned resistance to this peace and condemned Augustus as an offender against international standards.

Of course, Peter not only condemned his treacherous friend, but felt vexed with himself as well: Altranstädt was a serious failure of Russian diplomacy which, despite having received hints of the possibility of a Saxon-Swedish agreement being signed, he had not managed to forestall. Russia remained alone in the face of a menacing opponent; Stanislaus, behind whom just a day before there had marched merely a handful of people in all, now had become the full-fledged king, he had been recognized by foreign states, and in advancing against Russia Charles could leave him at the rear. After Altranstädt, Peter tried to find a replacement for Augustus. He offered the Polish crown to many: to Franz Rákóczi, the leader of the Hungarian rebellion, to the Duke of Marlborough, to Jakub Sobieski, to Eugene of Savoy, and to others. No takers were found, however, and the petty nobility started to go over to the side of Stanislaus I.

The ground in Poland was shifting under Peter's feet. He then started feverishly to seek intermediaries so as to make peace with the Swedes on condition of retaining Ingria for Russia. For this he turned to the English, the French, the Austrians, and the Dutch. But Charles listened to nobody. He would agree to peace only on condition of Russia's practical capitulation: demanding the restoration of all occupied territories and payment of a huge indemnity. At the same time in his typically uncompromising manner Charles insisted that Peter recognize Stanislaus I and declared that he "would sooner sacrifice the last inhabitants of his state than agree to leave Petersburg in tsarist hands."

Searches for a diplomatic resolution of the problem proved to be in vain—Austria and the other countries that had been drawn into the War of the Spanish Succession, upon seeing the Swedes in Dresden, took fright that Charles would intervene in the general European conflict; they therefore did not wish to antagonize him by mediation. An armed struggle with Charles alone became unavoidable for Peter. So he launched intensive preparations for the conflict.

Perhaps the most important thing of all that Peter did after Altranstädt was the decision taken in December 1706 at a council of war in the locality of Zolkiew near Lvov. After discussing the situation in Poland it was decided not to give battle to the foe on Polish territory, "because if some misfortune should happen, then it would be difficult to retreat, and therefore it is agreed to give battle at our own frontiers, when necessity will require it, and in Poland to harass the enemy at crossings and by diversions as well as stripping the countryside of provisions and forage." This plan was implemented in the Ukraine as well, right up to Poltava.

It should be noted that in general Charles was a peculiar statesman and commander. The campaigns in Poland had showed that by staging a swift march amid sometimes quite difficult conditions, he could destroy the enemy head-on, and then stand in one place for whole months calmly watching while the defeated foe gathered and regrouped his forces. There followed a new, swift, and triumphal thrust— and then a pause ensued anew. In the conflict with such a commander the army's mobility held great importance, or speaking bluntly, the strong legs that both Augustus and Peter had often demonstrated.

After Altranstädt the pause lasted almost a year. At the end of the summer of 1707 Charles led his troops out of Saxony into Poland and halted there until December, at the very end of which, despite the frosts, he moved into Lithuania. On 26 January 1708 he hastily broke into Grodno. The tsar only two hours earlier had speedily left the town. One can understand the anxiety of the Russian high command, for it was unclear where Charles would go: into Lithuania, toward Pskov or Moscow, or into the Ukraine. Charles turned southeast. A pause ensued for five months when the king halted near Minsk, and then in June he moved toward the Berezina. Near the small town of Holowszyn he forded the river and here for the first time encountered Peter's main army, commanded by Sheremetev.

It was no longer the army Charles had faced at Narva. It had passed the severe school of campaigns and engagements in Poland and the eastern Baltic. The military reforms had yielded their first fruits, the general level of military art and the training of soldiers and officers had matured, and the experience of large-scale operations had appeared. Furthermore, in size the Russian army of 135,000 outnumbered the Swedish army twofold. Even so, the battle at Holowszyń on 3 July 1708, which was the first big field engagement with Charles's main army, ended in defeat for the Russians. Noticing that the Russian army, which was covering the route toward Mogilev, had become strung out over several versts, Charles swiftly struck at the center of its deployment where the division of Anikita Repnin stood, and after a stubborn battle drove the Russian regiments from their positions, which brought about the withdrawal of the whole Russian army. In five days Charles was in Mogilev.

Peter ordered "an investigation launched" of General Repnin. The court-martial demoted Repnin to the ranks. His general's rank would be restored after the engagement at Dobroe, where Repnin displayed great selflessness.

But most important from the defeat at Holowszyń were lessons that would be applied later. On the occasion of this battle Peter wrote: "I am very thankful to God that ours did see the enemy a good bit before a general battle and that from this army of his one-third of ours sustained it and got away."[14]

On 28 August an engagement occurred at the village of Dobroe. A group of General Mikhail Golitsyn's troops attacked the Swedes and drove them back, and only the intervention of their main forces headed by the king forced Golitsyn to withdraw. Describing this engagement, Peter could not conceal his joy—he saw that in the action of his troops qualitative changes had taken place that were inspiring for the future, though they remained hesitant in action.

After Dobroe it seemed that nothing had changed. The Russians withdrew as before, but all the same their resistance had played its role: Charles was diverted all the more to the south, away from the shortest route to Moscow via Smolensk. It should be stressed that the Russian army's withdrawal was not flight. In withdrawing, the army constantly alarmed the Swedes with cavalry raids, blocked the roads, organized resistance at crossings, and, most important, created in front of the enemy a dead zone: villages were burned, grain, forage, and livestock were carried away or destroyed (this was called "stripping these localities"), and the populace was sent into the woods.

Charles did not succeed in a swift maneuver aimed at coming out onto the Kaluga road, and at the end of September there could no longer be any question of a march on Moscow during this campaign. On 28 September at the hamlet of Lesnaia (not far from the town of Propoisk) a detachment of troops from the main army under Peter's command overtook and defeated the corps of General Lewenhaupt

coming with a huge supply train from Livland in support of Charles.
Peter had followed Lewenhaupt long and intently, for the direction of
his corps's movement revealed Charles's intention to move not into the
Baltic but into Russia or to the south. Now came the moment when this
corps had to be liquidated.

The Russians' victory was weighty: the Swedes lost 6,000 or 7,000 men
and almost the entire supply train. The engagement on a small field,
one square verst in area, was drawn out and stubborn. The Swedes
withstood ten Russian attacks. By evening, as a military historian writes,
"as a consequence of the prolonged character of the battle, an intermis-
sion ensued and both sides awaited assistance."[15]

The source of this laconic conclusion, *The Journal of Peter the Great,*
was written by an eyewitness and therefore gives the sensation of a
person before whose thoughtful gaze a shocking picture arose:

> And on this field all of the people on both sides entered into the main
> fight, which continued some hours, where the enemy was driven from
> the field and went off to his supply train, and ours stayed on the
> battlefield, where eight cannon were taken and several banners; and
> since on both sides the soldiers were so tired that it was not possible to
> fight more, and then the enemy with his supply train, and ours on the
> battlefield sat down and rested quite a while at a distance in a line of
> half a cannonshot from a fieldpiece or closer to one another . . . (this
> instance was very surprising to see, as if the enemies were so meek
> among themselves and so close to each other as they sat resting).

This fearsome rest on the field soaked with blood did not last long.
Peter received reinforcement from the detachment of Rodion
Khristianovich Bauer, and "then ours attacked the enemy, completely
drove them from the field and took the remaining cannon and the
supply train and achieved complete victory, at the end of which there
began a great storm from the south with snow, and then night came at
once, and so the remaining enemy received a chance to depart,
whereas ours spent the night wherever the storm found them. . . ."[16]

Let's stop for a minute. It is amazing how in the minds of eyewitnesses extraordinary events of nature suddenly become part of these
events, even participants in them whether amicable or hostile. In moments of great tension a person suddenly perceives its mysterious image
filled with portents and meaning. In fact, who in a different, common
situation would have recalled the beginning snowfall and the swiftly
falling autumn dusk by the light of campfires? Just as amazing is the
description of the Ukrainian winter of 1708–9 by captured Swedes—
memoirists who saw in its horrors the causes of the impending defeat

near Poltava. The warriors of the Swedish king portray this winter as if they had been born in the Apennines and were describing the winter in Siberia near Verkhoiansk: here is spittle freezing in mid-air, birds falling from the hellish cold, trees and earth cracking from the frost, and other horrors the rumors of which were widespread in the West concerning Russia, a country of eternal cold, bears, and darkness.

Only a month had passed after Lesnaia when an event occurred that shocked Peter. On 28 October when Peter headed out of Smolensk toward the Ukraine he received sensational news from Menshikov: Hetman Ivan Mazepa had betrayed Russia and gone over to the side of the Swedes.

We shall oversimplify the matter if we see in Mazepa a man almost born to be a traitor, a moral monster who had long ago set out on the path of perfidy. Everything is much more complicated, for in the saga of Mazepa all the problems and tragedy of the Ukraine were reflected as if in a drop of water.

First, as concerns Mazepa's "treachery" as political crime: Petrine propaganda did everything to present Mazepa's deed as an unheard-of, unprecedented crime. But we need only turn to the history of the Ukraine after its entry into Russia to encounter a multitude of similar instances. Thus the successor of Bogdan Khmel'nitsky, the first hetman of the Ukraine, Hetman Ivan Vygovsky, broke relations with Russia after Bogdan's death, entered into contact with the Crimea and Poland, and in 1659 joined the Tatars in defeating the troops of voevoda Trubetskoi near Konotop. Khmel'nitsky's son Yuri, who replaced Vygovsky, returned to Russian sovereignty and, taking part in the war against Poland, at the most decisive moment when the Poles and Tatars had surrounded the army of Vasily Borisovich Sheremetev near Chudnovo in the fall of 1660, did not provide aid and even signed the Slobodishchenskii treaty whereby the Ukraine submitted to Poland. As a result Sheremetev's army was compelled to capitulate.

After the partition of the Ukraine into the Left Bank and Right Bank and the establishment of the system of a dual hetmanate, Peter Doroshenko, hetman of the Right Bank, became a vassal of Turkey and then entered into an agreement with the hetman of the Left Bank Ukraine, Ivan Briukhovetsky, who in turn after long service to Moscow and even gaining the rank of boyar revolted in 1668 against the authority of Russia. Thereupon Doroshenko, becoming for a time hetman of a united Ukraine, led his army against the Russian troops.

In 1687 Hetman Ivan Samoilovich, who had been dissatisfied with Russia's rapprochement with Poland, was accused by the Russian government of traitorous contacts with the Tatars and, blamed for the unsuccessful Crimean campaign, was deposed. By presenting a bribe of 10,000 rubles to Sophia's favorite, Vasily Golitsyn, Ivan Mazepa had taken over the hetman's mace.

Thus Peter, who represented the perspective of Russia, had every reason to say in 1723 in response to the Ukrainians' request to be allowed to elect a new hetman in place of the deceased Ivan Skoropadsky: "Because it is known to everyone that from the time of Bogdan Khmel'nitsky, who had come under the authority of our father of blessed memory, even before the late Skoropadsky all the hetmans had been traitors and what great calamity our state had borne, and especially Little Russia, from that."[17] At the same time it should be noted that the tsar was not entirely accurate: after the Pereiaslavl council of 1654 when the Ukraine had acknowledged Moscow's authority, Bogdan Khmel'nitsky had renewed his alliance with the Crimea and had entered into negotiations with King Charles X of Sweden about a protectorate, despite the insistent demands of Russia to break relations with Sweden, which was then at war with Russia.

The basic cause of these "treacheries" lay, of course, not in the personalities of the hetmans or the qualities of the national character of the Ukrainians, but in the peculiarities of the political and socioeconomic development of the Ukraine within the framework of the Russian state. For one hundred years after the celebrated Pereiaslavl council the Ukraine traversed a course from the "Articles of Bogdan Khmel'nitsky," in which a unique political system had been consolidated that included many elements of democratic structure and broad autonomy, to the practical liquidation of autonomy and the hetmanate and the conversion of the country into a regular guberniia of the Russian Empire settled by noble landowners and enserfed peasants. The subjection of the Ukraine to the Russia of autocracy and serfdom was not a smooth and painless process. The time about which we are speaking was part of this historical path of the Ukraine.

Many events occurred during Peter's reign that were shaped by earlier developments. With his typical despotism and in the rush of war Peter scarcely appreciated the peculiarities of the political structure of the Ukraine, seeing in the hetman merely a privileged executor of his own will. Disposing of the Ukraine's material and manpower resources in accordance with the tasks he was resolving through the war with the Swedes, the tsar did not consider whether these tasks corresponded to the interests of the Ukrainian people. In the same regard it should not be forgotten that the Ukraine of that time had dangerous neighbors such as the Crimean khan, the Turkish sultan, and the Polish-Lithuanian Commonwealth, in conflict with which blood flowed quite often.

Also giving rise to discontent were the burdens of fortification work, the digging of canals, and the quartering and levies connected with the maintenance and movement of troops through the Ukraine.

The national feelings of the Ukrainian cossacks were affronted by their frequently unceremonious treatment by officials and officers, whether Russians or foreigners in Russian service. Patkul's attempts to muster the free cossacks after the manner of recruits in the "German" style, the unceremonious conduct of the all-powerful favorite Menshikov, who had tried to order the council of elders about and even to subordinate the hetman to himself, all gave birth to discontent among rank and file cossacks, the council of elders, and the hetman himself.

There were also some circumstances that seriously influenced the situation in the year 1708. As we know, the Right Bank Ukraine, which had been under the authority of Poland, launched in the 1680s a struggle for reunification with the Left Bank under the aegis of Russia. The movement was headed by Semen Palei, Gurko, Samus', Iskra, and others who converted it in practice into a popular war. Having seized the main centers of the Right Bank, Belaia Tserkov' and Nemirov, the rebels had repeatedly appealed for help to both Mazepa and Peter. Yet the tsar, proceeding from his own interests, had maintained close relations with Poland and therefore had forbidden Mazepa to aid those in revolt. On this basis the Russian government had required Mazepa to persuade the rebels to capitulate to the Poles.

In the years 1700–1704 the Poles had drowned the rebellion in blood, and Palei had been seized and exiled to Siberia by Mazepa, who feared his influence and popularity. The representatives of the Polish-Lithuanian Commonwealth both at Birzhi in 1701 and later repeatedly demanded the cession of Belaia Tserkov' and the consolidation of the Right Bank for Poland. In 1707, when Charles XII took the offensive, Peter had given the Poles at Żołkiew assurances of the partition of the Ukraine into two parts. This, of course, went against the interests of the Ukrainians, for the Dnieper was for them not a border separating one Ukraine from another but its backbone.

Concurrently, the fate of the Right Bank was decided without any Ukrainian participation, and Mazepa, always submissive to the tsar's will, had meekly attempted to soften the conditions of the practical capitulation of the Right Bank. In a letter to Chancellor Golovkin of 23 October 1707 he wrote: "Of course, every private thing must yield to the common good. It is difficult for us to know the internal intentions of the great master by which he, thanks to the alliance with Poland, is ready to make her such a concession, but we expect no good from Poles in close proximity with them. If it is the great monarch's will to give Belaia

Tserkov' and other Ukrainian localities into Polish possession, then at least let his tsarist majesty's ministers confirm with the Polish ministers and specify that the Poles make no pretensions to the towns and localities located near the Dnieper—Kanev, Cherkassy, Chigirin and others. . . ." A little later, in 1713, the Right Bank was given to the Poles. The partition of the Ukraine had been reaffirmed.

Another circumstance concerned the processes going on in the "hetmanate" itself—the Left Bank Ukraine. In the conditions of wartime and reforms that reinforced centralization and the tsar's autocratic authority, among the Ukrainian council of elders serious apprehensions arose that Peter, the reformer of Russia, would not stop short of liquidating the hetmanate, which would fundamentally alter the Ukraine's political structure. The glaring example of Settlement Ukraine or southern Russia, where the cossack regiments were completely dependent on the local administration, was always on their minds. There were ample grounds for such apprehensions. As historian N.I. Kostomarov has written in surveying the known facts, "the matter concerned changes in the cossack style of administration of the hetmanate that were really being pushed for by Peter, who wished to recast his entire state on a new footing. The tsar had hitherto not touched the Little Russian order only out of respect for the advice of Mazepa, who found it inopportune to disturb the hetmanate in this regard, although in principle he had always avowed his approval before the tsar of the latter's plan of reform, whereby he had maintained Peter's good disposition."[18]

All these problems, apprehensions, and anxieties were aggravated a hundredfold when the Ukraine became the arena of war, when it seemed that the withdrawing Russian army would abandon the Ukraine any minute. It was no accident that in a letter to the council of elders after defecting to Charles XII, Mazepa would write: "And in the meantime the all-powerful and unwarlike Muscovite army, fleeing from the invincible Swedish troops, is saving itself only by destroying our villages and seizing our towns."[19]

The Poltava engagement of 1709, which sharply turned the wheel of history, often overshadows for us the pre-Poltava events and obstructs an adequate perception of the conduct of the people of that time. The situation was unclear; Peter was ready for the worst—Moscow was being hastily fortified, and the Baltic fortresses were being mined. Surely many in the Ukraine, and Mazepa first of all, were asking themselves: what will happen if Peter abandons the Ukraine or the commander of the Russian army, Boris Petrovich Sheremetev, should find himself in the desperate position of his ancestor Vasily Borisovich Sheremetev, who had capitulated in 1660 near Chudnovo?

Meanwhile, Mazepa had something to fear in case of Peter's defeat, for the hetman had always been the tsar's most obedient servant and had long since acted on the principle: "Wherever it will please His Tsarist Majesty to put me, there I shall be." Such a stance, which had in general become typical for the council of elders since Samoilovich's time, incited the cossacks' discontent. Here is one of many examples.

In 1706 Peter had turned over to Mazepa for execution the centurion of the Kiev regiment, Mandrik, who said what everyone knew and had been discussing. A local town ataman had reported that this centurion, traveling with him in the same vehicle, had said: "It will not be good for us in the Ukraine so long as this hetman lives, for this hetman is at one with the tsar in his thinking; the tsar in Moscow is destroying and banishing his own, and the hetman is causing the diminution of the Ukraine by various means and now, as I have heard myself, so many brave young men have fallen without any aid or hope because he often runs to Moscow to get instruction there in how to ruin this people."

It is hardly likely that the unfortunate centurion had ever read the letters to Moscow in which the old hetman himself had instructed Peter how to rule the Ukraine:

> Let the great master not have too much faith in the Little Russian people (a bit earlier he had written: 'our people is stupid and inconstant'), let him deign to send to the Ukraine without delay a good troop of brave and trained soldiers so as to keep the people of Little Russia in submission and loyal subjection. It is necessary, however, to treat our people humanely and amicably because if such a freedom-loving, yet simple people is angered, then it will be difficult to bring it into fidelity by harshness. I, hetman and cavalier, wish to serve His Serene Tsarist Majesty loyally till the end of my life, as promised before the Holy Gospel and to care for the maintenance of the Ukraine without wavering. . .[20]

In 1707–8 the military and political crisis set in, and Mazepa, considering all circumstances, understood that in the event of Peter's defeat it would be the last days for him, the tsar's protégé. These considerations led the hetman to the idea of betraying Peter. By entering into contact with Stanislaus I, he got in touch with the Swedish king as well. Finally, at the end of October 1708, fearing exposure, he resolved to flee to Charles XII. Yet he did not succeed in raising the Ukraine in revolt. For this there were both particular and general causes. Mazepa's act proved to be utterly unprepared. Apprehending the tsar's suspicions, he had dispatched without objection the greater part of his forces to other arenas of military operations—to Belorussia—and thereby had practically disarmed himself. That is why he defected to the Swedes with four thousand sabers in all, that is, with those he had on hand at the time.

Only much later was he joined by the Zaporozhians, and his forces grew to ten thousand sabers.

It is essential to give Peter his due, too. At this moment he displayed amazing willpower, determination, and focus. He immediately made two decisions that had enormous consequences. Foremost, in Peter's thinking, it was essential to forestall the spread of the mutiny, to prevent the Ukrainian army in Belorussia from joining Mazepa's side, and, furthermore, to elect a new hetman.

Then and there by special decree the Ukrainian people was relieved of the wartime taxes and impositions, which had supposedly been levied by Mazepa for his own purposes. Four days after receiving news of Mazepa's betrayal, Baturin—the hetman's capital—was captured and burned and part of the inhabitants slaughtered. On 7 November the council of elders, assembled at Glukhov by Peter's decree, selected as hetman the candidate designated by the tsar—Ivan Skoropadsky. On 8 November the church anathematized Mazepa. On 10 November his closest confederates seized at Baturin were publicly executed. Later the Zaporozhian Sech, the military settlement of cossacks on the lower Dnieper that had joined Mazepa, was devastated.

All the same, the chief reason that a revolt did not occur was that by this time the democratic structure of the cossack republic had degenerated, and the council of elders had long since evolved into a privileged estate endowed with land, riches, and authority and estranged from the great bulk of the cossacks and the peasants. Mazepa, a most blatant representative of the council of elders, had not been popular among the common folk as Bogdan Khmel'nitsky or Semen Palei had once been. Prior to his flight to the Swedes, he had done nothing to unite or to rally behind him a people who had already lived half a century under Russian rule and who, terrified by the reprisals at Baturin, the threats of the tsarist manifestos, and the horrors of war, distrustful of the cruel conqueror that had appeared without warning from across the sea, kept silent in response to the summons of the ex-hetman.

All this enabled Peter to write in one of his letters concerning the Ukraine: "This land has been just itself," although his feeling of distrust for the council of elders and the new hetman remained quite strong. Having thus resolved upon a general engagement near Poltava, Peter communicated this to all military commanders *except* Hetman Skoropadsky, so that "it not fly about," that is, there not be any leakage of information.

Let's return, however, to the fall of 1708. Charles's star had risen very high, and it seemed to Mazepa that not all was lost. Therefore, he persuaded the king not to leave the Ukraine for the winter, promising to incite the population against Russian rule. Even there no warm quarters awaited the Swedes; only devastated hamlets greeted their arrival and fortified small towns that had to be taken with great losses.

At this time Peter tried once more to enter into negotiations with the Swedes, proposing the previous moderate terms: Ingria including Petersburg and Narva in exchange for substantial compensation. Still Charles did not wish to listen to any talk of peace; he was raring for battle, risking his life by taking part in the minor skirmishes that were thrust upon him nonstop by the Russian high command.

The Swedish forces continued to melt away. To the civilian population of the Ukraine Charles was just as harsh and implacable: burdensome levies, fines, and corporal punishments were visited en masse on the populace of the small towns and hamlets that resisted. A partisan movement against the Swedes grew accordingly. In December 1708 Mazepa, perceiving that his position was fragile while the Ukrainians played the role of apprentices to Swedes who ignored them, decided to switch sides again. Colonel Apostol was dispatched with the news that Mazepa was ready to recant and hoped for forgiveness by offering Charles's head if circumstances permitted. The proposal was accepted, but contact with Mazepa was broken.

In the spring of 1709 the Swedish forces were concentrated in the vicinity of Poltava, the siege of which they undertook at the beginning of May. The capture of Poltava provided Charles with a powerful strong point on the Left Bank, and opened the road to Khar'kov and Belgorod and to the Crimea and Ochakov as well, although it may be that Charles aimed by besieging Poltava to force Peter into an engagement in the open field—in the hope of a clear-cut victory.

His calculation turned out to be true. After a siege of seven weeks the commandant of Poltava, Aleksei Kelin, informed Peter that the defenders were at the end of their strength and capabilities. Peter could not permit the surrender of Poltava. He ordered Kelin to hold out until the approach of the main army—Charles's wish had also become Peter's desire. On 8 June he wrote Grigory Dolgoruky: "We declare to you that we are determined to attack the enemy with all forces and with God's aid and at that time it is necessary for you, too, to attack on the other side with all regular and irregular cavalry and take care to cause good diversion and loss, as much as possible, to the enemy."[21]

On 20 June 1709 the Russian army forded the river Vorskla and arrived within several versts of Poltava. At its back was the steep bank of the river, to the right a deep ravine, to the left dense woods. The troops set up a fortified camp in front of which a rather narrow field stretched out reaching to Poltava. Across this field Peter ordered several earthworks thrown up—redoubts the fire of which would be impossible to avoid while advancing on the camp.

During the brief night of 26–27 June 1709 the Swedish army came out of its camp onto the field and deployed in battle formation. Wounded in a skirmish shortly before this, the king was carried on a litter, and the army greeted him. The commander-in-chief, Field Marshal Rehnskiöld, obeying the king's order, issued the command to advance. The Swedes moved forward in four columns.

This was a historic moment. Onto the battlefield had come one of the best armies in Europe that had not lost its superb battleworthiness since the time of Gustavus Adolphus, everything that distinguishes a national army recruited from a free peasantry as opposed to an army of mercenaries, of whom, however, there were some in Charles's army. At the head of 30,000 soldiers who had passed through the crucible of nine years of war stood experienced officers. The best Swedish generals—Rehnskiöld, Stenbock, Lewenhaupt, Rosen, Horn, Field, Sparre, the prince of Würtemburg, Hamilton, and Stackelberg—were on the field of Poltava that day. Finally, at the head of the army stood the great commander—the king who had never known defeat until this day.

One may imagine Peter's anxiety. He had no love of general engagements; he knew how often the destiny of a campaign, a war, or a country had been decided on the spur of the moment. In December 1708 he had written Fedor Apraksin: "I don't suppose this winter will pass without a general battle (because toward spring I am not without apprehensions), and this game is in God's hands, and who knows whom fortune will favor?"[22]

At the same time he understood that there was no other way than through a general engagement—such were the circumstances, such was the foe. And already at the end of 1708 Peter had been prepared for such a battle. He calculated that the Russian army had gained sufficient battle experience after Holowszyń, Dobroe, and Lesnaia, that the opponent had been much worn down by the constant maneuvering and skirmishing in the Ukraine, and that the previous tactic of fighting at river crossings would not be possible now. Finally, he feared that toward spring the king would be reinforced by the corps of General Krassow from Pomerania and the army of Stanislaus I.

It is hardly appropriate to describe in detail the celebrated engagement, glorified by Pushkin's pen. On the second page, the reader without special training will be confused by the details of who went where and did what. I suspect that not every author who has reproduced on paper all phases of the fight is himself in shape to recall and repeat everything fluently. Therefore, we turn to Peter's letter to Fedor

Romodanovsky written right after the engagement. In it the tsar lays out the course of the conflict and its results:

> We report to you about a very great and unexpected victory which the Lord God deigned to grant us through the indescribable bravery of our soldiers with little blood shed by our troops in such fashion. Today at daybreak the ardent enemy attacked our cavalry with his whole army of horse and foot which, although it withstood admirably, still was forced to yield to the enemy with great loss. Then the enemy came up to the front of our camp, against which all of the infantry was immediately led out of the entrenchment and deployed before the enemy's eyes while the cavalry was on both flanks. The enemy, catching sight of this, immediately advanced to attack us, against which ours advanced to meet them, and thus they met them and immediately drove them from the field. Of cannon and banners a multitude was taken. . . [Peter further enumerates the captured generals]. And to say it in a single word: all the enemy's army ended like Phaeton [i.e. died messily] (and concerning the king we cannot know yet whether he is with us or is abiding with our fathers). . . .[23]

To this it should be added that the Swedes, who had launched the engagement, had immediately been forced to resolve the problems that Peter had imposed on them. First was the cavalry clash mentioned by Peter; then, after driving off Menshikov's cavalry, the Swedes were forced to overcome the redoubts located directly in front of their advancing forces and defended by the Russian infantry. Because of poor reconnaissance the Swedes did not even know about these redoubts and at first took them for the Russian main forces. Overcoming the redoubts, from which an enfilading fire was directed, required rather complicated movements by the Swedes in the midst of which one of their columns became separated from the main force and was destroyed by Menshikov's cavalry. Then Lewenhaupt's advancing regiments fell under the fire of the Russian artillery at the camp. In general the artillery in this engagement played an important role (completely lacking with the Swedes). One may say that the engagement proceeded under the roar of hundreds of Russian fieldpieces, which at all stages of the battle inflicted great losses on the enemy. All this slowed down the Swedes' advance and allowed Peter to lead his army out of the fortified camp without hindrance. Emerging onto the field, it deployed by battalions in two lines, using linear tactics. It enjoyed numerical superiority (32,000 versus 20,000 Swedes).

The troops had been deployed by Peter in unusual fashion—the second line of battalions was located a substantial distance from the

first, beyond range of the enemy's fire. This created a dangerous rift in
the formation, but allowed them to avoid needless loss. At the decisive
moment the fresh battalions played their role. From the start of the
general engagement the Swedes attacked Repnin's division headlong
and broke the first line, driving back one of the battalions. Observing
the battle closely, Peter took command of a fresh battalion standing in
the second line and immediately led it to the point of the gap. Stubborn hand-to-hand fighting ensued, which soon spread along the entire
line. The culmination of the engagement arrived. The Russian battalions of the first line withstood the thrust and then went over to the
attack.

Let's halt for a minute. In the past three centuries the country's fate
has been decided in three general engagements: at Poltava in 1709,
Borodino in 1812, and Stalingrad in 1942–43. Notwithstanding the colossal differences among these engagements, they have something subtle in common: the initiative was with the advancing opponent, and at
the culminating point of the battle the fate of the engagement was
decided by the fortitude of the Russian soldier, who was able to with-
stand colossal pressure without flinching.

So it happened on the battlefield at Poltava. The pressure continued
no more than two hours before the Swedes, fearing capture of their
flanks, started to retreat.

The Russian troops did not pursue the enemy farther than the
woods, and "after the ending of this fortunate battle the master dined at
his supply train in chambers or tents and with him were all of our
generals, staff and senior officers, and also the captured Swedish generals."24

Analyzing the situation, many scholars have been perplexed: why
didn't Peter pursue the foe immediately? This becomes understandable
if we recall that Peter in creating a regular army was a consistent supporter of the doctrine of linear tactics. According to its principles, the
main task of the army in battle was to drive the opponent from the
field, "to occupy the battlefield." To abandon the limits of the battlefield for pursuit of the opponent was not recommended because of the
danger of breaking the formation of the infantry, mixing up the troops
in defiles, and losing control over them. To this it should be added that
the engagement had been preceded by a sleepless night, and then the
terrible strain of the battle was followed by the mortal fatigue of men
and animals. It is no accident that the "Comprehensive Relation" about
the battle stated that the cavalry had pursued the Swedes not more than
a mile and a half, "as far as they could go because of the exhaustion of
the horses." Peter himself wrote Ivan Musin-Pushkin on 13 August 1709:

"I have been sick more than two weeks here since the Poltava games, but now, glory to God, I have recovered. . . ."[25]

There are no grounds to suspect Peter of sympathizing with the old tradition (and the natural desire of people who have passed through death and fire) to celebrate victory with a shot of vodka right on the battlefield. It is not impossible, we may remark in jest, that precisely amid this table-talk to which Peter so magnanimously "treated" his captured "teachers," the idea arose of finding and inviting to the improvised earthen table the chief "teacher," King Charles, for whom were dispatched Golitsyn, Bauer, and then Menshikov. It should be noted that Charles also conducted himself like a gentleman, congratulating Peter with the victory, but he attempted at the same time to divert and delay his pursuers.

On 30 June, after an exhausting crossing, Mikhail Golitsyn's cavalry overtook the Swedes at Perevolochna, but they could no longer "invite" the king to the tsar. With a handful of intimates, his bodyguard, and Mazepa, King Charles crossed to the right side of the Dnieper, and the slow-moving General Volkonsky with his dragoons could no longer overtake him, about which Peter was very dissatisfied upon reaching Perevolochna. He arrived when the Swedish troops had already surrendered. This astonishing fact, when an army of 16,000 laid down its arms in front of a detachment of 9,000 cavalry, has given historians no rest for many generations. Apparently the similar decision of Commander-in-Chief Lewenhaupt, who had orders from the king to retreat toward the Crimea, was affected by many unfavorable factors: the three-day flight across the barren steppe, the shortage of munitions and provisions, the lack of means for crossing the two-kilometer-wide Dnieper, and finally the general demoralization and apathy of troops who had sustained complete defeat and were therefore easily misled by Golitsyn's military cunning in showing the opponent from afar "infantry" made up of dismounted riders and "cavalry" of horses only.

In general, both during the engagement and afterward the Swedes committed a host of mistakes; they had become victims of the strategy and tactics that they had adopted for the war. Peter, no matter how inebriated with victory, thought hard about the circumstances of the battle and the causes of defeat of such a powerful opponent as the Swedish king. Lewenhaupt recalled that after capitulating he was invited to dinner, where he sat at the same table with the tsar, and the latter questioned him about different episodes of the war, among others about Riga, to which, it later became known, Peter wished to lay siege in the near future. But then "he asked nothing more about Riga, but inquired why we had penetrated so deeply without covering our

rear. And why our king had not held a council of war. With what aim
had he come to Poltava? Why had we attacked the Russians in a place
where our position was most difficult? Why had we not used cannon?
Why after the first thrust had we withdrawn to the left and stood so long
in place? And why had the infantry and cavalry not met in converging
directions? We could not answer these questions any more than to let
him know that, indeed, we had not been consulted about anything.
Then he looked at Count Golovkin and mister Shafirov, who translated
his discourse into German, saying that he was quite astonished how it
could be that these generals knew nothing. . . ."[26]

In analyzing these questions, military historians may understand a
great deal, proceeding from Pushkin's well-known phrase: "To follow
the thinking of a great man is a most diverting art." But even for a
nonprofessional it is clear that Peter would have acted differently had
he undertaken such a campaign and entered into such an engagement.
A person cannot know his own fate, however, and only two years passed
before Peter, finding himself in a most difficult position on the Pruth,
repeated many of his opponent's mistakes.

Meanwhile, the victors counted their trophies. Beyond the almost
19,000 captives many arms and banners had been collected on the
battlefield. More than 9,000 Swedes were buried near Poltava. The Russian losses, if one believes the *Journal*, were comparatively insignificant—1,345 killed and 3,290 wounded. Peter was ecstatic over the
victory which, true to his typical realism, he called in the letter cited "a
very great and unexpected victory."[27]

And one more question: what would have happened had Peter's
army lost the Poltava engagement? Several eyewitnesses say with assurance that in case of catastrophe he intended to continue the struggle.
Possibly he was prepared in this regard to abandon the Baltic temporarily. This is how we should interpret Peter's letter of 3 December 1708 to
Apraksin from Lebedin in which he wrote that the fate of a general
engagement is in God's hands and "who knows whom fortune will
favor?" Further, he gives orders about the regiments stationed in the
Baltic region: ". . . therefore for every instance I have considered it
convenient for these regiments all to be in Moscow (which is a place
halfway between us and Piterburkh), and then we shall see where it will
be best to direct them by spring, for here in January everything will
show itself."[28] That is, a general battle would occur.

The Breakthrough:
From Poltava to Hangö

In the history of eighteenth-century Russia perhaps no other military victory yielded such rich fruits as Poltava. Peter managed to exploit the victory in the Ukraine optimally, seizing the initiative in both diplomacy and war. In the first days after Poltava he formulated and began to resolve several of the most important problems, one of which was the restoration of the Northern Alliance. Above all, it was necessary to restore the Polish throne to Augustus and to expel Stanislaus from Poland. On 6 July 1709 Peter sent Augustus a letter in which he urged him to begin active operations "without losing time" and promised as early as mid-July to enter Poland "for the completion of our common interests."[1] Astounding efficiency! It was based on a clear appraisal of the context and also on the fact that the army had really not been drained of blood by the Poltava engagement and after a rest might enter Poland, which indeed was done.

Before setting off for Poland the tsar tried to strike while the iron was hot by negotiating a peace with the Swedes. Josias Cederhielm, the royal secretary captured at Poltava, delivered Peter's new terms to Stockholm: the tsar was ready to make peace if Sweden yielded Ingria and Karelia and also conceded Vyborg. Peter proposed that the Swedes accept Russia's offer before their former adversaries, Denmark and Saxony, meddled in the war by taking advantage of Sweden's weakness after Poltava. In Peter's appeal to the Swedish people it was put thus: "To the aforementioned secretary it was explained at that time how angry with the Swedes were their majesties the kings of Poland and Denmark and that they would undoubtedly not fail to be avenged, wherefore on the contrary—if a good peace were to be arranged—no time should be lost in addressing the matter before the aforementioned powers might enter into alliance with us and unite with us. We, of course, hope that the aforementioned king [Charles], in view of his unfortunate position that is known to all the world, will recognize the moderation and modesty of our demands and will be inclined to display the same Christian and sincere inclination to peace with us. . . . But how little response from the side of the king and the Swedish Senate have these our praiseworthy proposals received!"[2]

In this excerpt of a propaganda leaflet there is not one false word. Peter really was ready at that moment to waive the interests of his own unfaithful allies for the conclusion of a peace on terms acceptable to both sides with the king who had fallen into difficulty. The diplomatic calculation was exact, and Peter was certain of success. On 13 August 1709 he wrote Fedor Apraksin: ". . . the royal secretary Cederhielm has been sent by us concerning all this to Stockholm via Riga, which will of course bring a decision. Also I hope that during the present instance [the Poltava victory] that which we have achieved with God's aid will start working for us."[3]

Inebriated with victory, Peter had forgotten for a time with whom he was dealing. Charles, sitting near Bender, did not wish "to follow" anybody and refused any negotiations with Peter, declaring that he would assemble a second army in place of the one that had perished at Poltava. Apprised of this, Peter even signed the appeal to the Swedish people cited above, predicting inescapable calamities for them in the future, after which he left for Poland to meet with Augustus.

Perhaps more than anybody else, Peter grasped the role of Poltava as a breakthrough event. In his mind, after Poltava, the general idea and concept, possibly not entirely distinct at the start of the conflict, of the war's further course finally took shape. Its crux was the intent to end the existence of the Swedish Empire, partitioning its possessions among potential allies on condition of preserving Russia's currently decisive role. An instruction to Boris Kurakin, who was dispatched on 23 October 1709 to the German electorate of Hanover for negotiations with elector Georg Ludwig, expressed the idea, perhaps not entirely clear in form but distinct in content, concerning the fate of the Swedish Empire after Poltava:

And if they [the Hanoverians] will rightly consider their own interest, then for them this near neighbor, the king of Sweden, due to Bremen and Verden can be dangerous, for their Swedish insatiability to expand their own authority is already known abundantly to their neighbors. And because His Tsarist Majesty, both for his own profit and for the other regions that share borders with the Swedes, has reason for security to consider, upon obtaining such a fortunate victory against the king of Sweden, how he might so restrain his power in advance so that he could be constrained by the previous and present terms not to harm both the Russian and the [Holy] Roman empires and other neighbors, as he did before.[4]

Further, according to Peter's plan, it was essential to include the king of Prussia in the alliance, who must act in concert with the kings of Poland and Denmark, "whereas the Swedish forces in Livland and Finland will be driven out by His Tsarist Majesty's troops, and Shonina [Scania] and Norway by the Danish [forces]. And so they may finish the matter easily and quickly with God's aid and, with each obtaining his intention, compel the Swede to peace. And for the maintenance of their own conquered territories they may in the future make a treaty of guarantee."[5]

After Poltava, Peter began to consistently implement the idea of partitioning the Swedish Empire. But first in October 1709 there was the meeting with Augustus at Thorn (Toruń). This was no longer a meeting of old friends after a long, forced separation. Peter had not forgotten Altranstädt.

Indeed, Peter was already dictating the conditions, one of which was the confirmation of supporters of Russia in the most important posts of the king's government. On 9 October at Thorn a treaty was concluded according to which the tsar promised to restore Augustus to the Polish throne, and the latter in turn was supposed to launch a struggle against the adversaries of Russia in Poland. In a secret article of the treaty it was envisaged that Augustus would be given Livland, whereas Russia might, "beyond the previously conquered localities, retain the province of Estland, wherein both their majesties are agreed."[6] Thus, under the press of reality Augustus had conceded Estland to Russia. This contradicted the Preobrazhenskoe treaty of 1699. As subsequent events showed, however, Peter did not intend even to fulfill the conditions of the Thorn agreement, violating them several months later in seizing Riga, which will be discussed below.

Soon after the Thorn agreement Vasily Lukich Dolgoruky concluded a treaty in Copenhagen restoring the Russo-Danish alliance and renewing Denmark's war against Sweden. Some days later Peter met with the king of Prussia, Frederick William I, at Marienwerder. The negotiations revolved around the allies' shares in the partition of the possessions of the Swedish Empire. Although Prussia had been preoccupied with the War of the Spanish Succession and had not entered the Northern Alliance, it promised not to permit the Swedish forces from Pomerania to pass through its territory into Poland. As a form of reward for cooperation Peter (in a secret article of the treaty) promised Frederick William "to obtain the town of Elbing [Polish Elblong] with its hinterland in such fashion that they will work to clear the town of the Swedish garrison and to install their own garrison. . . ."[7]

There, too, Peter gave written instructions to Boris Kurakin, who was supposed to persuade Georg Ludwig, the elector of Hanover and heir to the English throne, to provide aid to the Northern Alliance in the war with Sweden, promising him a solid chunk of the Swedish Empire—the towns of Bremen and Verden and their hinterlands. On 22 June 1710 the corresponding treaty was signed, and Hanover broke its alliance with Sweden. It was ratified by the elector the next day when news arrived of the fall of Riga.

The occupation of Riga was the most important point of the second part of the program worked out by Peter after Poltava, and it signified the final conquest by Russia of the eastern Baltic lands. In general, too, Peter had immediately evaluated the significance of the Poltava victory for the Baltic theater of military operations and for his beloved Petersburg. Also immediately after the engagement he had written Fedor Apraksin, who had been left behind in charge of Petersburg: "Now a finished stone has already been set in the foundation of Sankt-Piterburkh with God's aid."[8]

The main efforts were directed toward the seizure of Riga, the real capital of the Swedish east Baltic lands. The siege dragged on. The plague that had broken out decimated both the besieged and the besiegers. It carried off almost ten thousand Russian soldiers and sixty thousand inhabitants and soldiers of the fortress. This circumstance as well as Riga's strong fortifications put the success of a possible storm in doubt, and Riga was mainly subjected to continuous bombardment, which had been launched by Peter in person. On 4 July 1710 the capitulation of the garrison and town was signed. On 8 July Dynemunt (Dünamünde) on the Daugava fell, on 15 August the garrison of Pernov (Piarnu) surrendered, a little later Russian troops occupied the island of Øland (Saarema) and the fortress of Arensburg (Kingisepp) located there, and on 29 September Revel (Tallinn) surrendered.

Success in Livland and Estland was combined with success in Karelia: on 12 June Vyborg surrendered to the victor's mercy, and on 8 September Keksholm (Priozersk, earlier Korela). Thus, in a single summer all the east Baltic lands had come into Peter's hands.

In theory, on this basis it would have been possible to end the war as well. But Charles would never agree to this, as he was intriguing at this time in Turkish possessions, and Peter himself, for that matter, was filled with different, imperial ideas.

One circumstance linked with the surrender of Riga merits attention. Among the points of the capitulation was one that is exceptionally noteworthy: ". . . in order that the native Livlanders remain on the Russian side and in loyalty to His Majesty they have made the oath and signed it with their own hands." The new military administration of Riga knocked down everywhere the emblems of the kingdom of Sweden and set up those of Russia.[9]

On 16 August 1710 Peter signed a manifesto proclaiming the annexation of Estland to Russia. It was noted therein that "the Swedish king, because of his known stubbornness, gives us no peace, so that for the true attainment of this just ultimate purpose we have been compelled to direct our armed forces into Estland so as to consolidate control of its seaports and thereby defend ourselves from any invasion. In particular we have considered it essential with God's aid to control the town of Revel. . . ."[10]

All these actions signified only one thing—Peter declared the territory of the eastern Baltic littoral including Livland and Estland (despite numerous agreements with Augustus) henceforth to be part of the Russian state; their inhabitants were his subjects without the right to leave the country, like the Swedes, and were obligated to swear loyalty to the new ruler.

Peter reckoned on taking full advantage of the favorable situation in the Baltic. He drafted a plan to land a Russian corps from Danish ships in Scania, a territory on the Scandinavian peninsula belonging to Denmark that had gone to Sweden in the seventeenth century.

Still, in drafting plans for operations in the Baltic region it was increasingly necessary to look southward. Finding himself near Bender, Charles XII had not been simply passing the time but actively inciting the Turks to attack Russia, frightening them with the growing might of their northern neighbor. Immediately upon arriving in Turkish possessions, he had dispatched to Istanbul his secretary Neugebauer with a letter to the sultan demanding that Turkey play an active role in the north.

But losers hear things differently from victors, and for a long time Charles's efforts to push the Ottomans into war failed. On 3 January 1710 the Turks renewed the Constantinople treaty of 1700 with Russia. So great was the significance of the treaty with the dangerous southern neighbors for the fulfillment of Peter's Baltic plans that it was marked in Moscow as another military victory.

It should be noted that over the span of almost ten years Peter had displayed special caution toward the Turks and the Crimean Tatars. At the most critical moment, on the eve of the Poltava engagement in the spring of 1709, when an attack by the Crimea and Turkey might have placed Russia in a hopeless position, Peter had gone to Azov and had demonstrated his peaceful intentions to the representative of Turkey in the Crimea, Kapadzhi-pasha: he burned part of the Azov fleet. (Indeed, as Peter's letters show, this involved designated ships that had been specially taken to Azov for selection.) Moreover, rich gifts and money were sent to Istanbul. As a result the sultan prohibited the khan, who was already preparing for the campaign, from attacking Russia.

Nevertheless, war was not averted at the end of 1710: Peter's activities in Europe and in Poland, which particularly perturbed the Ottomans along with Charles's démarches, all played their role, and Turkey launched a war against Russia. For the first time in many years, fighting on two fronts was in prospect. Peter decided not to wait for the Turks to maneuver, but to move toward the southern frontier.

Why did Peter hasten to take the initiative before the intentions of the Turks and the Crimean Tatars were clarified, and why did he undertake a hasty advance in this region and not around Azov or along the Dnieper? The direction of the blow and the decisiveness and the speed of Peter's actions were governed by knowledge and sober appraisal of the situation. Peter guessed the direction of the Turks' possible blow—the Ukraine and Poland—and strove to avoid converting these lands into a zone of active operations of the Russo-Turkish War, for this would have sharply increased the risk of unpredictable political clashes. It was necessary to keep the war as far to the south as possible, out of range of the powerful corps of the Swedish general Krassow stationed in Pomerania, the numbers of which by the spring of 1711 had reached 26,000 men.

An important factor that defined the Danubian direction was the agreement with the Moldavian hospodar Dmitry Kantemir, who promised to support the Russian troops and the annexation of Moldavia to Russia. By a campaign toward the Danube, Peter also hoped to raise the south Slavic peoples against the Turks. "When the Lord God shall raise His sword-wielding right arm against the Basurman," Serbian patriots had appealed to Peter in 1710, "do not forget us, the least ones, by tsarist invitation and your own kindness, and we shall pay homage by our own service to our Orthodox tsar."[11]

These were not empty words, as the Balkan peoples saw in Russia their liberator from the Ottoman yoke. Peter did much to propagate these ideas, which found a response in a number of places in Serbia, Montenegro, and Albania where rebellions commenced. But these were soon suppressed; likewise dispiriting was the news from Moldavia that Peter's campaign had proved unsuccessful.

Put concisely, it turned out to be poorly prepared and conceived.

This concerned efficient reconnaissance, coordination of troop operations, and their supply with provisions and forage. In general, in looking at the emotional side of the enterprise, we might note that Peter had gone on this campaign with a sinking feeling. He did not display his typical optimism and faith in victory in the war the adversary had imposed on him. He was particularly concerned about Catherine and his daughters, which explains his proclaiming Catherine his wife.

Although Peter understood that (considering the conditions of war in the south) it was necessary to fight the Turks differently from the Swedes, nonetheless buck passing and foolishness were displayed on the part of the Russian commanders—the heroes of Poltava—that were severely punished on the battlefield. So it was that intuition had not misled the tsar.

On 7 July 1711 the Turks in the vicinity of the river Pruth interdicted the communications of the Russian cavalry with the main part of the army. Taking into account that the campaign was being carried out over waterless steppes ravaged by locusts, it was decided at a council of war not to go to the Danube, but on the contrary, as noted in Peter's *Journal,* "to retreat from the enemy while it is possible for all to happen [unite] and in a suitable place to give battle."

The withdrawal proceeded under the most difficult conditions. The Preobrazhensky Regiment, marching in the vanguard, repulsed continual attacks of the numerically superior opponent over some hours. At the same time it was necessary to drag along the heavy chevaux-de-frise—the infantry's most effective defense against the swooping attacks of the steppe-raiders' cavalry. Over six hours of withdrawal the army, fatigued by heat and thirst, covered only six versts and was forced to halt on the bank of the Pruth. Three times the camp sustained attacks by the Turkish and Tatar troops. The situation was becoming exceptionally dangerous, for the 38,000 Russians confronted no less than 140,000 warriors of Vizier Baltaci Mehmet.

Realizing that his troops were not in position to overcome the covering detachment of chevaux-de-frise, the Turkish commander resorted to a very effective means: trenches, approaches, and batteries were laid down right up to the Russian camp, and more than three hundred fieldpieces were emplaced in them that began bombarding the Russian positions. Further, the Turkish guns that had been set up on the other bank of the Pruth fired from the commanding heights at anyone who tried to come close to the riverbank and fetch water.

Most critical proved to be 9–11 July, when the fate of the army, Peter, and the country was decided. These three days are among the most dramatic in Peter's life. It is no accident that quite a few legends are linked to the battle on the Pruth. One of them concerns the so-called "Testament," Peter's letter to the Senate, known to us from *Curious and Noteworthy Anecdotes about Peter the Great*, a 1785 book by academician Jakob von Stählin.

"The Testament from the Pruth" has engendered heated disputes in the literature concerning its authenticity. The trouble is that neither the original nor a contemporary copy has been preserved. Therefore the document cannot be subjected to paleographical or textological analysis. It remains only to analyze its content. Here is the full text of the letter in translation from the German of Stählin's book:

> I inform you that I with all my army, through no fault or mistake, but through false information, being surrounded by forces four times as strong, and cut off from all lines of supply, look forward—unless with the special help of God—to nothing but complete destruction or captivity amongst the Turks. In the latter case you are no longer to look upon me as your Tsar and ruler, and are to do nothing which I tell you, even if I write it with my own hand, until I reappear amongst you in my own person. Should I perish, and authentic news of my death reach you, choose amongst yourselves the one most worthy to be my successor.[12]

I should say at once that I am among those historians who doubt the authenticity of the letter from the Pruth. Those who have argued this most cogently are the West German historian Reinhold Wittram and Nikolai Ivanovich Pavlenko. As the latter has justly remarked, "the setting on the Pruth is explicated in such general phrases that its compilation would have been accessible to any educated person who had on hand *The Journal of Peter I.*[13]

Quite a few other reasonable doubts arise in reading the letter. Pavlenko considers that Stählin, in inventing the letter, was motivated by the age-old urge of "the little man consumed by the dream of glorifying a great man through anecdotes." If one is to avoid such a sharply deprecatory evaluation of the personality of this exceptional cultural figure whose creativity is just beginning to be studied, then one may presume that Stählin, true to the accepted style of "anecdotes" of the eighteenth century, moralizing novellas "from the lives of the great," was not after the precision so prized by us and was recounting rumors then current in society about some "Testament" of Peter.

The situation on the Pruth really had taken such shape that at that very time there was reason to think about a testament.

Let's review the foregoing events. The surrounded army had been subjected to continual bombardment. "In the mean time," the tsar himself wrote subsequently, "the fire from the enemy batteries was increasing by the hour, yet it did not do much damage, for it was impossible to retreat further, but it had come to this: either to win or to die."

As we see, Peter obviously contradicts himself. Other sources tell us that the situation was becoming critical: the actions of the Turkish artillery had substantially worsened the position of the Russian regiments deployed on the field.[14] In Sheremetev's journal for 1711 it was noted: "And this night [8–9 July] for some hours before daybreak from the Turks and from us there commenced great firing from cannon and from small arms, from which in our supply train many people and horses have been hurt."[15] A flag of truce was sent out to the Turks, but they were silent—only their artillery spoke. Once more a flag of truce was sent out. Let's give Peter the floor again: "And then, when the response was delayed, at that time we sent to tell them that they should quickly give a response, whether they desire peace or not, for we cannot wait longer. Later, when the response to this message was also delayed, then we ordered the regiments to advance. And when this was done and ours had advanced several dozen paces, then the Turks sent at once to tell us not to move, for they accept the peace. . . ."[16]

Vice-Chancellor Piotr Pavlovich Shafirov was dispatched to the Turks. However, events had occurred the day before that, according to legend, were linked to Catherine, who was in camp with Peter. The cause of the Turks' desire for peace is explained as follows: without receiving an answer to the truce proposal, Peter had resolved to break out of the encirclement and had therefore given orders to prepare to march, after which he had gone off to rest in his tent. Catherine, on her own or on somebody's advice, held consultations with the top generals, who showed her that such a march would be suicidal. Then the tsaritsa persuaded Peter to send a new letter to the vizier, to which, secretly from the tsar, she appended all her valuables and money. This decided the matter: at the moment of the Russian advance the vizier, who had seen Peter's resolve to break out at any cost, agreed to negotiations.

The legend is supported by several facts. In *The Journal of Peter the Great* for 24 November 1714 it is noted: "November 24th, that is the saint's day of Her Majesty the mistress tsaritsa Catherine Alekseevna, the master himself placed on Her Majesty the newly instituted knightly Order of Saint Catherine, which order was instituted in memory of Her Majesty's presence at the battle with the Turks on the Pruth, where at such a dangerous time she was seen by all not as a wife but as a male person."[17]

Piotr Shafirov, in leaving for the Turks, received instructions. They stated the following:

1. Concede to the Turks all the conquered towns, and raze the structures on their lands, and if they are obstinate, then you are permitted to concede;

2. If there will be talk about the Swedes and about our conceding all conquests, then mention the cession of the Livland [towns]. If they cannot be satisfied with that alone, then yield the others a little at a time, except for Ingria. If they will not concede, then offer Pskov, and if that is too little, then offer other provinces as well. If possible, it would be better not to name, but to rely on the sultan's will;

3. If they will start talking about Lesczyński, permit them to;

4. For the rest, whatever is possible to satisfy the sultan in every way, so that he not strive much for the Swede.[18]

Having begun negotiations, the Turks did not hasten to complete them. The prolongation of the negotiations made the position of Peter's encircled army still more difficult. On 11 July, after receiving the first news from Shafirov, the tsar gave assent to all possible concessions except capitulation and surrender to captivity. But horses were needed for a breakout, and therefore Peter requested preliminary agreement at least about permitting the cutting of grass for the horses beyond the Turkish trenches. "My Lord! I have surmised from the word sent that the Turks, although they appear to be so inclined, are slow in regard to peace. Therefore, do everything according to your consideration, how God will instruct you, and if they will genuinely speak about peace, then concede everything they wish except slavery. And let us know today, of course, so that we may embark with God's aid upon our desperate route. If a genuine disposition to peace appears, and they cannot complete the treaty today, then at least make it today to cut beyond their entrenchment. The rest has been ordered orally. Peter."[19]

The last sentence seems noteworthy. What more could Peter have transmitted orally to his emissary after such terrible words for a statesman: "concede everything they wish except slavery"? I think that in this situation the single thing that the tsar could transmit in words was: "Don't spare the money!"

Impatiently awaiting news from Shafirov, Peter prepared to sell his own life dearly—the council of war by this time, despite the overwhelming superiority of the adversary, adopted a decision to break out if the adversary demanded capitulation.

Fortunately, Shafirov succeeded in reaching agreement with the vizier, and on 12 July the peace with the Turks was signed. It was, perhaps, one of the most onerous peace treaties that Russia was forced to endorse in the eighteenth century. Azov was restored to Turkey; Taganrog, Kamennyi Zaton, and Sakmara were destroyed. Russia promised not to interfere in Polish affairs, nor to hinder the passage of the king of Sweden back to his homeland.

That same day Peter ratified the treaty, and the Russian army left the trap. "And so," Peter wrote the Senate on 15 July, "that deadly feast has been ended by this." People and horses had grown weak and, as it was noted in Sheremetev's Journal, "they proceeded a little at a time because many horses had died from lack of fodder." With good reason many contemporaries believed that Peter had gotten off quite lightly, considering the position in which his army had been caught, surrounded by an adversary almost four times superior, without provisions and forage, with munitions running out.

En route to the Dnieper news had been received that the cavalry corps of General Rönn, which had been detached from the main army, had taken the Turkish fortress of Brailov by storm on 13 June in accordance with plans adopted earlier. For the first time Russian dragoons watered their horses on the Danube. But this victory was no longer needed, and Rönn abandoned the fortress to rejoin Peter.

The swiftly concluded peace on the Pruth was a terrible blow for Charles XII—his sworn foe had literally slipped out of Turkish hands, and the vizier had not bothered about his ally's interests. As Poniatowski, the former representative of Stanislaus I in the Turkish camp, wrote, when the peace was concluded and Peter left his camp on 12 July, the king of Sweden galloped up from Bender infuriated with the Turks for the hasty peace with Peter.

Immediately upon the conclusion of the peace and the exit from encirclement Peter wrote letters to his allies, Augustus and Frederick, in which he remarked that "for some inconvenience and especially as regards ours and the common interests with your majesty, we have not proceeded further in this war and have made an eternal peace with the Turks, about which we have issued a decree to our envoy Prince Dolgoruky to report in greater detail and love, wherein you will be pleased to believe him."[20]

The most onerous condition of the treaty was the return of the Azov region to the Turks. With his own hands the tsar had to destroy what had been created by huge efforts over fifteen years, what was so dear to him as a person and statesman. Now all the plans of consolidating the Azov region and constructing a town, a port, and a Volga-Don canal had been reduced to ashes; it had been necessary to destroy the fleet and for Peter himself to close the southern window with which he had linked grandiose plans for the future.

For Fedor Apraksin, who had been occupied as previously ordered with reinforcing the defenses of the Azov region, Peter's decree about yielding Azov and razing everything that had been built on the north coast of the Sea of Azov came like a thunderclap amid a clear sky. In the beginning Apraksin did not believe the report about the peace terms, and only a second letter from Peter convinced the faithful Fedor Matveevich of the bitter truth. The fate of the southern Petersburg had been decided irrevocably.

But Peter did not like to mourn losses for long, no matter how onerous they were—lots of matters awaited ahead. There is a phrase in the aforementioned letter to Apraksin revealing much of what Peter pondered after the Pruth: "It should also be considered whether it would not be desperate to wage war with two such adversaries and give up this Swedish war, the end of which already appears close in God's hope, for Pomerania follows as did Livonia. God preserve us if, being in two wars, we await a French peace whereby we would lose everywhere."[21]

A great deal of information is packed into these few lines. Most notably, Peter is glad that the Russo-Turkish War has ended, for this frees his hands to finish the Northern War. Its end appears very close to Peter; for that, in his opinion, it would suffice to conquer Pomerania.

Peter, however, was mistaken: the war had merely crossed its midpoint, and there were still ten years until that memorable day when the courier delivered the news of the Peace of Nystadt. The peace treaty of Utrecht was concluded in 1713, so that he did not succeed in avoiding the intervention of the great powers that had finished their War of the Spanish Succession. Finally, it proved much more difficult to conquer Pomerania than it had seemed on the banks of the Pruth.

At first, events transpired, as Peter had thought, very rapidly: already at the start of August 1711 the Russo-Saxon forces, after joining the Danes, had invaded Swedish Pomerania and laid siege to Wismar and Stralsund. In essence, the allies' troops were acting together for the first time in all the years that the Northern Alliance had existed. Furthermore, Peter reckoned on bringing Prussia and Hanover into the military operations against the Swedes. The rulers of these countries had something to ponder—forthcoming partition, perhaps, of the very richest part of the Swedish Empire. Nonetheless, the risk was great: the Swedish lion was still strong. The siege of Stralsund had to be lifted in the fall; the Danes had not delivered the besieging tools and could not blockade the fortress from the sea. At the same time differences appeared among the allies as mutual pretensions and offenses increased.

The differences also carried over into the following campaign. In drafting plans at the start of 1712 Peter already refused to go to Stralsund and decided to concern himself with the siege of another powerful fortress, Stettin (Szczecin). The main cause of the change in

Peter's plans that incited the allies' dissatisfaction was a desire to involve Prussia in military operations, "enticing" it with the promise of ceding Stettin. The disputes continued till autumn and ended only when the Danes and the Saxons started to besiege Stralsund, Wismar, Bremen, Verden, and Stade, and the Russians Stettin. Although the Danes soon occupied Bremen, Stade, and Verden, the campaign did not succeed. The Russian forces invested Stettin, but the Danes did not manage to bring up the siege artillery in time, and after sitting a long time under the walls of the fortress, Menshikov's army went off to Stralsund, where all the allies together had to taste the fruits of disagreement and delay. In mid-September the Swedish fleet reached Stralsund and landed the 10,000-man army of Field Marshal Stenbock, who at the end of October broke through the blockade of the fortress and broke out into a strategic expanse. Trespassing on the sovereignty of neighboring Mecklenburg, he occupied Rostock, and on 9 December defeated the Danish-Saxon army near Gadebusch.

In early 1713 one more north German state became a battlefield—Holstein. There at Friedrichstadt on 31 January Russian troops under Peter's command drove Stenbock from very favorable positions and forced him to retreat to the Holstein fortress of Tønning, where he was besieged by the allies. Soon Stenbock surrendered to the victors' mercy. So ended the Swedish field army in north Germany. Out of Sweden's former possessions along the seacoast remained only a few fortresses, weak garrisons awaiting their fate.

In the summer of 1713 Menshikov's army besieged Stettin. After intensive bombardment the fortress capitulated. Thereupon Menshikov transferred it, as had been promised by Peter, into the temporary possession (sequestration) of Prussia jointly with Holstein. This circumstance provoked the acute dissatisfaction of Denmark, which had long had accounts to settle with Holstein, the satellite of Sweden that had used the principality's territory to maintain constant pressure on Denmark's southern borders. Peter at first expressed dissatisfaction with Menshikov's "self-governance" and promised the Danes to regulate the Stettin problem. In fact, however, with the aid of sequestration he contrived to bring Prussia into the orbit of his own policy, and the Prussian king Frederick William signed a treaty according to which Russia guaranteed the annexation of Stettin to Prussia, whereas Prussia in turn guaranteed to Russia the incorporation of Ingria, Karelia with Vyborg, and Estland. Knowing the extreme caution of Prussia's policy, Peter contrived only with the aid of such a sweet morsel "to entice" into the guarantee—an important element of the system of international relations—the Prussian king avid for territorial annexations. The treaty was dated June 1714 when the concluding stage of Russia's conquest unfolded in the skerries of Finland. Peter attributed huge significance to the seizure of Finland, seeing in it one of the paths to peace with the Swedes. In a letter of 30 October 1712 he explains this to Fedor Apraksin in bright, figurative, if somewhat crude, language: ". . . this province is essentially Sweden's teat, as you know yourself, not only that [they obtain] meat and so forth but also wood from there. And if God allows us to Åbo this summer, then the Swedish neck will become easier to bend. . . ."[22]

In this same letter Peter devoted special attention to the construction of small-oared vessels. Acquainted with the topography along the Gulf of Finland's southern coast, marked by skerries, he understood that only with the aid of galleys, shear-boats, chalks, and careybashes would it be possible to move and supply troops. The tsar exerted much effort in increasing the galley fleet, which might offer at least some resistance to the powerful Swedish fleet cruising in the Gulf of Finland.

The idea of such a coastal war was wholly justified. Subsequently Peter, summing up the results of the campaign in Finland, thus evaluated what had occurred: "The end of this war by such a peace has been obtained not otherwise than by the fleet, for via land in nowise could it have been attained thanks to the location of the place, because in Finland one confronts passage on dry land with extraordinary difficulties, thanks to the rocky and narrow roads and the lack of fodder."[23]

In the spring of 1713 a huge oared fleet with a whole army of 16,000 men on board set off for Finland. The peculiar feature of military operations in the Finnish theater consisted of the fact that the Swedish land forces, sensing the superiority of the Russian army, avoided engagement, abandoned the seacoast, and went off deep into the interior of the territory, whither the civilian population also fled. The Russian naval force did not rush into battle with the Swedish fleet, which was superior in numbers of ships and firepower. Therefore Peter, who showed himself to be a brilliant strategist, took advantage of the superiority of shallow-draft oared vessels, carefully coordinating operations (literally before the eyes of the Swedish fleet) with the army moving along the coast. In sum, the shrewd combination of the army and the navy allowed him to occupy Helsingfors (Helsinki), Borgå, and Åbo practically uncontested. The Swedes were deprived of their last naval bases in the eastern Baltic region. The land army of Mikhail Golitsyn, whose talent for command blossomed in Finland, operated with success. Twice he inflicted defeat on the army of General Armfelt and finally managed to squeeze the Swedes out of Finland.

The campaign of 1714 is celebrated for the Hangö engagement, which has entered the annals of Russian naval history. In itself the engagement is exceptionally curious and reminds one of the intense finish of a chess match in which the attacking side, maintaining the initiative and ahead by only one move, does not allow the opponent the possibility of using his strongest pieces for defense.

When the Russian galley fleet moved along the coast from Helsingfors toward Åbo, reconnaissance established that the squadron of Admiral Wattrang was blocking the route of the Russian galleys. Sixteen Swedish ships of the line and five frigates with hundreds of cannon, standing off Hang Head—the end of the peninsula of the same name—were patrolling the breakwater and the approaches to the shore. Peter and his staff inspected the Hangö peninsula, which extended many kilometers into the sea, and noticed that at its base it had a narrow neck. It was decided to build planks on it and drag the galleys to the other side of the peninsula, thereby bypassing the barrier created at the head in the form of Swedish ships.

But Admiral Wattrang had not been asleep. He quickly guessed Peter's plan and decided to give battle to the Russians at the crossing. For this he divided the squadron: he dispatched Vice Admiral Lillie with twelve ships to the place where the Russians proposed to drag the boats ashore and Rear Admiral Ehrenskiöld with a frigate, six galleys, and three rock-boats to where the Russians intended to launch the galleys. He himself with six ships and three frigates remained in place at the tip of the peninsula off Hangö Head.

Peter also closely observed the operations of the Swedes. He immediately resolved to take advantage of what nature and the Swedish admiral had offered him. The former provided complete calm that early morning of 26 July, and the latter had cut his forces at the head by half. The detachment of Russian galleys circled the becalmed Swedish ships out to sea as sailors say, that is, farther from the shore, out of range of the powerful Swedish guns. A second detachment came after them. The efforts of the Swedish sailors to tow the ships with sloops out to sea did not work. Only at night when a breeze sprang up did Wattrang move his ships farther from shore. The morning of 27 July dawned. Again, as the day before, the sea was calm. A third detachment of Russian galleys moved toward the head and, taking advantage of Wattrang's maneuver the night before, encircled the Swedish squadron from the other side, which was now already close to shore. Wattrang hastily had to launch his sloops and tow the heavy ships back toward shore. But it was too late.

It's not hard to imagine what terminology the old sea wolf resorted to while standing on the flagship's bridge and watching as the Russian galleys, except for one that had run aground, rounded Hangö Head. He could not intercept their subsequent operations: the galleys had locked into the fjord that very detachment of Ehrenskiöld which was supposed to command the launching place of the Russian boats from the portage, and they were preparing for an attack. The Swedes rejected a proposal for surrender, and then three dozen galleys forming a half-moon moved against the motionless Swedish ships.

From the side it was, apparently, a grandiose spectacle that recalled the sea engagements of the Punic Wars. The furious fire from the Swedish ships, however, proclaimed that the eighteenth century was at the door. Twice the Swedish sailors repulsed the attacks of the galleys, but the third time the galleys closed with the opponent, and the infantry commenced boarding. After a three-hour fight the Swedes lowered their blue and yellow flags. Probably the water of the quiet fjord was reddened from the blood of the almost one thousand Russian soldiers and Swedish sailors killed and wounded in these hours. Admiral Wattrang no longer had strength to watch the triumph of the Russians. As soon as the wind sprang up, he left for the open sea.

Peter interpreted this engagement as a nautical Poltava. Although the two battles are not comparable in their military and diplomatic effects, one may understand the tsar: it was the first engagement at sea (and successful as such) by a state that ten or fifteen years before did not possess a single ship. The inspiring victory at Hangö Head was valuable not only in that respect. At the beginning of August 1714 Russian galleys seized the Åland Islands, located at the entrance to the Gulf of Bothnia, which represented a suitable base for subsequent military operations against Sweden itself.

In December 1714 news was received that Charles XII accompanied by four confederates had suddenly arrived at Stralsund after riding through Hungary, Austria, and the German states. After the Pruth his relations with the Turks had worsened, and they wanted by all means to get rid of the uninvited turbulent guest and urged him to leave for Sweden.

The king who struck everybody as strange did not smooth out matters with the Turks either. Moreover, in 1713 armed conflict broke out: the Turks stormed and burned the house where the king defended himself around the clock. Charles fought the janissaries hand to hand and was wounded and captured. The losses of the Turks, Tatars, and Swedes in this melee amounted to dozens wounded and killed.

After returning to Pomerania and then, after an absence of fifteen years, to Stockholm, Charles could no longer fix things. It was not just a matter of his having lost time while sitting in Bender, but also that

Sweden's material and human resources were practically exhausted at the same time that Peter had seized the initiative, attaining brilliant successes while the internal reforms in Russia had started to bear the fruits essential for victory. The forces of the allies had also been strengthened and after the saga at Stettin they had been joined by the Prussian troops. Along with the Danes and the Saxons they besieged Stralsund, which fell in December 1715. Charles XII, who had led its defense, left for Sweden on one of the ships. The balance of power was manifestly tilting in favor of the allies; the great empire of the Swedes had reached its last days.

BIRTH OF THE EMPIRE

The Realization of Peter's State Ideal

On 22 October 1721 Petersburg solemnly celebrated the conclusion of the Peace of Nystadt, which closed the book on the Northern War. The detailed descriptions of this event and the prints of the Petrine era that have been preserved permit us to imagine that unforgettable day.

The action unfolded at the Trinity Cathedral, where in the presence of the highest nobility, officialdom, and generals the Senate awarded Peter the titles "Emperor," "Father of the Fatherland," and "The Great." After a festive church service the text of the Nystadt peace treaty was proclaimed. Trumpets sounded, kettle drums and military drums thundered, the dense smoke from the cannon salute blanketed the bastions of the Peter and Paul and Admiralty fortresses, and the 125 vessels of the Russian fleet stood in the Neva (we recall Pushkin: "And the Neva is shocked afar by the heavy firing"). When the salute's echo and the cries of "Vivat" subsided, Peter addressed those present with a speech that he had carefully prepared beforehand.

In thanking the Senate for recognizing his merits and citing, by the accepted standards of the time, God's special blessing to Russia, Peter seemingly reminded those present of the well-known expression: "Trust in God, but keep your powder dry." Warning of the necessity to strengthen the armed forces, he turned to the past for an example and recalled the fall of Byzantium to the Turkish attack, seeing its demise in the neglect of the needs of defense.

Especially important is the third point of Peter's speech, when he speaks of "the reorderings begun in the state" that are essential to finish ("so as to bring them to completion") in order that later, making use of the opportunities provided by the peace ("advantages"), there could be trade with other countries "so that the people might have relief thereby."[1] (Recall the basic idea of mercantilism that the revenues from commerce represent the main source of the state's prosperity.)

What did Peter have in mind in speaking of "the reorderings begun"? Undoubtedly he was referring to the whole complex of transformations and, above all, to the tax, church, and state reforms implemented during the last years of the Northern War and to the elaboration of new principles of external and internal policy-making.

Even three years before this triumphal speech, in a decree of 19 December 1718, Peter had written about himself (in the third person as was the accepted style):

> Yet His Majesty, despite his own unbearable toil in this burdensome war in which he was compelled not only to wage war but also to train people in everything anew and to make ordinances and codes of war with God's aid brought everything into such good order that it has now become superior to the former forces and yielded fruits that are known to everyone.
>
> At present, in ruling he has not neglected civil administration, but is laboring to bring it into the same good order as military affairs. Wherefore Colleges have been instituted, that is assemblies of many persons instead of the bureaus in which the presidents, or chairmen, do not have the same authority as the old judges [bureau administrators] who did what they wished. . . .[2]

Prideful awareness of the stature attained in the war and in the military reforms resounds in these words—indeed when they were being written negotiations were under way with the Swedes on the Åland Islands, and the war was supposed to end any minute with victory for Russia! But even before termination of the war Peter publicly announced that he had already undertaken the reform of the state machine, a most complex task, and that he even knew how and through which instruments it would be possible to attain justice and order. In general, in the language of Peter the Reformer to bring something "to order" meant to organize a sharp break with the old order, and in this instance the reform of "civil administration" meant a basic restructuring of the administration of the country on new principles. The decree cited allows us to understand the logic of the reformer's thinking: having created an army strong in its regularity, he would use the successful experience of the military reform to embark on the creation of an equally strong regulated state.

At the base of the restructuring of the state structure lay ideas of state-building that were widespread in Europe and about which I spoke in the first chapter. I shall briefly recite the gist: inasmuch as the state is not a God-given but a human creation, man himself may also perfect it, convert it into an ideal instrument for the transformation of society and the upbringing of virtuous subjects, and make it into an ideal institution through which one may attain "the common good"—humanity's desired end, which is constantly receding like the line of the horizon. The ceaseless working of the state mechanism (we recall Leibniz's "timepiece") is achieved with the aid of perfected laws and the institutions that bring them to life. Peter fully shared these ideas, as has already been said. Hence it is understandable that he attributed great significance to the reform of the state structure.

Here it is essential to underscore once again one aspect without which it is hard to understand many phenomena in Russian history. This is the state's role in the life of society. It is huge. In many respects everything progressive and reactionary starts from above. For Russia it had long been natural that public opinion does not determine legislation, but legislation forms (and even deforms) public opinion and social consciousness in the most powerful manner.

Proceeding from the concepts of rationalistic philosophy and traditional notions about the autocrat's role in Russia, Peter attributed great significance to written legislation. He sincerely believed that the "right" law, promptly issued and consistently implemented in practice, could do almost everything, starting with providing the people with bread and ending with the correction of manners. This is precisely why the legislation of the Petrine era rudely interfered in private life and fulfilled the functions of an intrusive "policing of manners," which will be discussed in detail later.

The tsar was convinced that consistent fulfillment ("preservation" in Peter's terminology) of "correct" laws is the key to the general prosperity and flourishing of the country, a universal panacea for all difficulties and failures which, he assumed, arose owing to "negligence in the laws" and poor "order," that is, organization. The great reformer of Russia dreamed of creating complete and comprehensive legislation that would encompass and regulate his subjects' entire life. He dreamed of an ideal state structure, like clockwork, through which this legislation could be implemented.

One may speak of the emergence under Peter of a real cult of bureaucratic institutions, of the administrative office. Not a single public structure, from commerce to the church, from the soldiers' barracks to private homes, could exist without administration, supervision, or oversight on the part of specially created offices of general or special designation.

Peter had long nurtured the idea of creating a complete state structure, but only when no doubts of victory over Sweden remained did he resolve to realize his dream. As has already been mentioned above, in this very period in many spheres of internal policy-making Peter turned away from the principles of naked coercion toward regulation of social phenomena by means of the bureaucratic machine. As the pattern for the proposed state reform, Peter selected the Swedish state organization.

In reviewing this reform, like many other of Peter's transformations, one cannot avoid the question of the extent of his borrowing of Western European experience. Often in the historical literature this problem is decided one of two ways: either through originality or through plagiarism. Some historians consider that Peter merely applied the Swedish state system to Russian circumstances by adapting it, whereas others see complete originality in the reforms, with the exception of several details like the term "college."

It appears that when one speaks of mutual influence, such an either/or presentation of the issue is far from scholarly. It is essential to know how and to what extent that which is taken from other cultures facilitated the strengthening of the political, social, and economic structure of the society that borrowed it. Glancing ahead, we shall note that the undoubted borrowing of Western European, more precisely Swedish, state experience, facilitated as a whole the strengthening of the Russian Empire's statehood. In general, Peter turned to the Western European experience for his reform activities whether it was legislation, culture, military affairs or everyday life. Still, why was the Swedish experience used more thoroughly than that of any other country? This is connected not so much with the several elements of similarity in the socioeconomic conditions of both countries as with Peter's personal passions. Holding the Swedish military and state organization in high regard, Peter aspired to surpass Sweden by exploiting its own experience both on the field of battle and in civilian life. The words he proclaimed on the day of the Poltava victory in honor of the Swedish instructors defeated by the student who had surpassed them are memorable.

If we admit that this is only an appealing legend, we still cannot disregard an unquestionably authentic testimony. In Amsterdam in 1716 the Swedish commission-secretary Preis met Peter. In a letter to Stockholm, Preis recalled that Peter "said that for what he had learned about waging war and had taught his own people about war he was indebted to none other than his majesty [Charles XII]."[3]

It is not surprising that once he achieved military victory over such a "regulated" people as the Swedes—recall the military reform!—Peter began reorganizing the Russian state by means of that same "regularity."

The Swedish state system had been built on the principles of cameralism, the teaching about bureaucratic administration that had spread in Europe in the sixteenth and seventeenth centuries. Cameralism contained a number of features quite attractive to Peter. First was the functional principle of administration that envisaged the creation of institutions specializing in some sphere, such as finances, military administration, or justice. Second was the organization of institutions on the bases of collegiality, distinct regimentation of the duties of officials, specialization of chancery work, and establishment of uniform staffing and salaries. For readers familiar with present-day bureaucratic procedure it is hard to discern anything new in principle in this regard. In fact, it is staring us in the face, for we must compare it with what had obtained prior to the reform, that had been at bottom a medieval structure of administration with its characteristic lack of specialization and division of functions, mixture of territorial and functional administration, and lack of coordination in the duties of officials, their status, and payment for work.

Using the Swedish administrative experience and taking Swedish prototypes as a basis, Peter as a rule introduced structural changes necessitated by the peculiarities of Russia. Sometimes the changes bore a purely cosmetic nature. Peter's general principle of dealing with Swedish institutions was expressed repeatedly and consistently, an example of which is the decree of 28 April 1718: "All Colleges are now required on the basis of the Swedish code to write up all matters and regulations according to points, and in the Swedish regulation whichever are inconvenient, or unsuited to the situation of this state, these are to be taken under consideration. And, taking them so, report back whether they should be so approved."[4]

The reform of the state structure was begun at the end of 1717 and the beginning of 1718 when Peter drew up a peculiar program of forthcoming reforms: he specified the number and jurisdictions of the colleges, designated their presidents, and enjoined the latter to select "subordinates or their own comrades," watching particularly "that there definitely not be any relatives or their own creatures."

From the beginning the group of colleges of military and foreign policy offices was singled out—the War College, the Admiralty, and the College of Foreign Affairs.

The first three colleges occupied a privileged position in the system of state institutions thanks to the enormous significance that Peter attributed to the army, the navy, and the diplomatic service, and also thanks to the enormous role in administration that their presidents played. They were the foremost of Peter's first associates: General–Field Marshal Most Serene Prince Alexander Menshikov, General-Admiral Count Fedor Apraksin, and Chancellor Count Gavriil Golovkin. These colleges did not arise in a vacuum. As we recall, at the start of the Northern War the creation of the new army, navy, and active diplomacy had required different forms of organization distinct from the old structure. The War and Admiralty bureaus and the Ambassadorial chancery (Ambassadorial bureau) had been clearly oriented to specialization. Quicker than anywhere else, the new collegial methods of conducting business were instituted in them. All this eased the subsequent transition to the colleges.

Of all the colleges, the group of financial colleges—the base of bases of the cameral system—was singled out for special attention. The foremost fiscal college became the Camer-College, which oversaw all money revenue and budgetary income planning. Expenditures on state needs were made through the Staffing-Office-College, which played the role of a central cashier, whereas oversight and accounting for the work of the financial organs was entrusted to the Revision-College, which was independent of the other colleges. The tripartite division of the fisc had tremendous significance in the state administration. In the old structure of bureaus these three financial functions—revenue, expenditure, and accounting—had been carried out by each bureau independently. As a rule, the bureau itself levied taxes on the population that went for its own needs and came under its own accounting. Now everything was changed fundamentally; the financial overlap of the seventeenth century was consolidated.

The creation of the Justice College held the same significance. It immediately replaced several judicial bureaus and took judicial functions from many bureaus that did not have legal competence. A sudden unification and centralization of justice came about—indeed the preform period had been characterized by an intermixture of administrative and judicial functions, and it was no accident that the leader of a bureau had been called a "judge." With the formation of the Justice College a sharp change had come about, but its significance should not be exaggerated, for in the process of specifying the competence of the new college, numerous social and professional groups of the population "fell out" of its jurisdiction. Townspeople, merchants, entrepreneurs, and workers were taken into the jurisdiction of the Commerce College, the Mines and Manufactories College, and the Main Municipal Administration; military personnel were supervised by the War College and the Admiralty College, monastery servitors by the Synod, and so forth. This was the cost of the estate structure that had existed in Russia in the pre-Petrine era.

A special place in the administrative system was taken by the colleges that supervised commerce and industry—the Commerce College and the Mines and Manufactories College—which will be discussed in detail in the following chapter. In 1720 the central institutions were joined by the Main Municipal Administration, the chief duty of which was the administration of the towns, including both judicial and administrative authority.

The composition of the Petrine colleges during Peter's lifetime underwent substantial change. In 1721 the Spiritual College, or Synod, was formed and removed from subordination to the Senate. In 1722 the Manufactories College was detached from the Mines and Manufactories College, the Little Russia College was formed in the town of Glukhov for the administration of the Ukraine, and from the Justice College the Patrimony Office was made into a separate Patrimony College. The Revision and Staffing Colleges lost the status of central institutions and became offices of the Senate. In 1721 there were eleven colleges in all, whereas in 1723 there were only ten.

The colleges became the core of the central system of administration even though quite a few petty institutions were retained from the old bureau structure: the Palace, Postal, Printing, Medical, and Policemaster chanceries, the Preobrazhensky Bureau, and several others.

Constantly confronting the celebrated "Muscovite red tape" that was typical of the activities of the bureaus, Peter became convinced that in the work of the state machine maximum effectiveness could be achieved only through detailed regimentation of the activities of all institutions and each of the officials. This conviction of his fully corresponded to the cameral system, which was simply inconceivable without a document drafted and followed in detail, a regulation that specified everything essential for the existence of the bureaucratic institution: its functions, the duties of the officials, the routine of work, official procedures, and remuneration for work. Peter, however, went further than the Western European theorists and practitioners of cameralism. The idea of creating a whole hierarchy of regulations belongs to him. With the tsar's participation an unprecedented document was created, a peculiar regulation of regulations, the General Regulation of 1719–24. It contained the most general principles of the activity of the bureaucratic machine, of all state institutions. Each of them, moreover, had its own regulation that specified the peculiarities of the work of that particular institution. The duties of each official were written down, in turn, in the "duties" or instructions included in the college's regulation. Typical of the all-encompassing regimentation of Peter's thinking was the 1722 regulation of the Admiralty College, which he drafted himself and considered the prototype for the regulation of a central institution. In this regulation fifty-six duties had been entered, beginning with the president's extensive duties and ending with the brief and even jocular

duties of the provost: "He must see that in the Admiralty nobody defe-
cates except in the places appointed. And if somebody should defecate
in other than the appointed places, he is to be beaten with the cat of
nine tails and ordered to clean it up."[5]

Regulations, as Peter conceived them, were definitely not simply instructions. Here it is important to note that for Peter—the reformer of
the state—there was a characteristic urge to transfer military principles
into the sphere of civilian life and state administration. This was manifested both in the direct extension to civilian administration of military
legislation and in the attribution to laws defining the work of civilian
institutions of the significance and force of military codes.

Treating the regulation of a civilian institution like a military code
took on special clarity in Peter's decree of 20 January 1724: "Add to the
procurator's duties that the regulations be followed in everything just as
firmly as the military regulation and enjoin it strictly for all members
and subordinates, and extract from the regulation and read it as it is
read to the soldiers and sailors [from the Articles of War]." [6]

A similar attitude to civilian legislation led to the creation of a system
of punishing officials hardly different from that applied to the military.
In February 1722 Peter ordered that for truancy, civilians were to be
fined the same as the military. In October 1723 he began creating a
special code of punishments that divided all crimes into two categories:
state and private (individual). For state crimes brutal punishments were
laid down, up to and including death. It should be said that neither
before nor after Peter were there issued in Russia such a huge number
of decrees that punished state crimes with death. Peter composed a
special "explication" clarifying the reasons for the severity of the punishments for state crimes that concluded with "in scorn for one's duty."

The "explication" strikingly recalls in its ideas that part of the Articles
of War that discusses the duties of the general–field marshal, who might
ruin the army by two vices—cupidity and "negligence." Here we see the
very same thing—the apprehension that the state as well as the army
will fall from "negligence," lapse of discipline, and violation of instructions. Peter is inclined to consider the "bribery" and "negligence" of
officials even more harshly than the military crime of treason.[7]

Thus, for Peter it is typical to treat a state institution as a military
unit, a regulation as a military code, and an official as a military servitor.
Nikolai Pavlenko has rightly remarked: "For Peter institutions that resembled barracks seemed ideal, as did servitors of the institutions re-
sembling military ranks that executed decrees with the same dispatch as
soldiers and officers executed the military codes."

Another scholar, the American James Cracraft, who has devoted special attention to the military basis of Peter's personal life, writes that militarization appeared in everything: Peter not only dressed like a soldier, but acted and thought like a soldier. It is no accident, Cracraft contends, that Peter introduced into everyday public discourse the concept of the "generalitet" as "an estate of the realm equal in dignity to the body of senior civil administrators and to the hierarchy of the church."[8]

Military laws founded on principles proven by the dangerous experience of combat had shown convincingly, in Peter's view, the advantages of this military model. Military discipline is the means through which it is possible to inculcate in people love for order, labor, consciousness, and Christian morality. (One recalls the well-known joke of Koz′ma Prutkov, the literary hero of the nineteenth century: "In sight of ammunition at the ready how scorned are all constitutions.") The forthrightness of the Articles of War and its obvious effectiveness on the battlefield tempted Peter to extend the military basis both to civilian administration and to society as a whole. When you analyze the development of Peter's ideas about the state and the reform of administration this conscious orientation of the tsar to military prototypes, and the attribution to the state of features of a single grandiose military organism, strikes you in the face.

The structure of the chief element of this organism, the college, was rather simple: the college in itself (later it was called a "sitting") and the chancery were a business department in which the chancery servitors worked. Departments of the college were offices that supervised any particular branch of administration.

How did a college work? The General Regulation and the numerous supplements to it laid down a definite routine for the work of a bureaucratic institution. Its work consisted in oversight of the unity of time and place of bureaucratic action: at a specified time of the week or day and only in the college's building.

Actually this meant that on the day and hour appointed for the sitting the members of the college assembled in the audience-chamber for the session. The presiding person, the president, opened the session; the secretary announced the list of affairs to be reviewed, which were enumerated one after the other. Then ensued the most important secret of the collegial form of administration. Depending on the matter heard, a proposal for a resolution was worked out, each of those present beginning with the most junior in rank gave his opinion, and the majority decided the fate of the matter.

The General Regulation defined the collegial form of administration rather succinctly. But, in acquainting oneself with it, one sees that the single guarantee of the correct application of the collegial basis appears to be moral notions: the fear of offending God, betraying the tsar, or besmirching conscience or honor. Of course, in the institutions of that time there were quite a few persons for whom these notions would have been a moral law, but there were also many who might violate the provisions that required honesty and principles and who did not fear to incriminate themselves before God, the tsar, or a superior, or to contradict their own conscience, morals, and duty. All this, of course, was taken into account by Peter, who along with moral norms had introduced a series of juridical institutions implementing surveillance over the activities of officials—a subject that will be discussed later.

There were three kinds of servitors in the college: members of the college, chancery servitors, and so-called "lower servitors"—couriers, guards, watchmen, and soldiers. The central figure of the collegiate council was the president, who exercised the administration of the college in the tsar's name and therefore had a right to special respect from the members of the college.

The tsar-reformer did everything to ensure that the president in his authority would not recall the earlier single-person judge of the bureau. About this the aforementioned decree of 19 December 1718 had spoken, that is, at the very beginning of the reform: "Wherefore colleges have been instituted, that is assemblies of many persons (instead of the bureaus) in which the presidents or chairmen do not have such power as the old judges who did what they wished. In the college, however, the president cannot do anything without the agreement of his comrades, and likewise there are other great obligations that take away the old inclinations to do [wrong], as soon as regulations (or charters) will be published and the duties of all the colleges made known to the people."[9]

Peter laid great hopes on the institution's very mechanism, assuming that it would by itself force the officials to follow the laws of duty, honor, and conscience that guarantee collegiality. In looking over the protocols of the college, however, only occasionally do we encounter traces of disputes and disagreements among the members of the sitting. There are many reasons for this. On one hand, the college reviewed matters that basically conformed to the norms of legislation and therefore did not evoke disputes. The bureaucratic commonplace of resolving such matters did not presuppose disagreements if, of course, peace prevailed among the members of the college and nobody's special interests were involved. But, as a rule, these interests were manifested not at the sessions of the council of the college, but earlier, somewhere behind the scene.

On the other hand, there could not be any real equality among the council members. The presidents were, as a rule, the most influential of Peter's statesmen with whom it would have been risky to disagree. It is known that General–Fiscal Colonel Aleksei Miakinin attempted to unmask the financial machinations of Menshikov, who "persuaded" the subordinate military leaders to review the matter in such a way that Miakinin was sentenced to be shot for slander, whereas Menshikov got off scot-free. Recalling this story, a member of the War College—a certain modest Colonel Karaulov or one of his comrades—did not even consider opposing his powerful patron, the president of the college, who, according to the letter of the regulation, was his equal in formal terms.

Councilors and assessors constituted the bulk of the college members. Within the college, business was distributed among them.

The members were joined at the sitting in the audience-chamber by one more official, who was completely independent of the college and had important powers. This was the college's procurator, a post of extraordinary significance in the system of the Petrine bureaucracy. He oversaw the implementation of the institution's directives.

From the second group—the "chancery servitors"—the secretary occupied the most important position. His duties were close to those of the bureau's secretary and consisted of managing business: the receipt and processing of incoming correspondence, the preparation of matters for report, and the preparation and dispatch of decisions and outgoing documents.

In accordance with Swedish staffing arrangements, three new positions appeared among the corps of college servitors: notary, actuary, and registrar. The notary compiled the protocols of the college's sessions (therefore he was often called a protocolist), then sewed all the protocols into a book, and also kept track of "resolved" and "unresolved" matters. The actuary dealt exclusively with incoming correspondence, putting it through preliminary processing. The registrar conducted the subsequent systematization of correspondence as well as recording incoming and outgoing papers.

Secretaries, notaries, actuaries, registrars, and also translators and fiscals were the chancery's aristocracy as it were, sharply differentiated from the great bulk of servitors by their role in bureaucratic action, their salary, and their position. Clerks—the direct processors of files who were occupied, as in the past, with rewriting papers—constituted the chancery's plebes. In the bureaus there had been three forms of clerks: senior, middle, and junior subsecretaries. All of them turned up in the college even though they accordingly began to be called chanceryists, subchanceryists, and copyists.

The chanceryists, subchanceryists, and copyists made up the majority of those serving in the new institutions. The growth of the bureaucratic machine during the years of the reform occurred mainly on their account. On the eve of the reform the central administration had had 1,169 servitors in all, with the chanceryists composing 79 percent, or 924 persons. In 1723, when the reform was completed, the number of chancery servitors in Russia had more than doubled, reaching the figure of 1,962 persons, which amounted to 93.4 percent of the total number of servitors at the time (2,100 persons).

The general trend of a growing bureaucratic machine, which had been noticeable in the course of the state reforms, received further development in the post-Petrine era, and all the efforts of the higher authorities to curtail the machine were in vain. At our disposal are data from 1723 about the official work of the comparatively small Commerce College. During one year the college received from the Senate, Synod, colleges, and other institutions and also from private persons 1,684 documents. Furthermore, from the sittings 1,041 documents (resolutions, extracts) came to the chancery. In all 2,725 documents poured into the chancery. During the same period 1,702 "outgoing" documents were dispatched to other institutions. In sum, in one year almost 4,500 documents passed through the offices of the Commerce College. That same year this college had thirty-two servitors.[10] In other colleges there were many more: 228 persons in the Camer-College, 353 in the War College, and so forth. One must assume that the amount of paper passing through the bureaucratic conveyors increased commensurately. If we calculate the direct connection between the amount of paper and the number of servitors, then the 1,412 servitors of all the colleges must have worked on a minimum of 200,000 documents per year and therefore—for the first five years of work—not less than one million documents. The figure is impressive if one takes into account that the taxable population of Russia at that time amounted to no more than twelve million persons.

Incidentally, an even greater impression comes from a fact cited in the textbook *The Theory and Practice of Archival Work* (Moscow, 1980, p. 63). It turns out that in the USSR "in institutions, enterprises, and organizations . . . there are annually prepared up to 100 billion documents, which comprise no less than one billion files." It's easy to make a calculation: for each of the country's 280 million inhabitants no less than 357 documents are produced per year.

The reform of the central administration was introduced in tandem with reform of the higher administration. The crux of the reforms consisted of changing the structure, competence, and composition of the highest governmental institution, the Senate, for purposes of adapting it to the new system of collegial institutions.

The Senate's new position in the system of authority was reflected most fully in the "Duties of the Senate," a special instruction that defined the authority, structure, and procedures of the Senate under the new conditions. From 1718 through 1722 Peter reworked the proposed "Duties" six times—so important was this document for him.

The "Duties" immediately defined the high stature of the Senate as the preserver of state interests: "Once and for all it is stated—it is always fitting for the Senate to have ceaseless concern about the monarchical and state benefit, to extend the good and to thwart totally everything that could be harmful."

Accordingly, the responsibility of the senators themselves was raised: they were charged to safeguard their own dignity as the apple of their eye.

This caution to the senators was not accidental. Peter knew well the constant dissension that divided statesmen and which was manifested quite often at the Senate sessions. In a decree of 2 October 1718 to the senators and the presidents of the colleges Peter wrote with vexation: "And also upon arrival, whether for this matter or to the Senate, there should be no useless words or babbling, but speak at this time about nothing but the matter at hand. Likewise, whoever starts to speak, another is not to interrupt, but let him finish and then let another speak, as befits honest people, and not like old women haggling at market."[11]

The Senate occupied a key position in the Petrine state system. It concentrated judicial, administrative, and legal-consultative functions and supervised the guberniias and, above all, the colleges and other central institutions. At the start, in 1718, Peter directed that all the presidents of the colleges should be included in the Senate. The idea, of course, was a tempting one—the collegial principle pervaded the entire administration: the colleges would be administered by a college of the presidents of the colleges. Yet this idea soon had to be rejected: concentrating the duties of president and senator in the same hands did not yield the desired effect, and besides, the presidents were overloaded by work in their own colleges.

The Senate functioned according to collegial principles. The unity of place, time, and composition of a sitting, conditions essential for the Senate's activity as a bureaucratic institution, was preserved and specified by the "Duties."

The appointment and confirmation of practically all officials in the new institutions became an important function of the Senate. The rules according to which secret balloting was first introduced into Russia afford particular interest. These rules are called the "Mode of Balloting" and are dated 18 February 1720. Peter, apparently the author of the "Mode," foresaw the most petty details of the process of balloting.[12]

The most detailed description of all the nuances of voting is governed not so much by the unfamiliar innovation as by Peter's urge to arrange the whole procedure so that it would be impossible to falsify the results. Here and in other decrees Peter clearly exhibited his favorite ideas of detailed and harsh regimentation of all actions of the state machine, the only means, in the tsar's eyes, to guarantee legality and to prevent abuses. Here, too, as in the application of the principle of collegiality, failure awaited Peter: it is evident that separate democratic institutions operating in the general framework of authoritarian power and even in its interests are inevitably undermined. The choice of the box into which to throw balls in balloting depended least of all on how the officials would be seated beforehand and the box brought to them: the one elected was he who appeared suitable and needed by the leadership and who had been tapped beforehand.

The decree of 12 January 1722 occupies a special place in the history of the state reform. It obviously testifies to Peter's ability to take heed of a changing situation and correct the reform plans. Understanding all the absurdity of the situation whereby the presidents in the capacity of senators were supposed to judge themselves, Peter by this decree removed the presidents from the Senate and acknowledged the failure of his own venture to create a college of colleges. Furthermore, the decree deepened the reform of the Senate and laid down several new principles that strengthened the Senate's significance in the system of administration.

This decree created a most important control office in the autocratic state of the eighteenth century—the procuracy. Peter had long been moving toward its organization, appointing guards officers to the Senate to watch over the senators, then Vasily Zotov to the post of general-inspector. Here, finally, in 1722 according to a French prototype the general-procurator appeared in the state machine in Russia. In the first draft of the "Duties of the General-Procurator" he was called a specially trusted official, "an attorney from the master and from the state."

It would hardly be worthwhile to review one more bureaucratic position if the matter did not concern the creation of an entire institution headed by the general-procurator, a public institution of open surveillance. Besides the position of general-procurator, which was occupied by one of Peter's closest associates, Pavel Yaguzhinsky, a special procurator's office was formed under the Senate, the position of senior-procurator—assistant to the general-procurator—was introduced, and above all the position of procurator was introduced throughout the central institutions. The college and court procurators were independent of their own institutions and were subordinated directly to the general-procurator.[13]

Peter laid great hopes on the effectiveness of the procuracy's work. But in order to guard his system from official wrongdoing, Peter considered it essential to duplicate the institution of open state surveillance by an institution of secret surveillance. This concerns the fiscals—officials whose designated duties became sadly renowned in Russia.

The most important principles of the activity of the fiscality, an institution widespread in Western Europe, were secrecy and impunity. The fiscal did not bear responsibility for false delations, for, as a decree of 1714 affirmed, "it is impossible to keep account of everything in detail."[14] Documents convey to us the extremely negative attitude of contemporaries toward the fiscals. On one hand, the very nature of the activity of the secret overseers and delators in state service, who were protected by law from punishment for a false delation, caused them to be shunned, and their work was dirty, unscrupulous, and linked to tale bearing, and it trampled on moral standards. On the other hand, for officials prone to enriching themselves at the expense of the fisc, the fiscals' activity posed a real danger. Peter supported the fiscals by every means, presuming that when interests of state were involved it was essential to act in moral terms.

The Senate reform facilitated the development of the institution of the fiscality on an entirely new level. In 1723 a general-fiscal was appointed, and in 1725 the "Duties" that had been drafted by Peter for the general-fiscal and his assistant, the senior fiscal, were published.

A ramified institution of local fiscals had been created under the general oversight of the general-fiscal and the senior fiscal. The institutions of the procuracy and the fiscality were closely connected: the fiscals reported to the procurators and to the general-fiscal, who was subordinate to the general-procurator.

The procuracy and the fiscality were links in a single chain of state control that Peter had created in connection with the reform of the Senate and also in connection with the reform of the law courts. Even in the 1710s Peter had been seriously occupied with court reform, the purpose of which was, as aforementioned, to separate judicial from administrative functions. The formation of guberniias in 1708 had presupposed providing the governor with an assistant, the sheriff (*landrikhter*) to whom the supervision of justice was delegated. In reality, however, such a division of authority did not occur, and the notion of separating the court from the administration, as M.M. Bogoslovsky aptly remarked, merely "flickered under Peter."[15] But even that was quite a lot for the Russia of the time.

Peter made great efforts to organize and direct the flood of complaints coming into the central and higher institutions. In 1720 the office of Master of Requests was created under the Senate, headed by the senior master of requests, to whom petitions with complaints about officials of different ranks were sent. Concerning these the general-master of requests was supposed to report to the tsar and to the senators.

The creation of a new, full-fledged state machine, founded on the principles of cameralism—subordination, differentiation, regimentation—would have been impossible if the reform had not touched the lowest link of administration—the local offices. It was natural that the regional reform was introduced in tandem with the reform of the central and higher offices and was based on the very same principles. Furthermore, in creating the new regional administration the Swedish administrative experience had likewise been used, which was reflected in the proposals of Heinrich Fick, Peter's agent who had spent time in Sweden and had carefully studied the Swedish administrative system.

Fick's proposals, which reproduced the Swedish structure of local administration, were discussed in the Senate and were accepted as the basis with certain changes that took into account Russia's specific circumstances.

In Peter's directive of 9 May 1718 there is talk about analyzing and changing the Swedish regional system, which was tripartite in structure: parish (*kirkhshpil'*), district (*kherad*), and regional, at the head of which stood the official mentioned by Peter, the landkhevding. For Peter and his associates there was much to think about: the Swedish system was different in principle from the Russian, more precisely from what they wished to create.[16]

The lowest important link of Swedish administration was the parish. Its activities were based on the active participation in administration of the people, the peasants, and electors from whom entered the administrative and court offices of the parish. Moreover, an important role was played by the pastor, the highest moral authority in the parish. Having acquainted himself with the parish system, Peter and the senators rejected it completely: there could be no thought of any participation in administration by the people and clergy in the system of Russian autocracy. Refusing for Russia the system of lower elected ranks, the Senate directed: "There not be a *kirkhshpil'fokht* [parish warden] and electors from the peasants with the courts or in administration because all kinds of orders and dispatches come by order from the towns, and not from the churches; and besides in the district from the peasantry there are no qualified persons."[17] And this was said about a people who, acting on the regional and communal tradition of long ago, had once saved the country and the throne from destruction! Anyway, it is hardly surprising that authoritarian power and bureaucratic disdain for the "stupid" people went hand in hand.

Two other elements of the Swedish system were preserved. The province became the basic unit of regional administration. The eleven guberniias that existed at the time were subdivided into forty-five and then into fifty provinces. The guberniias were not abolished, although the governor's authority extended only to the province of the guberniia capital. It is noteworthy that in the future—under Catherine II (1762–96)—the Petrine provinces became guberniias.

The provinces were divided into districts in which land commissars were placed: overall leadership of the provinces was exercised by provincial governors, who were subordinated directly to the Senate, except for military affairs and court appeals in which they were subordinated to the guberniia governors. The instruction to the provincial governors adopted in 1719 made them full-fledged rulers in their provinces. Under their leadership were placed the offices of the kamerirs, or "supervisors of land taxes," and also the rent office, where money was kept. Furthermore, the provincial governors oversaw the chanceries for recruiting levies, investigatory affairs, provisioning, customs collection, and other institutions.

With the introduction of the second regional reform the network of local institutions became noticeably thicker than before, and it is no longer necessary to compare it with pre-Petrine Russia: the sparse districts looked like an anachronism in comparison with the powerful, ramified structure of guberniias, provinces, and districts.

The principles of cameralism had also been laid down at the base of the regional setup that arose by the end of Peter's reign. All the local institutions were closely linked to the corresponding central organs—the colleges. Uniformity and "regularity" had been instituted from top to bottom and accomplished through the unity of internal arrangement, clarity of mutual subordination, and identity of the competence of the personnel and the offices of one administrative level on the entire territory of the country. Henceforth, the bureaucratic principle of uniformity had been activated that often ignored each region's specific identity. Thus Kungur Province in Siberia did not differ at all in its setup from Starorusa in the northwest or Saratov on the lower Volga. The state that had been built on a regular basis was also supposed to aspire to uniformity: this facilitated, as it seemed to its creators, the realization of the decrees from the center and control over their implementation.

Peter's urge to organize the state according to military models naturally increased the role of the military in society and the state. There is no doubt that the state and military reforms had led to a quite definite division of the military and civil services, which was subsequently confirmed by the celebrated Table of Ranks. At the same time, however,

the Petrine reforms signified a broad expansion of the practice of utiliz-
ing professional military men in state administration. This was manifested not only in the ease of appointing military men to civilian posts,
but also in their frequent employment (especially Guardsmen) in the
capacity of emissaries of the tsar and of the higher institutions. It became commonplace to dispatch sergeants and officers of the Guards to
guberniias, provinces, and districts, where they were entrusted with extraordinary commissions and fulfilled the role of peculiar "trouble-
shooters" and "expediters." For failure to execute decrees they had the
right "to incarcerate in fetters, on a chain, and in irons" any officials
and hold them for an unlimited time.

It is relevant to recall that in abolishing the strel'tsy regiments that
had played such a major political role in the events of the 1680s and
1690s, Peter had scornfully called them "janissaries." At that time he
could scarcely have supposed that his cherished Guards regiments, the
flower of the Russian army, would fulfill the same function that the
strel'tsy had done in the time of Tsarevna Sophia, deposing and install-
ing rulers on the throne. The notorious palace revolutions of the eighteenth century, so typical for the political history of the Russian Empire,
reflected not just the struggle of political groupings that were hardly
distinguishable from one another in their aspirations and policies, but
also the exaggerated significance that the military element had assumed
in the public life of the capital and the empire.

The practice of using military men in the civil administration, which
may be partly explained by the critical situation at the start of the
Northern War, was not abolished in more peaceful times, but became
systematic and normal, underscoring the military-bureaucratic crux of
the empire Peter had created. It is important to note that the well-
known integration of civilian and military institutions led to the subordination of the former to the latter even in peacetime. This tendency
may be observed with special clarity in the history of tax reform, a
typical financial enterprise as a result of which the soul tax was introduced in Russia in 1724.

The reform of tax assessment was a direct product of the necessity to
resolve the problem of supporting the army in peacetime. Having finished the Northern and the Persian wars, Peter had no intention of
cutting back the huge army or of altering the program of building a
seagoing navy. The size of the regular army in peacetime did not decrease, but on the contrary, grew. If in 1711 the armed forces (infantry
and cavalry) had comprised 106,000 men (as specified by the staffing
regulations of 1711), then in 1720–21 the overall size of the infantry
and cavalry had reached almost 121,000 men while retaining the same

proportion of field artillery and not counting 74,000 garrison troops who had formerly been the field army's reserves.[18]

While the war was on and the army was on campaign or defending the frontiers, the problem of its maintenance had not seemed complicated. Extraordinary taxes and imposts, the forcible extraction of provisions, forage, transport, and the like from the population of other countries and from one's own citizens—all these and similar means of maintaining the army had been used in full measure, formally justified by the harshness of war. But with the arrival of peace the situation had to change. In 1718–19 the regiments had already begun returning home from abroad. Peter found a temporary, but important task for them: soldiers were assigned to major construction sites that required massive labor. These included fortresses, harbors, and canals. Thus, on 8 February 1717 Peter, informing the Senate of the army's imminent withdrawal from Poland, wrote: ". . . inasmuch as presently there is nothing for them to do anywhere, and they receive their salary free, I therefore consider it necessary to take half of them for work on the canal that will be built from Tosna to Tver', and so, upon receiving this decree, execute it."[19]

To occupy the regiments with construction work was to create a peculiar "labor army"—this was a temporary solution and, of course, did not fully resolve the acute problem of maintaining and billeting the troops within the country in peacetime. Therefore, Peter's imagination worked frenetically over this task, and at the start of the 1720s a solution was found.

The solution involved a reform of tax assessment begun in 1719 and basically completed in 1724. Its thrust was that instead of dozens of different petty taxes and imposts a single direct money tax was introduced that went directly for the army's needs. This soul tax was collected from all souls "of the male sex" entered on the tax rolls.

Besides its purely financial effect the reform led to an essential change in the fate of the regular army. According to the reformer's idea, which had been taken from the Swedish practice of maintaining the army in peacetime, the regiments were quartered directly among those same peasants from whom the taxes were collected for the maintenance of the soldiers and officers. This permitted one to shorten substantially the route of the money from the pockets of the peasants into the regimental cashboxes, for a series of intervening financial links was abolished.

The censuses, as a rule, were also carried out by the forces of the army itself, which detached substantial contingents of military servitors for that purpose. Thus the first census was instituted in the years 1721–

24. In 1725 Field Marshal Mikhail Golitsyn informed the War College of the chronic shortage of officers in the army. He wrote that "in the regiments there are no staff officers, as the greater part of them are with the census takers," that is, working on the census of the population. General data indicate that no less than 45 percent of the army's staff and senior officers were used in the capacity of census takers during the first census.[20]

For the collection of the soul impost from the peasants, so-called land commissars, responsible for the transfer of money to the regiments, were mustered from the local nobility. After the end of the Persian War and especially in 1724 the regiments themselves were stationed in the central guberniias around Moscow, the center of the gigantic circle of the resettled army.

Wherever the commander of the regiment lived, the regiment's headquarters was built, and in the localities that billeted companies, a company headquarters was set up. The companies were settled in a radius of 50–100 versts from the company headquarters, with Peter requiring that the soldiers be settled as densely as possible among the hamlets.

Besides the company headquarters, households were established for the officers and their servants, staff and quartermaster accommodations, and infirmaries. The following proportion was selected after careful preliminary calculations for the settlement of the troops: 47 peasants could maintain 1 foot soldier (at a cost of 28.5 rubles per year) by a soul tax of 70 kopecks, whereas 57 peasants were required for a cavalryman because the cost for him and his horse amounted to 40 rubles.

In this fashion the entire populace of the central guberniias were "assigned" to the army, the regiments of which they were supposed to accept and quarter on their own territory.

In general, the history of Russia had not known anything like it—the military aspect of Peter's tax reform meant that regular military detachments were stationed in practically every district of all guberniias except for Siberia, the population of which, because of the guberniia's remoteness, was limited to paying money for the maintenance of "its" regiments, which were left in the center of the country. The peasant population of all the other guberniias had to make a choice whether to billet the soldiers in their own homes, as had long been done, or to build special settlements for them with their own money and efforts, for which it was proposed to cut off lands from landlord and peasant fields. In this fashion, besides paying the soul tax the peasant population of Russia was either assessed the billeting obligation or had to make substantial compensation in the form of payments for building settlements.

The reaction of the peasants and landlords, on whose lands the regiments suddenly began to arrive and settle, was sharply negative: billeting—that most burdensome imposition of wartime—was now becoming a standing institution in peacetime, as it were. There is no denying the discontent that swept across the country, for it is well known that in later times disobedient peasants who rioted against the landlord or the authorities were punished by arranging to station in these hamlets soldiers, who literally ruined their hosts, raping and plundering. In short, billeting appeared more fearsome than mass executions and exile. It is no accident that through all of the subsequent history of Russia freedom from the billeting impost was looked on as a most desirable privilege, and a few of the most substantial villagers and townspeople succeeded in attaining it only by providing special services to the state or by giving large bribes.

Having made the billeting impost permanent, Peter naturally strove to soften its inevitably negative consequences, which he of course knew about. His greatest hopes were placed, as might be guessed, on laws that were supposed to regulate relations between the population and the army. The most important laws of this kind became the "Schedule of Payments" and the "Instructions for the Colonel" of 1724. Both documents had been drafted with the very active participation of Peter himself, the real inspirer of the tax reform. It should be noted that both documents presumed, first of all, the army's direct participation in collecting the soul tax, and second, made the colonel—the senior military commander in the localities billeting the regiments—the chief arbiter in all potential disputes and disagreements between the populace and the army.

The state institutions (local, central, and higher) represented a structure, similar to a pyramid tapering at the top, at the apex of which stood the autocrat, who exercised supreme unlimited authority.

In chapter 1 much was said about the political, ideological, and personal aspects of the authority of the autocrat Peter the First. Now, however, the state and bureaucratic aspect of this authority should be treated. There is nothing strange in posing the question this way: as soon as the autocrat stands at the apex of the bureaucratic pyramid he has created, then it is natural that he must fulfill a series of functions defined by the structure and functions of the pyramid.

In principle, organization of the central and higher institutions created by Peter did not presuppose the autocrat's participation in their activities. The reformer had attempted to resolve the principal task of creating such a bureaucratic machine, all the parts of which would work smoothly, according to the regulations adopted. This ceaselessly working machine was supposed to process all matters rapidly and efficiently, primarily by applying legislation in force. Quite a few of Peter's resolutions have come down to us in which he insisted that matters that fell under the corresponding principles be reviewed in the institutions without referring them directly to him: "Implement according to the state rules," "Resolve according to the rules forthrightly," and so forth.

Peter demanded that he be sent only disputed matters or those without precedent. Thus, in a decree of 19 December 1718 addressed to court procedure, it is said: ". . . if such a disputed new and most difficult matter actually be presented from petitioners which the Senate cannot itself resolve according to the Law Code without a report and without a personal decree from H.Ts.M., then report it, besides the petitioners (in which there is already necessity) to the Senate, to his majesty. . . . And, having received a decree, resolve it."

This directive was a consequence of established practice under which a multitude of petitioners besieged the tsar wherever he went. It was no accident that in this decree of 19 December Peter literally begged for mercy:

> Inasmuch as petitioners constantly bother His Tsarist Majesty with their complaints everywhere in all places and give him no peace, and although on their part it were easy to consider that for each his complaint is bitter and unbearable, at the same time it is fitting for each to consider what a multitude of them there are, whereas it is one person they petition, and he is surrounded by so much military and other burdensome work that it is known to everyone. And even if there were not such work, would it be possible for one man to look after so many? In truth neither for a man nor even for an angel, inasmuch as even for these (there is a definite place) for wherever he is present, he cannot be elsewhere.[21]

It is quite amusing that Peter publicly dispersed the slightest suspicion of his belonging to the host of angels. Noteworthy is the image in the given decree of a bureaucratic angel incapable of rushing everywhere at once. It was completely in the spirit of the time. As we have seen, the first Russian "regular" bureaucrats already wielded enormous authority and bore on their narrow shoulders the burden of unprecedented concern for the good of the people; they suffered from innumerable and impertinent petitioners who by their requests obstructed them from working for the latter's own "general good."

Peter demanded that he be given only the most important matters, accusations of state crimes. That same principle of selectivity was applied in the administrative sphere, which was reflected in the decree of 17 April 1722.

Thus it was supposed to be, ideally. How was it in practice? The materials prepared and partly published by the Commission for Publishing the Letters and Papers of Peter the Great allow us to judge the tsar's "functioning" as the leader of the state machine. During the years 1713–25 Peter dispatched in all 7,584 letters and decrees. If we divide them into two groups—before and after the state reforms, 1713–18 and 1719–25—then we shall see that after the formation of the colleges and the Senate reform Peter's individual activities did not decrease significantly. For the six years preceding the reform he dispatched 3,877 letters and decrees, whereas for the six years after the formation of the colleges and the reform of the Senate 3,707 documents were dispatched. Analysis of the content of Peter's decisions shows that the distribution of decrees according to branches of administration after the reform changed only slightly. As before, Peter was occupied with a mass of current affairs, which in principle should have been given out for decision to the state machine.

The breakdown of Peter's personal decrees by types is remarkable. Some decrees were completely written by Peter, others represent his resolutions on reports, still others are merely signed by his hand, and some were transmitted via some institution or officials.

Reviewing the corpus of laws that Peter worked with in the years 1720–25 (3,019 documents), it can be established that over half of them (more exactly 1,779 or 59 percent) were written by him alone or were shaped by his resolutions. It is remarkable that with the establishment of the new administrative system Peter's personal share in administration scarcely diminished in practice: in 1720 his "personal" decrees amounted to 54.2 percent of the total number of decrees issued that year; as a proportion of all personal decrees for each year they were 42.6 percent in 1721, 56.3 percent in 1722, 56.3 percent in 1723, and 62.4 percent in 1724–25.[22] By contrast, the number of decrees that Peter simply signed was quite small and remained stable from year to year. Hence it is hardly possible to say that with the implementation of the state reforms the tsar's load in resolving the bulk of ordinary affairs decreased, for which he constantly struggled.

Such a plethora of affairs directly reviewed by the autocrat should have had some organizational preparation; a mechanism should have existed through which the monarch could function in the system of state authority.

The Cabinet of His Imperial Majesty created in 1704, at the head of which stood Peter's cabinet-secretary Aleksei Makarov, became such a transmission link. Speaking in today's idiom, the Cabinet was the autocrat's secretariat in which under Makarov's leadership a whole staff of subclerks worked preparing documents for the tsar. Furthermore, the Cabinet managed the tsar's personal property and acted as his paymaster, for huge sums came into his cashbox from the salt impost.

It should be mentioned that over time the Cabinet's work became marked by a definite trend of intensifying bureaucratization of the autocrat's activities in executing the functions of supreme authority. With the reinforcement of the Cabinet's significance as a peculiar institution "under the master's person," to report anything, to denounce, to propose, and to request became synonymous with directing the corresponding document to the Cabinet, where it would be registered and reworked in order that later on, along with similar documents, it would be included in the form of "points" or "extracts" in a report to the tsar. The report read by Makarov with Peter's resolutions in the margins was returned to the Cabinet and became the basis for a decree or a cover letter from Makarov to the official to whom the "report" was directed.

In 1721 a document appeared with the designation "A prescription of how to keep order in the affairs in the Cabinet office." This document forthrightly insisted that the Cabinet is not a room, the emperor's working cabinet, where at tables loaded with papers the modest Makarov sits and writes with his aides, but a state bureaucratic institution with its own structure, procedures, staff, and even seal. There is no need to dwell on the notion that the Cabinet worked according to the same principles by which the whole bureaucratic machine of the time worked. "Regular" movement of papers is the main thing required of the institution.

Naturally every kind of bureaucratization that focuses on the movement of papers gives the figure of the bureaucrat pride of place. Aleksei Makarov became such a figure in the upper rungs of the administration in the Petrine era. In practice not a single document addressed to Peter bypassed him. Makarov was thus made the irreplaceable link between the emperor and the state machine. As Nikolai Pavlenko has shown in revealing the sources of Makarov's extraordinary influence, the cabinet-secretary's significance was so great that statesmen of diverse stature wrote about their own affairs to the tsar and to Makarov at the same time, requesting his assistance and providing additional information about the crux of the problem. Still there can be no doubt that both petty matters but also serious things—blunders in work and failures in ventures of the tsar himself—were hidden from Peter. Here the principle was a simple one: in order to report the matter to Peter in a favorable light, Makarov had to know the truth. Naturally, all this made statesmen dependent on the cabinet-secretary whose favor they craved—indeed in their careers and fates a great deal depended on how he reported things and what emphases he gave to a report.[23]

By the way, one can be certain that in each matter Makarov had a certain interest, however small, and that he probably was not completely candid with his correspondents or even with Peter himself. Some evidence has been preserved that confirms our suspicions. In the fall of 1724 an extensive anonymous letter was left for Peter. The tsar read it through and made many expressive comments in the margins. It was not the ordinary anonymous letter of some half-crazy "profit maker," schismatic, or complainant. Its author was extraordinarily well informed about the work of the Cabinet and the High Court—a temporary judicial organ that had been created to review serious state crimes. One may say that the delator was literally two steps away from Peter and Makarov and was, apparently, one of the chanceryists of the Cabinet or the High Court. The letter interested the tsar so much that he ordered it saved, and instead of burning it publicly (in the same envelope) according to law, a blank paper was burned.

Sharp anonymous criticisms were directed against Makarov. He was accused of having tremendous influence on the personnel of the High Court and of directing his servitors to prepare reports to the tsar that contained deliberate disinformation (naturally according to preliminary agreements with the persons involved). Upon receiving these reports in the Cabinet, he accepted them for Peter and the necessary resolution was added. In sum, the anonymous delator wrote, "according to the register Your Majesty deigned somewhere to sign with your own hand extracts of resolutions according to unjust proposals by him, Makarov, and others, and although you deigned to sign those unjust extracts of reports and thus punished some and knowingly ruined others due to him, Makarov, it was impossible for Your Majesty to see that those extracts were unjust, and they were believed."

The accusations were well founded and were backed up by many examples. The names of prominent statesmen who had colluded with Makarov were enumerated. The anonymous delator wrote that these statesmen "are indebted to this Makarov, for as far as important persons and matters of interest are concerned, heretofore and at present according to reports from fiscals and others, all of this had been hidden by him, Makarov, and nothing reported about it to Your Majesty, and till now there has been no inquiry into these matters."[24] Here we see in action the well-known principle of bureaucratic crime: "You give to me, I give to you." Opposite many points Peter made notations that affirm his intention to return to the anonymous letter later and to launch an investigation of his secretary's "clever tricks." At the end of 1724, however, Peter was already mortally ill, and fate preserved Makarov from great unpleasantness.

It is difficult to say now what feelings Peter experienced and what he thought as he placed on the margins of the delation nervous fat crosses—signs of particular attention. Perhaps he saw in Makarov's deeds the ordinary abuse of official position; perhaps he was fully aware that not only he administered the state machine, but that it also administered him.

Be that as it may, the role of Makarov and the Cabinet in the system of administration was enormous. It is important to note at the same time that a great number of reports were sent to the Cabinet from local and central institutions that were formally subordinated to the colleges and to the Senate. Nevertheless, the leaders of these offices, bypassing their superiors, wrote directly to the Cabinet, where all the threads of administration at the different levels thus came together. This was a blatant violation of the bureaucratic order requiring subordination as laid down and preached by Peter himself.

There were many causes for such deviations from the theory of cameralism. There were even causes stemming from the very nature of unlimited autocratic authority, when the tsar, the most zealous supporter of legality, as historian A.S. Lappo-Danilevsky wrote, "ultimately remained in many instances the supreme and sole level of appeal, for example in his own Secret Chancery, and he could always subject to his own judgment everything that he considered necessary and resolve matters according to those political purposes that he recognized as most suitable for the state."[25] There were subjective circumstances too— Peter's urge to enter into the heart of a matter, his desire to receive full and fresh information, and finally the impatience inherent in Russia's reformers.

It should not be forgotten, either, that for Peter's style of administration there were characteristic military-battlefield features, a consequence of whole decades of nomadic life when orders were given wherever and to whoever necessary. As historian F. Veselago has rightly remarked, "desiring the quickest execution of a matter, Peter often issued orders to whoever was closest at hand or who caught his eye, without informing his superior; thus orders coming down from commanders often ran into contradictory orders from the ruler going from the bottom up, from a subordinate to his superior."[26]

In short, notwithstanding his own strict decrees about the "regularity" of the state machine's work, Peter constantly interfered in its activities.

Bypassing the Senate, a flood of affairs in the competence of the Senate and the colleges came to the Cabinet, and from the Cabinet, likewise bypassing the Senate, decisions were dispatched that often defined the functioning of the state machine and even made policy. Sometimes the Senate tried at least to take account of the directives that bypassed it or that were adopted by Peter at sessions of the colleges and in other places, but it was all to no avail. The restless tsar, blatantly violating the very regulations he had adopted, interfered in matters not subject to his competence.

Apparently, the tsar's active involvement was essential in many cases in order to overcome the sluggishness of the bureaucratic machine and to correct deficiencies created by its own bureaucratic essence. It is worthy of note that after Peter's death several statesmen recalled with sorrow the "golden age" of the bureaus; the celebrated "Moscow red tape" seemed as common as a cucumber in comparison with the monstrous bureaucracy that the Petrine state reforms had spawned.

It should be said that in itself the creation of the bureaucratic machine, which had replaced the system of medieval administration based on custom, was a natural process. Bureaucracy is an essential element of the structure of modern states. Yet in the conditions of the Russian autocracy, when nothing and nobody limited the monarch's will—the sole source of law—when an official was not responsible to anyone except his superior, the creation of the bureaucratic machine became a peculiar "bureaucratic revolution," in the process of which the prime mover of bureaucracy was set into motion. Beginning in Petrine times, it started working according to its internal laws in pursuit of its ultimate aim—consolidating its own position—responding fluidly and flexibly to changes. All these features of the bureaucracy created by the Petrine regime permitted it to function successfully regardless of which ruler sat on the throne—clever or stupid, capable or passive. Many of these features and principles made for a cohesive caste of bureaucrats invulnerable to the present.

By means of the Petrine reforms a system was created in Russia unknown earlier. The statehood of the Russian Empire was like a building in the forest, and Peter, its engineer and builder, constantly introduced corrections and supplements that in his opinion were needed. To this construction he bent every effort: building the ship of Russian statehood till his last day and rushing to launch it into the waters of life and to thereby realize his own great state ideal.

The Serf Economy

During the introduction of the state reforms of 1719–24 central offices were created to administer commerce and industry: the Mining and Manufactories College (in 1722 it was divided in two, the Mining and the Manufactories colleges), the Commerce College, and the Main Municipal Administration. Before this, Russia lacked similar institutions (the Ore-digging bureau of 1710–11, resurrected in 1715 in the form of the Ore Chancery, could not compare with the Mining College in either designation or scope or level of centralization).

These bureaucratic organizations became the regulatory institutions for the national economy, responsible for implementing the commercial-industrial policies of the Petrine autocracy based on mercantilism and protectionism. The creation of a centralized administrative system for commerce and industry signified a turning point in economic policy-making of the Petrine state.

Confident after 1717 of quickly winning the war with Sweden, Peter launched a fundamental change of commercial-industrial policy. The crux of the change was the introduction of diverse measures of stimulating commerce and private industrial entrepreneurship.

On 8 April 1719 Peter, "from favor for the merchantry of the Russian state, decreed that there should be *only two state commodities: potash and weidash* (and those for conservation of the forests), whereas the other goods which have been sold by the state *are freed for trade among the populace.*"[1]

Thus were abolished after a decade and a half the state monopolies on the majority of goods that had been so burdensome and ruinous for the Russian merchantry; that is, freedom of trade was proclaimed. Implementation of the decree on freedom of trade and management of all commercial affairs was entrusted to the Commerce College, created that same year. It was occupied with so-called "commerce," that is, protection of commercial shipping, management of customs duties, the juridical aspect of trade, and so forth.

The measures for stimulating private industrial entrepreneurship were incomparably more substantial and diverse. Their basis was laid by the celebrated "Mining Privilege" of 10 December 1719. It authorized all residents of the country whatever their social status to prospect for minerals and to establish works. To found a works one had to present samples of ore to the Mining College, which after ascertaining the location of the find would deed the tract of land to the future entrepreneur and give him a "privilege"—the requisite document for the works confirming his rights and responsibilities.

An important facet of the new mining legislation was that it did not acknowledge a right of possession to the land on which the minerals and ores had been found: "If the owner himself does not have the desire to build and will not have the desire to enter into partnership with others, or cannot from his own deficiency, then he will be compelled to permit that others seek out and mine and process ores and minerals on his lands, so that God's blessings under the earth not remain without use."[2] Although the "Mining Privilege" had introduced a change in several branches of owners' rights to the land, the progressiveness of this norm of the "Mining Privilege" should not be exaggerated: in the Russia of that time everything belonging to the subject might at any moment be "appropriated by the master" and given to whomever he pleased. The landowner of Petrine times, whose father might be deprived of his estate without notice for failure to appear for muster, did not enjoy the security of a landed proprietor protected by law.

Another important initiative of the Petrine government was the practice of transferring state manufactories to private owners or, frequently, to whole companies specially created for the purpose.

The new owners received various favors from the state: an interest-free loan for several years, the right to add any entrepreneur to the company, customs-free sale of goods, and a high purchase price (in comparison to the usual) for the sale of goods to the state. To this it should also be added that the tariff confirmed in 1724 provided essential aid to entrepreneurs, facilitating the export abroad of native manufactories' production and hindering the import of identical foreign goods (with the aid of high customs duties).

All these measures of stimulating commerce and private entrepreneurship suggest, it would seem, that at the end of the Northern War fundamental changes had come about in the autocracy's economic policymaking and that a peculiar New Economic Policy (NEP) had arrived with its characteristic principles of greater economic freedom. But this illusion is quickly shattered when we look into the facts more closely.

As early as 18 January 1715 a decree had been issued defining the policy for light industry (more specifically, woolen cloth). It declared: "In order that we may cease purchasing uniforms from abroad in five years [as a decree of 1712 had ordained], woolen mills should be established in more than one location; and to that end: establish them in more than one location and, once they are established, transfer them to trading people assembled in a company, whether they wish it or are compelled to it, and to gain money for the mill yearly with ease, in order that it be easier for them to produce in this matter."[3] This brief decree contains the crux of all Petrine industrial policy of the last years. Previously, as at the start of the Northern War, the main aim remained to supply the army and the country with industrial goods. Now, however, a new path for resolving this task had opened up for Peter—creating trading and industrial companies. Since they had played such a positive role in the economic life of the Western European countries, Russia ought to have them too.

Companies intrigued Peter not simply because of the broad possibilities of organizing a venture that required the pooling of the capital of several entrepreneurs, but also because they constituted a peculiar commune the members of which, having poured their capital into a common pot, were linked by mutual interest and bore joint responsibility before the state. The state was interested in organizing companies and therefore included in the decree the phrase "whether they wish it or are compelled to it." Coercion remained, as we shall see below, a constant component of the Petrine "NEP."

It is important to note that the organizer and leader of the company often turned out to be in service to the state and holding, like Demidov, the rank of "commissar," could bring in others even against their will. Refusal to enter into a company and to offer one's own capital, like voluntary exit, could lead to serious complications. By a decree of 17 February 1723 company members might first be fined by the leadership of the company, then put in prison under the Mining and Manufactories College, which exercised general oversight.

In the last decade of Peter's reign the transfer of manufactories to companies and to private entrepreneurs became widespread, yet those liable to transfer were in the first instance enterprises more profitable for the fisc. In the official correspondence, profitability was set forth as the reason for transferring manufactories into private hands.

Stimulating private entrepreneurship and making "concessions" to merchants and industrialists, the state had no intention to withdraw from the economy. By the end of the Northern War a kind of new edition of the previous policy emerged. If earlier the state's influence on the economy had been one of compulsion through a system of prohibitions, monopolies, customs duties, and taxes, and through the direct participation of the fisc in trades and industries, now that the crisis justifying this intervention no longer prevailed, the whole weight of the burden was shifted onto the creation and activities of the bureaucratic machine of administrative control, which through codes, regulations, "privileges," accounts, and checks could direct economic life via a carefully devised network of peculiar sluices and canals in the direction needed by the state. Special colleges were also created for the guidance of this process.

It is important to note that in Sweden, whose state offices Peter considered exemplary, similar colleges likewise exercised royal authority as a whole on just these theoretical bases. Yet Russia's conditions differed greatly from Sweden's not only in terms of scale, culture, and the unusual intensity of industrial construction forced and financed by the state, but above all in the special severity of the regimentation, the ramified system of constraints, and the state's excessive oversight of its subjects' commercial-industrial activities.

We have no grounds to think that in the last decade of his reign Peter intended to loosen the tight administrative harness on the economy or, bluntly speaking, that he unwittingly facilitated the development of capitalist forms and the means of production that had become widespread in Western Europe. What had happened amounted to a shift not of principles but of emphases in commercial-industrial policy.

Looking carefully into the conditions for transferring manufactories, we discover that the companies did not exercise the rights of a capitalistic owner. Implemented was merely a variant of a peculiar lease, the conditions of which were clearly defined by the state, which had a right to change them, up to reclaiming for the fisc the works granted and even confiscating what had been built at the entrepreneurs' own "cost." Thus, in the "privilege" of 1720 for the copper-smelting works founded by Nikita Demidov "with his very own money" it was noted: "And therefore he, Demidov, is ordered to work and care for that copperworks, and to see that his mining venture is pursued and expanded satisfactorily; assure him that the works will not be taken from him, and from his wife and from his children and his heirs, so long as they operate the works in good condition." As we have seen, the state guaranteed to the entrepreneur ownership of his own works only for as long as the latter is "in good condition," that is, so long as the necessary production will be provided to the fisc without fail. Otherwise the enterprise could be confiscated.[4]

Timely fulfillment of state orders was the entrepreneur's main obligation. Only the surplus above that which currently is called the "state order" might he sell on the market. Thus, private entrepreneurship was firmly yoked to the state's cart by the system of state orders, which were primarily of military significance. On one hand, this of course protected the stability of sales by the manufacturers, who could be sure that the fisc would guarantee demand for their product, but on the other hand it discouraged technical and other kinds of innovation, and sharply undercut the significance of competition as a prime mover of entrepreneurship. This is why later attempts to introduce innovations into primeval works proved to be in vain, for there was no interest in their expansion and development as long as there were stable orders and demand via the fisc. The numerous privileges for a portion of the entrepreneurs worked in the same direction, for they signaled a compulsory liquidation of competitors.

Oversight and control of native industry were entrusted, as noted, to the Mining and Manufactories College. The "Mining Privilege" defined the rights of the new college with uncustomary breadth. The college exercised obligatory control over the activities of ore prospectors, granted permission to build works, set the prices for production, held monopoly rights on purchase of the production of manufactories in amounts set by itself, and exercised general control over the production and supply of goods. All administrative and judicial authority over the entrepreneurs and the workers was also in the hands of the Mining College.

At first both heavy and light industry had been united under the college's management. In 1722 a separation of the Mining and Manufactories colleges came about. In December 1723 the regulation of the Manufactories College was adopted, specifying that the new college's authority vis-à-vis the manufacturers was just the same as that of Mining College over the mine owners. The Manufactories College was supposed to patronize entrepreneurship in light industry in every way. According to the lawgiver's thinking, this would be achieved primarily via strict administration and control.

It was the right of the state to restrain the competition of entrepreneurs and to exercise oversight of the quality of the output produced, samples of which were periodically reviewed in the college. Furthermore, according to the regulation, the college was supposed to oversee production, to examine specialists, and later on "to institute a regulation for each manufactory." In a country where the General Regulation—that king of all regulations—was already operating and where each college, office, and position had or, at least, was supposed to have its own articles or regulations defining distinctly and in detail the functions of each institution and the obligations of each official, it would have been strange if each manufactory, private or state, had not had its own regulation that enumerated what was supposed to go on there, for the good of the state. Concerning this last point, the Manufactories

College was supposed to busy itself in caring for the manufactories.

Thus, under Peter, industry was created in which the chief was a special-ist bureaucrat-official who knew which branch should be developed and which should be retarded, who determined how much of what would be produced and how much each arshin* of cloth and pud† of iron should cost, who possessed tremendous authority over the entrepreneur and the conditions of his labor, and who decided the fate of the entrepreneur's business and prosperity.

The abolition in 1719 of the state monopoly on trade in traditional export goods expanded, no doubt, the opportunities of the Russian mer-chantry, whereas the protectionist customs tariff adopted in 1724 provided them with substantial advantage, safeguarding them from the competition of foreign merchants. The regulation of the Commerce College of 1724, as already mentioned, reinforced the new situation that had arisen as a conse-quence of the decrees abolishing monopolies. But the positive provisions of the regulation were nullified by the points following that firmly regu-lated the flow of cargo and stipulated the kinds of goods that were to be delivered to the different port towns in accordance with the privileges created for Petersburg, and with those general political considerations that the government deemed more important than observation of the newly enunciated principles of free trade. Therefore, the regulation enjoined that goods from Pskov and its region should be hauled directly to Narva, "whereas to Riga and to other places they are not to haul those goods that have been ordered to be hauled to Petersburg," and so on. Obviously, the administrative determination of the ports of trade was a manifestation of the state's command in the commercial sphere. In order to stimulate native commercial navigation and shipbuilding, the authorities categori-cally demanded that merchants desist from building vessels of the old style and ship their goods exclusively on expensive "new-model" vessels. These laws were extended even to the Pomor'e (northern maritime region), the population of which, for many centuries, navigated the northern seas. Violation of the prohibition on building ships of the old style threatened the Pomorians—who were born shipbuilders and sailors—with hard labor, as they were warned by the decree of 11 March 1719.

The state's influence on the economy was not limited to the authorities' direct intervention into commerce and industry. The socio-economic relations typical of Russian society as a whole permeated the manufactories, to a substantial degree deforming their features as po-tentially capitalist enterprises. The heart of the matter touches on the peculiarities of their use of the labor force.

---

*One arshin equals 28 inches.
†One pud equals 36 pounds.

The manufactories established at the beginning of the Petrine era had been provided with a labor force in a variety of ways. State enterprises and private owners used both a freely hired force and "assigned" peasants—the rural populace of the regions that as a rule adjoined the localities of the works' placement. The peasants, mainly those from state-taxed lands, worked off the state impost by laboring at the works. What did the "assigned" peasants do? As a rule, auxiliary work. In 1711 the Olonets peasants wrote in a petition: ". . . we work in all sorts of factory works, and cut wood in the forests and prepare charcoal, and dig ore, and smelt it, and haul without a break."[5] On paper, such labors were not supposed to exceed the state taxes in money terms. The works' management or owner compensated for the peasants' missing tax payments by deliveries of their production to the fisc. It should be noted, however, that the practice of "assignment" had been widely extended from the first years of manufactories' existence even in the pre-Petrine period. But, as already noted in similar cases, the scale of such practices under Peter was different: it included general and extended enlistment from near and far of state, palace, monastery, and privately held peasants at the most diverse construction sites, canals, and production centers. The new capital, fortresses, canals, and roads— everything that would later be called the infrastructure—were created under Peter by the immense efforts and exhaustion of the country's peasant population. I am speaking here of the hundreds of thousands of peasants who had been driven from all corners of the country with the exception of Siberia, the population of which paid money compensation for the working off of taxes at construction sites in the European part of the country, although it was not exempted from construction levies in the Urals and in Siberia. The peasant who traveled hundreds of versts to Taganrog or Vyborg, Petersburg or Voronezh, Briansk or Revel in order to work off the many months of labor dues became the most typical figure of Russian life on the roads of the Petrine era.

If one speaks of the basic, permanent skilled contingent of workers of Petrine manufactories who labored there for years and who achieved a moderately high level of skill, these were generally hired workers. For an enterprise to accept workers "by hire" from the street at the start of the eighteenth century did not pose any special complications. The differentiation of the rural population, the system of tax assessment that took account of the household and not each specific person, and the multitude of legal ways to avoid assessment or service, not to mention pre-Petrine Russia's simply untaxed strata of the population and the absence of a firm national passport system for the recovery of fugitives—all this led to the fact that in the large towns along the major land and river routes, as well as in the country as a whole, a substantial stratum of so-called "free and itinerant persons" grew up to provide the basic reserve of the freely hired labor force.

But not only persons free according to the law belonged to the category of "the free and the itinerant." Among them were quite a few declassed elements—the "freebooters" so familiar to us from the rebellion of Stenka Razin. "Thieving" along the big roads and rivers in summer, these "barebacks" settled down at the manufactories in winter. At the same time a substantial number of "the free and the itinerant" comprised peasants, including serfs who had fled from their lords and from state service, as well as peasant children who had lived from infancy at the works and had learned there the skills of weavers, blacksmiths, and so forth. In general, the law strictly prohibited the use at the works of the labor of fugitive soldiers, recruits, and landowners' serfs. In real life, however, these proscriptions were honored in the breech—fugitive peasants in great numbers turned up at the manufactories. Along with "the free" they also formed the basic contingent of a skilled work force at both state and private enterprises.

Criminals sentenced to hard labor also manned the manufactories. On 10 April 1722, for example, a special directive was adopted about banishing criminals along with their wives and children from the European part of the country to the silver mines of Dauria in eastern Siberia. The labor of convict women was used especially often in linen production. The sentence of "eternal banishment to the spinning court" is one of those most frequently encountered in cases involving women before the courts.

If, as noted earlier, problems of a free labor force had not arisen at the dawn of industrial construction, then at the start of the 1720s such a problem had not only arisen but had become acute. By this time important transformations of a social character had taken place. These, together with the acutely accelerated struggle against fugitives and the recruiting levies for the army of 250,000, became the main cause of the shortage of free work hands. With the introduction of the census for the soul (capitation) tax, which encompassed the entire Russian population of the country, a massive removal of fugitive peasants ensued including those from manufactories where they had been hiding in the form of "the free and the itinerant"—a category proclaimed illegal after the soul census. This provoked the anxiety of the state offices interested in filling deliveries to the fisc. The number of complaints about the removal of peasants increased also from private entrepreneurs.

Just then two of Peter's decrees were published that had serious consequences for Russian industry and the country's economy. On 18

January 1721 Peter signed in the Senate a decree permitting manufacturers to buy enserfed peasants for their own works. The main motives
of the government's actions, which had decided to change the traditional ban on buying peasants for representatives of the nonnoble commercial-industrial class, were the belief that manufacturers benefit the
state and a recognition of the need to encourage them.[6]

The significance of the decree cited is hard to overestimate—permission to buy villages with peasants for manufactories had irreversible
consequences; it signaled a decisive step toward converting industrial
enterprises, at which the capitalist mode had taken root, into enterprises of the serf economy, a variant of feudal property—a peculiar
patrimonial manufactory.

The decree established a special variant of landowner's property,
"villages attached to works," with a distinctively limited right of using
the property only for industrial needs. Yet serfdom was the sole basis of
limited as well as unlimited property in such villages, whether one
speaks of the serf's work on the lord's land or at a forge in the lord's
works.

Peter's second decree, which should be considered in detail, appeared approximately a year later, on 15 March 1722, and is linked to
the determination of the status of working people during the general
census of the population in 1719–24. In enumerating the factory population the census takers confronted a problem: what to do with working
people who did not belong to the owner of a manufactory? Almost all of
them were subject to the workings of the laws on removing fugitives
because, not being the manufacturer's property, they either were the
property of somebody else or had left the estates of monasteries, the
palace administration, state peasant, or town communes.

The decree of 15 March 1722, which had been drafted with Peter's
direct participation, came into being as a consequence of the
government's efforts to find a way out of the situation that had arisen.
The decree stipulated that the census takers should enumerate at the
works all the working people "whatever districts and whosoever people
and peasants they are, and having counted them, if from those same
districts . . . they be certified in registers submitted for souls of the male
sex, whether they have been registered and if registered, do not assign
them anew, and if they are not registered, then assign them to whichever villages and hamlets they will say, and place them in the assessment
on par with the others."[7] Putting it differently, on one hand, the government, concerned to conserve the number of taxpayers, ordered that
working people be entered in the soul-tax registers not at the enterprise
where they worked and lived, but in those hamlets and villages from

which they had gone off to the manufactory. On the other hand, the law, protecting the interests of industry, prohibited the removal of the worker-peasants from the works.

Thus the decree had the character of the judgment of Solomon whereby the fiscal needs of the state, which was interested in preserving the "taxed number" of assessed communes from which it collected the soul tax for the army, had been taken into account along with the proprietary interests of the landowners whose fugitives were obligated to pay dues, and also the interests of the manufacturers, who did not lose their precious work force. As often happened in Russia, however, the decree turned out to be good only on paper. The prescription of 15 March was not carried out—fugitive peasant-workers began to be taken from the works back to their previous owners. According to the materials that have come down to us, it is obvious that in the key issue the local authorities took the side of the landowners, the fugitives' owners.

Here it is desirable to direct attention to a characteristic particular. Working people, regardless of their actual position and the duration of their employment, were covered by the norms and criteria of the law that had fixed the estate structure of medieval Russian society. The law did not contain any supplements that might have taken account of the newly emergent reality—the manufactories and their related social strata, entrepreneurs and workers. In the social structure (and hence in the law that reflected it) there was no place for the estate of working people. Labor at a factory was not viewed by Petrine lawmakers, who were living in an era of intensive industrial construction, as an activity that might permit the person so employed to achieve a special status, a special place in the estate structure of society distinct from that of a peasant or a townsman.

Petrine lawmakers saw labor at an enterprise as one of the secondary occupations of the townsman, peasant, or person of mixed rank. Although a distinction was made at a place of production between permanent masters—workers who had long since become professionals—and temporary workmen and peasants, legislation and legal practice did not admit the difference: working people were viewed as serfs of the manufactory's owner, as his property. In fact, the lawmaker did not grasp the difference between entrepreneur-industrialists and the merchantry to which the former were often assigned.

This "blindness" of the law is especially evident in the work of the census takers, who conducted the census and who checked the number of souls present in each village, hamlet, town, and works. In enumerating the workers, the census takers overlooked the fact that the former had long since become skilled workers (possibly not in the first generation) separated from their estate, class, and social group. For everybody there was a single question: "From which ranks and which towns and districts are they?" and then in the registry the answers were set down: "from the peasants," "from the townsmen," "from the churchmen." That is, it was not the worker's social origin in the current sense of the word that was noted, but direct membership in the milieu from which he had once come.

Putting it differently, the census taker noticed the worker but did not recognize him as a representative of a special social group, similar to how the people of antiquity saw the color orange, but perceived it not as orange, but as a variant of yellow or red. In our case the cause of social "Daltonism" (color blindness) lay in the fact that something new was perceived as a variant of the old.

The aforementioned decree of 28 May 1723 was a direct consequence of similar notions about a working man whereby the worker (if he was not the property of the manufacturer or had not been "assigned" to a works) could enter only two statuses: as a furloughed peasant with a passport for temporary work at a factory, or as a fugitive in violation of the law and subject to immediate removal from the factory to his prior place of residence, where he had been registered with the other peasants in the assessment of the soul tax.

Now the significance of two decrees was becoming apparent: that of 18 January 1721 on the purchase of villages by manufacturers, and that of 15 March 1722 with clarifications of 1723 concerning the recovery of workers who were fugitive peasants. By these decrees Russia's industry could not develop except via bondage. After these decrees the proportion of freely hired labor in Russian industry started to decline markedly. State industry started to change over almost entirely to the exploitation of "assigned" peasants and developed a special institution of "recruits"—peculiar lifelong "industrial soldiers" obligated to discharge their recruitment not in the army but at the foundry or workbench.

The expansion of bondage also facilitated the practice whereby peasants who did not belong to landowners but who were laboring at factories started to be bound to the tax assessment wherever they had been found by the census, that is, at the factories.

The skilled workers and masters living at the factories were free persons and had not at first been subject to the soul tax, although they had been enumerated during the census. Their position was still acknowledged to be abnormal in a society where there were no longer free persons and where each was subject to taxation or service; by a decree of 1736 all free working people were proclaimed to be bondmen of the manufactory owners—the so-called "eternally committed" workers. In short, entire branches of industry started to use the labor of bondmen or of "assigned" peasants almost exclusively, with the exploitation of "assigned" peasants hardly differing in form from that of serfs. The entrepreneur could without supervision dispose of the labor of the "assigned" peasant, who found himself in temporary yet heavy and essentially bondaged dependence. A similar picture obtained with other factory owners too. Thus, the woolen cloth industry in general did not countenance free labor: the state, interested in supplying the army with native woolens, did not spare villages for the manufacturers of this branch. An analogous situation prevailed also in the metallurgical industry of the Urals. The census of 1744–45 revealed that freely hired workers constituted only 1.7 percent of the general mass of workers.[8]

It is hardly worthwhile to dwell on the ruinous consequences of the victory of compulsory labor in industry, which in total largely determined the country's economic backwardness compared with the economically developed countries of Europe. The use of bondage in the sphere of industry also deformed the formation of the Russian bourgeoisie that had just begun. As we know, in establishing manufactories, their owners received definite and substantial privileges. In particular, according to the "privileges," they were exempted from a series of imposts and from billeting. At the start of 1721, almost simultaneously with the decree about the purchase of villages for factories, a decree was issued whereby "the first that shall found a works is freed of service" to which he was subject as a townsman, a privilege that was seen as conducive to "making them [manufactories] multiply without difficulty."[9] This was quite an important privilege, for the entrepreneurs as well as the more substantial portion of the townsmen paid the lion's share of town taxes and provided many services in fiscal affairs. Singling out the manufacturers in estate, judicial, and fiscal affairs provoked discontent among the townsmen as a whole. This was reflected in a "Report" of the Main Municipal Administration of 1722. The Main Municipal Administration asserted that many merchants had entered industrial companies only to avoid general town obligations, and that the company men should be subordinated to town officials in determining their share of the payments. Peter heeded the request of the Main Municipal Administration and ordained that entrepreneurs who had already mastered the trade and were earning a stable return from it "are to be under the jurisdiction of the municipal administration in civil services and imposts along with other citizens."[10] This resolution was a step backward in the legal and fiscal formation of the social group of entrepreneurs. By taking entrepreneurs under the jurisdiction of the Main Municipal Administration (that was general for the urban community), the urban milieu was mixed up and the growing bourgeoisie was artificially leveled with the great bulk of the medieval urban community.

Apart from legal obstacles there were also economic circumstances hindering the formation of the bourgeois class under Peter. These comprised not only the entrepreneurs' dependence and the state's command in the economic sphere discussed earlier, but also the fact that the state's very stimulation of industry primarily had the character of bondage. This facilitated the development of bondage in industry and the decline in the role and significance of freely hired labor, the potential use of which had already been constrained by the autocracy's social and "regime" policy-making.

Yet providing the manufacturers with the right to use a purchased labor force cost entrepreneurs dearly (in both the direct and metaphorical senses of the word). As a result there occurred a "killing" of capital that went not for the improvement and expansion of production, but for the purchase of land and peasants. Thus, in 1745 Akinfy Demidov's twenty-two metalworks were valued at 400,000 rubles, whereas his estates and peasants were valued at 211,000 rubles. The Luganins' works cost 305,600 rubles, whereas the peasants and land cost 1.2 million rubles, that is, four times more.[11]

If we add to this that the furloughed peasant, who received a passport and went off in search of a livelihood, was exploited at the factory via the capitalistic mode so that later, having received the money, he paid feudal dues to his lord, it is clear that in the system of bondaged industry there was no room for the development of capitalism (and consequently for the formation of the bourgeoisie).

Finally, in exploiting the system of bondage in industry, the fisc was interested in the stable delivery of industrial output, for which indeed the entrepreneurs were encouraged by money and bondmen. Accordingly, the state looked quite benevolently on the request of manufacturers to introduce monopolies for the production of goods put out by this same manufacturer or for the purchase of needed raw materials. It is noteworthy that, in introducing such monopolies, the state saw their benefit in a purely fiscal capacity: the entrepreneur himself, the officials calculated, would be interested in ensuring that competitors not appear who might avoid fiscal payments.

The struggle against competitors with the aid of state decrees and "privileges" impeded the normal course of capitalist development in the country. Protected by "privileges" and provided with orders from the fisc, the entrepreneurs, as noted above, were not interested in perfecting production, for which it would have been necessary to invest large sums.

It is important to note that the deformation touched such an important sphere as consciousness. The manufacturer-entrepreneurs, "ensconced" in the general system of bondage, did not sense their social peculiarity, and a corporate class consciousness did not arise among them. At a time when, in the developed countries of Europe, the bourgeoisie not only was conscious of itself, but also had openly enunciated its pretensions to the authorities, to the nobility, and to the king, in Russia the trend was the reverse: manufacturers who received peasants strove to achieve a rise in their social status—to become noblemen. This tendency—the direct result of the development of bondage in industry—led to the fact that literally within one or two generations the representatives of the entrepreneurs had turned themselves into nobles completely dissolving into the privileged class. They had even forgotten the language of their own grandfathers and great-grandfathers who had originated from the peasantry and the urban community. The most striking example is the saga of barons Stroganov and Demidov.

And so, industrial construction under Peter led to two main results—the creation of a powerful economic base, so essential for a developing nation, and simultaneously the essential arrest of the country's capitalist development and movement along the path on which the other European peoples had been moving for a long time.

Producing the All-Russian Subject People

Building a new state structure was only part of the grandiose task that the great reformer of Russia had set out to accomplish. His field of vision encompassed not only the administrative structure, the economic policy, and military affairs, but also society itself—people and subjects. In the Petrine era society's structure underwent no less change than the structure of authority or the economy. Of course, we may speak about social changes as a consequence of the complex of reforms—military, tax, and so forth. In any event, the reformer did a great deal to transform the social structure itself and to realize the grandiose notion of "producing the all-Russian subject people."

As a result the social consequences of the transformations proved to be just as sweeping as in the economy, foreign policy, and other spheres. In fact the status of every social category was subjected to change.

Substantial changes came to the nobility's position. Indeed, the noble estate of the eighteenth and nineteenth centuries, in the form that has come down to us from literature, was formed or, better, organized by Peter. This is no exaggeration, for in pre-Petrine Russia there had existed a single estate of so-called service people that included both those who served "by descent," that is, by heredity, and those who served "by recruitment," that is, by muster on a voluntary basis.

The apex of the pyramid of service ranks was composed of the Boyar Council—the council ranks (boyars, cupbearers, lords in waiting, chamberlains, state councilors, state secretaries). Besides the council ranks, those serving "by descent" included table attendants, crown agents, Moscow court attendants, and town servitors (that is those serving from the list of the capital and from provincial towns). Joining the service people "by recruitment" were other petty service ranks: cannoneers, town cossacks, stockade guards, and the like. Close to them were the scribes. Although a social abyss separated the council ranks and "the recruited," the service estate was still unitary; the distinction between those serving "by descent" and "by recruitment" had been eroded, a fact that permitted an occasional scribe to be elevated to the Boyar Council. Neither was the service estate separated by an impassable barrier from the taxed estates—peasants and townsmen from whose numbers the servitors were recruited. It is curious that Peter still preserved this practice in the country's borderlands.

The unity of the service estate of the sixteenth and seventeenth centuries had been governed by the fact that for the duration of state service, wherever it was performed, the entire estate was provided with landholdings including those that were populated. In other words, unlike many other estate groups of Russian society, the service people enjoyed rights of land and serf holding, that is, the privileges that later on became a monopoly of the nobility.

The Petrine era destroyed once and for all the service estate. It broke into two categories: the greater part of those serving "by descent" were converted into noblemen (*shliakhetsvo*); the smaller part (predominantly those less substantial serving in the south) as well as those serving "by recruitment" entered the estate of state peasants that Peter had artificially created.

Of course, preconditions for the estate's stratification had been maturing little by little. Here one ought to mention the autocracy's merger of boyars and nobles, which had leveled all subjects when the descendants of appanage princes no longer enjoyed any privileges and competed in service to the ruler and in seeking his favor. The tsar, however, might selectively elevate some and demean others regardless of family origin.

This tendency toward consolidation of the service estate elite also developed owing to changes in the nature of service itself and of the system of rewards. Until the end of the seventeenth century service had retained a well-known periodicity and peculiar "seasonality": the servitors were assembled for inspection with their armed servants ("on horse with servants and armament") in order to return later to their landholdings with a sense of relief and, sheathing the saber and hanging up the pistol, to live peacefully until the next inspection. From Petrine times, characterized by incessant wars, the service of all categories became standing, and the system of remuneration was changed. For service in the regular army a money salary was paid. The servitors' landholdings, however, ceased to be a form of payment for service, becoming non-transferable in fact. They merged increasingly with the other form of landholding—the patrimony, that is, hereditary holdings. In 1714 both forms of landholding, conditional and hereditary, were declared thenceforth to be the uniform fixed property of the noble landowner.

For a long time the process of differentiating the servitors "by descent" from those "by recruitment" had also been under way. For the latter Peter's military reform played a fateful role. It ended the irregularity of the previous army. In place of the town cossacks, cannoneers, and so forth, regular garrison and field regiments appeared in which many of "the recruited" were assigned as rank-and-file soldiers. Part of "the recruited," however, lost their service and its corresponding privileges, were placed on par with the peasantry and the townsmen, and, like them, were subject to obligatory service. Thus "the recruited" were reduced to the position of the taxed, that is, the lowest categories of the population.

Social polarization proceeded gradually, of course, and it had been predestined from time immemorial by the distance that separated the Moscow boyar in principle from the Tambov town cossack, but still under Peter this process gained exceptionally rapid development. Peter imperiously intervened in its course, imparting the direction set by the reformer's ideas.

A huge role in changing the social estate's position was played by Peter's introduction of a new, distinctive criterion of service. That is, the principle of heredity was replaced by the principle of personal merit. In accordance with his own cardinal idea of service as the main obligation of his subjects and with his own conception of the autocratic monarch's role standing at the apex of the pyramid of ranks, Peter could not allow entry into the service hierarchy and movement along the ladder of ranks to be determined by a criterion such as heredity independent of the autocrat, instead of merit. In short, services to the tsar were not defined by laws but were dictated and changed by him at his own discretion.

Introducing the principle of personal merit greatly strengthened the autocracy's authority over the nobility. In place of the traditional estate of servitors "by descent" a military-bureaucratic corps of noblemen took shape; the obedient officer or official obligated to the ruler for everything displaced the previously wayward boyar or table attendant proud of the descent that had provided his social position.

At first much was done to halt the development and expansion of the old service estate. In 1695 appointments to table attendant and crown agent were ended, and in 1703 to court attendant. The roots that had fed the centuries-old servitors "by descent" were thereby torn out. At that time, too, appointments to boyar ranks were halted in practice. The Boyar Council, as noted earlier, although not abolished officially, literally died out over ten or twelve years without an influx of new elders.

It should be stressed that Peter did this deliberately and that it constituted one of the typical, though at first glance unexpected, features of his policy. Along with a fundamental rupture of the old institutions the tsar-reformer also abolished them by not supporting the traditions that had nurtured them. Also noteworthy is Peter's unwillingness somehow "to knock together" the old system of ranks with the one he was creating on the basis of the Table of Ranks. In discussing the table the Senate tried to propose such a thing: "Inasmuch as several persons have remained in the old ranks, namely boyars, cup-bearers, lords in waiting, state councilors, table attendants and others, it is therefore proposed: shall His Tsarist Majesty deign to assign them ranks like the others for life?" Peter ignored the senators' proposal.[1]

It should be added that many table attendants, crown agents, and other ranks of servitors "by descent" were taken into the regiments of the regular army, and not always as officers.

In the Petrine era the formation of the nobility proceeded not as a "rank" or a variant of the previous service estate, but as a unified corporation, a class-estate enjoying special privileges. At the same time Peter, though markedly favoring the nobility as a privileged estate, declined to loosen the harness or to remove the service obligations typical of the old estate of servitors. On the contrary, with the introduction of the regular army and the bureaucratization of administration these obligations became even more burdensome.

Noble status could have privileged significance only when its bearer served. The only nobleman worthy of respect, Peter suggested by his decrees, is one who serves. The 1712 decree to the Senate, which established an officer's superiority to the nonserving nobleman, is linked to Peter's views: "Tell all the nobility, that each nobleman in all instances (no matter what his family) is to respect and to yield first place to a senior officer and service, and this is designated only for officers, whereas for the nobility (who are not officers) it is designated only wherever they are sent."[2]

Peter worked out a system of converting simple noblemen into servitors, for the tsar really could not conceive of their life outside of service. The obligatory schooling of noble sons was a consequence, for without elementary education it was impossible to serve. Besides, as always Peter acted decisively. The decree of 20 January 1714 is unique in Russian history: the nobleman who has not acquired the basics of knowledge necessary for service is forbidden to marry: "Dispatch to all the guberniias several persons from the mathematical schools to instruct noble sons, except the single homesteaders and those of bureau rank, in ciphering and geometry and establish such a punishment that *he will not be free to marry* until he is schooled."[3]

Despite their parents' moans and groans noble adolescents were sent abroad at state expense (hence the term "pensioners" was applied to them) to be trained in diverse special skills. At home these functions were fulfilled by the Naval, Engineers, and Artillery academies to which noble adolescents were also assigned without any special regard for their own or their parents' wishes. Yet the most important school of the nobles was the Guards—the Preobrazhensky and Semenovsky regiments—where they were obliged to serve from a young age. Service as soldiers and sergeants, sometimes under the concerned and vigilant supervision of the tsar himself—colonel of the Preobrazhensky Regiment—was a harsh experience. Furthermore, Peter strove to bar entry into the officer corps to those nobles who had not mastered the rudiments of military service or had not passed through the school of the Guards. A special decree of 26 February 1714 governed this.

The autocracy needed not only soldiers and officers, but also officials for the institutions. The General Regulation had reinforced by legislative means the idea that the Russian nobility's civilian service was one of the most important forms of fulfilling one's obligations to the sovereign and the state. Therefore, a chapter was inserted into the General Regulation that envisaged the training of noble sons in chancery work.

Peter warned that just as service as a soldier was essential for the military, civil servants could not bypass the chancery and elevate themselves according to the Table of Ranks. From 1722 a special chancery post was inserted for sons of nobles, the chamber-junker, that was supposed to be fulfilled without fail.

In order that the pyramid of ranks would reproduce itself there existed in it (and in society as a whole) a clear subordination; the celebrated Table of Ranks—one of the important documents of Russian history—was created by Peter and his associates in 1722–24. It saw the light of day only after careful analysis of similar documents from the developed countries of Europe, documents that had been prepared in accordance with conditions in Russia. The Table introduced a new hierarchy of ranks (distinct from that of the previous service) that could be obtained by means of personal service, rising consecutively from rank to rank. All the ranks were divided into four categories: military (including infantry, Guards, and artillery), naval, state (civilian), and court (household). An important feature of the Table was that it established equivalents between the different categories. I shall give an example, citing the Table:

Class 4

	Army		Naval	State	Court
Infantry	Guards	Artillery			
major-general	colonel	major-general; major-general of fortifications	rear admiral; senior commander	presidents of the colleges and the State Budget Office; privy councillors; senior-procurators	senior master of court; senior chamberlain

In all, there are fourteen graphs of "classes" in the Table broken down vertically into six sections. Accordingly, in order to become a major-general (4th class), a man who had served in the ranks needed to enter the 14th class—to become an ensign or aide-de-camp under a lieutenant-general or brigadier, then be promoted to sublieutenant (13th class), then a lieutenant (12th class), rise into the captain-lieutenants (10th class), then into the captains or aides-de-camp under a general-field marshal (9th class), and then into the majors (8th class) and subcolonels (7th class). Having received the next status of colonel or occupying the post of senior-quartermaster, the officer would appear in the 6th class, and the post of brigadier or general-quartermaster would confer the 5th class. Only after this could he count on becoming major-general (see the table above). With successful service the major-general could move up to lieutenant-general and thereby appear in the 3rd class, from where he could stretch out his hand to full general (2nd class), and perhaps to general–field marshal at the summit of the military ladder in the 1st class. Corresponding to the general–field marshal were the general-admiral and the chancellor in the naval and state hierarchies, respectively.

Particularly important was the civilian hierarchy according to which those serving in the colleges and chanceries could be moved up:

14th class—junker of a college or equal rank
13th class—protocolist or translator
12th class—financial official or secretary of aulic court
11th class—lacking for civil servants
10th class—secretary of college
9th class—collegiate councillor
8th class—collegiate assessor
7th class—senior secretary
6th class—procurator

5th class—vice president
4th class—college president
3rd class—general-procurator
2nd class—actual privy councillor
1st class—chancellor

A special provision of the Table stating that candidates from the higher categories of the nobility are not excused from beginning service from the bottom reinforced the principle of personal merit.

With special fullness and even proverbial power the principle of personal merit is expressed in Peter's resolution on a point of the War College's report from 11 November 1724 concerning the criteria of determining eminent nobility. The War College had inquired: "Inasmuch as it is impossible to know which is eminent nobility, therefore definition is required how to consider eminent nobility: according to number of households, from one hundred and higher or according to the regulation about ranks, up to which class." To this Peter issued a resolution: "Eminent nobility is to be considered according to suitability."[4]

There is no doubt that the tsar invested merit and personal qualities in the concept of "suitability," that is, criteria not linked to origin or, as the War College had proposed, with the number of households or the attainment in service of a specified class in the Table of Ranks.

Here we are treating a very important subject—the right to make a career according to the Table of Ranks for representatives of other estates. There were many persons descended from taxed groups, even serfs and slaves, both in the army and in the state machine, who had made careers under Peter. In principle the previous system of the service estate had permitted this to be done even earlier. Nevertheless, the difference lay in the fact that Peter had distinctly defined in law the conditions under which a nonnoble could move up and become a nobleman. Climbing the ladder of ranks, he merged with the contingent of military and civil officials not as a foreign body but as a nobleman.

Peter's approach to eminence as a distinction defined by a person's personal merit and qualities did not touch the issue of democratizing the society's elite, nor did it introduce "bourgeois" criteria for evaluating a person. He merely opened the possibility for "those suitable," that is, capable and devoted to the sovereign's service, and for those descended from the lower strata of society to improve their social status, and to become members of the privileged estate, the criteria for their evaluation being that same "suitability." Objectively this should have reinforced the nobility and the entire system of authority, always in need of an influx of "fresh blood," with capable descendants from the lower strata.

An analysis made by M.D. Rabinovich of the composition of the Russian army's officer corps toward the end of the Northern War showed that those descended from nonnobles composed 13.9 percent of the total number of officers, with every fifth officer in the infantry a nonnoble by descent. This important political action strengthened the regime.[5]

From several documentary testimonies, one sees that Peter envisioned nobles' composing the entire governmental machine. By the decree of 31 January 1724 it was forbidden to assign nonnobles as secretaries of institutions so that they might not "emerge as assessors, councilors and higher."

The Table of Ranks determined the future of descendants from the other estates. To receive nobility one was required to advance to the 8th class.

There cannot be any illusions in appraising the general position of the noble estate in the state. As a whole Petrine policy toward the nobility was extremely tough, essentially binding, for the noble-officials and the noble-officers enjoyed much less freedom in all senses than those who had served "by descent" in the seventeenth century.

In this regard a question arises: can one call this bureaucratized, regimented nobility that was obligated to study in order then to serve and to serve in unlimited military and civil service (even those discharged from service "for old age and for wounds" for which they had often been examined by the autocrat himself were assigned to garrisons or "whoever will be suited to whichever occupation"), the ruling class-estate in the sense that we understand this, as applied to the times of Catherine the Great and Nicholas I?

It may be objected, to the contrary, that the nobles were the ruling class, for they enjoyed the right of owning lands settled by bondaged peasants whom they exploited. This is true, of course, but as applied to the Petrine era serf ownership was not the exclusive right of the noble class. Bondaged peasants and even slaves could be owned in the seventeenth and the eighteenth centuries by representatives of the service estate and the merchantry. Only subsequently did the nobility succeed in gaining the monopoly right on owning settled lands.

This point requires consideration. We must look more closely into what we term the right of owning settled lands. Actually, in the Petrine era the formal reinforcement of the nobility's landed property came about: temporary holdings, service estates, were merged with hereditary patrimonies into uniform landed property. This was achieved as a consequence of the decree of 23 March 1714—the celebrated decree concerning entailed property and single inheritance. But in and of itself this decree addressed completely different aims. Its direct task consisted of establishing such "order" in landowning that would furnish the state with constant military and civilian servitors from the nobles, "driving them out" of the villages. This was accomplished by prohibiting the division of fixed property among sons according to the decree of 23 March 1714.[6]

Peter cited several motives for so brutal a measure. First, he expressed anxiety about the fate of eminent clans that had been dissolved as a result of the fragmentation of hereditary holdings. Second, the current order of inheritance was, in the tsar's opinion, inconvenient and even harmful to the state, for state revenues from petty fragmented holdings might decline.

It would be possible to set forth many counterarguments in the debate over Petrine "political economy," but it is pointless in several respects. One may state only this: Peter was consistent in defending state interests; he did not shrink from any measures to provide for them, sacrificing in the process the estate interests of separate groups of the population among which were those usually considered privileged.

Thus, on one hand, in reinforcing noble property via the unification of patrimonies and service estates the state introduced, on the other hand, the right of using this property in an even stricter framework than the use of landholding in the seventeenth-century system of service, making a fiction of the gains from merging the two forms of property.

All of this taken together puts in doubt the categorical assertion concerning the nobility as the ruling class. It may be said only about the privileged estate of the military and civil servants of the Russian autocracy, whose privileges existed only so long as they punctually fulfilled their service. Otherwise the privileges were converted into nothing—into dust.

It was impossible for a nobleman of the Petrine era to avoid service by legal means, and the illegal routes were interdicted by very harsh decrees, threatening nobles with public punishment and publication of the names of "no-shows" on special boards nailed to gallows. More terrifying than moral humiliation for the nobleman was the confiscation of holdings for refusal to serve. Decrees promised to give part of the holdings of the "no-show" to delators.

It is hard to imagine what the Russian nobility would have been if Peter's principles had been consistently implemented after his death. The actual emancipation of the nobility and the development of its noble corporate consciousness (in the European sense of the word) came about in large part from its "unbinding" in the decades from 1730 to 1770, when the law on entail was first abolished, the term of service was limited, and the celebrated manifesto of 1762 appeared, the name of which speaks for itself: "On granting liberty and freedom to the Russian nobility." As we have seen, the bases for such an emancipation were more than sufficient.

The disintegration of the service estate led not only to the formation of the nobility, but also to the appearance of so-called single homesteaders, who had remained beyond the bounds that separated the tsar's privileged servants from the unprivileged.

Many factors exerted powerful influence on the formation of the juridical status of the single homesteaders. As servitors of the sovereign, they were concentrated predominantly in the country's south, in borderland military-administrative sectors—the Sevsk and Belgorod militia units—and in their social and economic position they stood closer to the taxed strata, more precisely to the peasantry, than to those who served the center "by descent."

The single homesteaders are reminiscent of the poor hidalgos who served in the vanguard of the Reconquista, the reconquest of Spain from the Moors. Just like the hidalgos, they lived on a dangerous border, and were then called "borderlanders" (Ukrainians) who settled virgin lands at their own risk and expense, guarding the frontier and gradually moving ever farther southward.

Despite the extension to the single homesteaders of the norms of service-estate rights, they were distinguished from the servitors of the center by their mode of life: they lived like peasants; the number of their serfs was insignificant.

The process of consolidating the status of single homesteaders as a special estate group had been under way for a long time, but in the Petrine era, like many similar processes, it was abruptly strengthened. The creation of the regular army cut short, as noted above, the old service-estate system of defense that had involved the servitors of the southern borderlands. For the single homesteaders the most important consequence of the reforms was to deprive them of a series of privileges, and above all of the freedom from direct taxes. To be sure, during the seventeenth century the servitors of the south had fulfilled certain dues along with state service, yet in the Petrine era a qualitative change occurred: the single homesteaders were not included in the regular army, whereas their taxes and dues began to be viewed as compensation for freedom from military service. In sum, in 1710 the single homesteaders were subject to the household assessment along with peasants, including those that they owned.

The ultimate status and estate features of the single homesteaders were still defined not as nobles but as peasants, in the course of implementing the Petrine tax reform—the introduction of the soul tax in 1719–24. Through the decrees on enumerating the population the government bluntly expressed its intention to include the single homesteaders in the soul-tax assessment.

Recognition of the single homesteaders as subject to the soul tax became the point of departure in defining the peculiarities of their juridical status, which in itself was quite a complex and confused problem. For the distinction between those serving "by descent" and those "by recruitment," on one hand, and the distinction between those serving "from the Moscow ranks" and those from the south, on the other hand, had been largely eroded: part of the Moscow ranks served according to the lists of the "borderland" Belgorod and Sevsk militia units, whereas part of those serving from these units had turned up through the force of various circumstances among the "Moscow ranks."

If at the higher rungs of the ladder of ranks the problem of specifying status was not particularly acute, then at the lower rungs—closer to "those recruited"—it was sharply exacerbated because here it concerned vitally important things: whether one was recognized as a nobleman and belonged to the privileged estate of the "well-born" or became a "base" peasant and taxpayer. In the Petrine era the question was posed precisely this way for the majority of single homesteaders.

The central authorities used tax reform to introduce a clear boundary between the nobility and the single homesteaders. Registry in the soul-tax assessment automatically freed one from appearing at noble musters, but in return it extended laws aimed at halting the flight of taxpayers and so forth to the single homesteaders, who were subject to assessment. In 1724 the Senate ruled that exemption from the soul-tax assessment could not be granted even by a charter from the Heraldmaster's Office confirming its owner's membership in the nobility, if such single-homesteader-noblemen "are already assigned to the regiments and the books are completed."

There was one more noteworthy factor in defining the juridical status of the single homesteaders as nonnobles who were close to peasants in position. In 1724 the inspector of Azov Guberniia, A. Miakinin, wrote that "it is impossible to consider the single homesteaders as landowners, for although they may have as many household people [as nobles], but only the most paltry inasmuch as they are themselves husbandmen, they therefore are subject to the soul-tax assessment and are equal to their own people."[7]

To put it differently, in the inspector's opinion the socioeconomic position of the single homesteaders was the reason for extending to them taxed status and assessment, and at the same time the assessment placed on the single homesteaders was the reason for equating them with the peasantry. It should also be noted that Peter's government, interested in preserving the contingents of irregular military forces on the dangerous southern frontiers and also in settling the southern borderlands, did not support the complete conversion of the single homesteaders into rank-and-file peasants. They retained the right of serf ownership and of purchase and sale of landed holdings; the central authorities obstructed the enserfment of the single homesteaders—a trend that was increasing with the extension in the eighteenth century of large-scale feudal landholding to the black earth regions of the south.

The single homesteaders were not a special estate. They entered the estate of state peasants that was forming at just that time as a result of the Petrine social reforms.

The idea of forming a new estate category first arose in 1723 when Peter (according to a notation in a journal of the Senate) had said: "State peasants are deemed to be those who pay the fur tribute, share-croppers, single homesteaders and others similar to that; Mordvinians, Cheremis, which will be explained in a decree."[8]

As we see, under the term "state peasants" the lawgiver understood the most diverse taxed population. The most substantial groups turned out to be the so-called black-plowing peasants of the Russian North, the so-called fur-tributary peasants (Russians and minorities) along the Volga, and likewise the familiar single homesteaders of the south. Besides them the newly formed estate took in the peasants of Siberia—the so-called cultivator peasants subject to labor dues in working "the sovereign's allotted fields," peasants who paid dues in money and kind, and "men of mixed ranks" who had settled in Siberian settlements from diverse categories: servitors, townsmen, churchmen, and so forth. The general number of state peasants was substantial—no less than 20 percent of the total number of taxpayers, that is, more than one million souls "of the male sex."

What united into one estate the coastal population of the White Sea region, the Tatars of Kazan Guberniia, the single homesteaders of the southern towns of Verkhnii Lomov and Elets, and the Siberian cultivator peasants of Ilimsk?

The answer is obvious: Peter's actions in forming the state peasant estate bore a typical fiscal-police character. The foundation for "sewing" the patchwork quilt of the new estate stemmed from the circumstance that all these petty estate groups did not belong to anyone personally; that is, they did not find themselves in bondaged dependence. Therefore, the state decided to unify all this motley aggregation of free people and convert them into a single estate controlled from above.

It is essential to recognize that in the Petrine period the autocracy's policy in regard to those groups of the population that served and those that were free from service took on a pronounced tendency to constrain their rights and to narrow their opportunities of realizing the advantages that they had as people who were personally free of bondaged dependence.

The very unification of diverse groups of the population into a single estate of state peasants was in itself not only and not simply a tax measure as it was an important social measure. Its ultimate purpose was to establish stricter state supervision and constrain the juridical rights and opportunities of free people, of the whole nation. Of course, these constraints were not like those the landowner imposed on his own bondaged peasants; they had the character of public rights. Taking into account the general tendencies of the development of the autocracy's strict social policy in the Petrine period, however, it is still necessary to recognize that the great reformer of Russia's "fashioning" of a new estate of state peasants bound to the tax assessment and constrained in territorial and social movement was converting the categories involved into peculiar bondmen of the state, while their conversion into the bondaged serfs of any owner was accomplished in the eighteenth century simply by a stroke of the autocrat's pen.

In the epoch preceding the Petrine era the autocrat's authority as the supreme sovereign had been extended to the whole population, yet this supreme right was not treated as the right of the landowner to dispose of his peasants. As a result of profound socioeconomic processes under way in the country there was a sharp increase in dependence on the autocratic state at the expense of people who had once been personally free, and the monarch's right in regard to state peasants in the post-Petrine epoch became exactly that kind, when it became common to "grant" state peasants—formally free subjects—to private owners.

The Petrine reforms brought important changes as well in the position of the great bulk of subjects, the peasants who were the property of secular and ecclesiastical feudal lords. Prior to the Petrine era the traditional division of the peasants of secular owners into "service-estate" and "patrimonial" had been retained according to the type of landed property. The peasants of the clergy were divided into church, episcopal, patriarchal, and monastery. With the introduction of the Petrine reforms this division lost its specific content because of the changes of a social and economic character that had occurred: from 1714 the difference between the service estate and the patrimony disappeared, after the church reform there were no longer any church or patriarchal peasants, the stables and palace peasants had been combined, and so on. In a word, in the new conditions intensive processes were under way merging the various strata of the medieval peasantry into the single class of modern times.

For the great bulk of the peasantry—those under landowners—serfdom, which had received juridical consolidation in the Law Code of 1649, had become an important leveling factor. The Law Code had inaugurated the beginning of not only the merger of the two basic varieties of peasants, those belonging to holders of service estates and patrimonies, but also the merger of peasants and bondmen, a category close in position to household slaves.

The institution of slavery had a thousand-year history and a well-developed law. Just after the juridical consolidation of serfdom an intensive process of merging bondaged peasants and slaves ensued, for serfdom had been strongly influenced by the norms of the older slave law. In other words, serfdom was approaching slavery in its worst manifestations: the peasant started to be seen as live property. Nonetheless, at the start of the Petrine era slaves differed essentially from bondaged peasants in that, working on the lord's land and in his household, the majority were not subject to assessment and did not pay taxes. Furthermore, a substantial part of them, the so-called limited-contract slaves, had traditionally enjoyed the right of manumission upon the death of their lord. Custom required that the dying lord liberate his own slaves, thereby completing a pious deed.

Under Peter the process of bringing bondaged peasants and slaves together was sharply accelerated. A big role in this was played by the tax reform. By this means, slaves were included in the soul census, a fact explained by concerns about the concealment of taxable peasants in the guise of untaxed slaves. In the end, all slaves were equated in tax obligations with the peasantry no matter where they lived—whether in the lord's townhouses or on rural holdings—or what their occupation, and thereby they automatically lost the right of manumission. Thus by a single stroke of the pen the thousand-year-old institution of slavery was abolished.[9]

Behind this stood not only Peter's fiscal considerations. As a rule the tendency to enserf slaves to lords had also been typical of the preceding era, yet the Petrine epoch changed the situation fundamentally. The major change in the fate of slavery was the fact that the social base on which slavery had been founded as an estate and an institution had been destroyed. The sources for replenishing slavery were sharply limited. After the Law Code of 1649, which had prohibited taxable peasants as well as servitors from entering into slavery, the sole source of slavery had become the so-called "free and itinerant." The Petrine regime with its strict system of social and administrative control cut off this last legal source of replenishing slavery.

First, a universal and consistent struggle commenced against fugitives and likewise against all of "the free and itinerant," who were placed outside the law and pursued as fugitives.

Second, having launched the Northern War, Peter saw slaves as a source for replenishing the army with live bodies. One may definitely assert that prior to the start of recruiting levies from the peasantry in 1705 Peter's young regular army had been created mainly out of slaves, who had been the majority among "the free" and "the recruited." Both the measures mentioned, and also the campaign against fugitives and "the itinerant," drastically undercut and eroded the milieu that had fed the institution of slavery.

The beginning of the enumeration and census of souls of the male sex was accompanied, as already mentioned, by the wholesale registration of slaves. Furthermore, the census takers made a count of freedmen, who were obligated promptly to seek out for themselves a place for registry in the tax assessment, because the position of a nontaxable subject outside service was untenable. In practice this signified that the majority of freedmen had to register with landowners in the tax assessment, and documents of enserfment were drawn up for them, making them serfs.

Here it is essential to note a peculiar paradox that emerged from the growth of serfdom. The Law Code of 1649, which stipulated the basic condition of limited-contract slavery—a deed of servitude "for the life of the lord"—had asserted at the same time the hereditary eternal dependence of the bondaged peasant on the landowner. By this very provision "legal scissors" were created in favor of the limited-contract slave, for he had the right of freedom by law that the bondaged peasant no longer had. To remove these "scissors," to abolish the slave's traditional but in the conditions of serfdom anachronistic right to freedom even on a limited scale, became the social aim of the tax reform whereby slaves were bound to landowners. Accordingly, slavery as an estate was liquidated the very same way.

So we see that by extending the soul tax to domestics, the majority of whom were just slaves, they became equal to bondaged peasants in every respect: they were forbidden to enter the army under the pretext that those left behind in the assessment would decline from the extra payments for them; in case slaves ran away, fines were imposed on those who harbored them for the years spent in flight ("spent years").

It appears that this action had far-reaching consequences in the history of the Russian peasantry. Slaves worked not only in the lord's household as stablehands, cattle drivers, gardeners, cooks, and artisans, constituting his so-called menials. Data for several districts indicate that the greater part of the so-called skilled and household people (more than 70 percent) were slaves; they did not have their own economy or plot of land like the peasants who worked exclusively in the lord's fields; and they lived in special "people's" and "servant" quarters, receiving at the same time the so-called "monthly"—food calculated for a month. The functioning of the institution of slavery constantly provided the lord's economy with a work force, and, it seems, the share of the slaves' labor in the economy of landowners was substantial. With the abolition of the institution of slavery the burden of work for labor dues was shifted to the shoulders of the peasants proper. This, apparently, is linked to the marked increase of the bondaged peasants' work for labor dues, the level of which, according to the data of Iu.A. Tikhonov, was approaching the limit of the physical possibility of exploiting a person.[10]

Peter had long had intentions of instituting order, as he conceived it, not only in the village but in the towns. However, the burdensome dues imposed on the urban communes in wartime had become the cause of the flight of townspeople from the communes or crossing into "other ranks" (peasants, servitors, churchmen, drovers). At the same time departure did not mean leaving the town or even changing occupation: in becoming a drover or somebody else's slave, a townsman was no longer subject to the urban commune. Such a well-known phrase, oft-repeated in the literature, from the regulation of the Main Municipal Administration, "so that the all-Russian merchantry, like a tumbledown house, be assembled again," was understood by contemporaries as a directive about returning taxpayers to the urban community who (as noted further in the regulation), "not wishing to serve with the townspeople and to pay dues, left the communities and somehow and some way entered into various ranks, both into the peasantry and into the indentured, and supposedly were given away for debts."[11]

But it would be incorrect to think that "assembling the tumbledown house of the merchantry" was Peter's end in itself. His thinking went further: he posed the task of rebuilding this house from the ground up in the new European manner. Peter decided to unify the social structure of the town, bringing in European institutions: urban councils, artisan corporations, guilds. All these institutions, which had deep roots in the growth of the western European town over many centuries, were brought into the Russian setting coercively, by administrative fiat. Without exaggerating, one may state that one fine morning the townspeople of all Russian towns awakened as members of guilds and artisan corporations.

This was done according to the regulation of the Main Municipal Administration adopted on 16 January 1721.[12]

To Peter's way of thinking everything was quite simple; it would not be difficult to implement the regulation's standards. Possibly, therefore, the assignment of the townspeople to guilds was carried out concurrently with their subjection to the soul-tax assessment. When it came to determining the number of taxpayers from the urban population (and it amounted not to 74 kopecks as it was for the peasants but 1 ruble 20 kopecks), the census takers did not start assessing a special levy on "base people" who were officially considered outside the urban commune, but out of concern for the optimal "taxed number" in each town, they started to include them in the general assessment for all townspeople. Nobody even thought about following the standard of the regulation of 1721. As a result, strange merchants appeared in the towns who were written into the census "rolls" like the "merchant" Nikita Popov, a former clerk who was registered in the Tver urban commune: "I, Nikita, have the trade of common work," that is, unskilled labor.[13]

Moreover, it is known that in pursuit of fulfilling the peculiar "plan" of scraping together the "taxed number," the census takers did not scruple to enroll in the merchantry beggars, "the free and itinerant," even serfs; the townsmen of Tver wrote in protest that in the assessment of the urban commune "our serf workers" and domestics had been included.

The beneficent principle laid down in the regulation proved to be the purest fiction, remote from the actual problems of the townspeople, a far-fetched and ruinous undertaking for the more substantial part of the urban commune. The point is that the enrollment of indigent members in the guilds increased the total tax from a given town. At the same time the old principle of intratown apportionment was preserved, at the basis of which lay the rule of determining the size of the tax from each member of the commune according to his "property and wealth," that is, his prosperity, regardless of the soul tax imposed on him. As a result, the burden of payments fell on the most substantial residents of the towns, who were obligated to pay for beggars and the indigent. In this way the town reform, though it led to the formal "assembling of the house of the merchantry" and imposing the soul tax on town residents, yielded no new impulses for the town's development. On the contrary, it hobbled the process of forming capitalistic relations in a place where they might have been developed.

Proceeding from the idea of preserving the old order, the government also delved into the question of the so-called "trading peasants" who lived in towns and who involved landowners' and state peasants in their affairs. If the peasants had settled in the towns before the start of the reform and had been brought into the urban assessment, they were simply registered in the soul-tax assessment as townsmen; a different fate awaited peasants living in town and not registered in the urban commune. All of them were subject to immediate expulsion to the villages. After removal such a peasant was assigned to the assessment there in the village, and then, having received a passport, he could return to the urban commune.

Establishing such an order had been Peter's intention, as expressed in the decree of 13 April 1722. Its crux was that the "trading peasant" might freely enroll in the urban commune by fulfilling two conditions: first, he and his posterity preserved eternally and inviolably dependence on his lord, to whom he was obligated to pay dues; second, in order to get into the urban commune, he was supposed to have trades valued at not less than 500 rubles—an enormous sum for that time.[14]

By legalizing the practice of the rural population's migration into urban communes in this way, Peter's decree set it in an extremely strict framework that was in fact a hindrance, for the establishment of a high qualification for enrollment in the urban commune permitted only a small number of peasants to settle into it. In the urban commune itself the peasant was not a full-fledged member and was obligated to pay high taxes on the sums declared. The law gave the peasant the opportunity to engage in trade and to establish himself in the town, but at the same time it guaranteed the lord's authority over him. It was as if the chain had been lengthened that constrained without rights the serf who intended to leave the village and fend for himself. In this case one may assert that the Petrine reform reinforced and intensified the old social structures—as before, he who entered the town's territory did not become free.

Furthermore, the Petrine reform intensified and unified three constraints for the subjects: on movement about the country, on the freedom to choose an occupation, and on social mobility—on movement from one "rank" to another.

On one hand, all of these constraints were governed by traditional estate principles that directed the state's efforts not only to the crude suppression of social movements, but also to the observance of social stability hallowed by tradition and the law, and the "rightfulness" of moving from one estate group to another. In preserving a monopoly of estate occupations and the corresponding specific social status of each estate, people saw the basis of the legal order, justice, and prosperity for society and state, whereas violations were seen as causing innumerable calamities. The economic growth of the Petrine era, for all its lopsidedness, led to certain shifts in social structure, and this was considered dangerous.

On the concept of a "division" of the estates' occupations rested
much of medieval social psychology, which lived on into the eighteenth
century. The merchantry and the townsmen fought for the preservation
of the exclusive right to commercial-industrial activity to which in the
Petrine era the nobility started to be attracted, sensing the lure of "easy
money" in that sphere of the economy, as were the "trading peasants"
who strove to penetrate into the town while avoiding the town obligations that were common for all the urban commune. From their side
the nobility, considering itself the most privileged estate, fought for the
limitation and even the prohibition of serf ownership by all the other
estates and so forth. Echoes of such struggles are heard in the legislation,
polemics, and petitions of the seventeenth and eighteenth centuries.

From the other side, the estate standards and constraints under discussion were especially intensified in the Petrine era. Peter's legislation
was distinguished by greater clarity in the regulation of the rights and
duties of each group of the population, whether one considers the old
or the newly risen estates, which has already been partly shown earlier,
and correspondingly a stricter system of prohibitions concerning social
shifts. There is no dispute that the Table of Ranks opened the path
upward to representatives of the lower estates, but it also established a
strict order of stratification and distinctly marked the boundaries that
separated the privileged class from the others. The previous practice of
uncontrolled social displacements became history. A role similar to the
Table of Ranks was played by the soul tax. Subjecting a person to the
soul-tax assessment automatically signified his consignment to the unprivileged estate and made it impossible for him to change social status.

As we have seen, the expression "producing the all-Russian subject
people" is not a pompous metaphor, but a real expression of serious
social changes that led to crucial alterations of status and of the fate of
all estate groups in Russian society. Peter's transformations of estates
were definitely oriented to the extension and strengthening of state
influence over society. Whether one considers the noble estate or the
urban commune, slaves or peasants, everywhere at the basis of social
policy the interests of the "regulated" state were placed in the forefront—interests that crudely subordinated and reformed or deformed,
accelerated or obstructed many natural social-class processes resulting
from the development of society from medieval to modern times.

One reform—of the church—which held special social and political
meaning, should be recounted in more detail, and this will be done in
the following chapter.

Reforming the Clerical Rank

In its consequences the reform of the church administration was one of the most important Petrine reforms. It should be noted that the tsar had been considering it for a long time. A turning point in the new policy toward the church had occurred after the death of Patriarch Adrian in October 1700. Among the letters informing Peter about it was one of 25 October from Aleksei Kurbatov, a well-known "profit maker" or voluntary inventor of various requisitions and taxes from the populace. In his opinion the patriarchal system of administering the church had become ineffective, so in selecting the new patriarch "it will be proper to wait until such time as you yourself may wish to review your autocracy in this regard."[1]

Peter fully exploited Kurbatov's advice and others like it: he made no move to select a patriarch, but instead on 16 December 1700 appointed Stefan Yavorsky, metropolitan of Riazan and Murom, as the so-called "overseer" of the patriarchal see. On 24 January 1701 the Monastery Bureau, which had been closed in the 1670s, was restored under the supervision of boyar Ivan Musin-Pushkin, a nonclerical figure who received full authority over the church's land and financial affairs. The same move placed its riches under the state's control and they started to be used for the needs of the army, the navy, and foreign policy.

Stefan Yavorsky's influence steadily declined over the years, and first place in the informal church hierarchy was assumed by Feofan Prokopovich, who had become archbishop of Pskov in 1718. An exceptionally well educated and talented man, Feofan was an utterly unscrupulous statesman who displayed true enthusiasm in every matter, even unseemly ones, that the tsar delegated to him. A profound knowledge of church and secular history, together with a brilliant mastery of dialectics and logic, enabled Feofan to justify forthrightly the necessity of a fundamental restructuring of the Russian Orthodox church on principles of collegiality and full subordination to secular authority. Taking part in the compilation of the reform's main document, the

Spiritual Regulation of 1721, Feofan presented the church reform as the pious act of a God-fearing monarch concerned exclusively with fulfilling his own Christian duty.

> Among the many cares derived from the obligation of our God-given authority concerning the reform of our people and of other states subject to us, we have given consideration also to the clerical rank. Perceiving in it much disorder and great deficiency in its affairs, we have experienced in our conscience no idle fear that we appear ungrateful to the All-High if, having received from Him so much good success in reforming not only the military rank but likewise the civil rank, we should neglect the reform also of the clerical rank. And when He, the impartial Judge, asks from us a reckoning concerning this great commission entrusted to us by Him, let us not be without reply.[2]

Needless to say, after everything that Peter did to the Russian church in "reforming the clerical rank," he would have had much to answer for in the other world. But the true purposes of the transformations were different all the same: the princely system of administering the Orthodox church with its elements of autonomy had become archaic and undesirable for the autocratic regime that which created a bureaucratic machine for servicing the requirements of its authority. Therefore in the course of introducing the state reforms the patriarchal administration was destroyed.

The *Spiritual Regulation* stated forthrightly the unacceptability of any independent force that might oppose the autocracy and lead astray "simple hearts." The advantages of collegial administration were obvious to the compilers of the *Spiritual Regulation*, for "the fatherland need have no fear of revolts and disturbances from a conciliar administration such as proceed from a single, independent ecclesiastical administrator. For the common people do not understand how the spiritual authority is distinguishable from the autocratic; but marveling at the dignity and glory of the Highest Pastor [i.e., the patriarch], they imagine that such an administrator is a second Sovereign, a power equal to that of the Autocrat, or even greater than he, and that the pastoral office is another, and a better, sovereign authority. Thus have the people, on their own, become accustomed to think."

This citation palpably sounds echoes of the struggle that had flared up in the mid-seventeenth century between Tsar Aleksei and Patriarch Nikon, who had raised the prestige of the patriarch's authority extraordinarily high. However, why was it necessary for the compilers of the *Spiritual Regulation*, the theorists of the church reform, to recall events more than a half-century old? I think it was because the patriarchal church in unaltered form (with a powerful personality on the patriarchal throne) might have become the single moral force able to resist the tsar-reformer and win widespread support from "simple hearts" dissatisfied with Petrine policies.

The establishment of the collegial system of administering the church was directed against just such a threat, for "an administrative college is under the sovereign monarch and has been established by the monarch," and likewise because "the very name president is not lofty, for it does not mean anything more than chairman; thus, neither he nor anyone else can think pretentiously of him. And when the people see that this conciliar administration has been established by the monarch's decree and the Senate's resolution, then they will remain all the more meek, and will largely abandon the hope of obtaining aid for their riots from the clergy."[3]

And so we see that unity of the people and the church was what Peter's autocracy feared!

The publication of the *Spiritual Regulation* in January 1721 begins the almost two-hundred-year history of the synodal administration of the Russian Orthodox church. The Spiritual College created by the regulation was soon renamed the Most Holy All-Ruling Synod and was officially made equal in rights to the Senate. Stefan Yavorsky became the president, Feodosy Yanovsky and Feofan Prokopovich the vice presidents. According to the decree of 11 May 1722 a special secular (more precisely military) official was appointed to oversee affairs and discipline in the Synod. The senior procurator was placed in charge of a special staff of church fiscals, whose functions were analogous to those of the secular fiscals. So that the two would not be confused, the church fiscals were given the fearsome name of inquisitors. They were subordinated to provincial inquisitors and, even higher, archinquisitors.

Ultimately the creation of the Synod, a state institution whose servitors might receive a salary in case of necessity, signified that the tsar was superior to the church's authority and had thereby become the head of the church. The emerging situation is clearly reflected in one of Nartov's anecdotes:

> His Imperial Majesty, attending a meeting of archbishops and observing the increased desire of several for the selection of a patriarch, which had been proposed by the clergy more than once, pulled out of his pocket with one hand the Spiritual Regulation prepared for such an instance and dispatching it, told them threateningly: "You ask for a patriarch, here is a spiritual patriarch for you, and to those who think

otherwise (he unsheathed a dirk with his other hand and struck the table with it) here's a steel patriarch for you!" Then he stood up and left. After that the proposal to select a patriarch was abandoned and the Most Holy Synod was established. In agreement with Peter the Great's intention to establish a Spiritual College were Stefan Yavorsky and Feofan Prokopovich who had been helping His Majesty in writing the Regulation. Peter designated the former chairman of the Synod and the latter he made vice-president, whereas he himself became head of the church of his own state and once, recounting the disputes of Patriarch Nikon with the tsar, his parent Aleksei Mikhailovich, he said: "It's time to constrain the authority not proper to the old man [i.e., the patriarch]; God willing, it is for me to reform the laity and the clergy, for them I am both master and patriarch."[4]

Creating the Synod and abolishing the patriarchate were the most striking but not the only evidence of the Russian Orthodox church's conversion into a state institution and its servitors into servants of that institution.

The Synod was introduced along with a reorganization of the church's internal social structure: unification of the hierarchy of church ranks, establishment of personnel rosters of church servitors, and a purge of undesirable and accidental persons from their ranks.

A noteworthy peculiarity of the church reform was that it was implemented in unison with the tax reform, and the census of souls that composed the basis of the latter was used for the enumeration and classification of churchmen. As an object of the census churchmen are first mentioned in a decree of 5 January 1720, when Peter, upset over the concealment of souls, ordained that the census "rolls" include "churchmen, except priests and deacons, for whom a special roster should be submitted and who are to be allowed a term of a half-year."

Thus, although at this stage churchmen had not been included in the soul-tax registry, their lowest strata—church servants—were enumerated separately from priests and deacons. The sense of this division became evident on 5 July 1721, when the Senate directed "children of archpriests, priests, and deacons and other church servants ... to be subject to tax collection along with other souls." Thus were the majority of churchmen suddenly converted into taxpayers.[5]

Such an unprecedented decision could not fail to provoke the clergy's discontent. The Synod was compelled to appeal to the Senate to exempt churchmen from the soul-tax registry, citing the fact that "servants are holy to the church, and besides many are indigent and live in great need." Furthermore, the Synod considered that "placing" the sons of priests and deacons in the soul-tax registry would lead to staffing difficulties, for as a rule the sons of clergy inherited their fathers' positions, which would be impossible with the extension of the soul tax to include them.

Peter took this circumstance into consideration: the instructions to the census takers of 5 February 1722 indicated that the soul tax should not extend to priests or deacons or their sons "who actually serve at churches," whereas in the absence of such offspring "two persons from the other church servants [could be assigned] to each church." Thus in Peter's thinking a reserve would be ensured to fill vacancies at churches with nontaxable persons.

For the estate of church servants such a government directive unfolded a real drama: church servants and sextons living at churches on the lands of nobles turned out to be in the soul-tax assessment along with the lords' peasants and automatically became serfs, for the law stipulated "to register in the soul-tax collection [those] on the patrimonial lands of that village, and whosoever owns the village owns them too."

That same year of 1722 the personnel rosters of church servants were set at one priest for every 100–150 parish households; all "the superfluous" were subject to taxation. Part of them succeeded in obtaining vacancies among the "budgeted" church servants, and some managed to remain in the parishes where they lived while being registered in the tax assessment, but many turned out to be in the assessment on noble lands. As the decree had foreseen, this led to the enserfment of such former churchmen. Thus there was established a direct link between their inclusion in the soul-tax assessment and their recognition as serfs.

To be "placed" in the assessment forever closed to the churchmen any return to the estate from which they had been excluded. A decree of 20 May 1724 finally made the churchmen placed in the assessment of the soul tax equal with taxable peasants in that the fine for harboring a fugitive former churchman was set at the same amount as the fine for a fugitive peasant.[6]

In such fashion the estate of churchmen had been divided into two parts. One of them, consisting primarily of priests, deacons, and other representatives of the clerical elite, was recognized as nontaxable, that is, privileged; the other part—church servants, unbudgeted priests and deacons, and their sons—merged with the taxable estates and lost the privileges of church servants.

"Imposition of order" in "the clerical rank" did not end there, however. During the reform the estate of so-called episcopal junior boyars was abolished, a special service "rank" in the church hierarchy that had rendered personal service to the patriarch and other church hierarchs. With the culmination of the process of forming the nobility as a special

privileged estate, the episcopal junior boyars were included in the nobility with one condition set forth by Peter: only those were to be considered noblemen whose grandfathers had served as episcopal junior
boyars. Thus were screened out "free persons" attached to the patriarchal household and, naturally, they were subjected to the soul-tax assessment along with other nonnobles.

With the same decisiveness and harshness the state assumed responsibility for the expansion of Christianity (Orthodoxy) among other denominations and pagans who constituted a substantial part of the
population of the state's borderlands. Peter was wholly dissatisfied with
the long and patient work of Orthodox missionaries; he set his hopes
on decisive, rapid, and radical measures with administrative pressure
and force applied to whole layers of society, settlements, tribes, and
peoples. Thus on 3 November 1713 a personal tsarist decree was issued
that stipulated: "In Kazan and Azov guberniias Bessurmen of the
Mohammedan faith are to be baptized in a half year at most."[7]

In order to encourage persons of other denominations and pagans
to convert to Orthodoxy, the newly baptized were given tax privileges, they
were rewarded with lands and peasants, and they were even freed from
criminal punishments, including death for murders and other grave
crimes. If the Synod had drafted a plan for baptism of the population, it
probably would have been promptly overfulfilled owing to such measures.

Thanks to the Petrine reform the powerful church organization became the champion of a secular, or more precisely, autocratic ideology.
The church pulpit became a tribune for propagandizing the autocracy's
initiatives in the form of special sermons "for the occasion" (Feofan
Prokopovich was especially masterful in composing them), and also
simply for the announcement of decrees which were read to parishioners before the start of the service "so that nobody excuse himself
through ignorance." From the pulpit were proclaimed anathema—
church condemnation of political criminals and everything unaccept-
able to the authorities or the autocrat. If the church anathema to
Mazepa is explained by the fact of his political betrayal of Peter, then a
certain Major Stepan Glebov earned anathema solely for cohabitation
with Peter's former wife, Evdokiia Lopukhina, who had been confined
to a monastery.

The extraordinary tsar-reformer may actually have seemed the Anti-
christ to many of the faithful, for he imperiously changed church traditions and dogmas that had taken shape over centuries. Thus in 1721, in
order to retain skilled Swedish mining masters in the Urals, he permitted Lutherans to marry the Orthodox; that same year during the celebration of the peace of Nystadt a seven-day ringing of bells, unusual for

Orthodoxy, was arranged; a great number of new prayers were composed in honor of the victories of Russian arms and other state events. From the Petrine epoch the so-called table holidays entered church life; marked by a solemn church service, the observance of table holidays was strictly obligatory. Among them in 1724 were the following: 1 January, New Year's; 3 February, the nameday of Crown Princess Anna Petrovna; 19 February, "remembrance of the marriage of His Imperial Majesty"; 30 May, Peter's birth; 25 June, Peter's coronation; 27 June, "the most glorious victory at Poltava"; 29 July, "the taking of frigates, first at Hangö, later at Grengam"; and so on. After Peter the number of table days grew, for they were supplemented by many requiems for deceased members of the tsarist family and so forth.

Matters did not end with the use of religious services for state purposes. It is important to note that in the Petrine era the attitude of the secular authorities to faith and the church changed fundamentally. They started to look on both as instruments for training faithful subjects. As the eminent church historian P.V. Verkhovsky wrote, "faith, which earlier had been valued in itself as a means to salvation . . . now began to be valued as something useful for the state, as a training and constraining principle very convenient for purposes of attaining 'the common good.' " This notion finds confirmation in numerous remarks and decrees of Peter.[8]

Peter did not consider it beneath himself, a secular ruler, to edit theological works, books, and sermons aimed at his subjects' religious training in the direction necessary for the autocracy.

We have already spoken of Peter's rationalism and his faith. He looked on the church pragmatically, solely as a school of training in morality, and he even devised peculiar aides for this school. Noteworthy is an anecdote passed on by Ivan Golikov about how Peter struck Vasily Tatishchev with a cane for satirizing holy writ, exclaiming: "I'll teach you how you ought to respect it and not break the chains that hold everything together . . . without inspiring free thinking fatal for good order."

But beyond the drafting of materials for the training of parishioner-subjects, great attention was devoted, one may say, to both the conditions and the regimen of such training. Going to church and performing all the necessary rites were seen not as a believer's internal call but as his obligation. On 8 February 1716 the Senate announced Peter's personal decree containing the following: "The great master has ordered decrees sent to archbishops in all dioceses and governors in the guberniias to order it announced in the towns and districts to all people of the male and female sex that they make confession to their clerical fathers each year. And if somebody does not make confession during the year, lists of their names are to be submitted by clerical fathers and parish priests to archbishops in the towns and to judges of spiritual affairs, and in the districts to priestly elders and local councilors, and the governors and local councilors are to impose fines on these people, three times as much as their income, and then institute confession for them."

Church attendance and confession were thereby converted into obligations of parishioners, the fulfillment of which was strictly supervised and documented. The priest who refused to inform on his parishioners was subject first to fines, and then "for that will be deprived of priesthood."[9]

Especially meaningful and harsh was the Synod's directive of 17 May 1722 violating the secrecy of church confession, one of the sacraments along with those of marriage, communion, and baptism.

According to the decree of 17 May,

> If during confession someone discloses to his clerical father an unfulfilled but still intended criminal act, especially treason or riot against the master or the state, or an evil design against the honor or health of the master and the family of His Majesty, and disclosing such an evil intention shows that he does not repent of it but indeed justifies his intention and does not forsake it, ... then the confessor must not only not give him absolution and remission of his openly confessed sins (for it is not a true confession if someone does not repent of all of his sins), but *must promptly report him at the prescribed places* pursuant to the personal decree of H.I.M. promulgated on 28 April of the present year 1722 in virtue of which, for words reflecting on the high honor of H.I.M. and prejudicial to the state, such villains are commanded to be apprehended with all dispatch and *brought to the designated places.*

In other words, for the priest hearing a parishioner's confession the guiding light must be the everyday law against enemies of the state, not the standards of Christian teaching that prescribe upholding the secrecy of confession.

It is noteworthy that the priest was supposed to not only inform on his parishioner but even go all the way as a delator: "proceed without delay to the designated place and there, where such crimes are investigated, declare everything he had heard about his evil intention explicitly, without hesitation, and concealing nothing."

Every priest, similar to a soldier or an official, swore an oath always to be ready for state service: "Whenever some secret matter, or a matter of any kind, arises that pertains to the service or to the benefit of His Imperial Majesty, which I shall be ordered to keep secret, then I will keep it in complete secrecy, and not disclose it to anyone for whom it is not necessary to know about it and to whom it is not directed that it be revealed."[10]

An astonishing oath! As if it were designated not for a pastor of God but for a secret operative of the office of political investigations. Indeed, a secret operative was just what the Russian Orthodox priest was supposed to be according to the letter and spirit of the Petrine decrees.

A special page in the history of the Russian Orthodox church ought to be devoted to Peter's attitude to monasticism. As we know, Peter did not hide his hatred and scorn for monks. "Parasites," "hypocrites," "bigots"—this is a partial list of the softest epithets the tsar used for them.

There were many reasons behind the Orthodox monarch's curtness and harshness. In the monastic milieu he had encountered the most serious opposition to his own initiatives; here lurked the most determined real and potential foes.

In 1701 monks had been forbidden to have paper and ink in their cells or to write anything. This had been done in order to halt the writing and even more the propagation of the numerous manuscript compositions aimed against Peter and his reforms. The significance of such compositions for counterpropaganda should not be discounted: their authors—representatives of the clergy and monks—were as a rule educated and talented persons, gifted in wielding the pen. An example may be cited in Avraamy, the abbot of the suburban Moscow Andreevsky Monastery and author of a celebrated "Epistle" containing sharp criticism of Peter's regime.

Knowing of numerous examples of violations of monastic communal life by the residents of monasteries, Peter saw them as proof of the uselessness and harmfulness of the contemporary monastic mode of life.

It is indisputable that by the start of the eighteenth century a crisis had arisen in monasticism as a socioreligious phenomenon. Besides other reasons for this crisis not cited here, it had arisen ultimately from the triumph at the turn of the fifteenth and sixteenth centuries of the "Josephite" trend in theology over the so-called "Nonpossessors," whose representatives had preached ideas of an ascetic, eremitic existence as God's servants, manual labor, and poverty. The triumph of the concepts of the "Josephites"—supporters and disciples of Joseph of Volokalamsk—had facilitated the church's progress on the path of enrichment, converting monasteries into very wealthy landowners and later serf owners, which led to the growth of the church's dependence on riches and thereby on the state, which, of course, was reflected in the morals of monastery residents.

By the way, one should not get too carried away with the image of the monkish glutton so widespread in the propaganda of Petrine and later times. The people in cassocks were diverse, and Peter must have known that. Perhaps the true reason for Peter's hatred of monasticism stemmed not so much from the image of sybaritic monks as in the ideal to which the ascetics aspired and owing to which they were independent of the authority personified in the mighty but earthly lord Peter. Intolerant toward all heterodoxy, even to passive resistance, the tsar could not countenance in his realm people preaching other values and another mode of life than those that he himself preached and that he considered best for Russia.

It should be mentioned that he had done a great deal to inculcate his own ideals in the life of monasteries, or rather to place them under state supervision and to compel the estate of monks to work for themselves.

It began, as one may easily surmise, knowing the previous history of "producing the all-Russian subject people," with a census of the monasteries and the binding of monks to them.

The next step was to limit the monks' subsistence. Peter stipulated that for each monk, subsistence be set at 10 rubles and 10 quarters of grain per person annually. All the rest went to the state budget, as it would be termed nowadays, via the system of the Monastery Bureau, which funded the monasteries' expenses. These limitations were a natural continuation of the secularization of monastery lands that had been introduced with the formation in 1701 of the Monastery Bureau. Although part of the patrimonies was subsequently returned to the monasteries, the great bulk of their revenues went to the state.

The encroachment on monasticism continued throughout Peter's reign. On 28 January 1723 Peter transmitted to the Synod via the senior procurator an order to launch a new census of monks and to ban new novices. At the same time it was stipulated to report monthly "how many of the present number of monks and nuns will be leaving . . . and in these vacant places to assign retired soldiers."[11] On 3 March 1725 an exception was made only for widowered priests.

It must be supposed that Peter's thinking in banning the tonsure of monks tended to convert the monasteries into poorhouses for retired soldiers, whose number was growing with each year of the regular army's existence. Indeed, Peter had long since embarked on the path of converting monasteries into poorhouses and had consistently followed it, considering that this comprised the monks' service to the state. The most consistent notions concerning the earthly duties of monks were expressed by Peter's personal decree to the Synod of 31 January 1724.

The decree forthrightly calls monks parasites: "The present life of monks is a form of diarrhea from the other laws and much evil comes from it, inasmuch as the greater part are *essentially parasites*. . . . What is the profit to society from this? Truly only the old proverb: neither for God nor for people, inasmuch as the greater part flee from dues and from laziness, so as to eat bread for free." The sole means for reforming such an outrageous situation, when part of his subjects flee from their obligations to the state, is in Peter's view "to serve outright beggars, the very old and the very young."

For this Peter stipulated that the complements of monasteries be set proceeding from the number of retired soldiers and "other outright beggars" assigned to them, for whom hospitals and poorhouses were established at the monasteries. The number of monks was supposed to be in the following proportions: one monk for two to four of the retired or beggars, "considering those with worse illnesses should have more servants, whereas those with lesser afflictions and the old should have fewer servants, or as will be regarded as best from the example of the Regulation about Hospitals, in age no younger than 30 years." The rest of the monks who remained "beyond the number in service" were supposed to receive land from the monastery "so that they produce bread for themselves" and provide a constant contingent for replacement of the natural decrease of monks in the monasteries. For nuns in the same situation, however, it was stipulated "to feed themselves by handicrafts instead of cultivation: namely, spinning at manufactory shops." Monks were forbidden thenceforth to live in cells; space for them was to be allotted only in special storerooms "in those same hospitals." All monks were subject to constant and vigilant supervision by both spiritual and secular superiors.[12]

Apparently Peter did not succeed in completely realizing his plans for restructuring monastic life; he died too soon, but the attempt to put the monasteries and their inmates in the service of the state is typical of him. The regulated state had no place for a single person uninvolved in some kind of service rank or assigned to a taxable community or at least to a poorhouse.

Integrating the church into the state system was deliberate and affected not only the administration of the church itself but also worship and religious doctrine. The faith, as historian P.V. Verkhovsky wrote, "was made into a means of testing political reliability and effecting state purposes."[13]

This thoroughly affected the methods of resolving the long-standing problem of dissent, which had rent Russian society after the reforms of Patriarch Nikon. From Petrine times the struggle against the schismatics—the main opponents of the official church—turned into a police action regularly implemented by the state itself. At the start a strict head count of schismatics, both men and women, was established. A double soul tax was levied on all of them; in this the government saw an important means to counter the schism. According to a decree of 14 March 1720, all schismatics were given a choice: either recognize the official church or pay a double tax. In both cases the schismatics were supposed to appear at a special Bureau of Church Affairs and report themselves and their offspring.

Special details distinguished the Synod's decree of 15 May 1722 that closed all possible loopholes for schismatics attempting to circumvent the legislation against preaching the schismatic religious doctrine. All schismatic manuscript books were subject to immediate surrender; another decree (of 13 October 1724) warned that "nobody dare to keep such doubtful and suspicious books and notebooks about the schism, neither secretly nor openly in any form *under threat of severe punishment.*"

Adherence to the schism was looked upon as an admission of legal and civic disability. Schismatics were ordered "not to be superiors in any affairs but only to be subordinates, and likewise in testifying not to accept them except among themselves and then on occasion."[14]

The decree issued at the start of the eighteenth century concerning special clothing for the schismatics was repeatedly confirmed, while among all of the "great beards" who paid the tax for wearing a beard the schismatics were supposed to be distinguished by a special sign on the clothing—a patch. In the dictionary of Vladimir Dal' we read: "Patch . . . a scrap of red cloth with a yellow stripe that the schismatics wore under Peter the Great." Undoubtedly the purpose of this decree was to single out the schismatics by a special mark on the clothing, subject them to public humiliation, and make them objects of universal surveillance. At the same time the law forbade them to wear red clothing, so that the patches not blend in with it. By a decree of 6 April 1722 officials were forbidden to accept petitions from schismatics "not in that clothing." Denunciation of violators of this law was likewise encouraged: "Also whoever catches sight of someone with a beard without such clothing, they should be brought under guard before the commandants or provincial governors and the fine imposed on them there, *half of which goes to the treasury and the other half to the captor,* and furthermore *his clothes.*" In 1724 special removable "annual" brass marks sewn on the clothes were introduced. The wives of schismatics were ordered to wear "cloaklike clothing and hats with horns."[15]

All these unprecedented measures in their systematic application, strictness, brutality, and humiliation led the schismatics to flee to remote places, and to numerous "incinerations," the self-immolation of whole communities—the sole form of the schismatics' protest against the coercion over conscience and person.

Concerned about the "regular" fulfillment of the duties of subject-parishioners, Peter's "regulated" state opposed every kind of self-directed activity, every kind of manifestation of unregulated religious initiatives and spiritual feats uncontrolled by the official church. Noteworthy in this regard is the Synod's decree of 16 July 1722 that the compilers of the *Complete Collection of Laws*, where it was published, called the decree "on the invalidity of willful suffering incurred through illegal acts."

The basis for this strange, to say the least, decree was the notorious affair of the schismatic disciple Varlaam Levin, who had addressed a crowd at Penza in 1722 with a summons to oppose the tsar-Antichrist. The case was extraordinary in that Levin had knowingly undergone suffering and death for an idea and, interrogated by senators under torture "on the wheel," had declared "that the people have hearkened to him and presently he stands on his previous opinion and wishes to die and *had wished by his own will to suffer and to die.*"

We must surmise that the courage of a man under torture who chose for himself the path of torment and death made an impression on the Senate and forced the authorities to address the people with a decree condemning "those who from ignorance and madness, or from their own extreme malice, willfully desire evil as the main foes to themselves and are deprived of health and life in vain, attracted by the name of suffering and beguiled by those most bitter torments and death for themselves." This was the greatest mistake, the compilers of the decree considered, for "not every kind of suffering, but *only suffering that is legitimate,* that is for known truth, for dogmas of eternal truth, for God's infallible law, *is useful and pious.*" There was no place for legitimate suffering in Russia, however, because "there has never been any reason to apprehend such truth from persecution in the Russian Orthodox state, *inasmuch as this cannot be.*"

To put it differently, there were no conditions for spiritual feats in the Russia of the pious Orthodox tsar because there were no reasons compelling anyone to undergo torment and death for an idea.

Furthermore, the authorities expressed distrust of such exalted self-directed activity; without a corresponding higher summons equated to a superior's order it is impossible to act, "the more so as we must not dare to undertake such a feat by ourselves without God's own inspiration, just as a warrior does not dare to enter battle without his superior's order." There must be discipline and order in everything, whereas tricks like Levin's are harmful and dangerous, and such "thrice-accursed little people" obtain cheap popularity, to use current language, "and are attracted by dreams of this future glory that flatter themselves: I shall be lauded and blessed by all as I shall suffer for this, history will be written about me, my praises will be spread every-where."[16]

No doubt the Petrine reforms led to the decisive triumph of secular principles over confessional and religious ones. At the same time it should be noted that the history of the second half of the seventeenth century shows that Russia had entered upon this path even before Peter, that it had been an imperious manifestation of the time and a peculiarity of the situation that had arisen in connection with Nikon and the schism. But the Petrine transformations are noteworthy not just for a speed and scope unseen earlier in society's transition to secular foundations, but for the consequences stemming from the conversion of the Orthodox church into a government institution. In some text-books and other works the Petrine church reform is portrayed almost as a victory of outright atheism. In fact, however, it was not that at all. The church started to serve the regime of autocracy and started submissively to consecrate all the latter's initiatives.

The conversion of the church into an office of religious affairs and the subordination of all its values to the needs of autocracy signified for the people the destruction of a spiritual alternative to the regime and to the ideas coming from the state and having their source in statism, statist concepts, and secular authority. The church, with its thousand-year traditions of preaching morals and defending the downtrodden and those subordinated by the state, the church, which in ancient times "grieved" for those put to death and which could publicly condemn a tyrant, became a submissive tool of the authorities and thereby largely forfeited the people's respect as a preserver of spiritual principles. The church lost its supreme moral authority. It is no accident that the peo-ple looked indifferently both on the subsequent ruin of the church under the autocracy's shroud and on the destruction of its temples. If one speaks of faith, however, then it was preserved only thanks to the parish clergy, those common priests who were always with their people and who shared their fate even in prisons and labor camps.

"The police is the soul of the citizenry"

The great reformer of Russia dreamed, as we recall, of reforming his subjects' mores with the aid of perfect "training" legislation and an ideal state structure so that each would acknowledge, without sparing his life, the need of service to the state, that is to say, to the master, for the sake of attaining the mythical "common good." The panacea for all — calamities and misfortunes that befell his subjects en route to the radiant future Peter saw in the creation of one more state mechanism, conceived as something all-encompassing and all-pervasive. The role of such a system, pervading all of the gigantic building of Russian statehood, ought to be played, to Peter's way of thinking, by the police. It is crucially important that the police be understood not simply as an institution, but also as a system of relationships, a mode of universal thinking in which the cult of state authority was taken to the limit.

The chapter "On Police Affairs" in the Regulation of the Main Municipal Administration of 1724 is "The Song of Songs" of the police as a culture:

> . . . the police has its own special standing, namely: it facilitates rights and justice, begets good order and morality, gives everyone security from brigands, thieves, ravishers, deceivers and the like, drives out disorderly and useless modes of life, compels each to labor and to honest industry, makes a good inspector, a careful and kind servant, lays out towns and the streets in them, hinders inflation and delivers sufficiency in everything required for human life, guards against all illnesses that occur, brings about cleanliness on the streets and in houses, prohibits excess in domestic expenditures and all public vices, cares for beggars, the poor, the sick, the crippled and other needy, defends widows, orphans, and strangers according to God's commandments, trains the young in sensible cleanliness and honest

knowledge; in short over all these *the police is the soul of the citizenry in all good order* and the fundamental support of human security and comfort.[1]

Behind each of these clauses is a string of specific measures of the authorities, but we shall speak of that later. Let's try to understand how Peter arrived at the idea of a state inspired by the police.

The urge to implement state surveillance over the private life of each person—to enter his house and family and to monitor his mode of life, everyday routine, and mores, even his external appearance—appeared quite early, at the very beginning of the eighteenth century. As has already been said, the idea of extending "regularity" (the concept that reflected the urge to uniformity and unification on the basis of western European principles about the sphere of public life), had been derived from the idea of "regularity" as the main means of achieving success in war, victory over the external foe. Victory over the domestic foe—the opponents of the reforms—was achieved not only by harsh punitive measures (the executioner's block, the galleys, Siberia, etc.), but also by expunging that which had been so hateful to Peter from youth—"the old"—a concept opposed to "regularity" and firmly linked to the beard, long sleeves, the apparent chaos of Russian town building, superstitions, and customs based on tradition. This victory was achieved (by analogy with the military) through the willful, forcible inculcation of "regularity" everywhere into the subjects' everyday life. As in a war, Peter's decrees about transforming everyday life, customs, and dress sound like orders, curt and harsh. These decrees were to be executed without thinking about their sense and ultimate aim.

The last year of the seventeenth century—1700—opened with a decree of 4 January with the following content: "Boyars and lords-in-waiting and state councilors and privy councilors, table attendants and crown agents, and Moscow servitors, and state secretaries and court attendants and all servitor and bureau ranks, and trading people and boyar people in Moscow and the towns are to wear Hungarian dress and caftans: long on the outside to the midriff, and shorter underneath than outside in the same fashion, and he who succeeds in making this clothing is to wear it till Epiphany of the present year 1700, whereas he who does not succeed in making it, is then to make and wear it, ceasing with shrovetide this year." Apparently at that time, too, the decree came out about shaving beards directed to the cited categories of the population. A second decree appeared on 16 January 1705. It stipulated that all servitors, merchants, and townsmen "henceforth from this the great master's decree are to shave beards and mustaches. And if someone will not wish to shave beards and mustaches, and will wish to go about in beards and mustaches, these are to be taxed "at rates from 30 to 100 rubles." Peasants, however, were to pay "two kopecks" upon entering town. Those who paid the tax were issued a special mark.[2]

In the history of Petrine times it may be difficult to find better known decrees. They have long since become the symbol of the radical nature of the changes implemented by the great transformer and the focus on bringing Russia into western European culture and its way of life.

Peter had begun the shaving of beards and changing of clothing immediately after returning from abroad at the end of August 1698, with the beards of the closest boyars coming under the clippers in the first instance; they were the first also to be ordered to appear at court in clothing of European cut. The example of wearing "new style" women's clothing was dictated to the tsar's closest female relatives—his sisters. There is no doubt that this action, unexpected by all, had been done not only for "the glory and beauty of the state and the military adminis- tration," as was written in the August decree (of 1701), but primarily as a conscious counterposing of the new, the contemporary, the comfort- able, and the desirable versus the old, the archaic, the uncomfortable, and the despised closely associated with the Moscow of the bearded strel'tsy, boyars, foes, and ill-wishers. Here Peter's typical demonstrative- ness and imperiousness were revealed, the desire to compel people to do what he and only he considered best.

Of course, we may laugh at the disgraced boyars—the old people standing humbly before the tsar with shaven chins in short, tight clothes. But looking at the print in which a man is depicted standing on his knees in the mud while a soldier with sheep shears shreds the skirt of a "prohibited" caftan, we may also sympathize with Petrine contem- poraries. Imagine for a second that you have just come out of the subway when you are forced to your knees in the mud in order to cut off your new winter coat even with the ground.

Apparently, for a long time it was possible to support the new fash- ions and manners only by force. Decrees were repeatedly issued threat- ening violators of the dress code with diverse punishments including exile to hard labor, but it was not easy for people to get used to the new dress and to the new look, which had been so radically altered in one day.

Some—especially schismatics—did not hide their dismay, for the tra- ditional dress was directly associated with piety. Others, on the contrary, concealed themselves and bided their time, but on coming home hastened to doff the hated clothes and to don what had been customary and com- fortable since youth, and sometimes they even risked appearing in public in the old clothes. It is noteworthy that the princes Dolgoruky, the leaders of the oligarchs exiled to Berezov in 1730, took with them to Siberia their beloved one-piece caftans, padded coats, and other old-fashioned clothes, which, apparently, they had worn at home throughout the Petrine era.

Finally, still others (and these were the majority, especially among youth) became accustomed to the new clothing and customs introduced by Peter through decrees, triumphant ceremonies, and entertainments. Journeys abroad, interaction with numerous foreigners, and training the young in European manners all left their mark—within two decades the cloaks, beards, and padded coats of their fathers seemed ridiculous to many nobles.

The state did not stop at regulating its subjects' hairstyles and form of dress. It brashly crossed the threshold of the private house, demanding not only that the ceiling be plastered (there are corresponding decrees), but also that people live "regularly." Hardly had they been born into the world than they were inscribed in specially established parish registers at churches; in time they were assigned to school, to a regiment, to a chancery, and to the soul-tax assessment. When they died they were to be buried in coffins of the stipulated type.

From 1705 a monopoly had been introduced on the sale of oak coffins, and a deceased person brought to the cemetery in an oak coffin or one made of pine logs would have to be transferred to a prescribed one made of planks; the priests were most strictly forbidden to bury in unprescribed coffins.

If the prescription about coffins may be explained by concerns to conserve the forests, then the strange decree of 12 April 1722 concerning gravestones at cemeteries, which were to be arranged, "dug in, and set in the earth with such moderation so that they lie even with the position of the place," is explicable only by Peter's typical striving for "regularity," without which "those stones that have been placed untidily and unsuitably confer ugliness on the holy churches, and make obstruction for processions that take place around those churches."[3]

In accordance with the new life-style the state actively introduced new, often uncommon stereotypes of behavior for a Russian person. This was achieved through legislation and the personal example set by the tsar himself and his entourage. A real aid for a nobleman entering the new life came from the celebrated *Honest Mirror of Youth, or a Testimony to Social Intercourse Collected from Various Authors* (1717). This work by an unknown author created a new stereotype of a secular person's behavior, depicting a highly positive image of a young man who avoids bad company, extravagance, miserliness, drunkenness, malice, gossip, and coarseness. He is supposed to be "bold, industrious and steadfast like a pendulum clock" and "respectful and polite in both word and deed, not easily insolent and not pugnacious."

Reading in the *Mirror* about what is forbidden we see that in real life crude manners reigned. An adolescent of Petrine times was advised at table not "to pick your nose or roll your eyes," to blow the nose "like a trumpeter trumpets," "not to blow on the soup so that it splatters everywhere," not to put his hands on the plate and feet everywhere; "do not squirm, and likewise do not pick your teeth with a knife"; and he was enjoined: "when eating do not chomp like a pig, and do not scratch your head." But at the same time one should not conclude from the *Mirror* that it exemplifies the particular coarseness of Russian life. The *Mirror* also includes quite a few recommendations that would not be amiss for people to know today. It is curious that I.V. Saverkina in her study of the *Mirror* has discovered much overlap in the advice to the young man given by the author of the *Mirror* and Lord Chesterfield in his *Letters to His Son*, which appeared twenty years later (plagiarism has been ruled out). Here is the vivid image of the English young booby hardly distinguishable from his Russian brother in arms:

When an awkward fellow first comes into a room, it is highly probable that his sword gets between his legs, and throws him down, or makes him stumble at least; when he has recovered this accident, he goes and places himself in the very place of the whole room where he should not; there he soon lets his hat fall down; and, taking it up again, throws down his cane; in recovering his cane, his hat falls a second time; so that he is a quarter of an hour before he is in order again. If he drinks tea or coffee, he certainly scalds his mouth, and lets either the cup or the saucer fall, and spills the tea or coffee on his breeches. At dinner, his awkwardness distinguishes itself particularly, as he has more to do: there he holds his knife, fork, and spoon differently from other people; eats with his knife to the great danger of his mouth, picks his teeth with his fork, and puts the spoon, which has been in his throat twenty times, into the dishes again. If he is to carve, he can never hit the joint; but, in his vain efforts to cut through the bone, scatters the sauce in everybody's face. He generally daubs himself with soup and grease, though his napkin is commonly stuck through a button-hole, and tickles his chin. When he drinks, he infallibly coughs in his glass, and besprinkles the company. Besides all this, he has strange tricks and gestures: such as snuffing up his nose, making faces, putting his fingers in his nose, or blowing it and looking afterwards in his handkerchief, so as to make the company sick. His hands are troublesome to him, when he has not something in them, and he does not know where to put them; but they are in perpetual motion between his bosom and his breeches: he does not wear his clothes, and in short does nothing, like other people.[4]

Of course, along with a series of general ethical prescriptions the *Mirror* brought into Russian society much typically Russian and which related specifically to Petrine times. The state wished to see not simply a well-bred man who had received an education and conducted himself properly in society, but above all a subject and a servitor. One's early years is preparation for service, and happiness is a consequence of assiduous service: "he who serves, so too is he paid, because he obtains happiness for himself." In the *Mirror* the requirement is stressed that the adolescent be "diligent in all services" and serve "with eagerness and care," displaying in the process special respect for superiors. It is noteworthy that the *Mirror* offers a notion of noble honor, but categorically demands that it be defended not by the sword but by lawsuits in the courts, for the nobleman ought to shed blood only in defending the Fatherland and the ruler.

Quite unexpected for us are the sections devoted to the behavior of women. A persistently stereotyped notion has arisen about the behavior of the pre-Petrine girl and woman according to the model of the Muscovite *Household Manual*—locked away in the women's quarters, meek, an often forgotten Mistress Gloom shrinking from the glances of outsiders. Only under Peter does she come out in public, for he was the real architect of women's society in Russia. But the *Mirror's* advice is aimed not at emancipating women but at inspiring them with greater modesty, meekness, temperance, and silence.

In the section "A Maiden's Chastity" the girl who has come out into the world is summoned, first of all, to modesty of behavior. She ought to rush away from the table if "there should happen to sit down beside her a coarse ignoramus who does not sit calmly with his feet"; she should not rejoice but "be vexed when somebody wishes to tempt her"; when she hears immodest conversation the maiden must not laugh and "thus encourage that," but act "as if she does not understand." To the contrary, "the irregular maiden laughs and converses with everybody, dashes about disreputable places and streets baring her breasts, sits down with other young people and men, rubs elbows and does not sit quietly, but sings dissolute songs, makes merry and gets drunk, hops on the tables and benches, lets herself be dragged into all corners and courted like a carcass, for where there is no shame humility will not appear."[5]

One must suppose that the changes of everyday life and manners that arrived with Peter proved to be quite to the taste of yesterday's female recluse, so that for the following generation of Petrine maidens it became a beneficent cause of women's emancipation to introduce some constraints.

Also introduced under Peter was a new form of entertainment—assemblies—which, it is true, hardly resembled the pastime of freely assembled people, but remind one of a peculiar secular service. It is no accident that the decree about creating assemblies was announced by the senior master of police on 26 November 1718 and began by explaining to the public: "Assemblies is a French word which cannot be expressed in Russian by one word, but to speak in detail: a free assembly or gathering in a house not only for amusement, but also for business, for one may see each other there and talk over every need, and also hear what is going on somewhere else, and at the same time amuse oneself. And in what manner these assemblies are to be arranged, this is defined below this point until it will become a custom." Notwithstanding that it was permitted at assemblies "freely to sit, to walk, and to play," at the same time it was strictly forbidden that "anybody accost or insult another, or dare to make a ceremony of standing up and accompanying and so forth under pain of 'the Great Eagle' " (that is, the obligatory drinking from a huge goblet after which a person fell down dead drunk).[6] As we see, teaching people to conduct themselves without constraint in Russia was possible only by force. Furthermore, the general-policemaster made a count of the guests at assemblies, so that their attendance was, apparently, obligatory.

In speaking about the numerous changes in people's lives during the Petrine era, it should not be forgotten that these were not merely changes in everyday life, manners, dress, and architecture. All these were manifestations of cultural reform. Its crux, as we know, involved a shift of the language of culture when its definite orientation gave way to the Western prototypes recognized as the best. Through this reform the foundations were laid of a new infrastructure on which a new culture could be developed.

A fundamental reorganization and expansion of the system of education took place: general and special primary schools appeared along with higher educational establishments, the dispatch of young men for training abroad was practiced on a large scale, and foreign specialists were invited who attracted Russian students. Furthermore, in the Petrine era the preconditions were laid for the development of science: the Academy of Sciences was created, the first libraries and museums functioned, and expeditions with scientific aims were dispatched to remote regions of the country.

One should not forget about the substantial expansion of the channels of information. Gazettes appeared along with much translated and original literature—all this, in concert with journeys abroad, facilitated the burgeoning stream of information about practically all aspects of the European scene of the time. It is important to underscore that art developed vigorously and in spheres that previously had been weakly developed in Russia. The artistic style of the baroque then dominant in Europe firmly established itself in Russia from the first years of Peter's reign, dictating the hierarchy of aesthetic values, defining fashions, and forming tastes.

For the new culture, openness and the secular were typically in opposition to the earlier, albeit rapidly eroding, confessional insularity of medieval Orthodox culture.

The scholarly literature has justly noted that Peter's cultural reform had been in large part prepared by preceding developments whose manifest features became basic for the culture of the Petrine era. This concerns the development of the baroque in the literature and art of the second half of the seventeenth century when the personal principle started to come to the forefront, when the value of man was acknowledged as such, particularly the practical, active man. The specialization of all forms of creativity was reinforced, and a gradual general secularization of culture occurred. The Petrine reforms "had been prepared not only by separate phenomena of the seventeenth century. They were a logical result of the entire growth of Russian culture that had begun a transition from the medieval type of culture to the culture of the modern era."[7]

Peter's role is great in this regard. Commenting on it, D.S. Likhachev essentially supports Prince Mikhail Shcherbatov, who reckoned that without Peter, Russian society would have lagged behind in its growth by two hundred years: "Without outstanding historical personalities the historical processes would not have changed their direction, but would have been strongly retarded; at the same time the transition of Russian culture from the medieval type to the kind of culture of the modern era would also have been retarded."

Certainly state personalities, or more precisely the personification of the state in them, exerted immense influence on Russian culture of modern, and indeed of contemporary, times. The state, with Peter at its head, transferred onto Russian soil many western European institutions of culture, financing and stimulating those spheres that seemed to be the most important and necessary at the time. In the conditions of Russia at the turn of the seventeenth and eighteenth centuries the state's organizing role in culture was largely unavoidable and essential. For in the absence of sources of financing culture, of trained personnel, and of concepts of the universe with a tradition of regarding science as an autonomous value, any other way to assimilate the new ideas of the developed European culture of the Enlightenment era might have dragged things out interminably, condemning Russia to backwardness in the comprehension of general human values.

At the same time, in patronizing culture and fulfilling the role of Maecenas, the state imperiously dictated its conditions and soaked it for ages in that ineradicable bureaucratic spirit that made the work of the writer, the artist, and the actor just another form of service guaranteed by a salary. Therefore, the outstanding figures of eighteenth-century culture toiled in the ranks of various "commands" and "chanceries," and entered the Academy of Sciences and Arts, whereas those not slotted into these systems felt insulted, like Aleksandr Sumarokov, the poet of the mid-eighteenth century who craved membership in the Academy of Sciences more than eternal posthumous fame as the first Russian poet. Peter's reforms led to the transformed culture's becoming distinctly state related and fulfilling, like the other reformed structures of the time, definite state functions in serving the needs of the autocrat's authority. It is natural that through the complex of cultural values and stereotypes the state exerted a powerful influence on the real life of people, whose habits and style of life were leveled, unified, and subordinated to the state principle. Of course, this unification pervaded by the police spirit manifested itself most distinctively of all in the towns, especially in Petersburg. It was in Petersburg that the Policemaster Chancery was first created, which should be considered the first functional police office. The general-policemaster was placed at its head. Among the chancery's duties were "to beget good order" and "to drive away disorderly living."

Deciphering these general principles indicates that police duties were quite broad. Building codes, fire safety, cleanliness on the streets, regulation of trade—this is far from a full list of the duties of the Policemaster Chancery. The chief one was looking after the residents. For this the chancery organized nightly patrols of townsmen united into tens, demihundreds, and hundreds and strictly ensured that "at night at unspecified hours nobody venture out, except eminent persons, and fires be extinguished, and no drink or goods be sold," in order that all speedily fight fires in accordance with special regulations and so forth. After Petersburg a Policemaster Chancery was organized in Moscow and then in other towns too.[8]

Yet the policemaster chanceries would have been manifestly impotent in the role of "the fundamental support of human security and comfort" in the whole huge country. The army, stationed in all the guberniias and districts, might have become a force that could have instituted order in the state. It had become the first in the history of Russia to fulfill police functions on the local level. This stemmed naturally from that important social role that Peter had given the army in the new system of administration after the war. Of course, it would be an exaggeration to assert that the army was stationed in the districts especially to implement police oversight, but we shall not twist the truth if we say that this purpose loomed large among the calculations of the tsar-reformer, who at the end of the Northern War pondered how to quarter the army most rationally.

A precondition of the creation of a general state system of police oversight and at the same time an essential condition of its wholesale introduction stemmed from the tax reform of 1719–24. The state was interested in seeing to it that the population punctually paid the soul tax. But the army was even more interested inasmuch as the soul levy went directly for its maintenance.

The colonel's duties specified by special laws, the "Schedule of Payments" and the "Instructions for the Colonel," included looking after the completeness and speed of the land commissars in collecting soul-tax monies; he likewise looked after the correct distribution and disbursement of the money collected in the district for the needs of his own regiment.

But Peter did not stop with turning over to the army functions typical of civilian financial offices. The colonel's fiscal duties were only one of the aspects of his main duty—"to oversee the rural police," or speaking more bluntly, to fulfill police functions. The "Schedule" and the "Instructions for the Colonel" devote special attention to the military's police functions in the districts.

The colonel was recognized as the head of the rural police in the district. He was obligated to oversee the nature of the mutual relations of army and populace, preventing potential violations and abuses.

Another important police function of the army was the suppression by arms of any "brigandage," including cases of resistance of bondaged peasants to lords and local authorities. The "Schedule" stipulated the regimental commander's strict responsibility for overseeing that in "his" and neighboring districts there were no brigands, and likewise the populace's responsibility under threat of "severe punishment" and banishment "to perpetual hard labor" to report to the colonel, who was obligated, also under threat of severe punishment, to catch such brigands immediately.

Gradually a whole police system was created at the basis of which lay principles of constant surveillance over the population and diverse constraints that applied not only to serfs but to all subjects. As the social constraints have already been discussed, here we shall review the constraints on movement about the country.

The "Schedule," and also the special decree "On the colonel's duties in overseeing the rural police in the districts," mostly prescribed a struggle against fugitive peasants. In the "Schedule," where there was a separate paragraph "On restraining peasants from flight," the colonel's duties were formulated this way: "The colonel and the officers are ordered to see to it that from the peasants who have been assigned to the regiment nobody flees, and if they learn that some are preparing for flight, to restrain them from it. Go in pursuit and catch those who flee. And order both those caught and those restrained to be punished by their lords."[9]

An important peculiarity of the norms of the "Schedule" and the decree was that they devoted less attention to capturing and returning fugitives than to nipping flight in the bud. This could have been achieved only by careful, vigilant surveillance of the population, and "prophylaxis" by encouraging denunciations of intended flight. At the same time it was most strictly forbidden to accept fugitive peasants in districts where they had not been registered for the payment of the soul tax.

The state's police functions in the social sphere were manifested with particular clarity in resolving the question of the so-called "free and itinerant." As we know, the legislation of the seventeenth century had recognized the existence of "the free and the itinerant" who, according to the Law Code of 1649, were those deemed to be outside the three social statuses that partly overlapped each other (the servitors, the bondaged, and the taxed). The Law Code stated that "free people" are those who are "not sons of fathers in service, and who are not in the ruler's service or the tax assessment anywhere, and who are not slaves or peasants or landless peasants under anyone." The presence of "free and itinerant" people, from whose ranks servitors, slaves, and workers were recruited, constituted a characteristic peculiarity of Russian medieval society that had become unthinkable with the construction of the Petrine "regulated" state.

It is noteworthy that in discussions in the Chamber for drafting the Law Code of 1700 concerning an article about accepting "free" people into the peasants and landless peasants it was decided: "This article is set aside . . . because after the first Law Code [of 1649] *there is nobody free except for churchmen.*"[10] After the church and tax reforms this could not be said even about churchmen, for in introducing the reforms Peter had carefully provided that nobody "got out" of service or the tax assessment or some occupation. The whole thrust of legislation and practice was to end once and forever all estate and social uncertainty, escape from tax liability, and avoidance of service. If according to the Petrine decree of 1722 each nun was supposed to learn spinning or handicrafts "two or three times per month from the time of receiving this decree without shirking," and according to another decree all village and town idiots as well as "the blind, and the badly crippled and the senile" were supposed to pay the soul tax (although, as indicated in the decree, "of course they have no occupation or support"), then it is understandable that the fate of "the free and the itinerant" was predetermined.

There was no place for the category of "the free" in the Petrine state's estate structure. They simply began to be equated with fugitives and criminal elements and to be persecuted accordingly. The principle of this policy was realized with special consistency during the tax reform. All subjects were supposed to be included either in service or in the tax assessment, and whoever was unfit for service or for paying taxes was assigned to a poorhouse "only so that . . . there be none without occupation and in idleness." So it was written in a decree about certifying petty servitors. This principle operated as applied to other estates too. Thus, a decree reviewing the staffs of scribes throughout the country noted that servitors not attached to the chancery staffs would be subject to the assessment and choose an occupation, "only so that none remain unassessed and sunk in idleness." Those unfit for service and retired soldiers were also admonished "that none of them be in idleness, but assigned to other services or to someone in domestic service." In like fashion the fate of "unbudgeted" churchmen and former slaves was decided.[11]

The measures in the struggle with "the free" were extended to the indigent too. On 6 April 1722 Peter "was pleased to order that the indigent in all localities be caught, and whoever will keep them or to whom they will turn, those shall be fined."

Therefore, other decrees also designated massive roundups of "holy fools," "idiots," "orphans and the poor," and beggars and similar vagabonds. For example, in January 1724 Lieutenant Timofeev, who was conducting the census in Nizhny Novgorod, reported to his superiors that he had seized from the Nizhny Novgorod pothouse (i.e., from a tavern) "naked men, who testified under interrogation that they had not been registered in any census registers anywhere," and they were dispatched "to former residences" for assignment to the assessment or to a poorhouse. The matter involved prodigal drunkards who had drunk up everything and had been living in taverns till warm weather; they were fortunate the latter had not been closed.[12]

Lieutenant Timofeev operated according to government resolutions about liquidating beggary and vagabondage. On 3 June 1724 a decree was prepared about a grandiose police action to enumerate and to register beggars throughout the country. It was proposed to conduct the action in one day—1 October—all at once in all localities, "where there are old, sick, and crippled beggars and orphans, both of the male and of the female sex, who were in poorhouses and hospitals and furthermore those who appear sick and crippled and who cannot feed themselves by work, and who are not assigned to anyone, and have not been placed in the soul-tax assessment." So that this action did not become known to the common people beforehand, it was categorically prohibited to open the envelope with the decree to the governors and the district officials before 1 October, and upon opening "all should begin enumerating at once the same day as soon as they unseal it."[13] The state, as we see, successfully executed the prescription of the Main Municipal Administration's regulation: "the police . . . care for beggars, the poor, the sick, the crippled and other indigents; defend widows, orphans and strangers according to God's commandments."

As a whole "the free and the itinerant" were viewed as an alien body in the social organism that posed a social menace. In certifying churchmen the census takers were required "to watch out in every way that from these itinerant there be no forgery. . . . Because from those that wander about without service one cannot hope for state benefit, but only an increase of theft."[14] This also cited the main reason for arranging the "sorting out of the common folk" under Peter—to apply to each person the criteria of state benefit and to evaluate a person accordingly, changing his status if need be.

The struggle with "the free and the itinerant" became part of a whole system of combating fugitives. It is natural that this struggle entailed bygone traditions from the pre-Petrine period. But again we cannot overlook the many quantitative and qualitative changes that occurred in connection with the reforms. The crux of the changes was not only the reinforcement of practical measures in the fight against fugitives, but a change in the lawgiver's approach to evaluating this widespread social phenomenon, when "flight began to be seen in general as unsanctioned departure by all who find themselves in the assessment or bondaged dependence."[15]

Such an expansive interpretation of flight reflected a new direction of policy that had become dominant during the formation of Peter's "regulated" state, or more precisely from the start of the tax reform, the soul-tax enumeration and census, which were used, as we saw earlier, for the "imposition" of a new social order in the country and which were included in the struggle against fugitives.

Here we shall single out the most important factor. At the turn of the seventeenth and eighteenth centuries the struggle against fugitives had been waged with the aid of special detachments of "searchers" dispatched to the places fugitives had settled (remember how the Bulavin rebellion began) and which, upon arrival in the designated region, apprehended fugitives, primarily bondaged peasants, and returned them to their former places of residence. Occasionally the owners of fugitive peasants were themselves compelled to take up the search and, upon finding them, to petition the authorities to assist in returning the fugitives. During the Northern War the government could not give the matter much attention. Furthermore, the demand for working hands at works, at construction sites, and in the armed forces had led the authorities to wink at fugitives.

The policy changes of Peter's government appear all the more striking beginning in 1721, when a series of laws intensified the struggle against fugitives as compared with the preceding period. Especially important is the law of 1 February 1721, which had been drafted with the tsar's active participation. It established a definite term for the return of all fugitives—a year and a half from the moment of the decree's publication. The contingent of those considered fugitives was abruptly expanded—added were the sons-in-law of fugitives, even if they had never fled anywhere themselves and lived separately from their fathers-in-law. This norm, by the way, had been unknown to the law of the seventeenth century. The decree doubled the fine for failure to return fugitives on time and introduced corporal punishments and banishment to the galleys for elders and stewards guilty of hiding fugitives.

Even more severe punishments awaited landowners who risked taking in fugitives after publication of the decree. Striving by cruel measures to create unbearable conditions for harboring fugitives, the law encouraged stewards and elders to denounce their lords if they compelled their own people to accept fugitives in hamlets. Denunciation might lead to all hamlets of such a lord being confiscated "irretrievably, whereas the delators for their true denunciation are to be made a reward, namely freedom from and a quarter share in those confiscated hamlets." Thus, by informing "where proper" on one's lord, one might not only receive freedom, but also become a landowner.[16]

The decree of 1 February 1721 and the supplement of 6 April 1722 became the juridical basis for the start of an unprecedented campaign of catching and returning fugitives. The military census takers, who were then implementing the census of male souls for "placing" them in the assessment of the soul tax, were preoccupied with this. All fugitives were obligated to be dispatched to their former places of residence and to be registered in the tax rolls. A remarkable peculiarity of the new, large-scale action, which employed the army throughout the country, was that the return of fugitives was implemented by means of those harboring them, who were obligated to present the receipt of the fugitive's owner concerning his exact delivery to the right address, and also that all fugitives were interrogated beforehand, often under torture, in the military chanceries that certified taxable souls.

The care exhibited by the census takers in certifying each estate and district, interrogations, face-to-face confrontations and torture at the first suspicion of submitting false testimony, threats of huge fines for harboring fugitives, apprehensions of denunciation, confiscations of property—all this overheated the situation in the localities and made it unbearable both for the fugitives themselves and for those who harbored them. Therefore in 1722–25 the chanceries that were certifying souls were literally swamped by cases of fugitives who had been brought in by the thousands by those harboring them. Fugitives voluntarily "presenting themselves" to the chanceries became widespread. Those who had been harboring fugitives—frightened by the decrees and the red tape in settling cases of flight and not wishing to be burdened by the return of those living with them—simply "expelled" the fugitives from the property, leaving them on their own.

Among those turning themselves in to the authorities were quite a few peasants with families. Why did they come to the chanceries in person? The problem of fugitives should not be oversimplified. Not every peasant, often burdened by a family, was able to flee to the Don or abroad. Not everyone even wished to flee, although the flood of fugitives to Poland rose sharply just at this time. As we know, a huge number of fugitives settled in the country's interior regions on palace, church, noble, and state lands. Here the fugitives established themselves with families and kin, built houses, and entered the assessment "in equality" with the local peasants—in short, they "grew into" the new places. The new laws struck most painfully not at vagabonds wandering from place to place, but at those peasants who had fulfilled, despite the law, their human right to choose a place of residence on earth and who aspired to live "freely without any state imposts and masters' dues." For thousands and tens of thousands of such peasants, return to a former owner or expulsion was a real calamity.

It was a calamity for the country as well. Even the census takers saw that. One of them, F. Chekin, reported that it was altogether senseless to return fugitive state peasants from state lands to their former places of residence because "in the former places from which they have departed, there are no households and no shelter and it will be impossible for them soon to establish household buildings and cultivated fields."[17] In 1723 it was decided not to return state and palace peasants that had migrated to other state and palace lands. No consideration was given to landlords' peasants. The authorities pursued especially strictly their return to their previous owners according to the letter of the law. To be sure, in 1723 one "indulgence" was allowed. Peter ordered that serfs living on palace lands not be returned if they had settled in whole villages or they composed no less than a third of the population. In this case the peasants were not freed from the landowner, but on the contrary the landowner received ownership over such a village along with the lands settled by the fugitive peasants. No doubt the tsar's decision in defending the existing social order could only be welcomed by landowners who thereby received new possessions.

Of course, not all peasants obediently went to the chancery. In the census takers' reports one finds that the peasants, "being fearful, a day or two afterward fled nobody knows where"; hamlets proved to be "empty because of the flight of the peasants to parts unknown"; and "the peasants fled from them en route nobody knows whereto."

Many went off to the Don. In discovering empty villages, the census taker of Azov Guberniia, A. Miakinin, surmised that the peasants had fled to the Don, for "besides the Don there is nowhere to go, for there is no such freedom anywhere in the all-Russian state except in those localities."[18] A curious admission! Many other sources confirm Miakinin's observation.

The growth of flight abroad, primarily to Poland, was a consequence of the massive police effort. In 1724 the Senate got word that the borderguards could not contain the fugitives and that at the checkpoints "come fugitives assembled in large numbers who do battle with firearms and cudgels against the dragoons as if they were enemies." The Senate directed the War College to reinforce the border cordons with army units and, "if any fugitives try to force their way through, then such miscreants are to be shot at with firearms." Once, the Senate discussed the problem of deploying the whole army along the border in order to create a powerful covering detachment in the path of the peasants leaving for Poland.[19]

The grandiose nationwide search for fugitives was no caprice of Peter's. It was a considered action that had been calculated along with others already mentioned earlier to lay down the bases of a social order corresponding to the general conception of the police state. The laws about fugitives implemented while enumerating the current population and placing it in the tax assessment were not temporary. They created the juridical basis for the struggle against all forms of unsanctioned movement around the country. The law about pursuing fugitives, or to put it differently, the ban on abandoning one's place of residence, which had also become the place of paying the soul tax, was extended beyond landowners' peasants to all of the population that had been included in the soul-tax assessment.

There can be no doubt that the laws on fugitives reinforced police surveillance of the country's population. The aforementioned decree of 6 April 1722 stipulated the return of all fugitives and payment of a fine for the years spent as fugitives—the so-called "residence"—except for those peasants who "are released to work as shepherds or in other work for hire, and not by flight." Further it was noted: "And henceforth by this decree landowners and clergymen and stewards and elders are to provide letters signed by their own hand to whomsoever is released for some work or simply for work whereby he might feed himself, to write it down precisely so that he not go about begging inasmuch as there is a decree about beggars and the crippled, whereas the healthy when caught are ordered to be sent to convict labor with punishment, for among those with such letters there have been many thieves, if not all of them, and do not accept anyone without such letters according to previous decrees."[20] The words "for some work . . . " to the end the decree were written by Peter himself and epitomize his distinctively strict thinking.

Peter's idea about passports—documents without which a person could not leave his place—was consistently brought into the aforementioned "Schedule" of 1724 defining the army's relations with the populace. It must be repeated that, as in many other cases, passports were not Peter's invention. Even in the seventeenth century the practice had existed of providing peasants who went away to work with special "subsistence tokens." Neither in the seventeenth century nor in the course of the Northern War had there existed the strict passport regime that appeared after the introduction of the laws about fugitives and with the start of billeting the army. The introduction of the soul-tax levy, which had been built on an enumeration of the country's entire male population, served as its basis, whereas reinforcing the general principles of police order in the country made the strict passport regime a reality.

On the eve of introducing passports the tsar was given a project whose author is not known. He welcomed the tax reform and believed the introduction of the soul tax should be used to strengthen surveillance over the population via a system of passes and passports. In the opinion of the project's author, it was impossible in general to allow movement around the country to all who desired it. Passports, which the projector named "patents with a coat of arms," need not be given out to more than a quarter of the population enumerated by the census. A landowner's trusted people would receive from the local rural councillor a set number of "patent"-passports for a given estate and

distribute them with great circumspection to those who wished to go off
for work. The "patent" was good only for five years, and without it the
peasant was considered a fugitive.

The project's author saw the system of "patent"-passports as universal, encompassing all categories of the population. Thus, merchants
would have "patents" specifying the route of their travels and listing the
goods conveyed.

The unknown author's enthusiasm for police truly knew no limits.
He devised a complex, refined system of surveillance over all subjects.
Everyone, upon returning from a trip, was supposed to present in obligatory order a letter given in the chancery of the town to which he had
traveled according to the passport. This letter was supposed to contain
confirmation "that he was there and not in other places, from which
each will be truly ascertained." The introduction of such peculiar certifi-
cations of travels—long familiar to Soviet readers—was supposed to
reinforce order and facilitate "the state's profit."[21]

It would hardly be worthwhile to dwell on the project of an unknown
fanatic of the police regime if his ideas had not been largely brought to
life in the "Schedule" of 1724 and other stipulations of the time. In
particular the "Schedule" stipulated: "Each peasant is allowed to feed
himself by work in his own district with written passes signed by his own
lord, and in the lord's absence signed by his steward and the parish
priest; without such passes one is not to go to other districts or more
than thirty versts from home and is not to be accepted for work; and
whoever will accept and will hold someone more than thirty versts away,
he shall be fined just the same as the fugitive."

For someone who wished to go to another district, the lord and the
parish priest were supposed to give a pass to the rural commissary, who
was charged to record information about such a peasant in a special
book and give him "a signed letter of passage from himself and signed
and sealed by the colonel whose regiment has permanent quarters in
that district," carefully checking that the pass ("release") from the lord
and the parish priest was authentic.

The peasant paid two kopecks to obtain a passport of the established
form. Knowing the "human" habits of local and other authorities, the
authors forewarned: "more than this is certainly not required and the
peasant is not to be held up more than two days, under threat of severe
punishment." In the letters of passage the term was strictly stipulated
(no more than three years) for which the peasant was being released
and beyond which it was forbidden to keep him at the places of work. It
was categorically forbidden to give out "letters"-passes to peasant families, and the authorities were forewarned: "though some peasant pre-

sent such a letter, it is not to be believed, and both at the checkpoints and at lodgings they are to be caught, and sent back under convoy to the former places and lords." There were quite a few other petty bureaucratic hooks and crooks that might be used to hinder the freedom of leaving for work elsewhere. Furthermore, while working, the furloughed peasant was forbidden to marry.[22]

The introduction of passports in 1724–25 resulted in the authorities' ability to control the population's movements, limiting them by temporal and spatial frameworks, which was almost immediately reflected in the economy. It has already been mentioned that many entrepreneurs at the beginning of the 1720s started to experience difficulties with the hired labor force that were also linked largely to the introduction of the passport regime.

Naturally, wherever something becomes more stringent, people strive to find an illegal outlet, to deceive. One of the methods to circumvent the law immediately became the fashioning of false passports. To prevent this the authorities introduced printed passports. They were supposed to be given out not by the rural commissaries but by the district and guberniia administrations. All of a sudden a new problem arose. As local officials wrote the Senate: "if a district is extensive, for example, Moscow, Novgorod, and Nizhny Novgorod or many others like them, one from such a district is not free to hire himself out in another district or to go to work without having received a passport from the district, but must go one hundred or two hundred versts to the provincial governor in town, and will have expended his last on the road before he has obtained work to pay the dues."[23]

In other words, in order to go off to work at a distance of forty versts, one had to trek two hundred for a passport! Another Russian characteristic, red tape, is well known to us when for weeks peasant-petitioners "drag themselves around town for passports."

Execution and discipline—that is what was most required of all subjects. Quite a few methods and institutions enabled the authorities to supervise execution of that which had been ordered. As noted above, the police was not merely an institution or an office, but presumed a special social conduct, a special way of thinking. It is logical that under Peter we encounter the full-blown institution of denunciation, an authentic culture of denunciations.

To be sure, denunciation did not arise with Peter. Researchers date the appearance of legal norms for denunciations ("delations") to the time of the rise of Muscovy, when the grand princes, striving to bind to themselves newly arrived servitors, included in the "corroborating charters" (deeds sealed by oath) clauses not simply about the vassal's fidelity to his new suzerain, but also his obligation to denounce plots against the latter: " . . . where I learn or hear of any miscreant against my own master it is for me to tell my own master the grand prince without any cunning according to this corroborating charter."[24]

Similar treaties of personal service were later replaced by public-legal records of service fidelity, which also included clauses about "delation." The Law Code of 1649 included the already traditional norm concerning denunciation, supplementing it with a norm on punishment for failure to denounce.

A peculiarity of the law on failure to denounce was that the duty of political denunciation also lay on all of the traitor's relatives. This alone made voluntary departure abroad fearsome too—relatives became hostages and were considered participants in the flight of the accused, which was equated with state treason.

Grigory Kotoshikhin, a scribe of the times of Aleksei Mikhailovich who fled abroad, wrote in his work about Russia that a fugitive's relatives were tortured with such questions: "why did he send to another state, is he not inciting some fighting people against Muscovy wishing to take over the state, or for some other malevolent plot and at whose direction?"[25] As we know, the investigators had many methods of "getting to the bottom" of treason cases.

Another noteworthy feature of the law about "delation"-denunciation was that it extended exclusively to political (state) crimes, among which figured "assembly and conspiracy or any other evil intent" against the tsar, attempts against his health, and treason.

Right here an essential distinction is drawn between the traditions of old Russian law and the law of the Petrine era. First of all, Peter abruptly extended the framework of crimes considered state crimes and subject to laws on denunciation and failure to denounce. Beyond the aforementioned traditional state crimes (intent against the sovereign's health, riot and rebellion, treason) their number was expanded to include "spoliation of His Tsarist Majesty's fisc," that is, embezzlement of state property.

In 1723 Peter drafted a decree about dividing all crimes into "state" and "private" ones. Such a division should have become the basis of the new law code that was being drafted after 1719. Included among the number of state crimes were all crimes of malfeasance; hence the criminal official, "as a violator of state laws and his own duty," was subject to capital punishment. Peter's explanations on this account have already been reviewed: official crimes ruin the state worse than treason does.

Besides malfeasance, state crimes also encompassed quite a few others that the subjects were obligated to denounce as state treason or

impending riot. Among the crimes subject to denunciation were concealment of souls from the census, harboring fugitive peasants, cutting forest
reserves, failure to appear for inspection and service, belonging to the
religious schism, and preaching the schismatics' teachings.

In general under Peter there was a tendency to subsume under state
crimes all kinds of acts committed despite state laws. The legislation
evolved a generalized type of enemy to the tsar and the Fatherland—
"the violator of the decrees and the prescribed laws." No matter who he
was—dignitary or bondman, soldier or son of the tsar—his fate was
supposed to be resolved the same way.

Besides increasing the number of state crimes that fell under the
workings of the laws on denunciation and responsibility for failure to
denounce, Peter actively and somewhat successfully facilitated expanding the practice of mass denunciations, which also enables one to speak
of a blossoming culture of denunciation. This was achieved by diverse
methods.

First and foremost was the creation of a state system of denunciation
in the person of special state officials, the fiscals, whose obligations,
according to the decree of 5 March 1711, entailed "secretly watching
over all affairs and looking into unjust courts, and also into the collections of the fisc and so forth," and later in the Senate's presence un-
masking the criminal detected. If, however, a denunciation was not
confirmed, the fiscal need not worry: under the threat of severe punishment and "ruin of the entire estate," judges had no right to prosecute
him for false denunciation and "neither hold it against the fiscal at all,
nor vex him."[26]

Creating the institution of state fiscality in 1711 held colossal significance, for its activities, hallowed by the state's authority, became exemplary and the model for all subjects' conduct. Its very existence was
supposed to inspire delators of every stripe. Peter's decree of 25 January
1715 directly addressed this. Outraged over the distribution of plac-
ards—anonymous letters—Peter wrote that their authors might forthrightly bring in their denunciations: "And if somebody has doubts
about this, that if he appears he will suffer, it is not true, for nobody can
prove that there has been any punishment or recrimination to any
delator, whereas favor has clearly been shown to many." Although delators were not guaranteed secrecy for their activities, the authorities
strove to avoid publicity as much as possible so as to preserve the cadres
of secret operatives.

Second, with the fiscality's appearance material encouragement for
denunciation became the norm, which had not been specified in the
Law Code of 1649 but had been known in the practice of political

investigation in the seventeenth century. In a special decree of 23 October 1713 encouraging delators to denounce "violators of decrees and the prescribed laws and pillagers of the people," it was underscored: " . . . whoever learns about such criminals should come forward without any apprehension and report it to us ourselves, only so long as he reports the truth. And whoever will report truly on such a miscreant, then for such service he will be given his wealth both movable and immovable. And, if he is deserving, rank as well. Permission is hereby given to people of every rank from the most eminent even to the cultivators."

Third, state offices were ordered to treat denunciations very carefully and to assist delators. The newly formed courts of appeal were directed to accept for processing cases not only from denunciations by fiscals, but "even from someone who is not a fiscal and reports on somebody."[27]

The principle of denunciation from anyone was repeatedly confirmed, "from the most eminent even to the cultivators." Through denunciation anyone—bondaged peasant, slave, relative, neighbor, and so forth—could reckon on snatching a large sum to improve his own position substantially.

Fourth, the institution of fiscality in the narrow (state) and broad (public) sense created an atmosphere of impunity for false denunciations. Although formally a false denunciation was prosecuted by law, the law did not relate to the fiscals or to their voluntary assistants who made mistakes.

It should not be thought that denunciation was the delator's voluntary doing. As had been the case in the preceding epoch, failure to denounce remained one of the gravest crimes.

Everybody was obligated under threat of punishment to report about a completed or a contemplated crime. This was demonstrated quite clearly in the legislation cited earlier concerning priests' violation of the secrecy of confession. The priest who did not report a parishioner could be subjected to capital punishment. It appears that such a law became the apotheosis of the culture of denunciation, no longer leaving a single secret corner in a person's life or soul.

The roots of the institution of denunciation and fiscality therefore reached back to the period preceding Peter, but under him sprouted extraordinarily luxuriant growth. This blossoming of denunciation was justified morally inasmuch as all means were permitted within the framework of the "regulated" state if the purpose was the good of all subjects and the populace.

The reader might have certain associations with the culture of denunciation that flourished after 1917, when the slogan hurled by Stalin's People's Commissariat of Internal Affairs—"Every citizen is a collaborator of the NKVD"—did not seem so fantastic. One also recalls the fact that only recently has the review of anonymous letters been abolished, and that in current criminal legislation responsibility is envisaged for failure to report about thirty-one forms of crime, that figure including some not regarded as grave. Current jurists consider that there can be no discrepancy between law and morality and that denunciation, firmly associated with immoral conduct, ought to be excluded from legislation.

The creation of a statewide police system and the introduction of new principles of social interaction are most distinctively expressed in the phenomenon of Petersburg, the city conceived as the "regular" capital of the "regular" state, as an exemplary city. It is really no accident that the type of building in Petersburg and its architecture were later copied in the building of more than two hundred provincial towns of eighteenth-century Russia.

Petersburg was not thought of as the capital at first. A city-fortress on the first clod of conquered land, Petersburg defended the tsar's new possessions. But over the years the tsar devoted more and more attention to it. He linked it not merely to his own successes in war—Petersburg was becoming a notion, a symbol of everything new that had gone into the concept of the reforms. Peter built his own city like a ship, laying its keel upon principles of town building and architecture new to Russia. Seizing land from the enemy and marshes for his own town that contrasted markedly from the old capital, he loved it the same way that he hated Moscow, which vexed him by its architecture, people, and customs, and which teemed with unpleasant and terrifying memories. There was none of that here, in a land of new buildings, full of the freedom of creativity, which did not limit the tsar in any way. Just as a father is enthralled by the insignificant successes of his own child that are invisible to the world, so Peter was moved by the streets bordered by puny little trees that grew in the Summer Garden. "Paradise"—that's the term the tsar often used in letters referring to his own city, feasting his eyes on its creation, "like a child that is growing into beauty."

For Peter it was natural to identify ideas of the new with the ideas of the regular, as new ideas were brought into a systen via different principles than before. Dreams of a world of regularity were supposed to be embodied on the banks of the Neva. Therefore the tsar devoted great attention to regulating the construction of Petersburg and the life of its residents. This regulation was detailed and intrusive.

As we know, at first the city was built spontaneously; primary attention was devoted to defense and to constructing its citadels. But during

the decade from 1710 onward construction took on a planned character, with the most consistently new principles starting to be implemented on Vasil'evsky Island. Here, according to Peter's concept,
was to be the city's center, built the way that all of Petersburg and all
other cities would be built.

On Vasil'evsky Island completely planned buildings according to the
approved projects of "exemplary" type houses were first erected.

A decree strictly enjoined all landowners to build only on Vasil'evsky
Island, and to build masonry buildings of a size corresponding to the
number of households in the lords' possessions. Those reluctant to
settle on the subsequently celebrated island risked a lot: "And if someone
even after this announcement will not take these places and build their
houses according to the decree: those will be severely punished according
to His Tsarist Majesty's decree as condemners of the decree."[28]

But those who began building were also supposed to fulfill strictly all
standards of building "according to architecture," that is, according to
the plan. Otherwise everything could be razed. In 1721 it was ordered
to build stone houses not only in a line but also compactly in the form
of peculiar barracks. Peter considered that by this means one might
economize on a great deal of scarce stone.

Let's look at one more decree. In the spring of 1718, many substantial residents of Petersburg "for the novelty of this place people of
various ranks are given at no cost fully equipped sailing and oared craft,
with orders that each will own them forever." All the owners of small
craft were obligated every Sunday at a special signal to proceed to a
designated place and to engage in exercises under sail. It was strictly
ordered beforehand that those who failed to appear for these review-ex-
cursions more than twice per month would be fined, as would those
who went home from the "exercises" without permission.

Both decrees are quite remarkable and even somehow linked together, although one concerned the necessary conservation of building
materials, whereas the other instructed the city's residents in the use of
sailing and oared river craft. But this did not exhaust the decrees'
meaning. They contain the realization of the reformer's great dream.
As if looking at his city through the years, the tsar saw its compact
uniform buildings similar to those of western European cities. Before
Peter's thoughtful gaze arose the multicolored façades of the houses of
his beloved Amsterdam standing in a solid wall and reflected in the still
waters of the canals on which stylishly dressed residents play every Sunday
on yachts and small boats to the sounds of music. Indeed it is no accident
that Peter had ordained: "All canals and the streets on both sides of them
are to be in breadth as against the Herengracht in Amsterdam."[29]

Probably this was the way that Peter wished to see his "New Amsterdam," in the name of which he built, rebuilt, razed, compelled, and expedited. But Petersburg was not Amsterdam, and its inhabitants had almost all been sent there from the depths of Russia by the tsar's decree (if not exiled, for under Peter it is well known that Petersburg was a place of hard labor for criminals). Not all Petersburgers were fated to be immediately inspired by the tsar's dreams and sympathies, and to many it probably seemed very strange to build one's house up against a neighbor's house on the huge marshy desert of Vasil'evsky Island, built in a style so unlike that of the traditional Russian dwellings in which their forefathers had been born. Equally strange, accustomed as they were to the chaotic and in itself convenient building of Russian towns, would have seemed houses built in one line along the canals then feverishly under construction and the channels of which, because of the irregular waters, quickly turned into foul-smelling swamps.

Therefore, the plethora of Peter's wrathful decrees stigmatizing the disobedient seems natural.

By decrees "under heavy fine" were laid down the dimensions of chimneys, the form of roofs, the placement of fences and stables on the lot, the building material and its coloring, the width of bridges, the order of digging ponds and their dimensions, the installation of "cast-iron balusters with iron poles," turnstiles served by sentries from the townspeople, who may have a bathhouse and who may not, the depth of piling, the order of pasturing livestock, and many other requirements.

At the same time it is important to note that Peter's numerous decrees regulating the life of Petersburg give hardly any reasons why the residents' life must be this way and not some other. It must not be forgotten that explicit justification of the prescribed was characteristic of Peter's "training" legislation as a whole. Here, however, in a sphere so directly affecting every person we find none.

We shall begin with the fact that the removal of the capital to the banks of the Neva is not explained at all. Furthermore, it is not known which year the Petersburg period of history began. One may provisionally consider it to be 1713, when the court and the higher government institutions transferred to Petersburg. The wholesale resettlement of nobles, merchants, and craftsmen to the new city was not explained in any way. No reason was given for shifting the center of the city to Vasil'evsky Island. The year 1724 began with a decree about completing the transfer of all nobles who had been building houses in other regions of the city in the course of 1725. "And if anyone's house will not be finished in 1726," the tsar-transformer threatened, "from such violators is to be taken by decree half of their hamlets irrevocably, actually it will be for brick and plaster, and reports are to be given to the Policemaster Chancery so as to certify that it is true." Concurrently those "who in 1725 do not move" were forewarned, "and from them all their houses will be torn down, but they too, the householders, will themselves be sent forcibly to live on Vasil'evsky Island in rude huts."[30]

Imagine yourself for a minute, reader, in the place of a person obediently fulfilling the ruler's will who moved to the marshy "Paradise." With much labor and huge expense he built a house "according to architecture" somewhere on the city's Moscow or Petersburg side whither every stone had to be hauled over dozens of versts. He settled into it and turned over a new leaf, adapting to the new conditions that were similar to exile, when suddenly they read him a decree about resettling on Vasil'evsky Island, according to the ruler's will. And similar decrees, like snow on the head, often fell on the inhabitants of the new and also of the old capital and of the country's other towns.

With unbelievable effort the city was created. It was not like Russia's other cities; it was not just regular, but even military. The military element often came to the forefront. The assertion of historian V.V. Lapin does not seem especially exaggerated that in the Russia of the eighteenth and nineteenth centuries it was not the army that was under the state, but the state that was under the army, that the capital of the Russian Empire would look like a desert if the buildings, fortifications, and monuments linked in one way or another with the army, military affairs, and the successes of Russian arms had suddenly been withdrawn from it.

In fact, let's look around: the Peter and Paul Fortress and the Admiralty, the General Staff and the Staff of the Guards corps, the Field of Mars and the War-Campaign Chancery, the Alexandrine and Rostral columns, the Rumiantsev Obelisk, the barracks of the Horse Guards, the Pavlovsk and many other regiments, the first, second, and third Naval Cadet Corps, the Military-Medical Academy and the hospital of the Finland regiment, New Holland, the Arsenal, the Guardhouse on Haymarket Square, the monuments to Suvorov, Kutuzov, and Barclay de Tolly, the St. Nicholas of the Sea, Preobrazhensky, and Izmailovsky cathedrals—all these are only the more costly of Petersburg's hundreds of monuments as the empire's military capital.

"Regularity" and the military element set into the idea of Peter's city, it might seem, ought to have conferred the weight of the barracks, the despondency of the dusty parade ground, and the tedium of endless monotonous lines. But this did not happen. Built on a marsh by a wave of the tsarist hand, it bore the stamp of illusion, the lightness of a phantom, a mirage, the Northern Lights that had visited the city earlier.

Almost at once, however, this gave birth to the somber, phantomlike folklore that stems, in the words of Aleksei Tolstoi, from that same Petrine clerk who glimpsed a nightmare on a dark staircase and called out in a tavern: "Petersburg is to be empty!"

"Since then, probably, it has been believed that Petersburg is unclean. At one moment eyewitnesses saw how the Devil drove along a street of Vasil'evsky Island in a cab. Another time at midnight amid a storm and high water the bronze emperor tore himself away from the granite boulder and galloped through the streets. And once a privy councilor passing by in a carriage was accosted by a corpse—a dead official—who pressed his face to the glass."

Also important is another factor in the history of Petersburg—the "regular" city. The people and their life, memories, and feelings enlivened the layout of the Petrine plans and made the city alive, memorable, many-sided. The despondent lines stretching from water to water became lifelines.

> Oh, you lines!
> In you has remained the memory of Petrine Petersburg.
> The parallel lines were once laid out by Peter. And some of them came to be enclosed with granite, others with low fences of stone, still others with fences of wood. Peter's line turned into the line of a later age: the rounded one of Catherine, the regular ranks of colonnades.
> Left among the colossi were small Petrine houses: here a timbered one, there a green one, there a blue, single-storied one, with the bright red sign "Dinners Served." Sundry odors hit you right in the nose: the smell of sea salt, of herring, of hawsers, of leather jacket and of pipe, and nautical tarpaulin.
> Oh, lines!
> How they have changed: how grim days have changed them!

One poet (Andrei Belyi) is echoed by another (Joseph Brodsky):

> Neither country nor graveyard
> Do I wish to choose.
> To Vasil'evsky Island
> I shall come to die.
> Thy dark-blue façade
> I shall not find in the dark.
> Between faded lines
> I shall fall on the asphalt . . . [31]

The Imperial Idea

Thus, by the beginning of the 1720s the ship of empire had been framed by the great carpenter, and amid the sound of the last salvos of the Northern War she was already afloat. Now it was time for the last question: just where was this ship heading? (Recall Pushkin: "whither are we to sail?") What were the aims of the reigning helmsman?

On 7 April 1716 the last Swedish fortress in Germany, Wismar, had fallen. The Swedish Empire had ceased to exist. But still there was no peace, and Peter in 1716 had attempted to implement his long-standing idea of a combined assault by the allied navies on the Scandinavian coast. Soon, however, this notion had to be relinquished: the Swedes had artfully prepared their coastal defenses. Peter's refusal, in turn, provoked Denmark's dissatisfaction, which demanded the withdrawal of the Russian expeditionary corps from Jutland.

By this time, especially after the Swedes' expulsion from continental Europe, relations among the allies had started to deteriorate. The Northern Alliance turned into "a little club of friends." The cause was nearing its finale—dividing what had been taken from Sweden—and the allies glared distrustfully at each other, and especially at the young giant: Russia. Indeed, with Russia's entry into the Baltic, the foundation of Petersburg, and the appearance of the Russian navy, documents record the constant attention of the European powers to Russia's activities. Peter's intentions became obvious by the end of the Northern War.

In 1715 in instructions to envoy Boris Kurakin, dispatched to England for negotiations about the mediation of the great powers in reaching peace in the North, Peter did not mince words about the most important condition to be achieved:

> . . . of that which has been conquered he will be pleased in concluding peace to concede to the Swedish crown the town of Åbo along with other localities of the Grand Duchy of Finland, leaving some barrier toward Vyborg, whereas about Riga and Livland he is pleased

to declare that these His Tsarist Majesty *is certainly not able to concede to the Swedish crown*, for by that means he would bring into eternal danger all his other hereditary gains from the Swedes as well as the other conquered places and would thereby give a means to the Swede at the slightest occasion to enter into war in H.Ts.M.'s lands and would thus cause H.Ts.M. more loss than profit in always keeping great forces in those places.

In other words, Peter figured that leaving Livland to Sweden meant creating a threat to Petersburg. Further, Peter thought that it was impossible to fulfill the numerous promises to hand over Livland to the Poles or to their king, "for this crown, as one that is inconstant and subject incessantly to the times, might easily lose them in the meantime to the hands of the Swedes or to somebody else who will concede the provinces." Furthermore, the tsar pointed out that his conquests had required great expenditures and he wished to recoup these at the expense of the new territories, for "he alone bore all the burdens and expense in this war, and in defending the king and the Polish-Lithuanian Commonwealth from Swedish attack, took this town and these provinces with his own forces and expense and in the treaty about surrendering these places the nobility and citizenry of that province and town had yielded to Ts.M. on condition that they be in the possession of H.Ts.M."

The new interpretation of earlier agreements provoked protest from the Polish-Lithuanian Commonwealth. Both sides turned to history, which proved without difficulty that the forebears of its ruler had earlier held the East Baltic provinces. As early as 1714 the Russian envoy to England had started to voice on the official level the notion that "not only Ingermanland and Karelia, but also the greater part of Estland and Livland had belonged to the Russian crown since ancient times."[1]

At present it hardly makes sense to seek after priority of seizure—it is clear that the lands of Livland and Estland belonged to those who had lived there for centuries, the Letts and the Ests. Yet at that time, at the beginning of the eighteenth century, it was too early to speak of the national political consciousness of these peoples, and in the dispute about priority he who was stronger was right. The stronger proved to be Russia, which ruled these territories for two hundred years.

The fate of Livland and Estland really upset only one of Russia's allies—Poland. Prussia did not interest itself in it. From Russia it fruitlessly tried to get Polish Elbing, which had been captured by Russian troops in 1710, and offered proposals more than once to Russia about partitioning Polish territories. Prussia, like both Denmark and Hanover,

with England and Holland standing behind them, was seriously worried
by Russia's increasing interference in German affairs. This had a complex nature and varied causes.

Once Peter had achieved the Poltava victory, he turned to Germany,
for in the conquest of Sweden's German possessions he had grounds to
see the shortest route to peace with the stubborn king. In resolving this
strategic task, however, Peter was also motivated by obvious imperial
notions that involved expanding and strengthening Russian influence
in both neighboring and more distant lands. This did not mean that he
intended to take Sweden's place in Germany by ruling her German
provinces. Peter was a sober enough statesman who understood that in
the emerging international context, Pomerania's remoteness from Russia made such thinking unrealistic and that an attempt at its realization
would lead to numerous dangerous and unnecessary complications. He
pursued his aims by a different route.

The differences of interests among the German principalities, and
those of the great powers that were not reluctant to fish in cloudy
German waters, gave Russia many possibilities to influence the situation
in Germany by using various forms of intervention. One of the most
tried-and-true devices was marriage policy. It is hard to overestimate the
significance of dynastic marriages for almost any of the monarchical
states of Europe in the eighteenth century. Blood relationships held
tremendous significance in European politics, and marriage combina-
tions were one of the important aims of diplomacy. Peter was a reformer in this sphere of Russia's politics, too, for he ended the
Romanov dynasty's "isolation by blood." The first attempt was made in
1710, when Peter's niece, Anna Ivanovna, the daughter of his older
brother Ivan (and future empress), was given in marriage to Frederick-
William, Duke of Kurland, and was almost immediately widowed. Peter
insisted that Anna leave for Kurland and live there under the supervision of representatives of the Russian government. From this time Russian influence became dominant in this vassal principality of the
Polish-Lithuanian Commonwealth.

Great significance accrued to the very fact of the marriage in 1710 of
the heir to the Russian throne, Aleksei, to Princess Charlotte of
Wolfenbüttel. In the 1720s intensive negotiations were pursued for a
marriage of Louis XV of France with Tsarevna Elizabeth.

In 1712, pursuing Stenbock's army with the allies, Russian troops
entered Pomerania's neighboring duchy of Mecklenburg-Schwerin and
stayed there for a long time, for it was a convenient place for winter
quarters for a landing force against Sweden. Russo-Mecklenburg relations were not limited to questions of supporting the Russian expedi-

tionary corps, however. Almost at once Peter launched negotiations about a marriage of Duke Charles Leopold of Mecklenburg with his niece Ekaterina Ivanovna. The duke found himself in conflict with his own nobility, who did not accept his absolutist ways and numerous caprices. In the person of Peter and his troops he reckoned on finding support and he was not mistaken. According to the marriage alliance signed by Peter on 8 April 1716, Russia was supposed "to obtain by military means for the duke and his heirs complete security from all internal disruptions without any payment for expenses." For this Mecklenburg was obligated "to allow into Mecklenburg nine or ten Russian regiments at the duke's own disposal for the security of common advantages and with tsarist salaries, where they are to be until the end of the Northern War, and not be taken back without the most extreme need," and also "to defend him, the duke, from all unjust complaints of the Mecklenburg nobility hostile to him and to bring them to submission." Furthermore, Peter promised with the end of the war "to obtain for Charles Leopold the Swedish town of Wismar."[2]

The ink had not yet dried when it turned out that it was impossible to fulfill the treaty; a scandal had erupted among the allies. Russian troops were not permitted into the surrendered fortress of Wismar by the Prussian-Hanoverian Danish commanders. This extraordinary event nearly spilled over into armed conflict between Russia and its allies. It reflected the apprehensions with which Denmark, Prussia, and especially Hanover had observed Russia's growing strength in northern Germany, the more so as the elector of Hanover, who had become the king of England and dreamed of turning his electorate into a powerful domain, had pretensions to the Swedish possessions. Of course, he did not wish to have the Russian army as his neighbor in Mecklenburg. Not appreciating the situation, Peter had touched an exceptionally tender spot in Germany and had upset the political balance in this region, provoking alarm in Hanover and the other principalities that were closely linked to Mecklenburg by political, family, and economic ties.

Nevertheless, Peter's intervention into Mecklenburg affairs was maintained and even strengthened. The tsar emerged as an arbiter in the dispute of the Mecklenburg nobility with the duke, and, knowing the Russian autocrat's political sympathies, it is not hard to guess which side he upheld. In 1716 the Mecklenburg nobility revolted against their own sovereign. In response the Russian command arrested the ringleaders, rumors circulated about the impending deportation to Russia of all those dissatisfied with the duke, and the flight of noble families from Mecklenburg ensued. Although Peter soon withdrew his main forces from Mecklenburg to Poland, a limited contingent was left there. The nobility continued to complain to the supreme suzerain—the (Austrian) emperor of Germany—about the duke for summoning the tsar "to deal with" his subjects by armed force, and about the tsar for indulging Charles Leopold's ambitions. The matter became widely known in Europe—after all, it involved a constituent part of the German (Holy Roman) Empire. Peter, though he avoided extreme actions, was still completely on the duke's side. In February 1718 he interceded for Charles Leopold at the imperial diet at Regensburg, with a request "to grant him peaceful possession of his lands and let it be known that in the contrary case he, the tsar, would firmly support him, the duke, and would defend his rights most strongly with assistance." Besides such outright threats to the German princes Peter's entourage discussed a proposal for connecting the Baltic and German (North) seas via a network of canals through Mecklenburg territory and the creation there of a transit point for Russian goods, which might thus avoid paying the Sound tolls levied by the Danes on all vessels passing through the straits of the Sound and the Belts.

Thus, with Peter's active participation the "Mecklenburg Question" cropped up and convulsed European political circles for a long time. All attention would have been riveted on it if concurrently another had not arisen—the "Holstein Question"—in which Russia had likewise taken an active and far from disinterested part.

Its plot went back far into the past. In 1713 the king of Denmark had invaded Schleswig-Holstein and occupied Holstein adjacent to the Danish frontier. This had become possible because of the manifest weakening of Sweden, which had provided support to the dukes of the Holstein-Gottorp house related to the kings of Sweden (the young duke Charles Frederick was a nephew of Charles XII). From 1714 the statesmen of Holstein, in the first instance Bassewitz, had approached Peter seeking a new patron and had made several enticing proposals. The issue was that Charles Frederick, the son of Charles XII's sister, might inherit the Swedish throne in view of Charles's childlessness and might unite Sweden and Holstein under one crown. Bassewitz offered Russia an alliance and with it a "marriage treaty" of Peter's eldest daughter, Anna Petrovna, and Charles Frederick. At first Peter was cautious, responding that "in attaining . . . the Swedish crown he does not refuse to help the young duke, but for this the king of Prussia's agreement is necessary, and it is improper to make a treaty about this beforehand, for the king by youth is still far from a natural death [Charles XII was thirty-two at the time], yet he will try to obtain for him, the duke, Finland."[3]

But gradually Peter's sentiments and actions were becoming bolder and more definite, which evoked an extremely negative reaction in Copenhagen. Thus arose the "Holstein Question" in the resolution of which the same hand is observed as in the resolution of the "Kurland" and "Mecklenburg" questions, although the situation became less favorable for Peter with the end of the War of the Spanish Succession.

The appearance of these "questions" and, more broadly, the acuteness of the principal one—the partition of the Swedish legacy and Russia's role therein—brought the Northern Alliance to the brink of collapse. This was particularly facilitated by the position of the king of England, George I, who was displeased by Russia's growing might in Germany and feared that Russia's actions would undermine the bases of Anglo-Dutch trade in the Baltic. England even became the instigator of a frankly anti-Russian alliance that included, besides herself, Holland and France and into which she was likewise drawing Denmark and Prussia.

All this led to the beginnings in May 1718 of separate Russo-Swedish negotiations on the Åland Islands. These had been ripening long since and had started from a "chance" meeting of the Swedish minister Görtz and the Russian envoy Boris Kurakin during a stroll in the woods near the castle of Loo, close to Utrecht. To be sure, the "chance" meeting had been prepared by long contacts through various intermediaries.

The Russian position at the negotiations, which was set forth by Jacob Bruce and Andrei Osterman, amounted to a demand for Swedish cession of Ingria, Karelia, Livland, Estland, and Vyborg. Finland from the river Kiumen' would go to Sweden. The Swedish representatives Gyllenborg and Görtz insisted on the return of Estland and Livland to Sweden. Further negotiations were proceeding toward a rapprochement of the Swedish and the Russian points of view.

But in mid-December 1718 it became known that Charles XII had been killed in Norway at the siege of the Danish fortress of Frederiksten. A story exists that he perished from the bullet of a traitor from his own suite, the French secretary Sicre.

The king's sudden death abruptly changed the situation. The younger sister of the deceased, Ulrika Eleonora, succeeded him, which led to stronger English influence at Stockholm. Görtz, the mainspring of the Swedish-Russian rapprochement, was arrested and executed in March 1719. The English plan of regulating matters, which stemmed from the ambitions of Hanover and English commercial interests, also envisaged compensation for Sweden's territorial losses, but only at Russia's expense. Concurrently English diplomacy made efforts in connection with apprehensions about the fate of Poland, which then seemed threatened by partition between Prussia and Russia (that Prussia had such plans is beyond doubt), and also strove for a punitive expedition against the duke of Mecklenburg, Charles Leopold. At the beginning of 1719 a Hanover-Wolfenbüttel army entered Mecklenburg and set up a commission to administer the duchy in the name of the emperor of Germany. Thus was Russia finally forced out of Mecklenburg. Peter, acutely interested in peace with the Swedes, now had no intention of helping his foolish relative and proposed that Charles Leopold make peace with the nobility and the emperor.

In 1719 the Åland negotiations were renewed with the participation of a Prussian representative, but soon they were broken off entirely. Peter understood that peace could be hastened only through arms. Circumstances nudged this too—in the summer of 1719 the Hanoverians signed a peace with the Swedes, and Prussia was also on the way to peace with the Swedes.

The military operations against Sweden in 1719–21 were conducted along the Swedish coast and directly on its territory. The Russian seagoing fleet by this time was superior to the Swedish in all respects, which was demonstrated by the Ösel engagement in May 1719 and later in the Grengam (Granhamn) battle of 27 July 1720. The Russian ships engaged in convoying galleys and transports, which waged the campaign along the Swedish skerries, landing troops on the islands and the seacoast. The raid by the Russian forces bore a clearly expressed punitive-demonstrative character.

The destruction of villages, hamlets, and towns was intended to demonstrate that the tsar's intentions were serious if the Swedes persisted further in declining peace. The glow of fires from burning settlements in the vicinity of Stockholm and the stream of fugitives into the capital were supposed to convince the royal family of this. The threats of the Petrine manifesto addressed to the Swedish populace after Poltava started to come true.

The naval victories of 1720 reinforced Russia's hegemony in the Baltic despite the presence of an English fleet there, and in the spring of 1721, punitive raids were launched anew with the participation of cossack forces. In the summer Russian detachments that landed near Ymeo met no resistance and devastated and burned 4 towns, 509 hamlets, and 79 estates with 4,159 households, 12 ironworks, and other installations and carried off thousands of puds of copper, iron, and 556 head of horned cattle.

Broken by these raids and the terrifying devastation in general, which knocked Sweden out of the ranks of the great powers, and also by the inaction of its new ally, England, the Swedish government embarked on a renewal of the peace negotiations with Russia, which began in April 1721 in the small Finnish town of Nystadt. It was fated to enter history with the peace concluded on 30 August 1721.

Sweden forever renounced the eastern Baltic region in favor of Russia, which by a secret article promised to pay monetary compensation of two million thalers by September 1724.

By the end of August 1721 the main aim for which Peter had lived—conquering an outlet to the Baltic Sea—had been brilliantly attained. Russia had obtained not only the "patrimonies and grand patrimonies" once taken by the Swedes, but had also participated in the partition of the Swedish Empire, seizing Estland and Livland.

But what was next? It is clear that egress to the Baltic had been needed by Peter not for the satisfaction of his own pride and not even for the restoration of justice. Peter was a son of his time, a time when the concepts of mercantilism and protectionism dominated statesmen's minds. The state was supposed to enrich itself with the aid of gold and silver, which was gained by an active trade balance and a predominance of exports over imports—such was the cluster of ideas in which the mercantilists' concepts circulated. Peter, as we know, attributed great significance to the growth of commerce as the basis of the state's might and his subjects' prosperity. He considered the state's lack of seaports through which it could conduct commerce an abnormal phenomenon. Likening the state to a living organism (a frequent device in the mechanistic philosophy), he writes: by means of ports, "this artery, the state's heart can be healthier and more profitable. . . ."

Therefore one may speak of the dominance of trade politics in the general system of Russian foreign policy after the peace of Nystadt. Many currents of Petrine diplomacy are linked to this dominance. The most crucial was the so-called "Sound Question." Its crux was that Denmark had for centuries levied imposts on all vessels passing the straits of the Sound and both Belts. Sweden had enjoyed the privilege that its ships could pass the straits without dues. On 7 November 1721 the Russian envoy Aleksei Petrovich Bestuzhev-Riumin (the future chancellor under Elizabeth) proposed to Peter to take advantage of one of the articles of the Treaty of Nystadt, according to which the Baltic towns that went to Russia preserved all of their privileges and rights including also the right of free passage through the Sound. In other words, goods from Petersburg were subject to duty, whereas those from Riga, Pernau, or Revel were duty free. Peter immediately seized upon Bestuzhev's idea.

Often we cannot trace back the plot of one international conflict or another: either the sources have not been preserved, or there never were any. Here, however, the conflict had begun from an envoy's specific letter and the answer thereto. Some readers will laugh, thinking, what a conflict! But everything is measured by the standards of its time, and for the Baltic region the "Sound Question" was one of the most important for six whole years, for it involved powerful powers, above all, Russia. Her might was appraised and feared. The French envoy to Russia, Jean-Jacques Campredon, wrote his government about Peter: "at the least demonstration of his fleet, at the first movement of his troops neither the Swedish nor the Danish nor the Prussian nor the Polish crown dares to make a hostile move or to shift its own forces from one place. He alone of all the northern rulers is in a position to compel respect for his own flag."[4]

The distress in Copenhagen after the corresponding demarches of Bestuzhev was great, for Peter had linked the "Sound Question" to the "Holstein Question" already known to the reader.

In the plans for an active, not to say aggressive, policy the "Holstein Question" was exceptionally fruitful. It would allow one to keep Denmark in "irrevocable uncertainty," for, bordering on the south, Holstein constantly threatened its soft underbelly. Denmark was also distressed by talk about the possibility of digging a canal from the Baltic Sea to the North Sea (the future Kiel Canal) and the creation of a free port for Russian goods. This would have been a serious blow to Denmark's economy, for the collection of the Sound tolls constituted an important item of revenue. Besides, Duke Charles Frederick was, as we recall, a nephew of the childless queen of Sweden, Ulrika Eleonora, and therefore Russia actively supported the Holstein party in Stockholm, which dreamed of seeing him on the Swedish throne.

As we know, in 1720 the regime of absolutism was liquidated in Sweden; the hereditary aristocracy came to power. Russia in the person of Peter and his resident envoys did not miss the opportunity to intervene in Sweden's affairs, actively supporting the aristocratic "republicans," for in the absence of a powerful absolute authority Peter saw the most reliable guarantee that revanchism would not get firmly established in Sweden and that, diverted by the rivalry of parties and weakened politically and economically, it would not menace Russia. It is astonishing, but one of the conditions of the Treaty of Nystadt was the point according to which Russia promised not only not to intrigue against the order that had arisen after the oligarchical "revolution" of 1720, but even that "everything that will be plotted against it and will become known to His Tsarist Majesty he will seek in all ways to hinder and to forestall." Such a stance of the powerful neighbor tremendously impressed the Swedish elite, which had just become firmly established in power. Therefore, when negotiations began about making an alliance, the Russian representatives set conditions that if the Swedes would not seek a successor to the throne other than the Duke of Holstein—the fiancé of Anna Petrovna—then "we must not only abide by the Nystadt treaty, but also everything that the state ranks will propose even more for the maintenance of their own prerogatives and liberties and when it is proposed we shall guarantee it for all time."

A consequence of these negotiations was the defensive alliance of Russia and Sweden for a term of twelve years signed on 11 February 1724—a document unique in the history Russo-Swedish relations (hostile for the most part). In this situation Peter showed himself as a subtle diplomat and, being a statesman of the possible, on the whole, achieved the impossible—he drew yesterday's irreconcilable foe into an alliance advantageous above all for Russia, which had become the actual mistress of the Baltic. As often happens, the crux of the agreement was concluded in secret articles. The first of these provided that Sweden and Russia would obtain for Holstein the return of Schleswig; the second, that Russia and Sweden must make all efforts "to defend the Polish Republic under its liberty, repelling all opposing ventures and plots in that matter." Speaking more bluntly, the emperor of Russia would oppose Augustus's feeble absolutist impulses just as he had done in the case of Sweden, taking care for the preservation of the regime of the noble republic in Poland, for this did not permit Poland to strengthen itself and to mount resistance to Russia's ever-growing influence in Polish affairs.

Also important was the treaty's third article: Russia permitted Sweden duty-free export of grain, hemp, flax, and mast timber.

The alliance with Sweden became a powerful weapon against the influence of England in the northern region, where it had lost its earlier firm position in Stockholm, and especially against Denmark, which persisted in its own interpretation of the Sound tolls. It is also important to note that Russia was not consistently antagonistic toward England. Peter was ready to normalize relations on the basis of parity and a recognition of spheres of influence in the Baltic.

On the whole, however, Russian policy in the west after Nystadt was distinguished by activity, particularly in Germany, where the interests of several large powers met head-on.

Russia's influence in Kurland had grown immeasurably. Peter had acted very thoughtfully and subtly. The Russian emissaries, acting in the name of the widowed duchess Anna Ivanovna, bought up the domains once mortgaged by the dukes of Kurland. As a result of these private-legal operations the possessions of the dukes and their corresponding seigneurial rights passed to Anna (read: Russia).

The activities of Petrine European policy, of course, received a uniformly negative appraisal in the political circles of those countries that also dreamed of reinforcing their own influence in Germany, the Baltic region, and Poland. Among these were England, France, Austria, and Prussia, which was raising its head. An extremely peculiar expression of this relationship became the so-called "Political Testament" of Peter the Great, which received wide publicity and has been extremely popular even until now when one discusses the foreign policy of tsarist Russia and the Soviet Union.

As in the case of the "Pruth Testament," there is neither an original nor a contemporary copy of the "Political Testament," and apparently none will ever fall into the hands of historians because it does not exist. The "Testament" was first published in France in the 1830s. Some historians date its appearance to Napoleon's campaign in Russia, when the emperor of the French needed arguments against his northern opponent. Others maintain that the "Testament" was composed by the notorious chevalier d'Eon, famous in the mid-eighteenth century for his adventures in male and more frequently in female dress. He asserted that he had found it (during his stay in Russia) in the Peterhof palace. In the meantime the "Testament" is not cited in a single document of Peter's successors, although the necessity of it was palpably felt, especially in the time of Elizabeth, who constantly declared her fidelity to Peter's "principles." The text of the "Testament" is littered with many absurdities, patently reflecting ignorance of the international context of the Petrine era.

In a word, we have here an obvious forgery, the purpose of which is to justify in public opinion the necessity and justice of fighting Russia. Nonetheless, the forgery has enjoyed long popularity. The causes of this phenomenon lie not only in its service as a trusty weapon for Russia's undiscerning opponents, but also in that Russia in its actions from the eighteenth to the twentieth centuries has very often confirmed the ideas voiced by the author of "Peter's Testament." In other words, while wholly denying the document's credibility it is essential to note that its author captured many general tendencies of Russia's imperial policy of the eighteenth century and extrapolated them to earlier history, more precisely to Peter's era. It is indisputable that the great reformer became the founder not only of the Russian Empire, but also of imperial policy, the principles of which were successfully developed by his successors, particularly Catherine II. We touched earlier on the Russian Empire's policy in Germany and the Baltic region. Let's turn to the Asiatic aspect of Peter's imperial policy.

The celebrations of the long-awaited peace with Sweden had hardly ended when the Russian army set off for a new war, this time marching down the Oka and the Volga to Astrakhan and onward into Persia. What provoked this new conflict, which cost the Russian people some thirty thousand lives and substantial expenditures that were very appreciable for a country that had survived the excruciatingly protracted Northern War?

Quite a few theories have been put forward about the causes of the Persian campaign. I think that at bottom lay the same causes that had impelled Peter into the struggle for abolition of the Sound tolls. Knowledge of the conjuncture of international commerce persuaded the tsar that money might be earned not only by the sale of native raw materials and goods in the West, but also by direct trade with the East. Particularly great profits were provided by the transit trade in silk, spices, and other rarities of India and China. It is known that as early as the time of Ivan the Terrible, Russian autocrats had dreamed of shifting the great silk route from the Near East to Russian territory. These enticing dreams of the Russian tsars were stimulated a good bit by the periodic attempts of English, Dutch, and other merchants to find a route to the riches of India via the plains of Russia. But all these dreams and attempts, receiving no development, crumbled, only to be reborn anew. The causes of the failures were many, starting with the fact that the Baltic seaboard was not controlled by Russia throughout the seventeenth century and ending with misapprehension of the traditional nature of the great silk route through the Middle and Near East and of the influence of powerful groupings of Oriental merchant-intermediaries that controlled the export of goods from India and China.

Peter resolved to change the situation fundamentally and to shift the trade route between Europe and the Orient in such a way that it would pass through Russia—only this may explain one of the tasks he set for Volynsky's embassy to Persia: ". . . is it possible to make some obstacle to the Smyrna and Aleppo trade, where and how?" He saw the preconditions of success in the emergence of Petersburg, the achievement of peace in the Baltic, the development of shipping, the construction of canals, and, finally, the rise of a proper manufacturing industry capable of supplying goods to the Indian market.

It would also be incorrect to deny the influence of the general imperial idea, so widespread in European civilization of the modern era (we recall Napoleon and Paul I), that only he is truly wealthy who rules India—the fabled treasure house of humanity. We may speak of the existence of a peculiar "India syndrome" that has enthralled conquerors, for there is no world empire without India. This syndrome did not spare Peter either.

It is difficult to determine when Peter's "Oriental idea" arose, but we may say quite definitely that it was after Poltava, and more precisely after the Pruth, which had stymied the Black Sea thrust of Russia's policy. During 1714–17 Peter tried several routes to India. A beginning was made in 1714 with the expedition of Colonel Buchholtz, who was dispatched from Siberia Guberniia in a southerly direction to check into rumors of gold deposits on the river Erket. Encountering Kalmyk resistance, Buchholtz withdrew. Likharev, who replaced him, was commissioned to go to Lake Zaisan, to build a fort there, and "to reconnoiter a route from Lake Zaisan to Erket. How far is it and is it possible to reach? Also, are there not headwaters of the rivers that fall into Zaisan, and do they flow into the Darya River or into the Aral Sea?"

It is noteworthy that Peter, not having an accurate map before him, tried to find a water route to Central Asia and onward to India. It is essential to hold the rivers, he instructed his emissaries, to establish forts on their banks, and, having gained a foothold, to move on by boat.

Concurrently, Peter probed another route to Central Asia from the eastern shore of the Caspian. In 1714 he gave the Senate a task: "Send to Khiva (to the khan) congratulations on the khanate, and from there go to Bukhara to the khan, seeking some matter of trade, whereas the real matter is to find out about the town of Erket, how far it is from the Caspian Sea and whether there are not any rivers from there, or though not from the place itself, then in proximity to the Caspian Sea."

On the basis of legendary information Peter supposed that a dam existed whereby the waters of the Amu-Darya flowed into the Aral Sea instead of the Caspian. Alexander Bekovich-Cherkassky, head of the expedition organized in 1716, was directed to establish a fort at the former mouth of the Amu-Darya into the Caspian and then to proceed southeast along the former course of the Amu-Darya—the Uzboi—to the supposed dam, to select a site for establishing one more fort—a base for the advance into Central Asia. Further he was supposed to move into Khiva along the river: "Travel to the khan of Khiva along the riverbank, and keep the route along that river and inspect its course carefully, and likewise the dam, to determine if it is possible to direct that water now into the old course [i.e., into the Caspian], and for that to close the other mouths into the Aral Sea, and how many people are required for that work." As we see, the palm for priority in the transformation of nature through the diversion of rivers (with a different purpose than now, to be sure) goes to the first Russian emperor.

Particular interest is raised by another point of the instructions to Bekovich: "Also request boats from him [the khan of Khiva] and on them send merchants along the Amu-Darya River to India, ordering that they traverse it as far as the boats are able to go [i.e., to its headwaters], and from there go to India, marking the rivers and lakes and describing the water and land route, and especially the water one to

India by that or other rivers and return from India by the same route, or if he hears in India of a better route to the Caspian Sea, then return and describe it."[6]

It is important to note that sailors were included in the expedition, and under the guise of "merchants" traveling to India it was first proposed to send the professional navigator and cartographer Lieutenant Kozhin, who was commissioned by Peter at the same time to buy ostriches in "East India from the Mogul," so confident was Peter that Kozhin would get to Delhi.

The spirit is captivated by the ideas of the tsar, who dreamed with the aid of canals and the diversion of rivers to arrange things so that at one time one could board a vessel in Petersburg and disembark on the shores of India. Enormous energy, the scale of Peter's thinking, his profound faith in the unlimited possibilities of seafaring and engineering in combination with the persuasiveness of "force of arms"—and all this with the natural ignorance of the geography of this region that had not been explored by Europeans—made Peter's plans not so fantastic for his contemporaries as they may appear to be now.

Having built and settled the Krasnovodsk fort in 1716, Bekovich then set off toward Khiva. But at the approaches to the khanate's capital his entire detachment was destroyed by the khan's troops, and Bekovich himself perished. His unfortunate fate became a proverb: "He was lost, like Bekovich," we read in the dictionary of Dal'.

The failure of Bekovich's expedition did not stop Peter. In the summer of 1718 he decided to try to penetrate into Central Asia, more precisely into the Bukhara emirate, not from the north but from the south via Persia.

For this, the embassy of Florio Beneveni was dispatched to Central Asia. The expedition reached its destination only after three years, and its members remained there as hostages until 1725. During this time Peter thoroughly worked out a last, in his opinion more reliable, variant to India via Persia. The tsar resorted to this variant in 1716 when Lieutenant Kozhin was sent by boat "for a survey of the route and harbors on the Caspian Sea" and "positions" on the map. In 1718 this work was continued by Urusov, who was commissioned to map with particular care the western shore of the Caspian from Astrakhan to Gilian, "to survey carefully the harbors and rivers and which craft may put in where, also whether it is possible to go there by scout boat in view of the threat of storms." Further on in this decree Peter added in his own hand: "If there are no harbors, then is it possible to go along the shores, inasmuch as we hear it is shallow, and if such scout boats as we have cannot be portaged, then is it possible to portage flatbottomed ones and where?" As we see, Peter's interest in the Caspian seaboard was quite specific even four years prior to the Persian campaign. Speaking plainly, he was seeking places for future landings and choosing the type of assault craft.[7]

Parallel with the efforts by sea, a deep diplomatic reconnaissance was mounted in the form of the embassy of Artemy Petrovich Volynsky, who was dispatched to Persia in 1715, that is, almost concurrently with Bekovich's expedition to Central Asia. Although Volynsky was not ordered to build forts and divert rivers, his commission went far beyond that of a purely diplomatic mission. The instructions to Volynsky, the aim of which was to reconnoiter Persia's condition and to clarify the best route to India, attest to this most vividly.

Volynsky proved to be in Iran at a moment of most profound political crisis. One after another the peoples subject to Persia revolted: the Lezghians, the Kurds, the Lurs, the Baluchis, the Armenians. The greatest danger was posed by a rebellion of the powerful Afghan tribe of the Ghilzai, which had begun in 1709 in Kandahar and soon changed from liberation to conquest. Breakdown reigned in the center, where the inept and weak-willed Shah Husain was in power.

Analyzing the country's political condition, Volynsky informed Peter: "I think that this crown is approaching final ruin if not revived by another shah, they cannot defend themselves from either the enemies and their own rebels, already few places remain where there is no rebellion, they are all falling one after the other. . . ."

Summing up the situation, Volynsky proposed taking advantage of Persia's weakness for territorial gains.

Upon returning from the embassy, Volynsky was named governor of Astrakhan and at Peter's behest began preparing the political and material base for the impending campaign into Persia.

Peter was waiting only for the end of the Northern War. In August 1721, the month of the signing of the Peace of Nystadt, the Lezghian prince Hadzhi-Davud seized Shemakha and destroyed the trading stalls in which Russian merchants had been involved. Volynsky immediately wrote Peter, urging him to use the incident as a pretext for an attack on Persia.

Peter assured Volynsky on 5 December that "it is most fitting not to miss this chance, and we have already ordered a substantial part of the troops to march to the Volga for winter quarters, and from there they will set out for Astrakhan in the spring."[8]

Launched in the spring of 1722 by a manifesto that declared war on Persia for the purpose of recouping the losses of the Russian merchants in Shemakha and for the salvation of the Christians of the Orient from Moslem domination, the campaign was entirely successful: Derbent fell in August, the fort of the Holy Cross was established (a very symbolic crusading name), and Baku fell the following summer. The senators rushed to congratulate the tsar and "toasted joyfully the health of Peter the Great, who had entered upon the path of Alexander the Great." But, although the shah's army offered no resistance, the campaign proceeded in difficult conditions because of the unusual climate and the population's hostility. The situation was complicated in that Ottoman Turkey, perturbed by the movement of Russian troops and exploiting Iran's weakness, invaded eastern Armenia and occupied eastern Georgia including Tbilisi. Russia found itself drawn into a serious conflict; in the spring of 1723 war with Turkey appeared unavoidable. The threat from Turkey seemed more serious to the new shah, Tahmasp II, than that from Russia, and soon the embassy of Ismailbek was dispatched to Petersburg, where in September 1723 he was compelled to sign a peace treaty by which the Caspian strip of Daghestan, Shirvan, Derbent, Baku, and also Gilan, Mazandaran, and Gorgan (Astrabad) went to Russia forever. In exchange Russia was supposed to provide the shah with aid against the Afghan rebels.

A Russian corps of eight thousand entered Gilan and occupied its capital of Resht. Never had Russian soldiers gone so far south, to the latitude of Dushanbe and Athens. Peter was delighted with the war's outcome and congratulated his intimates with the annexation to the empire of the "new rag." Through this peace his dreams of gaining the riches of the Orient started to come true.

Preparing to affirm his hegemony in Iran, Peter ordered Dutch merchants informed of the changed situation in the region from which great quantities of raw silk went to Europe, pointing out that "this trade is quite secure, and that we shall give them every possible aid."

Peter knew what he was talking about—talks were under way with the Turks about partitioning Iran's possessions. In the summer of 1724 the corresponding treaty was signed. According to it, Turkey guaranteed Russia's conquests, and Russia Turkey's, namely the eastern Trans-Caucasus, Azerbaijan, and part of western Iran including Hamadan. Of course, because the true aims of the war had been different from those declared in the manifesto of 1722, there was no mention of the fate of the Orthodox Christians of the Trans-Caucasus (as earlier in the case of the Balkans). Only the Georgian tsarevich Vaktang received a charter according to which he was permitted "to retreat into our state." In case of Persian resistance to the partition, Russia and Turkey, according to the treaty, were supposed to operate jointly.[9]

As to Peter's further plans, we may judge by his "points"—decrees to General Matiushkin commanding the Russian corps in Persia. His first task was considered to be strengthening the forts in Derbent and Baku and finishing the fort of the Holy Cross. Because the Russian forces were stationed only in Gilan, the task was posed of moving to the southeast, taking Mazandaran and consolidating control in Astrabad.

According to Peter's thinking, the new colonies needed to be seized economically and revenue gained from them. For this it was proposed to resettle Armenians and Russians in them.

Many sources indicate Peter's intention to organize the resettlement of Russians and Christians in general to Gilan and Mazandaran. In September 1724 the tsar instructed General Rumiantsev, who was dispatched for the demarcation of the Russo-Turkish border in the Trans-Caucasus: ". . . inasmuch as your route will be either through Armenia, and also because there are many Armenians in Georgia, therefore try as far as possible to persuade them to go to Gilan and live in other places there and, if they will be many, we shall expel the Persians and give them the places where they had been living. . . ."

In another letter to Rumiantsev he wrote: "If the Turks start talking to you about this, then answer that we ourselves did not incite the Armenians, but they begged us in unity of faith to take them under our protection . . . it is only necessary to take into account the lands belonging to somebody specified in the treaty, whereas there is no need to hinder peoples from migrating to one or the other side. For the Porte it will still be advantageous when the Armenians leave because then it can rule their lands without resistance. Add, that if the Porte wishes to invite the Busurmen from the provinces acquired by us in Persia, then this will not be opposed by us." Matiushkin, however, received direct orders to settle the Armenians and to rid himself of the Moslems. On 2 June 1724 he was ordered: "Take care in every way to incite the Armenians and other Christians to go to Gilan and Mazandaran and take up residence, and as for the Busurmen do so very quietly so that they don't find out how many it is possible to take away, and precisely from the Turkish faith. Also when you get your bearings, find out how many of the Russian nation to settle there at first."[10]

Intending to consolidate his hold on the southern shores of the Caspian for a long time, Peter was brimming with optimism, for he figured he was standing at the gates of the treasure house of Asia. His conversation with Fedor Soimonov during the Persian campaign is noteworthy in this regard. A naval officer, Soimonov told the tsar about the need to seize the northeastern route to India via Kamchatka. Soimonov recalled that Peter had answered as follows: "Listen, I know all that, but not now, and it is distant; have you been in the bay of Astrabad? Do you know that from Astrabad to Balkh in Bukharia and to

Vodokshan [Badakhshan in Afghanistan] and by camel it is only 12 days' travel, and there in all of Bukharia is the center of all oriental commerce, and you see the mountains and banks along them stretching to Astrabad itself, [and] nobody can block that route."[11]

And so, in 1724 at death's door Peter was working out a broad, impressive program of colonial development of the captured territories. Even then he was thinking about new conquests, especially in the direction of the Trans-Caucasus. The conquered provinces along the Caspian would serve as the bridgehead for this. In the spring of 1724 Peter gave out assignments to the diplomats and the military men who, like Volynsky, would reconnoiter the Caucasus.

There can be no doubt that conquest of the Trans-Caucasus and, accordingly, war with Turkey was the next thrust of Peter's imperial policy in the Orient.

What about India? Apparently Peter intended, having created and fortified a bridgehead on the southern shore of the Caspian, to move farther south. But there is no hard information about this. There is, however, information about other, completely unexpected probes for the route to cherished India. This entailed outfitting a secret expedition by sea to India with a stop at Madagascar.

As we know, at the turn of the seventeenth and eighteenth centuries many pirate bands, which had been forced out of the Caribbean basin, found refuge on Madagascar. The situation on Madagascar is described by Daniel Defoe in his entertaining novel, *The Life, Adventures and Piracies of the Famous Captain Singleton*. The pirates' position was extremely unstable, for the English and the French severely persecuted brigandage on the seas. At that time the idea arose in the pirate "Republic" of requesting protection from some European ruler in order to unite Madagascar to his realm. Such proposals were made to the Dutch and to the French. In 1718 one of the chieftains of the pirates, Kaspar Morgan, visited Sweden and received a charter according to which he would thenceforth be the king of Sweden's viceroy on Madagascar. In 1722 the Swedes dispatched to Madagascar the expedition of commodore K.G. Ulrich on the frigate *Jarramas*, which got only to Spain and, after staying at Cádiz several months, returned to Sweden. Although this expedition, like the Swedes' whole plan, had been shrouded in secrecy, Peter got word of it, gaining information from sailors who had entered his service, among whom was an experienced sailor and naval commander, the Swede D. Wilster, who had been made a vice admiral of the Russian navy. In the summer of 1723 at Peter's request he compiled a note about the Swedish efforts to establish a base on Madagascar and how the pirates had been permitted to become subjects of the king

of Sweden and "to fuse with the Swedish population on the aforementioned islands for all together to remain united in all fidelity as subjects
of the crown of Sweden for the first centuries." In conclusion, Wilster
recommended that Peter get in touch with Morgan directly in order "to
confer prosperity on His Imperial Majesty's intention according to
every wish."[12]

In November 1723, at a time when the navy had already finished the
campaign season, Peter issued directives about launching preparations
for the expedition, with all of this shrouded in particular secrecy. For
the expedition, which was entrusted to Wilster, beautiful frigates of
Dutch construction were assigned—the *Amsterdam-Galei* and the
Dekrondelivd, which were manned by the navy's best sailors. The frigates
were ordered to take on supplies for eight months and to mask themselves
as trading vessels. They were supposed to avoid busy sea-lanes and sail
southward not through the English Channel but "around Scotland and
Ireland . . . so as not to cause anyone any suspicion." The instructions
given to Wilster envisaged India as the expedition's final aim. En route the
ships were supposed to drop by Madagascar, and Wilster was commissioned to invite the pirate "king" into the Russian emperor's service.

The unusual season for the preparations, their haste and secrecy—all
this was done in order to beat out a similar expedition by the Swedes.

Even with the very richest imagination you have difficulty visualizing
the Russian flag over a fort in the bay of Antongil on the island of
Madagascar. Nevertheless, these plans were close to realization. From
Madagascar, Wilster was supposed to sail on to India. According to a
special instruction, as Russia's plenipotentiary ambassador he was supposed to reach the Great Moghul "and by all means . . . incline him to
allow commerce to be conducted with Russia." It is important to note
that the organization of this expedition coincided with the conclusion
of the Russo-Persian peace of 1723, according to which the Persian
provinces along the Caspian went to Russia. The coordination of two
such different events was implemented by one man—Peter. But the
expedition did not occur.

On 21 December 1723 the ships left Rogervik, but they were immediately struck by a squall, and the *Amsterdam-Galei* sprang a big leak.
They had to go into Revel to repair the frigate's hull. For this it was
necessary to put her on her side. During the careening in January 1724
disaster struck—the frigate's gunports had not only not been caulked,
as was prescribed during such operations, but they had not even been
closed. The *Amsterdam* capsized. Most managed to save themselves (except for sixteen men), but the expedition had to be postponed. Peter
gave orders to assemble new ships, but they proved to be without sheep-

skin linings, which preserved ship bottoms from mollusks in the South Seas. There were no skins in storage . . . in a word, it went on like that, as so often occurs in dear old Russia.

In sum, preparing the ships for the cruise dragged on, and Peter ordered the expedition postponed in February until a better time. By this time he had received precise information from the aforementioned commodore Ulrich about the collapse of the pirate "republic" and the colony's depopulation. From this the tsar could conclude that it was hardly worth risking this adventure in Madagascar.

But the notion of searching for a sea route to India did not desert Peter. At the end of his life he decided to clarify the possibility of a northern route, and, following the expedition of Ivan Evreinov and Fedor Luzhin that had been dispatched in 1719, he sent Vitus Bering to the Far East with the task of studying the possibility of a passage between Asia and America. Concurrently, the tsar strove to incorporate the Persian provinces as quickly as possible. Fulfilling his plans, the government of Catherine I subsequently expanded its possessions to the north and south from Resht, occupying towns, fortifying them, and building forts, one of which received the name of Ekaterinopol.

Who knows what would have happened had the tsar lived a few more years? The notion of the conquered provinces as a bridgehead to the Middle East had some foundation. At least, one should listen to Artemy Volynsky, who knew well Peter's Oriental policy and who later remembered: "According to His Majesty's designs, his concern was not for Persia alone. For, if matters had succeeded for us in Persia and his exalted life had continued, of course he would have attempted to reach India, and he nurtured intentions even to the Chinese state, which I was honored from His Imperial Majesty . . . to hear myself."[13]

HERITAGE AND HEIRS

"To whom shall I leave the planting described above?"

On 28 January 1725 Peter died. A decree on this occasion stated: "Inasmuch as by the will of almighty God the most radiant, most regal Peter the Great, emperor and autocrat of all the Russias, our most merciful master, this January 28th departed this fleeting world for the blessings of eternity. . . ."

The great reformer of Russia painfully departed this fleeting world that is so dear to everyone. Quite a few legends and rumors have grown up around Peter's death, and silence about them in the scholarly literature has only facilitated their wide currency. According to the conclusions of specialists of the Leningrad Military-Medical Academy named after S.M. Kirov who have studied the materials concerning Peter's illness and who kindly gave me the opportunity of becoming acquainted with an unpublished article on that topic, the tsar's death occurred as a result of nitric poisoning. Its cause "was either swelling of the prostate, which in its final stage led to the retention of urine and to the development of uremia, or the development of a stricture in the urethra as a consequence of infection." It is important to note in this regard that in the opinion of many specialists the infectious process in the urethra could have been a consequence of Peter's being ill with gonorrhea, but not with syphilis.[1]

Peter died without leaving a testament. Yet in literature (M. Voloshin) and in public consciousness the legend lives on that shortly before dying he tried to issue directives about the heir to the throne: "Leave everything . . ." Peter supposedly wrote in faltering script. Except for these two words nothing more could be deciphered.

The source of this version is the "Notes" of Henning Frederick Bassewitz, a courtier of Duke Charles Frederick of Holstein. "Very soon after the holy day of the Lord's Baptism in 1725," writes Bassewitz, the emperor felt the attacks of the disease that ended with his death. All were very far from the idea of considering it fatal, but this error did not last even eight days. Then he was given Holy Communion according to the rites prescribed by the Greek Church for the sick. Soon from the unbearable pain his shrieks and groans resounded throughout the palace, and he was no longer in a condition to think with full awareness about the arrangements that impending death required of him. A terrible fever kept him in almost constant delirium. Finally, in one of those moments when death gives its victim some respite before the final blow, the emperor regained consciousness and expressed a wish to write—but his burdened hand outlined letters that could not be deciphered, and after his death one could read only the first two words of what he had written: "Leave everything. . . ."

He had himself remarked that he was writing unclearly, and therefore he had cried out for them to summon Princess Anna, to whom he wished to dictate. They ran for her; she hastened to come, but when she appeared at his bedside he had already lost consciousness and the power of speech, which were not regained. In this condition he lingered another thirty-six hours.[2]

As rightly remarked in the literature, the point of this account was to persuade readers that Peter had intended to leave the throne to his eldest daughter, Anna Petrovna, the wife of Duke Charles Frederick of Holstein, Bassewitz's suzerain. It is perfectly obvious that by means of notes written many years later Bassewitz wished to burnish the prestige of the new duke of Holstein, Anna Petrovna's son, the future Peter III.

Even allowing that Bassewitz reflected events that actually occurred, they still would not have had real consequences, for, even if it had been possible to decipher the words Peter scratched on a scrap of paper or on a slate, this could not have become a formal state document concerning the succession. A whole series of generally accepted procedures was necessary to recognize it as possessing juridical force: consecration of the document, public oath of the tsar's executors, and so forth. In any case, whether this was legend or not, Peter died without having managed to designate a successor. Most probably neither the fifty-two-year-old tsar himself nor his intimates had thought about such an unexpected and rapid demise. When, however, death hovered over his pillow it was already too late to do anything.

It is difficult to believe that Peter had not thought about a testament at all—indeed he had long been gravely ill. But even if he had acknowledged death's approach it was certainly not easy for him to decide to whom the throne and the empire should be left as a legacy. Consequently, he might have put off proclaiming a successor.

In pre-Petrine times the question would have been resolved quite easily: by law the throne passed via the direct male line of descent—from father to son and onward to grandson. If such an order had been maintained, the heir should have become Peter's grandson, Peter Alekseevich, the son of Tsarevich Aleksei. Yet the whole complexity of the problem stemmed from the fact that Peter in the so-called "Charter on the Succession to the Throne" of 22 February 1722 had violated this tradition, fundamentally altering the order of succession: thenceforth the autocrat reserved for himself the right to designate an heir according to his own wish.

The situation leading to the formulation of the "Charter" was governed by the tragedy that had occurred in the tsarist family not long before 1722. Its first document was completed on 3 February 1718 when Tsarevich Aleksei Petrovich renounced all rights to the throne. This was already the denouement of the conflict between father and son that had unfolded from a long prior history.

Almost from infancy Aleksei—Peter's son (born in 1690) by his first wife, Evdokiia Lopukhina, who was banished to a monastery in 1698—had proved to be on the remote periphery of the tsar's interests. As a living and unpleasant reminder of the unsuccessful first marriage, and indeed of the "Muscovite life" so hateful to Peter in general, he could not have become close to his father. Such closeness became even less likely later when a new family was presented to Peter. Catherine, who bore Peter other heirs and who dreamed, like every mother, of a favorable future for them, had scant need of a stepson. One must suppose that the boy, forcibly taken at age eight from his mother (under interrogation he called her "Mama") and who grew up among strangers, could not forget his mother. But Peter forbade Aleksei from seeing Evdokiia—the nun Elena of the Pokrovsky Monastery in Suzdal—and once, on learning that the seventeen-year-old tsarevich had clandestinely traveled to his mother for a meeting, had been beside himself with rage.

Apparently, the cause of the prolonged family conflict was also linked with the fact that Peter in raising his own son (like his subjects as well, by the way) proceeded from pedagogical concepts then widely current: he set an allowance for Aleksei, designated his teachers and governors, confirmed the program of his education, and—preoccupied with thousands of urgent matters—had assumed that his heir was on the right track, and if not, then the fear of punishment would right matters. As often happens in life, however, pressure on the child's personality gave birth to dissimulation, a desire to find a counterbalance to the father's dictates. A powerful hidden opposition to everything that stemmed from the tsar manifested itself in feelings of "loathing" for his person, which led as a result to misunderstanding and rejection of the grandiose affairs that constituted the principal meaning and purpose of Peter's life.

The well-known prewar Soviet film *Peter the First*, in which Nikolai Cherkasov played the role of Tsarevich Aleksei, has formed in public consciousness the image of the heir as a personality insignificant, pliable, neurasthenic, and mediocre. In real life it was probably not so. It should not be forgotten that Aleksei was Peter's son and, one would think, inherited many of his features, which, however, the unfavorable circumstances of the tsarevich's life strongly warped. Persistence turned into senseless stubbornness, wit gave way to malice, energy to carousing with intimates "organized" into a special "company" like the father's "Most-drunken conclave" in which there was not one man who discerned the sense of the conflict growing from year to year between father and son.

Neither did family life succeed for the tsarevich. At Peter's direction in 1711 Aleksei, manifestly against his will, became the husband of Crown Princess Charlotte of Brunswick-Wolfenbüttel, whose feelings did not interest anybody either. Alien to each other, Aleksei and Charlotte, like many other dynastic pairs, were merely pawns in the political game started in the post-Poltava period by the Russian tsar, the Polish king, and the Austrian emperor—a relative of Charlotte's. This marriage, as may be guessed, was an unhappy one. Also alien to Aleksei were the children that soon appeared—Natalia and then Peter. Charlotte died in 1715 bearing Peter.

Jumping ahead, we note that Aleksei did not organize any conspiracy against Peter; he found himself constantly on the defensive and hardly ever took the offensive, for during his father's life that was tantamount to suicide. One may only say for certain that the tsarevich impatiently bided his time, which would arrive with his father's death. The tsarevich did not have any kind of definite, distinct "restorationist program," although certain hints of a plan for the future reign gradually took shape.

We may hypothesize that the tsarevich on taking power intended to reverse his father's active imperial policy that had become so obvious toward the end of the Northern War. It is not ruled out that the political opposition, which Peter had driven deep underground but which hoped to rise again with Aleksei Petrovich's accession to power, spoke through the tsarevich. The materials of the investigation of Aleksei definitely attest that even among the tsar-transformer's confederates (especially among the hereditary elite) as well as among the clergy there were quite a few who sympathized with the tsarevich.

Peter, through his own channels, probably received information about the attitudes of the tsarevich and his entourage, and about the elite's and the clergy's sympathy for him.

However complex the relations of father and son may have been, the latter boldly looked ahead, for the future would be his. The fact that the tsarevich was the official and sole heir gave him special power in anticipation of his hour and allowed him, albeit covertly, to oppose his father without fearing the consequences—because the tsar had no alternatives. Things continued in this way until 1715, when exceptionally important events took place in the tsarist family. Peter wrote his son a decisive letter containing accusations of indolence and insubordination. At the end of the letter Peter got to the real point: "If not, I will have you know that I will deprive you of the succession, as one may cut off a useless member. Do not fancy that, because I have no other child but you, I only write this to terrify you. I will certainly put it in execution, if it please God; for whereas I do not spare my own life for my country and the welfare of my people, why should I spare you who do not render yourself worthy of either? I would rather choose to transmit them to a worthy stranger than to my own unworthy son. The 11th day of October 1715 at Sankt-Piterburkh. *Peter.*"[3]

Why was this fateful letter dated October 1715, although the relations between father and son, as is obvious from the text cited, had been troubled for a long time? Why exactly did Peter first voice the intention to deprive the recalcitrant son of his legacy?

Of course, it was not accidental; Peter had been thinking about the future ever more frequently, whereas Aleksei's conduct inspired no particular hopes. The tsar understood that his heir would not continue what he had begun. By the mid-1710s the tsar's health, sapped by war and illnesses, had begun to incite the anxiety of those around him and even of Peter himself. Furthermore, Peter was preparing to leave the country in order to achieve a final breakthrough in the war with Charles XII on the shores of Germany and Sweden. Therefore, the question of the succession had become acute in Peter's consciousness and required radical resolution, in the tsar's accustomed style.

On 29 October of that same year, 1715, fate intervened to tie the noose even tighter—Catherine gave birth to a boy, Crown Prince Peter Petrovich. Responding on 31 October to Peter's letter, Aleksei, obviously hastening to forestall the tsar's probable wish, declared that he was renouncing the throne not only because he felt himself incapable of bearing the burden of power, but also because he now had gained a younger brother.

A simple renunciation from the succession was not enough for Peter, however, and three months later he sent his son a "Last Admonition." (We note in passing that the exchange of messages by persons living alongside each other in Petersburg was not accidental; evidently in sending his son peculiar official warnings, Peter was interested in creating and preserving this correspondence.) The tsar gave the tsarevich a choice: " . . . so I cannot resolve to let you live on according to your own will, like an amphibious creature, neither fish nor flesh. Change therefore your conduct, and either strive to render yourself worthy of the succession, or turn monk. I cannot be easy on your account, especially now that my health begins to decay. On sight therefore of this letter, answer me upon it either in writing, or by word of mouth. If you fail to do it, I will use you as a malefactor."[4]

Aleksei agreed to this and on the next day answered his father: "I will embrace the monastical state, and desire your gracious consent for it. Your servant and unworthy son, Aleksei."

Soon Peter went abroad and from Copenhagen wrote on 26 August 1716 a letter to his son (as if he had not received Aleksei's agreement to enter a monastery), demanding an immediate decision: either take the true route and go to Copenhagen, where the Russian army and navy were preparing an assault on the Swedish coast, or be tonsured as a monk at once.

Such an irreconcilable and harsh stance by Peter made Aleksei's position untenable: the twenty-six-year-old secular layman did not, of course, wish to enter a monastery, although he had been compelled to give his agreement, evidently supposing that this was more a pedagogical threat than an unavoidable and impending reality. But he expected nothing good from a forthcoming meeting with his father; most likely, both understood that Aleksei could no longer "change his manner," as demanded by his father.

Aleksei decided to flee, to hide from his father and his fate. He had no strength to mount resistance to Peter's despotism, which subordinated everybody and everything to the state's aims, but neither did he wish to renounce the throne or even less to enter a monastery, so he decided on a terrible crime for a Russian subject—fleeing abroad, which was state treason. Having reached the possessions of the Austrian emperor in the fall of 1717, he requested (and obtained at once) political asylum. Undoubtedly, this flight was an act of desperation, the protest of a man who found himself trapped, an attempt to break the ring tightening around him.

Terror drove Aleksei. He was given no rest by the oppressive notion that his party had lost, and, rejecting monasticism, he was doomed to terrible trials and, possibly, to death. In fleeing to neutral Austria, he had had no definite plan for the near future; he craved rest and wished to remove the tension that had seized hold of him after his father's harsh messages.

A refugee, the tsarevich was still not completely convinced of the rightness of his choice; most likely he was tormented by doubts, which were in fact used by Peter Andreevich Tolstoi, who, dispatched by Peter, managed to persuade Aleksei to return while it was not too late to submit and correct his error.

During several conversations Tolstoi contrived to bend the tsarevich to his will, artfully combining affectionate exhortations with crude threats. He firmly promised Aleksei his father's pardon and in confirmation showed him a letter of the tsar's in which he wrote: "If you fear me, I assure you by this present, and I promise to God and his judgment, that I will not punish you, and if you submit to my will, by obeying me, and if you return, I will love you better than ever."[5]

Concurrently Tolstoi threatened the tsarevich with incessant pursuit, scared him with the Russo-Austrian war that Peter supposedly wished to launch, and promised that if Aleksei tried to flee to Italy the tsar himself would come after him. After long vacillation the tsarevich decided: "I shall go to my father on condition that it be permitted for me to live in a hamlet and that Efrosin'ia not be taken from me." Of course, both conditions were promised him on the spot.

It cannot be ruled out that the tsarevich's favorite, Efrosin'ia, on whom he doted (she was expecting his child), talked him into "obeying his little father." Efrosin'ia, who had immediately fallen into Tolstoi's snares, was virtually the only person from the tsarevich's entourage not subjected to torture in the dungeons of the Secret Chancery and who emerged dry from waters stained by the blood of dozens of people.

On 3 February 1718 the tsarevich was brought to Moscow, to the Kremlin, where he renounced the succession. The tsarevich took this ceremony for his pardon.

Overjoyed with this good reception, Aleksei did not notice the low rumble of the approaching tempest.

It was coming closer and was inescapable—one only needed to know Peter. Even if we grant that he was a sincere father in pardoning a prodigal son, as a ruler he had to bring the case of the traitor Aleksei Petrovich Romanov to an end, and as we know, in Russia traitors always have accomplices.

Reading the investigatory materials—and the case had already begun the day after a peaceful family dinner at Preobrazhenskoe—one sees how purposefully the search for accomplices proceeded: the investigators' urge to detect conspiracy and to place Aleksei at its head is too open. I don't know whether the tsar himself believed in the existence of such a conspiracy, but there is no doubt that through investigations, trials, threats of repression, and terrible executions Peter consciously frightened his political opponents. The bloody case of Aleksei, which stunned society at the time, was supposed to paralyze the resistance of the opposition to the reforms and to the tsar personally, just as the bloody strel'tsy executions had done earlier.

At the same time, Peter, as a sober statesman, distinctly understood that even Aleksei's public renunciation in favor of Peter Petrovich would not guarantee preservation of the throne for Catherine's son. Although the elite and the other subjects swore fidelity to Peter Petrovich, Peter saw that many did so hypocritically, while several refused outright to recognize the legality of such an act.

Thus, on 2 March 1718 at church in Preobrazhenskoe, scribe Illarion Dokukin shouldered his way up to Peter and handed the tsar a standard printed example of the oath of fidelity to Peter Petrovich, which all subjects were obligated to sign after the corresponding church ceremony. On the place left for the signature had been written in Dokukin's hand: "For the undeserved removal and expulsion from the all-Russian tsarist throne preserved by God of the sovereign tsarevich Aleksei Petrovich by Christian conscience and the judgment of God and the most holy Gospel I do not bow and do not kiss the life-giving cross of Christ, and by my own hand I do not sign; ... although for this, tsarist wrath pour down on me, being in this the will of my Lord God Jesus Christ according to His holy will for truth I, servant of Christ, Illarion Dokukin, am ready to suffer. Amen, amen, amen."

This was a daring public challenge to the will of the omnipotent autocrat. Right there in church Dokukin was arrested and in prison gave testimony about the reasons for his extraordinary civic act: "On the oath he signed by his own hand he, Larion, sympathizing with him, the tsarevich, that he is the one born and from the true wife, whereas the heir tsarevich Peter Petrovich he does not recognize as true because it is said that although the present sovereign lady tsaritsa is a Christian, but when the master will be no more, and tsarevich Peter Petrovich will reign and then she, the tsaritsa, will communicate with foreigners and for Christians there will be obstacles because she is not of native origin."[6]

Two weeks later Dokukin was subjected to public execution by breaking upon the wheel, and unable to endure the inhuman torment of prolonged execution, recanted, was taken down from the wheel, "pardoned," and beheaded. Other cases similar to this were launched. The gears of the repressive machine (a special Secret Chancery headed by Peter Tolstoi had been created for the investigation of Aleksei's case) started to gather momentum, seizing in their teeth more and more new victims.

The investigation of the case of the state criminal Tsarevich Aleksei Petrovich was marked by special severity, and the torture of those under investigation in the first half of 1718 went on incessantly. Sister Elena (Evdokiia Lopukhina) was brought to the torture chamber as well, who admitted that she had maintained a criminal correspondence with her own son. The torture apparatus did not spare the tsarevich either, and it cannot be ruled out that the tsar himself interrogated him under torture.

In the summer of 1718 a case was launched by a denunciation of several servants, who recounted that they knew how Peter, on an estate not far from Peterhof, had tortured the tsarevich. Andrei Rubtsov, a servant of Count Platon Musin-Pushkin, testified that once "when he was with his lord, Platon, at an estate where the master-tsarevich was, at one time his lord ordered him that when His Tsarist Majesty would come to the estate, he should not take note at that time: they will be torturing the master-tsarevich, said he." Later Rubtsov testified, "when His Tsarist Majesty drove up to the estate, he, Andrei, was sent away from his hut and he stayed in the woods far from that estate, and at that time in a barn on that estate there was shrieking and groaning, but who it was he knows not, and about three days after that he saw that the master-tsarevich said that his arm hurt and ordered the arm wrapped with a handkerchief near the hand, and they wrapped it."

Reports that the father himself was torturing the tsarevich evidently produced an anguished impression on the people privy to this secret. One of the witnesses, the wife of tavern-owner Andrei Poroshilov (who learned of the tortures from the aforementioned Andrei Rubtsov), recounted: "When Andrei Poroshilov came home in the evening from the estate of the master-tsarevich, and sat in the room weeping, and she, Irina, asked Andrei what he was weeping about, he replied: 'The master at his own son's estate was torturing the tsarevich.' "[7]

In the summer of 1718 the investigation of Aleksei's case was largely finished, and on 24 June a Supreme Court consisting of the highest military and civil ranks unanimously condemned the tsar's son to death on charges of conspiracy and attempting to seize the throne.

A day after the delivery of the sentence, on 26 June, the tsarevich, who was being held in the Trubetskoi bastion of the Peter and Paul Fortress, died unexpectedly. This death, however, was about as surprising as the death of Peter III, Ivan Antonovich (Ivan VI), and Paul I.

How Tsarevich Aleksei died we shall never, probably, know. The *Registry Book of the St. Petersburg Garrison Chancery* contains a notation for 26 June: "That same date in the sixth hour after noon, being under guard in the Trubetskoi bastion in the garrison, tsarevich Aleksei Petrovich departed this life." The Hanoverian resident Weber reported that the tsarevich, upon learning the sentence, had suffered an apoplectic stroke. The Austrian resident Pleyer in one report repeated this point of view but in another, reports the circulation of persistent rumors about the tsarevich's death by the sword or axe. The Dutch resident De Bie wrote his government that Aleksei died "from dissolution of the blood vessels." This report was opened, Chancellor Golovkin and Vice-Chancellor Shafirov arranged a formal interrogation of De Bie, and the resident revealed his informant, the midwife M. von Gusse, who was interrogated in the fortress along with her daughter and son-in-law. Historian Nikolai Ustrialov, who collected all this information, believed the tsarevich died from the tortures he suffered even on the day of the sentence's announcement.[8]

One cannot ignore one more very interesting document, a letter from Guards Captain Alexander Ivanovich Rumiantsev to a certain D.I. Titov concerning the tsarevich's execution. The letter has come down to us in copies. As always in such cases, historians are divided: some speculate that the letter is a later forgery; others, however, consider it authentic.

Rumiantsev describes the scene of the tsarevich's murder thus:

> Then we, as much as possible, quietly went through the dark passageways and with the same caution opened the door of the tsarevich's bed-chamber, as it was slightly lit by the lamps burning before the icons. And we found the tsarevich asleep, with the bedclothes scattered as if from some terrible nightmare, and still groaning at times loudly, and in truth really ailing, so that Holy Communion had been administered the evening of the same day that the sentence had been read from fear that he not die without having recanted his sins, from that time his health had become much better and in the words of the surgeons he was given strong hope for complete recovery. And none of us wishing to disturb his peaceful repose, sitting among ourselves we were saying: "Would it not be better to give him up to this death and thus spare him from terrible torment?" Yet conscience pressed on the soul that he not die without prayers.
>
> Thinking this and steeling himself, Tolstoi quietly shook him, the tsarevich, saying: "Your Tsarist Majesty! Get up!" He then, having opened his eyes and not sensing what this was about, sat in the

bedroom looking at us in confusion, without asking anything.

Then Tolstoi, coming closer to him, said: "Master-tsarevich! By a court of the most eminent people of the Russian land, thou hast been sentenced to death for many treasons to the master, thy parent, and the fatherland. Hence we, by His Tsarist Majesty's decree, have come to thee to execute this judgment, therefore by prayer and recantation prepare thyself for thy departure, for the time of thy life is already close to its end."

Hardly had the tsarevich heard this than he raised a great howl, summoning help, but not obtaining any success from this, he started bitterly weeping and saying: "Woe is me, poor soul, woe is me born of tsarist blood! Would it not have been better for me to be born from the humblest subject!" Then Tolstoi, comforting the tsarevich, said: "Master, as thy father has pardoned all thy transgressions, and he will pray for thy soul, but as a master-monarch he could not pardon thy treasons and violation of the oath, fearing thereby to subject his fatherland to some misfortune, therefore cease the groans and tears, a trait of women only, accept thy lot, as befits a man of tsarist blood and express thy final prayer for the forgiveness of thy own sins!" But the tsarevich did not heed that, but wept and cursed His Tsarist Majesty, calling him a child-murderer.

And as we saw that the tsarevich did not want to pray, then taking him under the arms we put him on his knees, and one of us, who exactly (from terror I do not recall) started saying to him: "Lord! Into Thy hands I commend my spirit!" He however, not saying this, wanted to straighten his arms and legs and tear himself away. That one, Buturlin I think, said: "Lord! Receive the soul of Thy servant Aleksei in the realm of the righteous, as a lover of humanity disdaining his transgressions!" And with this word they laid the tsarevich on his back on the bed and, taking two pillows from the head, they covered his head and pressed down until movement of the arms and legs stilled and the heart stopped beating, which was done quickly because of his weakness at the time, and what he said then nobody could make out, for from terror of impending death his reason became clouded. And as this was completed, we then laid out the tsarevich's body as if he were sleeping, and praying to God for his soul, quietly went out.

And the death of the tsarevich became known about noon that day, that is 26 June, as if he had died from a stroke of the blood. . . .[9]

The historians who doubt the authenticity of this document have found quite a few contradictions that could not have been in a letter of Alexander Rumiantsev, who was closely acquainted with Aleksei's case. Also the addressee is little known to scholarship, and the purpose of such a dangerous missive is unclear. In reading the whole letter, one notices turns of phrase and words close to the written speech of a man from the clerical milieu, yet Rumiantsev was a true soldier and not a particularly well educated or intelligent one.

At the same time one cannot discard the idea that the letter became known from copies, and it is quite possible that in copying it the letter was edited and supplemented. Such things have happened more than once with literary sources. Yet, despite doubts of the letter's authenticity, one cannot help but be astonished by its drama, vivacity, and detailed communication of all elements of this truly Shakespearean scene: the execution-murder of the unsuitable heir visibly unfolds before our eyes. In order to compose this shocking scene without having in hand the case of Aleksei, which was hidden for a century and a half in deep secrecy, and without knowing all the circumstances that accompanied it, one would need, no doubt, the talent of a great hoaxer or a dramatist. In the same breath one should never forget that the most talented dramatist is life itself, after which one only succeeds in writing it down.

The tsarevich's death gave birth to a wave of rumors and gossip. One of the unfortunate "clients" of the Secret Chancery said under torture: "And that the whole people is cursing the master, and this he said, but he heard it at the Obzhornyi [now Sytnyi] Market, all sorts of people stood in small groups talking among themselves about the death of the tsarevich, and in the conversation they cursed him, the master, and said that the whole people is cursing him, the master, because of the tsarevich." Another person under investigation testified about his companion that supposedly he said "that when the master-tsarevich was no more and at that time the master from joy broke out the frigate's flags and promenaded in front of the Summer Palace."[10]

Which was true! On 27 June 1718, the day after the tsarevich's death, Peter solemnly celebrated the regular anniversary of the Poltava victory. We shall never know what was in his soul, but perhaps by this symbolic act before the eyes of the shaken capital Peter strove to show that for him there was nothing higher than the values of the state, in the name of which he had sacrificed everything, including his son's memory.

After the tsarevich's death in all important official documents the name of the new heir to the throne, Peter Petrovich, is cited ever more often. It seemed that the acute dynastic crisis had already passed, life had returned to its customary course, and nobody looked up as fate went on "like a madman with a razor in hand."

Not a year passed after the death of tsarevich Aleksei before Petersburg buried his official successor—on 25 April 1719, after a brief illness, the three-year-old heir Peter Petrovich died.

This terrible blow, the destruction of all Peter's plans, was completely unexpected; the boy had grown up healthy and merry. "Shishechka"

[Little Boss] was his family nickname and Peter treated his son tenderly, as is very evident in his correspondence with Catherine.

On 26 April 1719 at the funeral service at the Trinity Cathedral as the body of Peter Petrovich was carried out, a most expressive and ominous scene took place, which was later carefully clarified by the investigators of the Secret Chancery. The Pskov rural councillor Stepan Lopukhin, a distant relative of Evdokiia Lopukhina, said something to his acquaintances and then burst out laughing. Standing beside him the clerk Kudriashov explained to those present at the funeral the reason for the blasphemous laughter: "So long as his, Stepan's, candle has not gone out, there will be time for him ahead." Denounced and seized, Kudriashov confessed from the rack that "he said that his, Lopukhin's, candle had not gone out because the grand duke remained alive [Peter, the son of Tsarevich Aleksei, the same age as the deceased heir], expecting that there will be good for Stepan Lopukhin ahead."

Yes, Peter's candle had really gone out, whereas the candle of the hated Lopukhins burned brightly. The orphaned Grand Duke Peter Alekseevich, left by his grandfather to the whim of fate, was growing up, feeding the hopes of all the great reformer's foes.

This could not fail to trouble the tsar. Hence on 5 February 1722 he adopted the aforementioned "Charter on the Succession to the Throne," unique in Russian history, which legalized the autocrat's right to designate as successor to the throne whomever he deemed fit. It is no accident that the law's preamble cites the precedent of Ivan III, who had at first named his grandson Dmitry as the heir, and then changed his mind, entrusting the throne to his son Vasily. The name of Grand Duke Peter Alekseevich is not mentioned in the "Charter," but one can read it palpably between the lines. There, too, the true sense of Peter's action peeps out, as he had supposedly said: "I shall give the throne to whomever I please, only not to the Lopukhins' ilk—destroyers of my life's work!"

Even in the complex situation that arose after the death of the heir to the throne, Peter, as always, did not lose his head. Right after publication of the "Charter" of 1722 he took the following important step: on 15 November 1723 he issued a manifesto on the impending coronation of Catherine. The basis for this decision was provided by the tradition of Christian states, and in particular the Byzantine Empire, to which the Russian grand princes and tsars, as we know, considered themselves to be the successors.

In May 1724 in Russia's main church, the Assumption Cathedral of the Moscow Kremlin, the ceremony crowning the wife of the first Russian emperor took place, which was solemnly announced to the whole country. In the description of the ceremony it is underlined that Peter himself placed the crown on Catherine's head. Although during the coronation festivities there was no talk about the succession, all observers clearly understood what had taken place in the Assumption Cathedral. The French emissary Jean-Jacques Campredon reported to Paris: "It is extremely and especially noteworthy that, contrary to custom, the rite of anointing was executed over the tsaritsa so that she has thereby been recognized as ruler and mistress after the death of the tsar her husband."[11]

A question naturally arises: why, eight months after the empress's coronation, had the dying Peter not proclaimed his intention to transfer power to her? I think not only that the tsar, as already indicated, did not expect a sudden death—strong attacks of illness had become common for him in recent years. The main reason for the tsar's vacillation stemmed from the profound conflict in the family in the fall of 1724 occasioned by the case of Villim Mons, which shocked Petersburg society.

But before addressing this theme, we should say something about Catherine, who did not leave the dying tsar's bedside in the anguished days of January 1725.

Catherine had appeared in Russian history in 1702, when among the captive residents of the Swedish fortress of Marienburg the seventeen-year-old girl Marta, who had been living in the family of Pastor Gluck, caught the fancy of Field Marshal Sheremetev. In the literature, opinion is divided about her origins: according to some information, Catherine came from a family of Livland peasants, the Skavronskys; according to others, she had been born in Sweden and only later moved to Livland.

Gossip links Catherine's appearance around Peter with the name of Menshikov, who had taken the young hostage from Sheremetev and then handed her over to the tsar. "Katerina is not native and not Russian," testified one soldier in the Secret Chancery, "and we know how she was taken into captivity and brought under a flag in only a shirt and put under guard and our sentry officer dressed her in a caftan. With Prince Menshikov she cast a spell on His Majesty."

In regard to "a spell" I cannot say anything definite, but it is obvious that over the span of many years Catherine and Menshikov had been allies. The reason for this was simple: secretly scorned by the ruling hereditary elite as new arrivals from below, they needed one another's support to counter their foes.

The impression about "a spell" as some magical means to bewitch the tsar finds confirmation in the colossal influence that Catherine possessed over Peter. Having become the tsar's favorite in approximately

1703, the captive of Marienburg gradually acquired ever greater influence. In her own life she traveled the route of Cinderella, who raised herself from "washerwoman" and concubine to "most gracious sovereign lady empress."

A stern despot, a man with an iron character and will, Peter treated Catherine with unusual tenderness and concern. Their surviving correspondence reflects this extraordinarily high tone of personal relations. ". . . I am greatly bored without you"; ". . . for God's sake, come soon, and if for some reason it is impossible to be here soon, do write, because without you it is sad for me that I neither hear from nor see you . . . God grant, to see you in joy soon"; "I hear that you are bored, and for me too it is not without boredom either"—similar admissions are sprinkled through the letters of the tsar, who was quite miserly with tender words and who received mutual admissions and touching gifts. These relations were maintained not for a year or two, but more than twenty.

There is no doubting that Catherine's huge influence on Peter, which contemporaries noted, was a consequence of what is called the same in all times: love, heartfelt attachment, trust. Undoubtedly this was a most rare marriage for a crowned ruler built on other than dynastic and political bases. By the way, there was politics here all the same: by marrying a "washerwoman," the tsar-reformer threw down as it were a challenge to the old society, considering suitability before eminence. This transformation of a concubine—one of the tsar's many "mistresses"—into a wife and an empress was due exclusively to her subtle understanding of Peter and her adaptation to his customs and manner. A woman not only uneducated but probably illiterate, she was wise in everyday life and evinced a deep, sincere interest in his aims, which elicited a corresponding reaction—indeed we know how much sincere feeling can do. In Peter's letters to Catherine we see how this iron person who admitted no weakness bared himself: he sought from Catherine no particular aid, but heartfelt sympathy and involvement, for as we know, the fate of him who stands above all is almost always inner loneliness.

And then this whole idyll collapsed precipitously in the late fall of 1724. On the evening of 8 November, unexpectedly for the entire court, Villim Mons (brother of Anna Mons and chamberlain to Catherine) was arrested, as were several people close to him. Mons's papers were sealed and delivered to Peter, and an investigation was launched that the emperor presided over in person.

Formally, the Mons case, which began from investigation of a denunciation against him, involved numerous bribes he had received from various people, including the foremost in the state. It became known that Menshikov had given the chamberlain as a gift a horse "with accoutrements," Prince Vasily Dolgoruky had given him "brocade for an outer caftan," Tsaritsa Praskov'ia Fedorovna, the widow of Peter's older brother Ivan Alekseevich, gave him the revenue from her Pskov estates.

It is quite remarkable that the investigation into the matter of bribes to Mons—and such cases usually dragged on for years—was pursued with extraordinary speed: many of the arrested and those implicated in the case were not even interrogated. On 14 November a high court sentenced Mons to death as a bribe taker. Peter then and there confirmed the court's decision: "Execute according to the sentence," and on 16 November Mons was beheaded on the Trinity Square.

One must suppose that the investigation of bribery had almost immediately taken a backseat if, of course, it had been the cause from the start and not a pretext for the arrest and execution. One need not exercise any special subtlety to understand that Tsaritsa Praskov'ia Fedorovna gave Mons estates while Menshikov gave him a stallion not for the good looks and urbane manner of the empress's young chamberlain, but for the influence that Mons enjoyed. Indeed this influence, as is not difficult to guess, was based on the special attention that the forty-year-old Catherine paid to the twenty-eight-year-old chamberlain.

Foreign observers reported that the investigation of the Mons case caused serious discord in Peter's family and tense scenes between the spouses.

Peter's extremely peculiar attitude toward problems of marital fidelity is known. Peter personally never limited himself in anything, and he was always surrounded by those who are delicately called "mistresses"—it must not be forgotten that Catherine had emerged from their ranks. Furthermore, Catherine herself "presented" women to Peter and even joked in letters on that account.

By recognizing and even encouraging Peter's marital liberty, Catherine as it were tore away the curtains behind which the influence of some other "little mistress" might arise and become strong without the empress's knowledge. Yet that which was allowed the emperor was impermissible for his wife. A consequence of this was the bloody Mons case.

One might think that the crux of the conflict was not so much in jealousy, as might be thought at first, as the serious apprehension that this saga incited in the tsar from the political point of view. Intending to leave the throne to his wife, the tsar unexpectedly confronted the Mons case and, perhaps for the first time, contemplated whether the fate of his great legacy might ultimately prove to be in the hands of some adroit knave like Villim Mons. I don't think that Peter had any illusions concerning his wife's aptitude for practical matters, for she had never bothered with statecraft.

Had the great reformer only known that the system of succession, the bases of which he had laid down, would become one of the causes of the chronic instability of Russia's eighteenth century, and that in cutting off Mons's head he was not forestalling the threat of favoritism—that constant, corrupting companion of harsh despotism whatever political clothing it put on ...

All of the foregoing is supposition, but it cannot be denied that this may explain Peter's swift and decisive reprisal against Mons and his manifest indecision and reluctance, dangerous for the country's fate, in designating his own successor.

Peter put off the decision, figuring at first on recovering his health, but when "from the unbearable pain his shrieks and groans resounded throughout the palace ... he was no longer in a condition to think with full awareness about the arrangements that impending death required of him." At the same time, as another observer, the Dutch resident De Wilde, wrote, "he was suffering so much that the tsaritsa did not dare to speak with him about it. . . ."[12]

In this fashion it happened that on the night from 28–29 January 1725 the fate of the throne was decided not in the room where the emperor was dying, but in an adjoining one where Peter's collaborators, his "principals" and "fledglings," had gathered and tensely awaited bulletins about his condition. They did not sit with folded hands.

The biggest of the "fledglings" was the Most Serene Prince Alexander Danilovich Menshikov—a striking, extraordinary personality, the most talented of Peter's collaborators, who was distinguished by brains, initiative, and organizational and command talents. Over three decades Menshikov had made a mind-boggling ascent up the service ladder, starting as Peter's orderly and ending his career as a generalissimo.

The possessor of immense riches and estates that exceeded in size some foreign countries, wrapped in the laurels of glory on battlefields and on the construction sites of Petersburg, he remained insatiable for money, honor, and power even when he was a simple orderly to the young tsar. Avid with greed, he desired only one thing on the day of Peter's death—to maintain and further strengthen his influence and his power. Therein was the logic of the political conflict, the logic of Menshikov's whole life.

It should be noted that in the last years of Peter's reign, Menshikov had lived in constant anxiety: relations with the tsar (the nuances of which decided much more in a courtier's fate than the mountain of awards and riches) had not been as good as before. Peter in fact became alienated from Menshikov and in the 1720s no longer wrote Al-eksashka such tender notes as in 1709: "I announce to you that I have this moment arrived here, and will be spending the night two miles from Khar'kov or in Khar'kov (only don't be jealous where I will be spending the night)."[13]

Therefore Peter's death, on one hand, naturally exacerbated Men-shikov's anxiety about the future, but on the other hand gave hope of reinforcing his compromised position: for Menshikov the most desir-able resolution would be Catherine's accession to power, for it was no secret to anybody that over the span of two decades Catherine had invariably supported him, and had interceded for the Most Serene caught embezzling at those moments when the axe had almost been poised over his neck. As already noted above, Catherine exhibited to-ward Menshikov some kind of special sympathy and, if one may say so, a sense of social solidarity based upon a commonality of the interests of newcomers from humble origins who had elbowed their way into the highest echelons of power through the tsar's favor and their own abilities.

In the impending conflict Menshikov had every chance to triumph, that is, to make Catherine empress—possibly even against the will of the dying Peter, if that will should diverge from the prince's wishes. It is no exaggeration to say that behind him stood the army and the Guards, in his hands were the levers of the state administration. Furthermore, he had powerful allies who desired the same thing as he did, the accession of Catherine in order to maintain power and privileges.

Some documents call them in the old Roman fashion "principals," underscoring their special position at court and in the state. There were only a few "principals"—they can be counted on the fingers of one hand: Chancellor of the Empire Count Gavrilo Ivanovich Golovkin, General-Admiral Count Fedor Matveevich Apraksin, Privy Councillor Count Peter Andreevich Tolstoi, Procurator-General Count Pavel Ivanovich Yaguzhinsky, and General–Grand Master of Ordnance Count Jakob Danilovich Bruce.

Perhaps the most colorless among them was president of the College of Foreign Affairs Chancellor Golovkin. He was manifestly lesser in native ability than his deceased predecessor—Fedor Matveevich Golovin—although, like Peter's other collaborators, he worked rather than sitting on his hands. As the leader of the foreign policy office, he made no clumsy mistakes and was a careful executor of the tsar's will. It is possible that just such a man was necessary for Peter in that sphere of state administration, which the tsar himself—a true diplomat and subtle statesman—had supervised directly and constantly over the span of de-cades. In many critical political situations, the chancellor conducted himself quite cautiously, not giving in to emotions, closely weighing his own actions, and maintaining that splendid silence that, as the masters of aphorism say, if it does not show brains, then neither does it show a lack of stupidity.

Fedor Matveevich Apraksin, president of the Admiralty College, had never been celebrated as an experienced naval commander and organizer of naval affairs. In this sense his position under Peter, who literally lived for the sea and the navy, was approximately the same as Golovkin's. But, in contrast to the latter, Apraksin enjoyed Peter's special trust and even, apparently, access to his household. Several of Peter's letters have been preserved that testify to the well-known warmth of the tsar's relations with his general admiral. Attention should be paid to them, because the list of addressees of similar missives of the stern tsar is quite short.

The most senior in the company of Peter's "fledglings," Peter Andreevich Tolstoi, was in 1725 about eighty years old. His long life had been complicated and tortuous: beginning his political career in the camp of Peter's rivals and the Naryshkins, actively supporting Sophia and the Miloslavskys, he reoriented himself fairly quickly and managed to curry favor with the new ruler. At the beginning of 1697, as a fifty-two-year-old family man, even a grandfather, he was dispatched along with noble adolescents to study naval affairs in Italy, which could not help but please the tsar. Yesterday's table attendant very rapidly managed to adopt the life-style and manner of thinking characteristic of the Petrine entourage, and soon he became one of Peter's closest collaborators.

By character he was undoubtedly a born diplomat, a shrewd tactician. A subtle psychologist, he contrived to find a common language with the most diverse people and to achieve the aims that Peter set before him. It needs to be noted that these aims were exceptionally complex: as emissary to Istanbul and head of the first standing Russian representation at the sultan's court, he managed splendidly to arrange the diplomatic and reconnaissance service in the capital of the Ottoman Empire, supplying the Russian diplomatic office with most valuable and trustworthy information (remember the situation on the eve of the Pruth campaign of 1711).

The high point of Tolstoi's diplomatic career was the delicate operation of finding and returning from Austria Tsarevich Aleksei in 1717. It should not surprise us that right after this diplomatic mission Peter Tolstoi was commissioned to head the specially organized Secret Chancery of Investigatory Affairs, which was preoccupied with Aleksei's case. Tsar Peter knew his people: Tolstoi was not simply an efficient executor of his will but also a cruel, unscrupulous man, ready to pursue the aims set before him, to waive ethics, and, if necessary for the cause, to murder, about which there is testimony.

In writing about Tolstoi, scholars have recounted an anecdote: at one of his drinking bouts, Peter, who personally did not especially abuse the gifts of Bacchus, as we know, remarked that the company included one cunning fellow who, feigning to be dead drunk, watched covertly after his drinking companions—such simple souls as Admiral Fedor Matveevich. Accosting him—it was Tolstoi—Peter allegedly said: "O head, head, if thou weren't so smart, I would long ago have ordered thee cut off."

Sentiments with multiple meanings! It has happened more than once in history that the most hardened executioner has become he who, tormented by terror for previous sins, is compelled to prove to the ruler his own commitment over and over. I think that neither Peter nor Tolstoi ever forgot about Peter Andreevich's loyal service to Tsarevna Sophia, and, remembering that the bones of the rebellious strel'tsy and all who supported them had turned to dust long before, Peter Andreevich served Peter with even greater effort, sparing neither himself nor his victims.

Peter paid liberally for this service: after the Aleksei affair Tolstoi became an actual privy councillor, a senator, an owner of extensive estates, and president of the Commerce College. Therefore, on that already tense night of 28–29 January 1725 Count Tolstoi had special reasons to be agitated: the accession to power of the executed tsarevich's son would have meant inexorable disaster for the tsar's loyal servant. Hence it is not difficult to understand on whom the cunning old man would place his wager.

Of course, among Peter's closest collaborators there could not be equality. Indeed, concerning Menshikov's undisputed leadership I shall not speak in detail, merely citing as an example the signatures of Petrine generals and dignitaries on a letter to the tsar: "From near Golovchin, 2 July 1708. Alexander Menshikov. Thy servant Boris Sheremetev. Your servant Gavrilo Golovkin. Your servant Prince Grigory Dolgorukoi."[14]

To be sure, direct proof of the ranking of Peter's "fledglings" does not exist, but one may cite indirect evidence. Take as an example the accepted system of signatures of official persons on official documents. If we review one after another the dozens of Senate protocols preserved over several years, we may establish a certain regularity in the order of signatures, although formally all members of the collegial Senate were equal. As a rule the signatures of the senators go in two columns. For example:

Menshikov	Golovkin
Apraksin	Matveev
Musin-Pushkin	Dolgoruky et al.

Protocols have been preserved, by the way, in which the columns of signatures have blanks, obviously left for those who were supposed to sign each "in his own place."

The following regularity is observable: Menshikov always signs immediately after the protocol in "first place." Only occasionally, as in the prototype cited (on one level with his celebrated autograph scrawled in gigantic "printed" letters—testimony to the far from brilliant literacy of the honorary academician and member of the London Royal Society), did Golovkin or Apraksin set his fancy signature down alongside.

Still more expressive is the placement of signatures of the dignitaries when Menshikov missed a session of the Senate, which happened quite often. On the majority of such protocols for 1723 Apraksin's autograph is placed higher than the autograph of Chancellor Golovkin, whereas Tolstoi, Bruce, or somebody else never dared to place his own signature higher than those of Apraksin or Golovkin.

It is perfectly obvious that, notwithstanding the formal equality of the members of the senatorial college, the significance of each differed, and the leadership of some and the subordinate position of others were governed by a combination of many causes, rooted in the relations that had taken shape outside the Senate's session chamber. A conflict was going on, of course, for power and influence. Sometimes it was imperceptible and bloodless, but real nonetheless. Comparing the protocols with the signatures of Apraksin and Golovkin for the years 1719–20 and 1723, one cannot overlook that in 1719–20 Golovkin placed his own name higher than Apraksin's, but two years later he did not dare to do this and signed only after Apraksin, which with the obvious repetition that is manifest through a great quantity of material could not have been accidental. The signatures of Bruce, Tolstoi, and other senators were never placed above those of Apraksin and Golovkin for the same reason.

Standing aloof from these magnates was another most influential man of the Petrine epoch—Procurator-General Pavel Ivanovich Yaguzhinsky. When one reads materials about him, it is not difficult to recognize that Peter knew how to select associates, assigning them to just those posts that suited their character and ability. Yaguzhinsky, like many of Peter's other associates, came from humble social origins. Having made his way up by zealous service, he possessed many virtues of the administrator: punctuality, activity, initiative, performance. At the same time he was severe, unrestrained in speech. The tsar in 1722 appointed

precisely such a man procurator-general, whose duties included overseeing implementation of the laws in the Senate and other state institutions. Officially called "the crown agent of the ruler and the state,"
Yaguzhinsky had the right to report directly to the tsar.

Tested in action many times, he enjoyed Peter's special trust and had
made "justice his craft." Sitting in the Senate behind a special desk, he
sternly watched how the senators labored in fulfilling their duty. Punc-
tual in transmitting and executing the tsar's will, autonomous and active in the matters delegated to him, he appeared as the official "eye of
the ruler" and simultaneously as a thorn in the side of many of Peter's
dignitaries, who dreamed like all bureaucrats at all times of peaceful,
unhurried service without the exhausting selflessness and exaltation so
characteristic of Peter, of service that would bring honor and content-
ment and, if possible, modest income as well, besides the salary. The
incorruptible procurator-general with his deliberate candor and subtly
calculated daring was a man extremely inconvenient for the magnates,
especially for Menshikov, with whom Yaguzhinsky was constantly in conflict. In short, on the eve of Peter's death it was quite impossible to
leave out of account the public fighter for state justice, the more so
because he was Chancellor Golovkin's brother-in-law. Using the services
of the aforementioned Bassewitz, Menshikov and others drew Yaguzhinsky to their side.

In the end, the cohesion of the "fledglings" decided the fate of the
throne: on the night of Peter's death Guardsmen loyal to them surrounded the palace, preventing Catherine's opponents from proclaiming the son of Tsarevich Aleksei emperor. After a short consultation of
the magnates, in which several were prepared to question Catherine's
right to the throne, the united "principals" triumphed. The empress
was proclaimed Catherine I, whom, as Bassewitz reports in his "Notes,"
"they begged not to refuse the throne," which she, in meeting the
ardent wishes of her subjects, did not do.[15]

Peter's death became an important political event in the life of Russia and all Europe. Along with the great reformer an entire era in the
life of Russian society receded into the past, an era, in the considered
judgment of contemporaries, never to be repeated.

On the day of Peter's burial Feofan Prokopovich, sharing the sentiments of many, expostulated: "What is this? To what pass have we come,
oh Russians? What do we see? What are we doing? We are burying Peter
the Great! Is this not a dream? Is it not a nightmare for us? Ah, genuine
the sorrow, ah, how well known is our misfortune!"[16]

There is no doubt that the impassioned words of the brilliant orator,
which impress even two and a half centuries later, as well as the lengthy

The Mice Bury the Cat

and elaborate ceremony of the burial, never seen previously, were accompanied by the tears and profound grief of the numerous crowds escorting Peter on his final route to the Peter and Paul Cathedral.

But people, as always, remain people. They grieved over the loss and at the same time, attending the hours-long ceremony, probably froze, tired. They probably talked about trifles, thought about their daily routines, about the future. One may say with assurance that not everybody sobbed at the burial and not everybody shed sincere tears, but only "dabbed the eyes," looked more at the society that had gathered so as later to recount it at home, to talk a bit of scandal, to have a laugh. Soon after Peter's death a woodcut started circulating around the country.

This woodcut, often known under the name "The Mice Bury the Cat," depicts mice encircling a burial sleigh on which lies a cat with remarkably accented whiskers, accompanied by a rhymed text in which the nameless authors strive to make fun of the hypocritical grief of some, to show the unconcealed joy of others, and in general to celebrate the liberation of all the insulted and persecuted mice in the cat's life. A subtle connoisseur of woodcuts, I.M. Snegirev, comments on the message of this image and the woodcut's corresponding popularity:

> Like the wolf in relation to the sheep, so also the cat in relation to the mice have occupied from bygone times in fables and parables their allotted role: both are oppressors and tormentors, whereas the sheep and the mice are the oppressed and the suffering. . . . The cat

treats a captured mouse like an experienced cat-hangman, who first
extracts from his victim by slow tortures admission of his committed
and even uncommitted crimes, then expels life from it in such a way
that it feels it is dying. . . . The mice—these are the subjects oppressed
by the cat, their ruler. The traits and actions of people are imputed to
these animals.[17]

Students of the woodcut, the greatest of whom was D.A. Rovinsky, have
found in this folk portrayal, tinged with crude but, as always in anecdotes,
accurate and merciless humor toward the powers that be, many realia of
the Petrine era, and indeed elements of the procession at the first
emperor's burial. Here are eight mice, a parody of the eight stallions of
Peter's funeral hearse, and here is a mouse "Malan'ia from the Finns
driving a sleigh full of fritters"; Malan'ia herself is a parody of Catherine
"who walks like a foreigner and speaks Swedish." Among the mice who
have assembled for the burial from all over the country are many "locals"
from Karelia, Sliushin (the folk name for Schlüsselburg), and Okhta.

After the sleigh come those insulted by the cat: "There is an old gray
hearth rat in spectacles from whom the cat has torn the butt to pieces.
. . . An Okhta mouse transfer (i.e., transferred by decree for residence
in Petersburg on the Okhta) carries its own baby wounded by the cat. . . .
A baby mouse with an injured snout carries a fried fish." Here come
many mice from the borderlands: "Trenka from a poor house on the
Don sings jolly songs, proclaiming that it is good to live without the
cat. . . . The Tatar mouse Arinka also plays on the bagpipes" and so on.[18]

But for the participants in the burial from the ruling elite there was
no street humor, of course. Upon awakening the day after Peter's
death, they could not help but sense that the situation had changed
radically, that henceforth things would never again be as they had been
under Peter, for everything that Peter had done, rightly or wrongly, had
been sanctified by his enormous authority, his truly unlimited power
that had been received long ago and which by right of birth did not
require proof and justification. The dignitaries closest to him were under
the powerful influence of the reformer's personality; they looked on the
world through his eyes; hence many shortcomings and vices of the system
they thought were easily correctable, whereas the resolution of even the
most complex problems seemed simple because Peter had always taken
upon himself all the responsibility for the consequences as the country's
true leader, the brains and soul of the grandiose cause launched by him.

After his death everything changed. Catherine could not rule; the
weight of administration and the burden of responsibility now lay on
the "principals," who, setting out together to take on the heavy burden

of supreme authority, bore it with various degrees of zeal and effort and quarreled and intrigued against each other. The reforms were not completed, and, standing in the unfinished Peter and Paul Cathedral at that moment, when the coffin with Peter's body was placed in the tiny chapel (from which it was transferred to the prepared tomb only in 1731), they beheld a striking allegorical picture of the country's condition at the moment of Peter's death: the splendid gigantic bell tower with an angel on the spire had been raised to head-spinning heights, while the walls along the entire perimeter of the huge cathedral were no higher than the height of a grown man. But if the brilliant Italian architect Dominico Trezzini had had a plan of construction for the cathedral approved by the tsar and knew for sure what and when to build, then Peter's brilliant suite had received from the deceased emperor neither directions nor advice nor any kind of plan for what needed to be done. Indeed, Peter himself never had any fully drafted plans of reform: he had, as a rule, only hints of specific reforms; in much he was guided by intuition, a general understanding of what needed to be done, whereas he often acted haphazardly, neglecting to explain anything in the meantime. With him died that grandiose laboratory of thought, which alone had long determined everything without exception in the country.

The orphaned "fledglings" had to brave unknown roads at their own peril, often making policy from circumstances and not from considered plans. Even though Menshikov was the recognized leader of the government from the first days of Catherine I's reign, and did not encounter any special resistance among the ruling elite, he did not display either the breadth or the scope of Peter's thinking, he did not even master his devices of administration so as to imitate at least the continuation of the previous course, and indeed apparently he did not particularly aim at that: life placed on the agenda dozens of urgent problems requiring attention and resolution.

Politics, as we know, is the result of diverse and different kinds of factors and submerged currents that cannot be ignored in setting the course of the ship of state, without the risk of running it aground. Now is the time to address these factors.

Finding themselves in power, Menshikov and the others confronted grave problems of domestic policy that had matured long before Peter's death. The year 1725 was only the second peaceful year of Peter's reign. From 1695 wars had stretched out almost without a break: the Northern War had succeeded the Turkish War; the Persian War had succeeded the Northern War. The country was going through a severe postwar crisis—a direct consequence of overburdening the national economy in

the war years. It was manifested in the growth of arrears in paying both
the old household tax and the new soul levy, in the intensification of
peasant flight, in the palpable discontent of diverse strata of society.

Financial affairs were particularly troubled. The army had constantly
swallowed the greater part of revenues, and even so was short of money.
The total sum of arrears from 1720 through the beginning of 1726 had
reached, according to calculations of the War College, 3.5 million rubles with the annual soul levy of 4 million. It was obvious that ruination
as a consequence of the wars and the reforms exhibited a chronic
character. It was aggravated in the first years of peace by a terrible
national calamity—harvest failure and famine. In 1721–24 grain prices
shot up sharply, and the mortality of the populace rose. The situation
had changed little by the year of the tsar's death.

Numerous documents speak of peasant discontent with the
authorities' policies in the 1720s. The peasants consistently pressed to
be "forgiven" for the accumulated arrears and fines, and for the exclu-
sion from the assessment for the soul tax of the dead and the fugitive
(which would have removed extra payments from those who remained). The peasants demanded their liberation from building regimental quarters and for the curtailment of recruiting levies.

Villages and towns were full of rumors about impending changes—
the inevitable companions of a change of central authority. "Truly it is
sinful," Provincial Governor Tormasov of Poshekhona wrote the Cabinet, "that it is possible to take from them [peasants] and not only at
that time [earlier], but now too it is not possible to right things without
difficulty, it will only provoke stubbornness and echoes throughout the
district that the established commission is drafting a report and when it
is drafted, then all arrears will be set aside."[19]

Oh, this eternal Russian faith in the workings of commissions! The
one actually set up in 1726 did not even review the question of arrears.

The fragility of the government's position is explicable by the fact
that, after Peter's death, the nobility, squeezed into uniforms, started to
exhibit dissatisfaction and to set forth more candidly its own pretensions to power. The nobles demanded the adoption of effective measures in the struggle against fugitive serfs and the abolition of fines and
charges "for the concealment of and the failure to report souls" during the
census. They flooded government institutions with petitions asking for
favors, exemptions, grants of land, and "little hamlets and little people."
Compelled to perform lifelong service in the army and the state offices, the
nobles persistently begged for at least long leaves in order to establish
order on their estates, where only old men and children remained. In
February 1725 an investigation was launched into the case of Colonel

Yushkov, who had declared that he did not wish to honor Peter's ashes: "What is there for me to do with a corpse? I have been released to the village, and was not often with him when he was alive." Another lord wrote in a petition in March 1727 that "from the year 1720 I have not been in my hamlets, and without supervision the hamlets have come to complete ruin."

Discontent with government policy was also expressed by the higher clergy, which under Peter had been as quiet as water, as low as grass.

In the summer of 1725 investigation began into the scandalous case of Archbishop Feodosy Yanovsky, the actual head of the Synod, who had exhibited open disdain for Catherine I and had come out in the Synod with "seditious" talk containing anti-Petrine sentiments.

There is no doubt that these and much similar testimony had taken shape in those very factors that had exerted strong influence on the course of the post-Petrine ship of state. As always happens in such situations, changes ensued with striking swiftness.

On 2 February 1725 Yaguzhinsky already proposed that the senators discuss the question of reducing the soul-tax levy, which had spurred so much discontent, by four kopecks, "so that in the present instance the favor shown the populace will be felt." Yaguzhinsky's proposal, which the senators endorsed, Catherine I immediately "deigned graciously to approve," and the 74-kopeck soul levy was reduced to 70 kopecks.

In October of that same year the Senate (on the procurator-general's initiative again) reviewed a report "On the maintenance of the army in the present time of peace and how to bring the peasants into a better state."[20] The very name of the report speaks clearly about the crux of the most important dilemma of domestic policy: how, without weakening the army and navy, to improve the position of the peasantry, which was suffering from imposts, low birth rates, hunger, and abuse by the authorities.

The new government was constrained to begin working out the bases of its own policy, distinct from the Petrine one, taking into account a series of objective factors, the workings of which had been weakened under Peter but which in the new climate could no longer be ignored. With the decisions of 2 February and, more exactly, with the discussion of the senate report in the fall of 1725, the general tendency of revising the Petrine legacy started to grow, doubts about the correctness of the different reforms resounded more candidly and extensively, and the rivulets of criticism gradually began to swell into a flood that started to wash away the bases of Peter's policy, which even a day earlier had seemed unshakable. The scent of counterreforms filled the air.

The people who had come to power were guided not only by the objective circumstances of the country's postwar position, but also by a mass of subjective calculations and intentions. Soon they began to use criticism of a series of the most important Petrine reforms for purposes of strengthening their own service and political position, striving thereby to acquire political capital, yet in the process they—"Peter's children till the end of the century"—failed to put forward any fundamentally new alternative. This was revealed with particular clarity in the activities of the Supreme Privy Council, which was formed in February 1726, a year after Peter's death.

It is essential to note that Peter's "fledglings," in implementing measures simply heretical for Petrine times, were guided not merely by urgent demands or their own political ambitions. They were constantly glancing into that corner of the political scene where, in a circle of aristocratic families, a boy was playing—the grandson of Peter the Great and the son of the unfortunate Aleksei. The aristocratic upper crust— foremost the Dolgoruky and Golitsyn clans—had not managed in the crucial hours of Peter's death to maintain their positions against the pressure of the grouping of the "newly" eminent Menshikov and company. They did not come forth as opponents of Catherine's policy either, but during her short two-year reign their actions grew steadily as Grand Duke Peter matured and powered the wave of criticism of the Petrine legacy. Huddling around Catherine's throne, they saw that the empress's health was steadily failing, and a year after Peter the Great's death the "Peter factor, Peter's grandson," had already become perhaps one of the most crucial in the political game, when those who lost were at best exiled to Solovki in the far north.

The people close to the young grand duke were strong by their corporate feeling, traditional aristocracy, and family ties. They rejected the reforms and, shaking the hated wigs, remembered their beloved "good old days." It so happened that two and a half years later fate gave them a chance to turn the Petrine ship, which had continued to move by inertia, back to the past.

But . . .

> Far from it. Peter's shade
> Stood awesome among the magnates,
> What had been could not be raised anew,
> Russia was moving forward,
> The same ones sailed her amidst the same waters.
> —Alexander Pushkin

But that is another story, and a long one at that. . . .

Conclusion

Peter the Great's life ended in 1725, but his life in historiography had only just begun. Debate will never end concerning the role and significance of Peter and his reforms, and likewise debate about Russia's fate and her place in the world. It is hardly worthwhile to get involved in the age-old debate and to calculate, like the late eighteenth-century historian, Prince M.M. Shcherbatov, how many centuries our country would have needed to arrive at its present state if the great reformer had not entered its history. . . .[1]

Peter was there, and that changes everything, even our perception of the times preceding the Petrine reforms. In Peter's hands, as M.P. Pogodin wrote, "the ends of all our threads are joined in a single knot. No matter where we look, everywhere we meet ourselves in this colossal figure who casts his long shadow over all our past and even eclipses our early history, who at present seemingly still stretches his hand over us and who, it seems, we have never lost from view, no matter how far we have gone off into the future."[2]

These words, written almost 150 years ago, are especially topical at present, when our society has entered an era of transformations, on the depth, consistency, and radical nature of which the fate of our children and grandchildren depends. Therefore, the historical experience of reforms and reformers in Russia is so important for us. For many years we in the USSR, convinced that we were creating an exceptional society, regarded any historical parallels as inaccurate, particularly those that went past the notorious dividing line of 1917. Now, however, persuaded of the cardinal defects and grave vices of the system that had taken shape and wishing to change it, we are looking into the past groping for analogies, seeking the sources of many phenomena and processes that trouble us today, and pushing the "lower" chronological limit of these searches farther and farther back in time: 1937, 1929, 1917, 1861, 1825, 1801, and so on. To seek out these sources is essential, so as not to commit errors pregnant with catastrophe, so as not to take consequences for causes. In this regard addressing the theme of "Peter and the present day" is logical and natural.

Our interest in this theme is the sharper for two fundamental reasons. On one hand, we see that a great many realia of the Petrine era have entered into contemporary life in Russia, that society in the USSR grew from historical soil sprinkled with the juices of Petrine ideas. These remain firmly in public consciousness and in our genes.

The Petrine era brought not only impressive achievements and brilliant military victories that facilitated the strengthening of national self-consciousness, the victory of secular over confessional principles in culture, and the inclusion of Russia in the general European family of nations. The Petrine reforms were also the apotheosis of statism that in practice left no place until now for other (nonstate) forms of social existence. The era of the Petrine reforms was the time of the foundation of the totalitarian state, the graphic preaching and inculcation into mass consciousness of the cult of the strong personality—the boss, "the father of the nation," "the teacher of the people." It was also the time of the start-up of the "eternal prime mover" of a native bureaucratic machine that has worked until now according to its own internal laws alien to society. This was the all-encompassing system of supervision, the passport regime, the fiscality and the use of informers without which our "administrative-command system" could not exist. Peter's era witnessed, too, vices typical of society in the USSR: apathy, social dependency, lack of external and internal freedom for the individual. Finally, triumphs on the battlefield coexisted with a real cult of military force, militarism, and the militarization of civilian life and of consciousness, with the imposition of one's own will on other peoples through naked force, with the knocking together of an enormous empire, and with the crystallization of stereotypes of imperial thinking that have been preserved in public consciousness even now.

On the other hand, the Petrine reforms rivet our attention, for they have become forever the symbol of the breakthrough, distinguished by ferocious contempt for compromise, by radicalism, even by revolution. The idea is not new—even Alexander Herzen had written: "In Peter, beneath the imperial purple, one senses a revolutionary."[3] Later this notion of "a revolutionary on the throne" was often repeated in the literature in various configurations; it was often brought back, counterposing Peter's time and personality with that which was happening in society even centuries after him. Noteworthy in this sense is the poem "Russia," by Maximilian Voloshin, who strove to capture the fateful link of the times.

Great Peter was the first bolshevik,
Who plotted to overthrow Russia,
Inclinations and morals apart,
For hundreds of years, toward her looming distant future.
He, like we, knew no other route,
Except decrees, executions and dungeons,
For the realization of justice and truth on earth. . . .[4]

Right here the most important, fundamental problem of transformations on Russian soil arises: by what means and by what route to realize truth and justice for universal happiness? Should it be by the route of coerced progress, when it is considered normal and permissible to sacrifice one part of the people for the bright future of the rest, when coercion and compulsion in their most varied forms are chosen as the means to achieve lofty aims? Peter the reformer proceeded precisely along that route.

The idea of progress through coercion has seemed (and still seems) enticing and attractive to many. Through it one may achieve the desired noble aim easily and quickly. This idea has materialized, as it were, the burning desire of many reformers of Russia for immediate and very radical change, the urge to achieve results "right now and right here."

It cannot be said that the idea of a resolute and systematic break with the past came to Peter all of a sudden, or that it took shape as a theory and was then realized according to plan. Most probably, at first there was no sort of sensibly worked out plan of transformations, but only a passionate desire on the part of the young tsar to get out of the exceptionally unfavorable circumstances in which he and Russia found themselves after the unsuccessful start of the Northern War. Applying extraordinary measures possible only in those conditions, Peter managed to achieve significant and impressive results in a short time. Much hindered him, but much also favored him: unlimited autocratic authority, organizational talent, willpower and energy joined with merciless brutality and the toleration essential to a statesman of such great stature, intelligent assistants, the country's inexhaustible potential, the gifts of its people, and so forth. In sum, the extraordinary measures, which yielded such tangible results—above all, the brilliant victory over Sweden, one of the strongest states in the world of that time—were recognized as universal and, most important, as the only suitable means in Russia's conditions to attain the "common good" to which her great reformer aspired to lead the country.

Coercion, which constituted the crux of the extraordinary measures, was fixed in the laws, it was laid down in the structure of the state's administrative-repressive machine, and it was reflected in the whole system of hierarchical authority. It was in the varied forms of coercion, which became the regulator of the system Peter created, that its totalitarianism was exhibited.

Of course, it would be wrong to simplify everything. The Petrine reforms had roots in the past, in the economic and social development of preceding eras, and in the traditions of central authority and subordination in Russia. Peter sharply intensified the processes under way in the country; he forced it to make a gigantic leap, carrying Russia all at once through several stages that she inevitably would have had to traverse sooner or later.

At the same time, all of Peter's revolution possessed, however paradoxical it may sound, a distinctively conservative character. Modernization of the institutions and structures of authority for the conservation of the fundamental principles of the traditional regime appeared to be the ultimate aim. We are discussing the emergence of the autocratic form of rule that lived on until the late twentieth century and that affected the structure of the new authority after 1917, the formation of the system of estate groups without rights that became a serious brake on the process of developing an essentially medieval society, and finally serfdom, which was reinforced in the course of the Petrine reforms. . . . Russia's future is more tightly bound up with its past than may appear at first glance. And the figure of the great reformer towering in the distant past compels us to look back in order to remember the lessons taught by Peter, in order to move forward more surely.

Notes

List of Abbreviations

ALOII—Arkhiv Leningradskogo otdeleniia Instituta istorii SSSR Akademii nauk SSSR (Archive of the Leningrad Section of the Institute of History of the USSR of the Academy of Sciences of the USSR)

ChIOIDR—Chteniia Imperatorskogo obshchestva istorii i drevnostei rossiiskikh pri Moskovskom universitete (Readings of the Imperial Society of History and Russian Antiquities at Moscow University)

DPS—Doklady i prigovory Pravitel'stvuiushchego Senata, vols. 1–6, St. Petersburg, 1880–1901 (Reports and Resolutions of the Governing Senate)

PBPV—Pis'ma i bumagi Petra Velikogo, vols. 1–12, St. Petersburg and Moscow, 1887–1977 (Letters and Papers of Peter the Great)

PSZ—Polnoe sobranie zakonov Rossiiskoi imperii, vols. 2–7, St. Petersburg, 1838 (The Complete Collection of Laws of the Russian Empire)

SIRIO—Sbornik imperatorskogo russkogo istoricheskogo obshchestva (The Collection of the Imperial Russian Historical Society)

TsGADA—Tsentral'nyi gosudarstvennyi arkhiv drevnikh aktov (The Central State Archive of Old Documents in Moscow)

ZA—Zakonodatel'nye akty Petra I, compiled by N.A. Voskresensky, Moscow and Leningrad, 1945 (Legislative Documents of Peter I)

Zhurnal—Zhurnal ili Podennaia zapiska Petra Velikogo, St. Petersburg, 1770 (The Journal, or Daily Notes, of Peter the Great)

Introduction

1. M.P. Pogodin, "Petr Velikii" in his *Istoriko-kriticheskie otryvki*, I (Moscow, 1846), 341–42.

2. Xenia Gasiorowska, *The Image of Peter the Great in Russian Fiction* (Madison, 1979); Nicholas V. Riasanovsky, *The Image of Peter the Great in Russian History and Thought* (New York, 1985).

3. M.M. Shcherbatov, *O povrezhdenii nravov v Rossii* (Moscow, 1986).

4. S.M. Solov'ev, *Istoriia Rossii s drevneishikh vremen*, bks. 7–9 (Moscow, 1962–63).

5. V.O. Kliuchevskii, *Sochineniia*, vol. 4 (Moscow, 1958).

6. *Pis'ma i bumagi Petra Velikogo*, 12 vols. (St. Petersburg and Moscow, 1887–1977).

The Personality of the Reformer

1. M.M. Bogoslovskii, *Petr I*, vol. 1 (Moscow, 1940), 193.

2. M.I. Semevskii, *"Slovo i delo"* (St. Petersburg, 1885), 273–76.

3. A. Nartov, *Rasskazy o Petre Velikom* (St. Petersburg, 1891).

4. N.I. Pavlenko, "Petr I" in *Rossiia v period reform Petra I* (Moscow, 1973), 72–73.

5. "Suzhdenie damy o Petre Velikom," *Literaturnaia gazeta*, 41 (1841); translated in Eugene Schuyler, *Peter the Great* (New York, 1890), 1: 285–86.

6. F.V. Berkhgol'ts, *Zapiski kamer-iunkera*, pt. 4 (Moscow, 1860), 35, 101–2.

7. ALOII, f. 270, d. 101, l. 712.

8. Iu. Iul', *Zapiski* (Moscow, 1900), 101–2.

9. Ibid.

10. *SIRIO*, 39: 58.

11. D. Perri, "Povestvovaniia o Rossii," *ChIOIDR*, 2 (1871), 179; John Perry, *The State of Russia under the Present Czar* (London, 1967), 278–79.

12. F. Prokopovich, *Pravda voli monarshei* (St. Petersburg, 1722), 17–18, 26–27.

13. *ZA*, 69.

14. *Zhurnal*, I: 344.

15. Nartov, *Rasskazy*, 89–90.

16. Semevskii, *"Slovo i delo,"* 273–76; James Cracraft, *"Some Dreams of Peter the Great,"* in Cracraft, ed., *Peter the Great Transforms Russia*, 3rd ed. (Lexington and Toronto, 1991), 242–43.

17. Perri, "Povestvovanie," 179; Perry, *State of Russia*, 278.

18. *ZA*, 483.

19. Prokopovich, *Pravda*, 17–18, 26–27.

20. Nartov, *Rasskazy*, 54; Ia. Shtelin, *Podlinnye anekdoty o Petre Velikom*, pt. 1 (Moscow, 1820), 11–12.

21. *From Max Weber: Essays in Sociology*, ed. and trans. H.H. Gerth and C. Wright Mills (New York, 1958), 245–52.

22. Solov'ev, *Istoriia Rossii*, 18: 553.

23. *ZA*, 155.

24. *PBPV*, 2: 45.

25. Solov'ev, *Istoriia Rossii*, 17: 61.

26. *PSZ*, 7: 50.

27. Nartov, *Rasskazy*, 82.

28. Berkhgol'ts, *Zapiski*, 2: 605; Shtelin, *Podlinnye anekdoty*, 2: 13–14.

29. ALOII, f. 270, d. 88, l. 323.

30. *PBPV*, 9, pt. 1: 190–91.

31. *Bumagi Petra Velikogo* (St. Petersburg, 1872), 18.
32. Iul', *Zapiski*, 122–23; V.A. Nashchokin, *Zapiski* (St. Petersburg, 1842), 8.
33. Nartov, *Rasskazy*, 35, 43.
34. Kliuchevskii, *Sochineniia*, 4: 221.
35. *Materialy k istorii russkogo flota*, vol. 3 (St. Petersburg, 1872), 359.
36. N.G. Ustrialov, *Istoriia tsarstvovaniia Petra Velikogo*, vol. 6 (St. Petersburg, 1859), 348.

The Narva Confusion

1. Ustrialov, *Istoriia*, 2: 285.
2. *PBPV*, 1: 94.
3. I.I. Golikov, *Deianiia Petra Velikogo*, vol. 1 (Moscow, 1837), 99.
4. V.E. Vozgrin, *Rossiia i evropeiskie strany v gody Severnoi voiny* (Leningrad, 1986), 64–70.
5. *PBPV*, 1: 262.
6. Ibid., 164–65.
7. V.D. Koroliuk, "Izbranie Avgusta II na pol'skii prestol i russkaia diplomatiia," *Uchenye zapiski Instituta slavianovedeniia AN SSSR*, 3: 200; Bogoslovskii, *Petr I*, 2: 88–89.
8. Ustrialov, *Istoriia*, 3: 312–13.
9. N.N. Bantysh-Kamenskii, *Obzor vneshnikh snoshenii Rossii (po 1800 god)*, pt. 4 (Moscow, 1902).

"Seek to overthrow the foe"

1. *Zhurnal*, 1: 23–24.
2. *Ocherki istorii SSSR, XVII vek* (Moscow, 1955), 448.
3. *PSZ*, 5: 204–5.
4. *DPS*, 2, pt. 2: 307–8; G. Aleksandrov, "Pechat' Antikhrista," *Russkii arkhiv*, no. 10 (1873), 2073.
5. L.G. Beskrovnyi, *Russkaia armiia i flot v XVIII veke* (Moscow, 1958), 41–48.
6. D.F. Maslovskii, *Zapiski po istorii voennogo iskusstva v Rossii*, vol. 1 (St. Petersburg, 1891), 93–96.
7. *PSZ*, 5: 319–20.
8. P.O. Bobrovskii, *Proiskhozhdeniia "Artikula Voinskogo" i "Izobrazheniia protsessov" Petra Velikogo po "Ustavu Voinskomu" 1716 goda* (St. Petersburg, 1881), 32–46, 124–27.
9. *PSZ*, 5: 213–14.
10. Ibid.
11. I.A. Bykhovskii, *Petrovskie korabely* (Leningrad, 1982), 10.
12. P.A. Krotov, "Sozdanie lineinogo flota na Baltike pri Petre I," *Istoricheskie zapiski*, 116 (Moscow, 1988), 313–31.

Industrialization Petrine-Style

1. B.B. Kafengauz, *Istoriia khoziaistva Demidovykh v XVIII i XIX vv.*, vol. 1 (Moscow and Leningrad, 1949), 52–59.
2. Ibid., 76.
3. E.I. Zaozerskaia, *Razvitie legkoi promyshlennosti v Moskve v pervoi chetverti XVIII veka* (Moscow, 1953), 130.

4. N.I. Pavlenko, "Torgovo-promyshlennaia politika pravitel'stva Rossii v pervoi chetverti XVIII veka," *Istoriia SSSR*, no. 3 (1978), 59.

5. *PSZ*, 5: 66.

6. A.I. Aksenov, *Genealogiia Moskovskogo kupechestva XVIII veka* (Moscow, 1988), 34–35, 44–45.

7. Pavlenko, "Torgovo-promyshlennaia politika," 63–65.

8. *PSZ*, 6: 296.

9. E.V. Anisimov, *Podatnaia reforma Petra I: Vvedenie podushnoi podati v Rossii, 1718–1728* (Leningrad, 1982), 27ff.

10. Ibid.

11. Ibid., 27; *PSZ*, 4: 292–94.

12. Beskrovnyi, *Russkaia armiia*, 26–28.

13. *DPS*, 1: 382.

14. *Bulavinskoe vosstanie* (Moscow, 1939), 136–37, 161.

15. *PBPV*, 7, pt. 1: 160.

16. *PBPV*, 8, pt. 2: 479–80.

"It's difficult for a man to know and direct everything sight unseen"

1. *Ocherki istorii Ministerstva inostrannykh del* (St. Petersburg, 1902), 36.

2. *PSZ*, 4: 397.

3. Ibid., 588; *ZA*, 196.

4. *ZA*, 199–200.

5. *ZA*, 201–4.

On the Roads of War: From Narva to Poltava

1. *Zhurnal*, 1: 43–44.

2. *PBPV*, 2: 84, 63, 75.

3. *PBPV*, 2: 82–83.

4. *Zhurnal*, 1: 56.

5. Ibid., 57.

6. Ibid., 70, 72.

7. Bantysh-Kamenskii, *Obzor*, 4: 20.

8. Vozgrin, *Rossiia i evropeiskie strany*, 79.

9. "Vospominaniia K. de Turvilia o pokhode Karla XII v Rossiiu," *Voprosy istorii*, no. 3 (1989), 126–27.

10. *PBPV*, 3: 1060.

11. *PBPV*, 3: 52; vol. 1: 458.

12. "Vospominaniia K. de Turvilia," 126.

13. *Zhurnal*, 1: 143–44.

14. *PBPV*, 8, pt. 1: 16, 28.

15. B.S. Tel'pukhovskii, *Severnaia voina* (Moscow, 1946), 75.

16. *Zhurnal*, 1: 168.

17. ALOII, f. 270, d. 103, l. 554; M. Grushevskii, *Ocherk istorii ukrainskogo naroda* (Kiev, 1911), 339.

18. N.I. Kostomarov, *Mazepa* (Moscow, 1883), 183.

19. Ibid., 220, 226.

20. Ibid., 185–86, 188, 206.

21. *PBPV*, 9, pt. 1: 227–28.
22. *PBPV*, 8, pt. 1: 334.
23. *PBPV*, 9, pt. 1: 227–28.
24. *Zhurnal,* 1: 197–98.
25. *PBPV*, 9, pt. 1: 260, 344.
26. D.M. Sharypkin, "Russkie dnevniki shvedov—poltavskikh plennikov," in *Vospriiatie russkoi kul'tury na Zapade* (Leningrad, 1975), 72–73.
27. *Zhurnal,* 1: 220–22.
28. *PBPV*, 8: pt. 1: 334–35.

The Breakthrough: From Poltava to Hangö

1. *PBPV*, 9, pt. 1: 247.
2. A.V. Florovskii, "Zabytoe vossvanie Petra I k shvedam posle Poltavy (1709)," in *Poltava* (Moscow, 1959), 362.
3. *PBPV*, 9, pt. 1: 341–42.
4. Ibid., 430–31.
5. Ibid.
6. *PBPV*, 10: 459.
7. *PBPV*, 9, pt. 1: 426.
8. Ibid., 231.
9. *Zhurnal,* 1: 274–75, 278.
10. *PBPV*, 10: 285–86.
11. A. Kochubinskii, "Snosheniia Rossii pri Petre Velikom s iuzhnymi slavianami i rumynami," *ChIOIDR,* 26 (1872), bk. 2: 27; PBPV, 11, pt. 1: 119, 153.
12. *PBPV*, 11, pt. 1: 314–15.
13. N.I. Pavlenko, "Tri tak nazyvaemykh 'zaveshchaniia' Petra I," *Voprosy istorii,* no. 2 (1979), 136, 138; Peter's letter is translated in Cyprian A.G. Bridge, ed., *The Russian Fleet under Peter the Great,* Publications of the Navy Records Society, vol. 15 (London, 1899), 14.
14. *PBPV*, 11, pt. 1: 570–71.
15. B.P. Sheremetev, *Voenno-pokhodnyi zhurnal 1711 i 1712* (St. Petersburg, 1898), 54.
16. *PBPV*, 11, pt. 1: 422–23.
17. *Zhurnal,* 1: 422–23.
18. *PBPV*, 11, pt. 1: 313.
19. Ibid., 317.
20. *PBPV*, 11, pt. 2: 10–11ff.
21. *PBPV*, 12, pt. 2: 197–98.
22. Ibid.
23. Tel'pukhovskii, *Severnaia voina,* 159.

The Realization of Peter's State Ideal

1. *ZA,* 159.
2. Ibid., 65–66.
3. "Izvlecheniia iz donesenii Preisa o prebyvanii Petra Velikogo v Gollandii v 1716 i 1717 godakh," *ChIOIDR,* 2 (1877), 4–5.
4. *ZA,* 60.
5. *PSZ,* 6: 591.

6. *PSZ*, 7: 205.

7. *ZA*, 131–32.

8. N.I. Pavlenko, "Petr I," in *Rossiia v period reform Petra I*, 86; James Cracraft, *The Church Reform of Peter the Great* (Stanford, 1971), 6–7.

9. *ZA*, 65–66.

10. TsGADA, f. 276, op. 1, d. 7, ll. 15–77.

11. *ZA*, 226.

12. *ZA*, 235.

13. *ZA*, 309ff.

14. *PSZ*, 5: 89.

15. M.M. Bogoslovskii, *Oblastnaia reforma Petra Velikogo* (Moscow, 1902), 42.

16. *ZA*, 60.

17. *ZA*, 61.

18. Beskrovnyi, *Russkaia armiia*, 39–49.

19. *Bumagi Petra Velikogo*, 342.

20. Anisimov, *Podatnaia reforma*, 84.

21. *ZA*, 377.

22. ALOII, f. 270, d. 94, l. 393–94.

23. N.I. Pavlenko, *Ptentsy gnezda Petrova* (Moscow, 1984), 252–57.

24. TsGADA, f. 16, d. 183, ll. 1–4.

25. A.S. Lappo-Danilevskii, "Ideia gosudarstva i glavneishie momenty ee razvitiia v Rossii so vremen Smuty i do epokhi preobrazovanii," *Golos minuvshego*, no. 12 (1914), 31.

26. F.F. Veselago, *Materialy dlia istorii russkogo flota*, pt. 3 (St. Petersburg, 1866), 367.

The Serf Economy

1. *PSZ*, 5: 734.

2. Ibid., 761.

3. Ibid., 5: 137.

4. *Otdel rukopisei Gosudarstvennoi Publichnoi biblioteki im. M.E. Saltykova-Shchedrina*, f. 1003, d. 11, ll. 105–6.

5. A.M. Pankratova, *Formirovanie proletariata v Rossii (XVII-XVIII vv.)* (Moscow, 1963), 339.

6. *PSZ*, 6: 311–12.

7. *PSZ*, 6: 516.

8. N.I. Pavlenko, "Sostav rabochikh na kazennykh predpriiatiiakh i zavodakh Urala po perepisi 1744–1745 gg.," in *Akademiku B.D. Grekovu ko dniu semidesiatiletiia: Sb. st.* (Moscow, 1952), 301.

9. *PSZ*, 6: 311.

10. *PSZ*, 7: 155.

11. Pavlenko, "Torgovo-promyshlennaia politika," 67–68.

Producing the All-Russian Subject People

1. V.A. Evreinov, *Grazhdanskoe chinoproizvodstvo v Rossii* (St. Petersburg, 1887), appendix, 77.

2. *PBPV*, 12, pt. 1: 25.

3. *PSZ*, 5: 78.

4. *ZA*, 149–50.

5. M.D. Rabinovich, "Sotsial'noe proiskhozhdenie ofitserov reguliarnoi russkoi armii v kontse Severnoi voiny," in *Rossiia v period reform Petra I*, 171.

6. *PSZ*, 5: 91. Significant material on this theme has been presented in the research of Marc Raeff, such as *Origins of the Russian Intelligentsia: The Eighteenth-Century Nobility* (New York, 1966).

7. TsGADA, f. 9, otd. 1, bk. 53, ll. 534–36.

8. Anisimov, *Podatnaia reforma*, 180ff.; *PSZ*, 7: 316.

9. Ibid.

10. Iu.A. Tikhonov, *Pomeshch'i krest'iane v Rossii* (Moscow, 1974).

11. TsGADA, f. 248, bk. 1888, ll. 332.

12. *PSZ*, 6: 295.

13. M.Ia. Volkov, "Goroda Tverskoi provintsii v pervoi chetverti XVIII veka," in *Istoricheskaia geografiia Rossii XII-nachalo XX veka* (Moscow, 1975), 150–60.

14. Anisimov, *Podatnaia reforma*, 198–99.

Reforming the Clerical Rank

1. P.V. Verkhovskii, *Uchrezhdenie dukhovnoi kollegii i Dukhovnoi reglament*, vol. 1 (Rostov on the Don, 1916), 111.

2. *PSZ*, 6: 314; *The Spiritual Regulation of Peter the Great*, ed. and trans. Alexander V. Muller (Seattle and London, 1972), 3.

3. Verkhovskii, *Uchrezhdenie*, 1: 318; *The Spiritual Regulation*, 10–12.

4. Nartov, *Rasskazy*, 71–72.

5. *PSZ*, 6: 406.

6. Anisimov, *Podatnaia reforma*, 228.

7. *DPS*, 3, pt. 2: 1014.

8. Verkhovskii, *Uchrezhdenie*, 1: 631–32.

9. *PSZ*, 5: 196.

10. *PSZ*, 6: 685–89; *The Spiritual Regulation*, 6; Cracraft, *Church Reform*, 238–39.

11. *PSZ*, 7: 432.

12. Ibid., 226–33.

13. Verkhovskii, *Uchrezhdenie*, 1: 643.

14. *PSZ*, 7: 355.

15. *PSZ*, 6: 641–42.

16. G.V. Esipov, *Raskol'nich'i dela XVIII veka*, vol. 1 (St. Petersburg, 1861), 8–46.

"The police is the soul of the citizenry"

1. *PSZ*, 6: 297.

2. *PSZ*, 4: 282–83.

3. *PSZ*, 6: 653.

4. L. Chesterfil'd, *Pis'ma k synu, Maksimy, Kharakhtery* (Leningrad, 1971), 13; *The Letters of Philip Dormer Stanhope, 4th Earl of Chesterfield*, ed. Bonamy Dobrée, vol. 6 (London, 1932), 460–61.

5. *Iunosti chestnoe zerkalo* (St. Petersburg, 1719), 25–88.

6. *PSZ*, 5: 598.

7. D.S. Likhachev, "Byla li epokha petrovskikh reform pereryvom v razvitii russkoi kul'tury?" in *Slavianskie kul'tury v epokhu formirovaniia i razvitiia slavianskikh natsii XVIII-XX vv.* (Moscow, 1978), 171–74.

8. *PSZ,* 5: 727, 575–76ff.

9. *PSZ,* 7: 314.

10. S.N. Valk, "Sud o krest'ianakh v Palate ob Ulozhenii 1700 g.," in *Akademiku B.D. Grekovu,* 236.

11. TsGADA, f. 350, d. 126, ll. 154v.–155.

12. *PSZ,* 6: 642; Anisimov, *Podatnaia reforma,* 250.

13. *PSZ,* 7: 299.

14. *PSZ,* 6: 720.

15. E.I. Zaozerskaia, "Begstvo i otkhod krest'ian v pervoi polovine XVIII veka," in *K voprosu o pervonachal'nom nakoplenii v Rossii (XVII-XVIII vv.)* (Moscow, 1958), 159.

16. *PSZ,* 6: 360.

17. TsGADA, f. 248, bk. 1891, ll. 145–46.

18. TsGADA, f. 248, bk. 688, l. 105.

19. *PSZ,* 7: 276.

20. *PSZ,* 6: 639.

21. TsGADA, f. 9, pt. I, bk. 45, ll. 33v.–42.

22. *PSZ,* 7: 315–16.

23. TsGADA, f. 248, bk. 390, l. 201v.

24. G.T. Tel'berg, *Ocherki politicheskogo suda i politicheskikh prestuplenii v Moskovskom gosudarstve XVII veka* (Moscow, 1912), 129–30.

25. G. Kotoshikhin, *O Rossii v tsarstvovanie Alekseia Mikhailovicha* (St. Petersburg, 1884), 58–59.

26. *PSZ,* 4: 643–44.

27. *ZA,* 361, 364.

28. *PSZ,* 6: 161–62.

29. *PSZ,* 7: 260.

30. *PSZ,* 7: 196–97.

31. Andrei Belyi, *Peterburg* (Moscow, 1978), 35–36; Andrei Bely, *Petersburg,* trans., annot., and intro. Robert A. Maguire and John E. Malmstadt (Bloomington and London, 1978), 12–13; I. Brodskii, "Stansy," *Raduga,* no. 2 (1988).

The Imperial Idea

1. *Materialy dlia istorii russkogo flota,* pt. 4 (St. Petersburg, 1867), 79–81; Bantysh-Kamenskii, *Obzor,* 4: 213.

2. Bantysh-Kamenskii, *Obzor,* 2: 107.

3. Ibid., 2, 80.

4. *SIRIO,* 52: 146.

5. *PSZ,* 6: 424.

6. ALOII, f. 270, d. 81, ll. 179–80.

7. Ibid., d. 87, l. 221.

8. Ibid., d. 93, 672; d. 98, l. 340.

9. Ibid., d. 104, 76; d. 107, l. 58.

10. Ibid., d. 107, 100, l. 312.

11. Solov'ev, *Istoriia Rossii,* 18: 377.

12. F. Tumanskii, *Sobranie raznykh zapisok i sochinenii,* pt. 9 (St. Petersburg, 1788), 229, 238.

13. A.I. Zaozerskii, "Ekspeditsiia na Madagaskar pri Petre Velikom," *Rossiia i zapad: Istoricheskii sbornik,* I (Petrograd, 1923), 102.

"To whom shall I leave the planting described above?"

1. G.M. Iakovlev, I.L. Anikin, S.Iu. Trukhachev, "Materialy k istorii bolezni Petra Velikogo," 8–9.

2. G.F. Bassevich, *Zapiski o Rossii pri Petre Velikom* (Moscow, 1866). See also Pavlenko, "Tri tak nazyvaemykh zaveshchanii," 139–42.

3. Ustrialov, *Istoriia*, 6: 346–48; Friedrich Christian Weber, *The Present State of Russia*, vol. 2 (London, 1968), 101–2.

4. Ibid., 350; Weber, *Present State*, 2: 105–6.

5. Ibid., 112; Weber, *Present State*, 2: 109.

6. G.V. Esipov, *Raskol'nich'i dela*, 1: 158–67.

7. Esipov, *Liudi starogo veka* (St. Petersburg, 1880), 126–39.

8. Ustrialov, *Istoriia*, 6: 185–88.

9. Ibid., 623–26.

10. Esipov, *Liudi*, 139, 135.

11. *SIRIO*, 52: 220.

12. Bassevich, *Zapiski*, 172.

13. *PBPV*, 9, pt. 1: 200.

14. *PBPV*, 8, pt. 2: 430.

15. Bassevich, *Zapiski*, 633.

16. F. Prokopovich, *Slova i rechi*, vol. 2, pt. 1 (St. Petersburg, 1761), 127.

17. I.M. Snegirev, *Lubochnye kartinki russkogo naroda v Moskovskom mire* (Moscow, 1861), 125.

18. D.A. Rovinskii, *Russkie narodnye kartinki*, bk. I (St. Petersburg, 1861), 391–401ff.

19. TsGADA, f. 273, d. 28625, ll. 6v., 22.

20. TsGADA, f. 9, otd. l, bk. 33, l. 92.

Conclusion

1. M.M. Shcherbatov, "Approximate Evolution of the Length of Time Russia Would Have Required, in the Most Favorable Circumstances, to Attain by Her Own Efforts, without the Autocratic Rule of Peter the Great, Her Present State of Enlightenment and Glory," in Marc Raeff, ed., *Russian Intellectual History: An Anthology* (New York, 1966), 56–60.

2. Pogodin, "Petr Velikii," 335.

3. A.I. Gertsen, *Sobrannye sochineniia*, vol. 7 (Moscow, 1956), 173.

4. M. Voloshin, "Rossiia," *Iunost'*, no. 10 (1988), 78.

For Further Reading

This brief overview will focus on recent literature in English not cited in the author's notes.

Two convenient guides to recent historical literature on Petrine Russia are by Philip Clendenning and Roger P. Bartlett, *Eighteenth Century Russia: A Select Bibliography of Works Published since 1955* (Newtonville, MA, 1981), and by David R. Egan and Melinda A. Egan, *Russian Autocrats from Ivan the Great to the Fall of the Romanov Dynasty: An Annotated Bibliography of English Language Sources to 1985* (Metuchen, NJ, and London, 1987).

Four new editions of important primary sources have appeared in the past twenty years: P.P. Shafirov, *A Discourse Concerning the Just Causes of the War between Sweden and Russia 1700–1721*, with an introduction by William E. Butler (Dobbs Ferry, NY, 1973); Ivan Pososhkov, *The Book of Poverty and Wealth*, edited and translated by A.P. Vlasto and L.R. Lewitter (Stanford, 1987), which includes a lengthy and insightful essay by Professor Lewitter along with superb annotation; *The Travel Diary of Peter Tolstoi: A Muscovite in Early Modern Russia*, edited and translated by Max J. Okenfuss (DeKalb, 1987), splendidly illustrated and copiously annotated; and James Cracraft, ed., *For God and Peter the Great: The Works of Thomas Consett, 1723–1729* (Boulder and New York, 1982). Additional maps and graphic materials may be found in Robin Milner-Gulland and Nikolai Dejevsky, *Cultural Atlas of Russia and the Soviet Union* (New York and Oxford, 1989), and in Russian with an English summary, N.V. Kaliazina and G.N. Komelova, *Russkoe iskusstvo petrovskoi epokhi* (Leningrad, 1990).

A selection of international scholarship is handily presented by James Cracraft, ed., *Peter the Great Transforms Russia*, 3rd ed. (Lexington and Toronto, 1991), a volume in the well-known D.C. Heath series Problems in European Civilization. Incidentally, the two earlier editions by Marc Raeff (1963 and 1972) contain quite different selections (a comparison of the three might be instructive). Older synthetic accounts are now also available in translation: S.M. Soloviev, *History of Russia*, vol. 29: *Peter the Great: The Great Reforms Begin*, edited and translated by K.A. Papmehl (Gulf Breeze, 1981), and vol. 25: *Rebellion and Reform: Fedor and Sophia, 1682–1689*, edited and translated by Lindsey A.J. Hughes (Gulf Breeze, 1989). Another famous account is Voltaire's *Russia under Peter the Great*, translated by M.F.O. Jenkins (Rutherford, NJ, 1983).

More recent scholarly accounts, each revisionist in its own way, are the superbly illustrated volume by James Cracraft, *The Petrine Revolution in Russian Architecture* (Chicago and London, 1988), Lindsey Hughes's provocative biography of Peter's half-sister, *Sophia: Regent of Russia 1657– 1704* (New Haven and London, 1990), and the stimulating essay by George Barany, *The Anglo-Russian Entente Cordiale of 1697–1698: Peter I and William III at Utrecht* (Boulder and New York, 1986). For Russia's role in European diplomacy, see also Andrew Rothstein, *Peter the Great and Marlborough: Politics and Diplomacy in Converging Wars* (New York, 1986).

A heavily statistical treatment of the Russian economy is provided by Arcadius Kahan, *The Plow, the Hammer and the Knout: An Economic History of Eighteenth-Century Russia*, edited by Richard Hellie (Chicago and London, 1986). Less statistical and more focused is Hugh D. Hudson, Jr., *The Rise of the Demidov Family and the Russian Iron Industry in the Eighteenth Century* (Newtonville, MA, 1986).

For a sweeping synthesis of Russian military history, see William C. Fuller, Jr., *Strategy and Power in Russia 1600–1914* (New York, 1992). The evolution of the modern Russian army is traced in authoritative fashion by J.L.H. Keep, *Soldiers of the Tsar: Army and Society in Russia, 1462–1874* (Oxford, 1985). A well-informed treatment of the Petrine navy is offered by Jacob W. Kipp, "Peter the Great and the Birth of the Russian Navy," International Commission of Military History, Records of the 7th International Colloquy on Military History, Acta No. 7, Washington, D.C., 25–30 July 1982: "Soldier-Statesmen of the Age of the Enlightenment" (Manhattan, KS, 1984), 113–39.

Somewhat statistical or "Cliometric" in approach are the monographs by Gary Marker, *Publishing, Printing, and the Origins of Intellectual Life in Russia, 1700–1800* (Princeton, 1985), and by Brenda Meehan-Waters, *Autocracy and Aristocracy: The Russian Service Elite of 1730* (New Brunswick, 1982).

On the church and religion, important studies have come from the pens of Robert O. Crummey, *The Old Believers and the World of Antichrist: The Vyg Community and the Russian State 1694–1855* (Madison, Milwaukee, and London, 1970) and Gregory L. Freeze, *The Russian Levites: Parish Clergy in the Eighteenth Century* (Cambridge, MA, 1977) and from a series of articles on Feofan Prokopovich by James Cracraft, "Feofan

Prokopovich," in J.G. Garrard, ed., *The Eighteenth Century in Russia* (Oxford, 1973), 75–105; "Feofan Prokopovich: A Bibliography of His Works," *Oxford Slavonic Papers*, n.s. 8 (1975), 1–36; "Did Feofan Prokopovich Really Write *Pravda Voli Monarshei?*," *Slavic Review*, 40 (1981), 173–93; and "Feofan Prokopovich and the Kievan Academy," in Robert L. Nichols and Theofanis George Stavrou, eds., *Russian Orthodoxy under the Old Regime* (Minneapolis, 1978), 44–66. In the last named collection, Alexander V. Muller discusses "The Inquisitorial Network of Peter the Great," 142–53. Concerning Peter's own religious views, see L.R. Lewitter, "Peter the Great's Attitude toward Religion: From Traditional Piety to Rational Theology," in Roger P. Bartlett et al., eds., *Russia and the World of the Eighteenth Century* (Columbus, 1988), 62–77. Oxford University Press published in 1992 a study by Paul Bushkovitch, *Religion and Society in Russia: The Sixteenth and the Seventeenth Centuries.*

On matters cultural and intellectual, see the revisionist sketch of the origins of modern theater in Simon Karlinsky, *Russian Drama from Its Beginnings to the Age of Pushkin* (Berkeley, Los Angeles, and London, 1985). Three revisionist essays by Max J. Okenfuss are "The Jesuit Origins of Petrine Education" and "Russian Students in Europe in the Age of Peter the Great," both in J.G. Garrard, ed., *The Eighteenth Century in Russia* (Oxford, 1973), 106–30 and 131–48, and "Technical Training in Russia under Peter the Great," *History of Education Quarterly* 13, no. 4 (Winter 1973), 325–45. The same author's stimulating essay *The Discovery of Childhood in Russia: The Evidence of the lavic Primer* (Newtonville, MA, 1980) may now be supplemented by the articles of Gary Marker, "Primers and Literacy in Muscovy: A Taxonomic Investigation," *Russian Review* 48, no. 1 (1989), 1–20, and "Literacy and Literary Texts in Muscovy: A Reconsideration," *Slavic Review* 49, no. 1 (Spring 1990), 174–89.

A brief, incisive, well-illustrated sketch is presented by L.R. Lewitter, "Peter the Great and the Modern World," *History Today*, 35 (February 1985), 16–23. Related images are studied by Daniel L. Schafly, Jr., "The Popular Image of the West in Russia at the Time of Peter the Great," in Roger Bartlett et al., eds., *Russia and the World of the Eighteenth Century*, 2–21. Anisimov's interpretation of the woodcut "The Mice Bury the Cat" is challenged by Dianne Farrell, "Laughter Transformed: The Shift from Medieval to Enlightenment Humour in Russian Popular Prints," in the same collection, 157–76. The same publication includes an essay on the Petrine police official Anton Devier (c.1675–1745) by William Rogle, "Antonio Manuel de Vieira, 1697–1745," 577–90. A companion piece on Russian prints is Dianne Ecklund Farrell, "Medieval Popular Humor in Russian Eighteenth Century *Lubki*," *Slavic Review* 50 (1991), 551–65.

A new anthology on Russian women's history, *Russia's Women: Accommodation, Resistance, Transformation,* edited by Barbara Evans Clements, Barbara Alpern Engel, and Christine D. Worobec, contains two essays related to the Petrine era and its background: Nancy Shields Kollmann, "Woman's Honor in Early Modern Russia," 60–73, and Valerie A. Kivelson, "Through the Prism of Witchcraft: Gender and Social Change in Seventeenth-Century Muscovy," 74–94.

On scientific policies and institutions, see Valentin Boss, *Newton and Russia: The Early Influence, 1694–1796* (Cambridge, MA, 1972), and Ludmilla Schulze, "The Russification of the St. Petersburg Academy of Sciences and Arts in the Eighteenth Century," *British Journal of the History of Science* 18 (1985), 305–35. Technical education is insightfully explored by W.F. Ryan, "Navigation and the Modernisation of Petrine Russia: Teachers, Textbooks, Terminology," in Roger Bartlett and Janet M. Hartley, eds., *Russia in the Age of the Enlightenment: Essays for Isabel de Madariaga* (London, 1990), 75–105. For biographical sketches of three leading physicians in Petrine Russia, see the encyclopedia entries by John T. Alexander, "Bidloo, Nikolaas," *Modern Encyclopedia of Russian and Soviet History* (Gulf Breeze), vol. 47 (1988), 83–87; "Erskine, Robert," vol. 48 (1988), 67–70; and "Posnikov, Dr. Peter," vol. 51 (1989), 228–32, the last being supplemented by the same author's "Dr. Peter Posnikov: A Biographical Note," *The Study Group on Eighteenth-Century Russia Newsletter,* no. 18 (1990), 18–20. A meticulously revisionist and well illustrated account of Russian eastward expansion is by Raymond H. Fisher, *Bering's Voyages: Whither and Why* (Seattle and London, 1977).

Recent documents and studies of Mazepa and Ukrainian politics include *On the Eve of Poltava: The Letters of Ivan Mazepa to Adam Sieniawski, 1704–1708,* edited and annotated by Orest Subtelny (New York, 1975), a publication of the Ukrainian Academy of Arts and Sciences in the United States; Orest Subtelny, *The Mazepists: Ukrainian Separatism in the Early Eighteenth Century* (Boulder and New York, 1981); Theodore Mackiw, *English Reports on Mazepa, 1687–1709* (New York, Munich, and Toronto, 1983); and Orest Subtelny, *Domination of Eastern Europe: Native Nobilities and Foreign Absolutism, 1500–1715* (Kingston, 1986).

John T. Alexander

Index

EVGENII V. ANISIMOV, born in 1947 and educated in Leningrad (St. Petersburg), is a senior research scholar at the St. Petersburg Branch of the Institute of Russian History, Russian Academy of Sciences. His first book, published in Russian in 1982, on Peter's tax reforms, was followed in 1986 by *Russia in the Mid-Eighteenth Century: The Struggle for the Heritage of Peter the Great.* The present work is a revision of his third book, *The Time of the Petrine Reforms*, published in 1989. Dr. Anisimov has been a visiting fellow at the Kennan Institute for Advanced Russian Studies (1991) and the Russian Research Center, Harvard University (1993).

Translator JOHN T. ALEXANDER is professor of history at the University of Kansas. His many books include *Catherine the Great: Life and Legend* (1988), *Emperor of the Cossacks: Pugachev and the Frontier Jacquerie of 1773–1775* (1973), and *Bubonic Plague in Early Modern Russia.* He edited and translated S.F. Platonov's *The Time of Troubles* and is the translator of a forthcoming English-language edition of Evgenii V. Anisimov's *Russia in the Mid-Eighteenth Century.* Professor Alexander is currently at work on a comparative study of Peter I and Catherine II.

Series editor DONALD J. RALEIGH is professor of history at the University of North Carolina, Chapel Hill. He is the author of *Revolution on the Volga: 1917 in Saratov* and is now at work on a sequel to that study. Professor Raleigh is also editor of *Soviet Historians and Perestroika: The First Phase*, editor and translator of *A Russian Civil War Diary; Alexis V. Babine in Saratov*, and translator of E.N. Burdzhalov's *Russia's Second Revolution: The February 1917 Uprising in Petrograd.* He edits the quarterly journal *Russian Studies in History.*